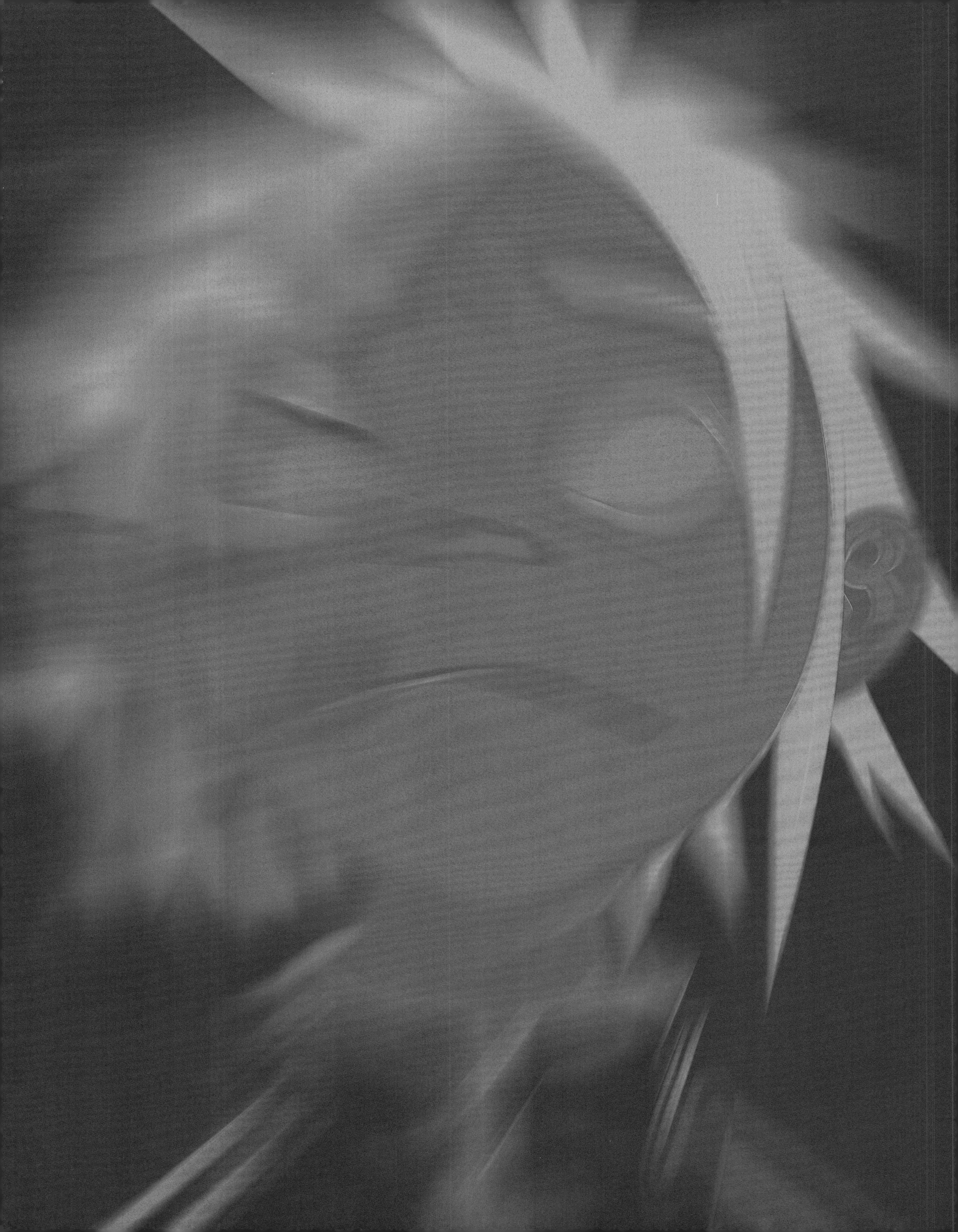

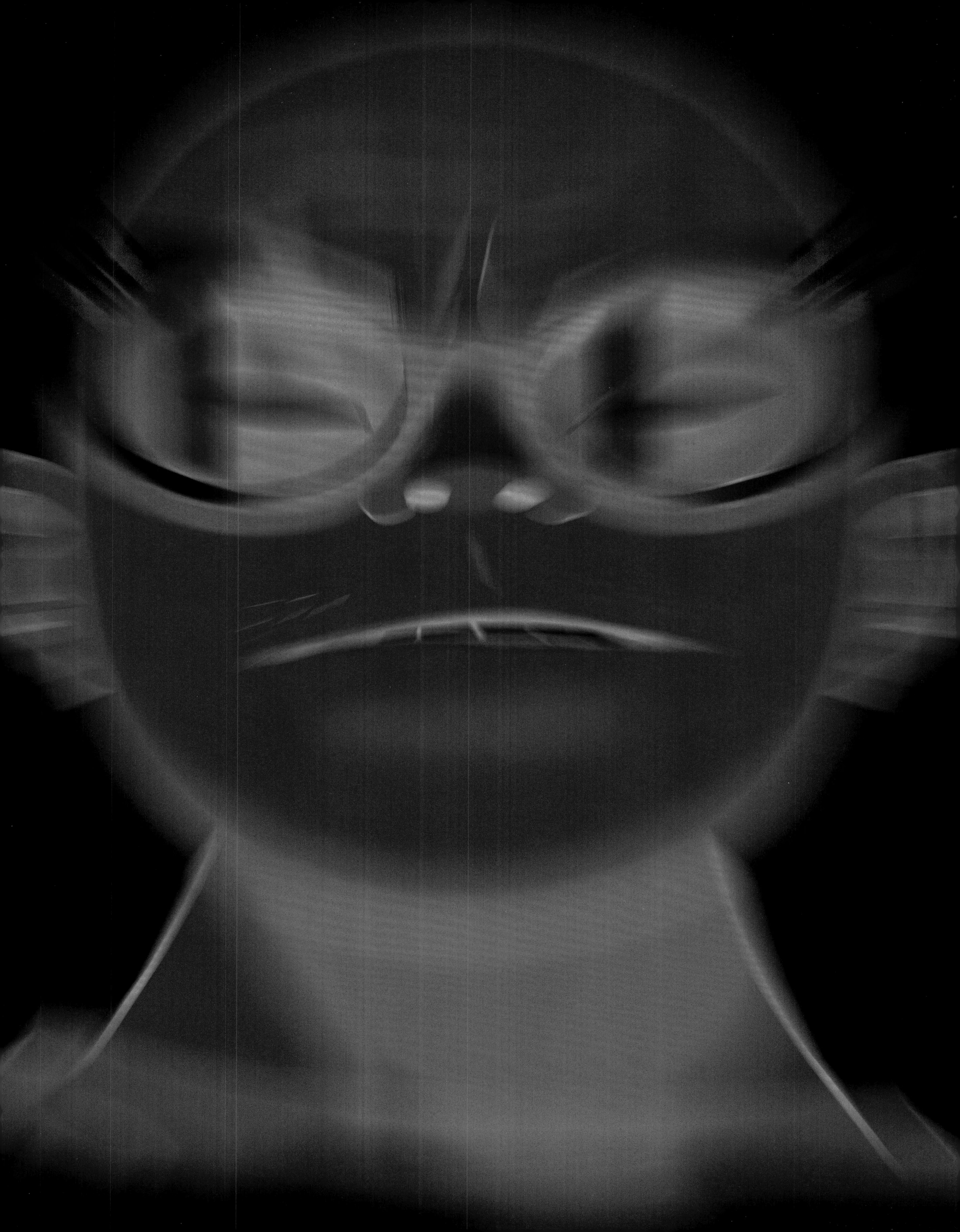

THE GORILLAZ ART BOOK

By Murdoc F. Niccals

Friends, fans, art lovers, and anyone who bought this book by mistake.
Let me start by saying what a massive bloody honour it is to be writing
this foreword. An honour for you, the owner of this book, and also
for the publishers, who begged me to bang out a few words to boost
sales. And who can blame them? A Murdoc Niccals endorsement is like
her majesty's royal seal, only much better cos she'll slap hers on
anything.

At first I was understandably sceptical about the idea of an 'art
book' - sounds like a load of Jackson Pollocks, the sort of thing you
keep in the bog next to the potpourri. But when they explained that
the subject of this collection was me, I was bang up for it! 'Think
of this book, Murdoc, as some talented artists coming together to
celebrate a much more talented artist.' Paraphrasing a bit but that
was the gist.

So it's with great pleasure that I present to you this homage to the
visual enigma that is Murdoc F. Niccals: Gorillaz founder, cultural
übermensch, and occasional life-drawing model. Granted, there are
a few pictures of other people in here too, so best just thumb past
those, or even better, use sticky labels to mark the pages with the
Murdoc pictures, like I've done with my copy.

All that remains to be said is thank you. Firstly to the artists, for
attempting the impossible by trying to capture my vital essence on
canvas. Every artist needs their muse, and I'm humbled to be yours.
That's something we've got in common, actually, because my muse is
also me. (Picasso's was 90% proof absinthe, which explains why his
drawings were so shit.) Thanks also to everyone else who made this
book possible - from the important people in suits, all the way down
to my typist 2D, who is tapping this out while I lay back sipping my
absinthe daiquiri. But most of all, thank you to Art itself, without
which the world would be a grey, depressing, but probably quite
efficiently-run dystopia.

Your ever-humble muse,

Jamie Hewlett

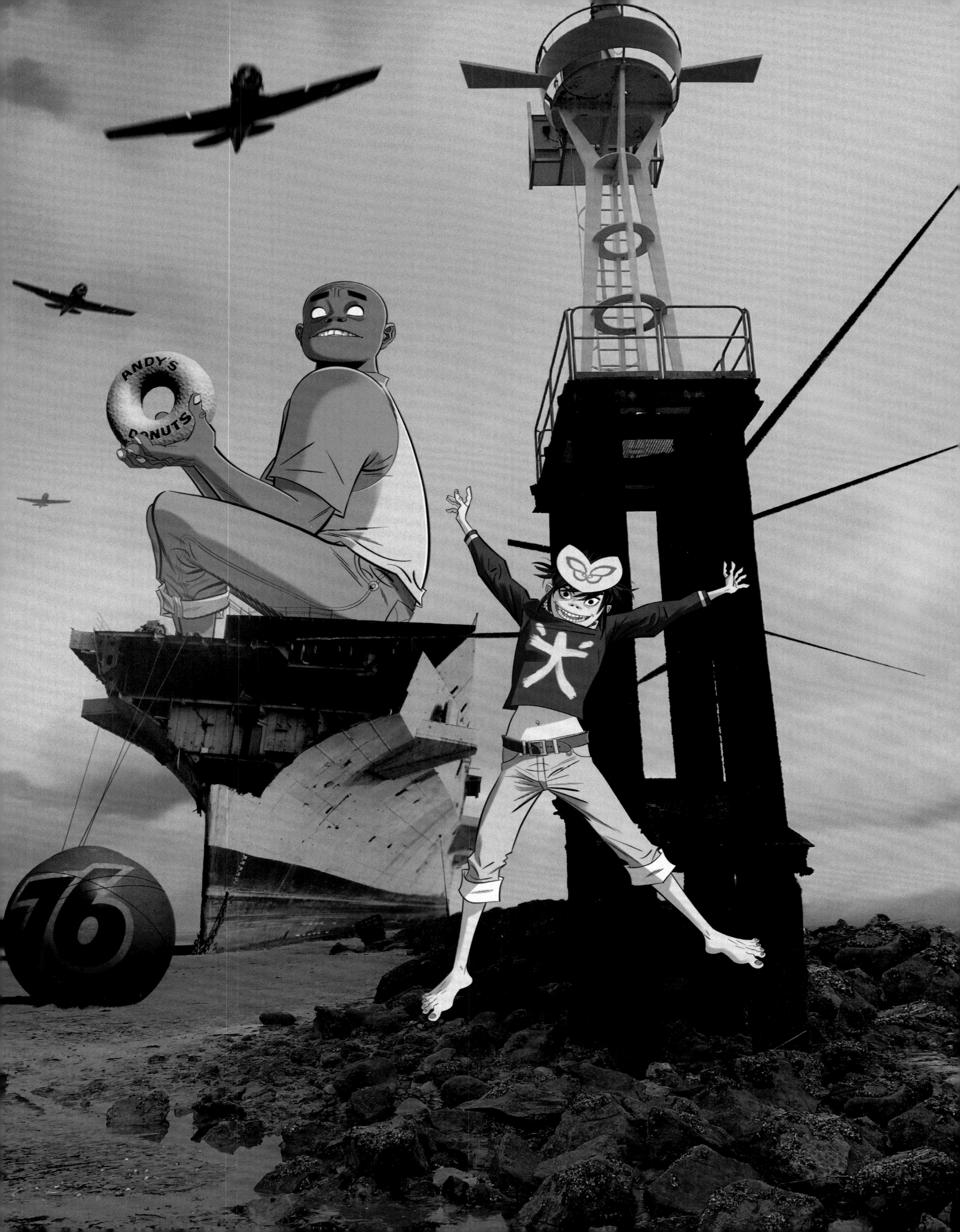
ANDY'S
DONUTS
76

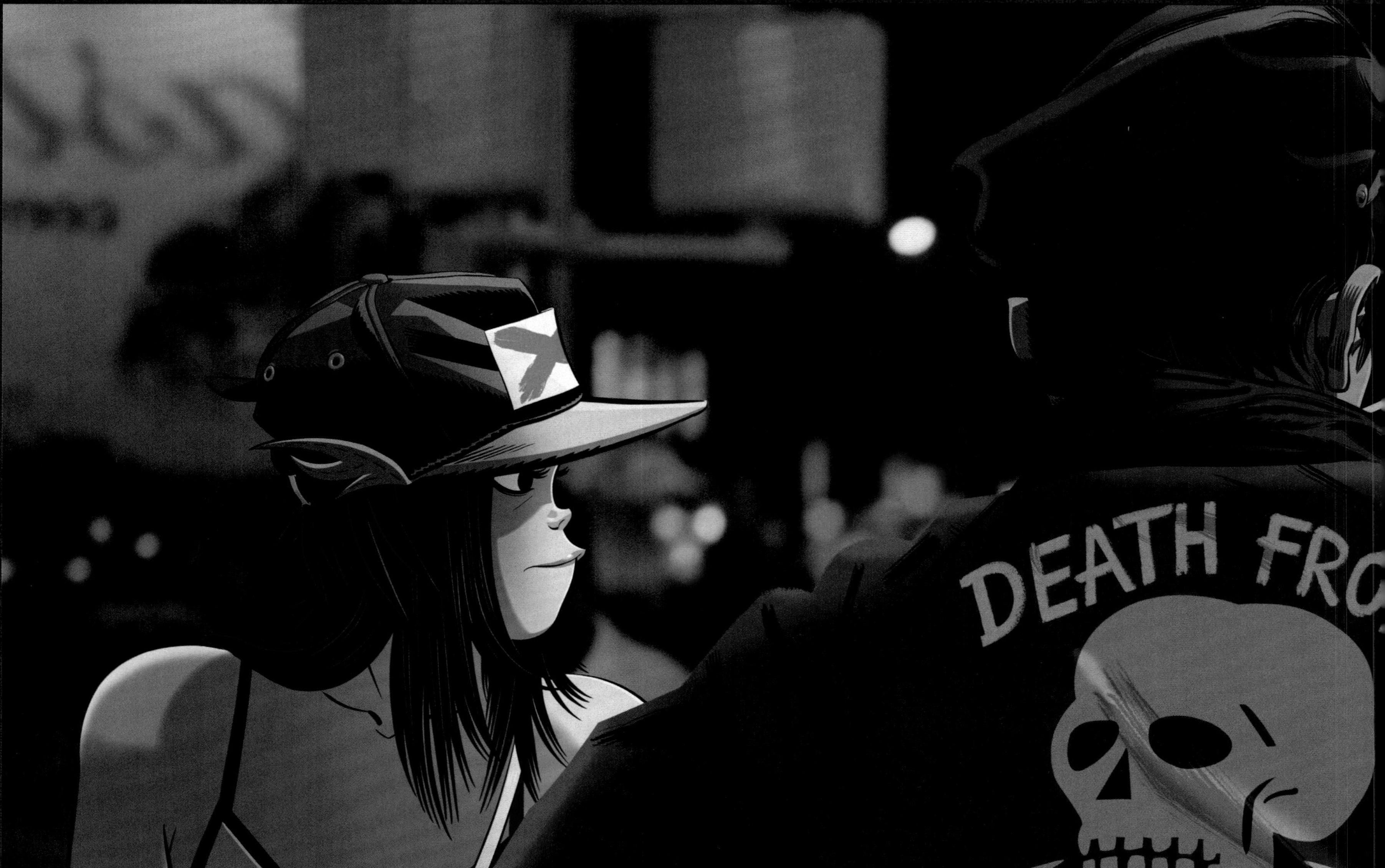
DEATH FRO
BELOW

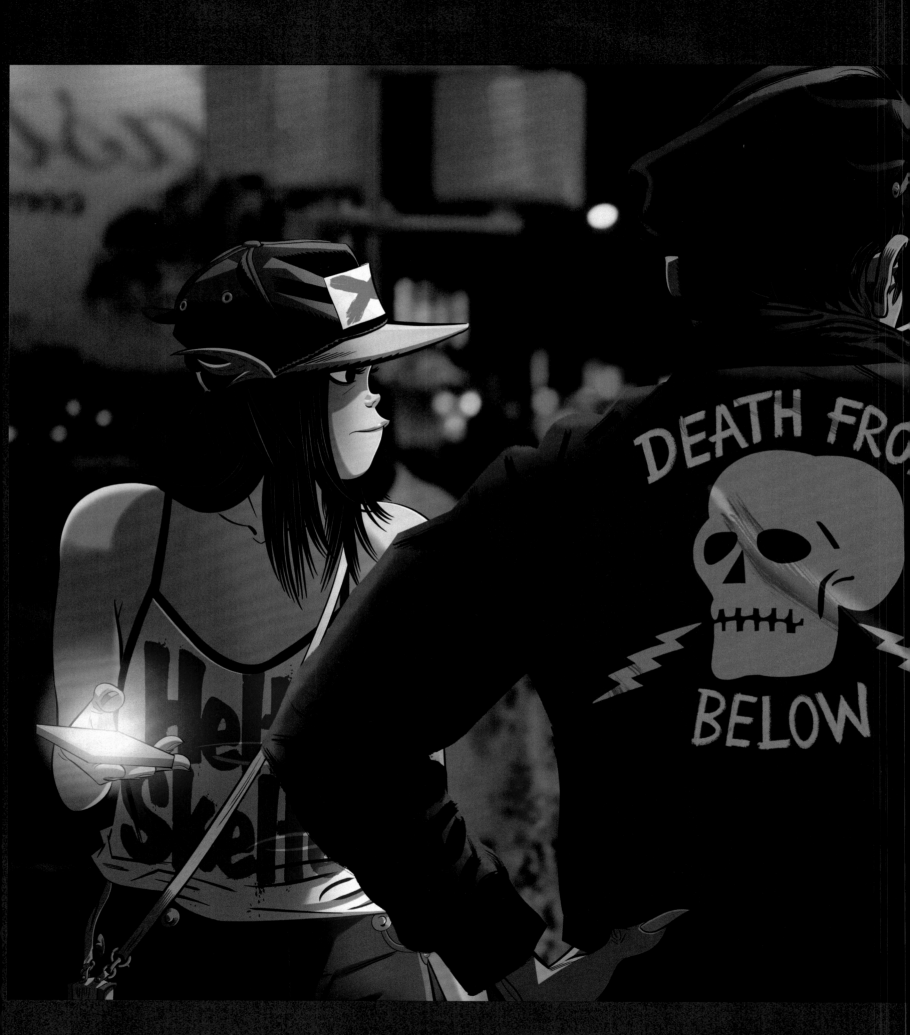

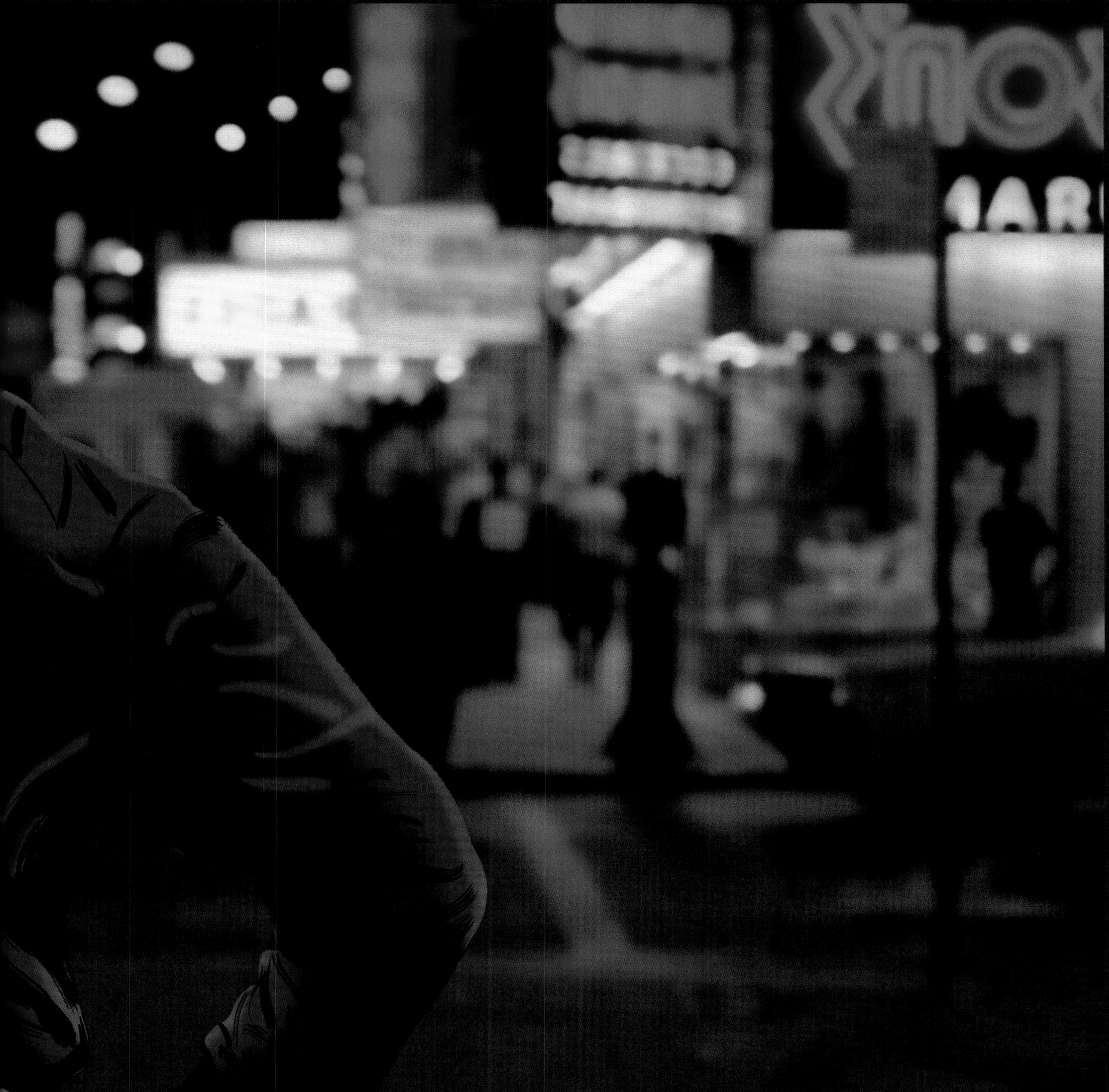

Up to Lexington, One Two Five

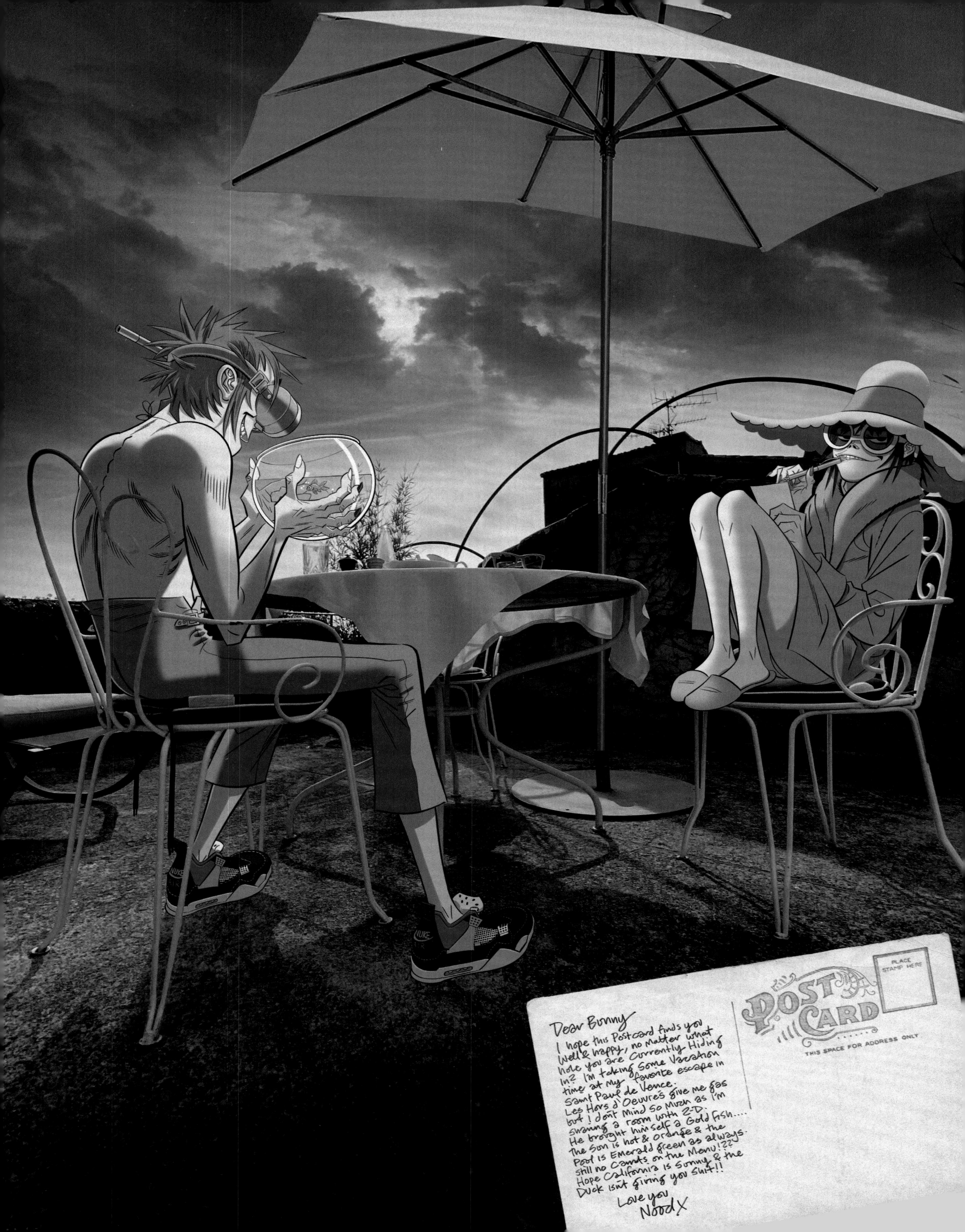
POST CARD
PLACE STAMP HERE
THIS SPACE FOR ADDRESS ONLY
Dear Bunny
I hope this Postcard finds you
Well & happy, no Matter what
hole you are Currently Hiding
In? I'm taking Some Vacation
time at my favorite escape in
Saint Paul de Vence.
Les Hors d'Oeuvre's give me gas
but I don't Mind so Much as I'm
sharing a room with 2-D.
He brought himself a Gold fish....
The Sun is hot & orange & the
Pool is Emerald green as always.
still no Carrots on the Menu!??
Hope California is Sunny & the
Duck isn't giving you shit!!
Love you
Nood X

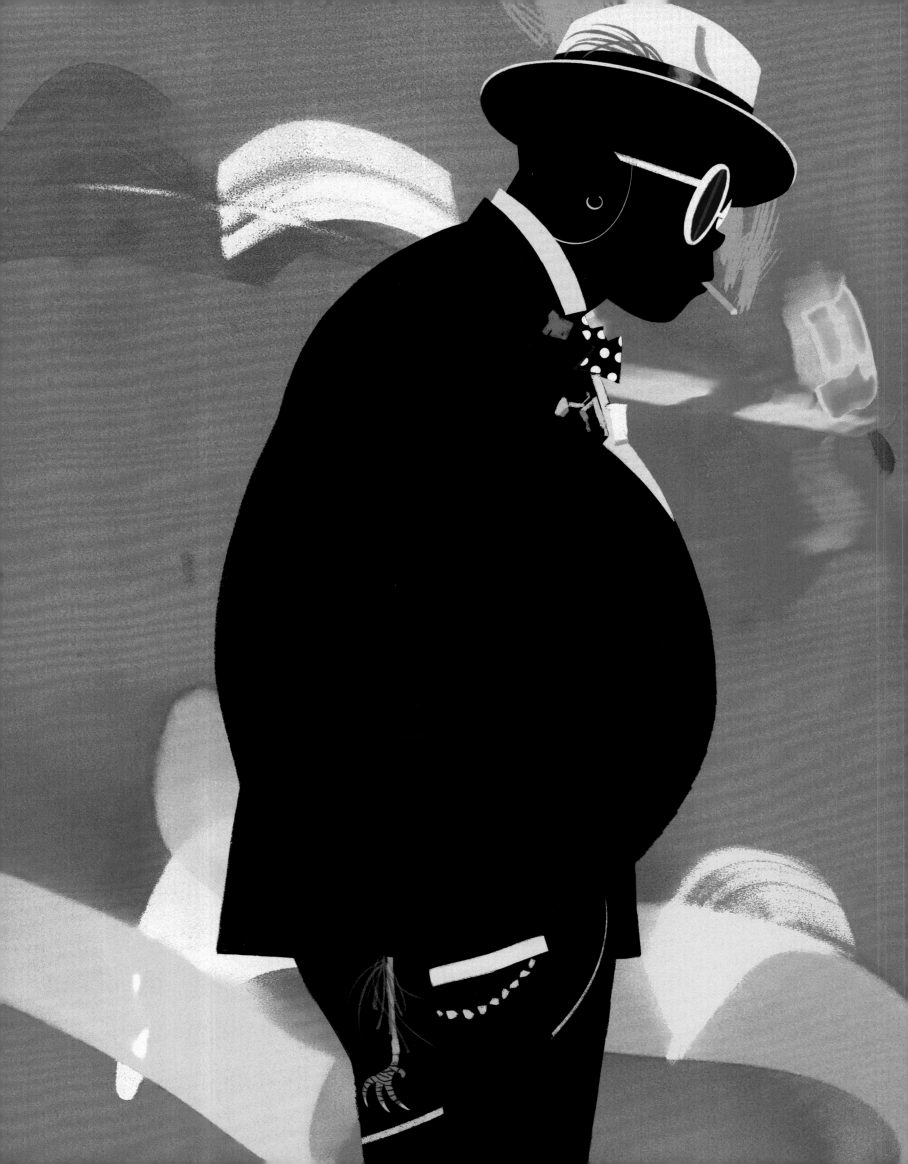

Hutson Lee Hobbs

The Blues Singer.

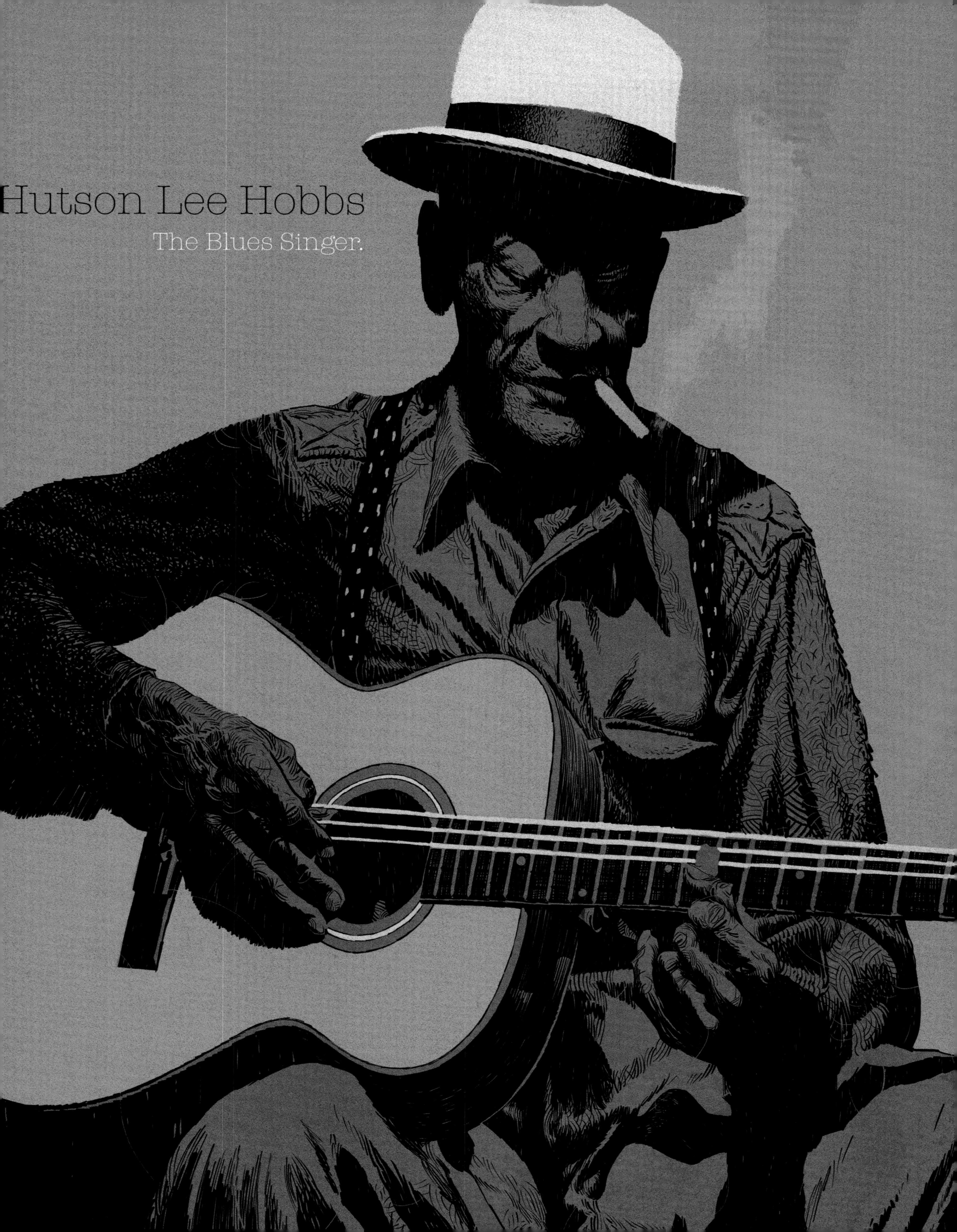

MVRDIAS TITVS NICCALVS

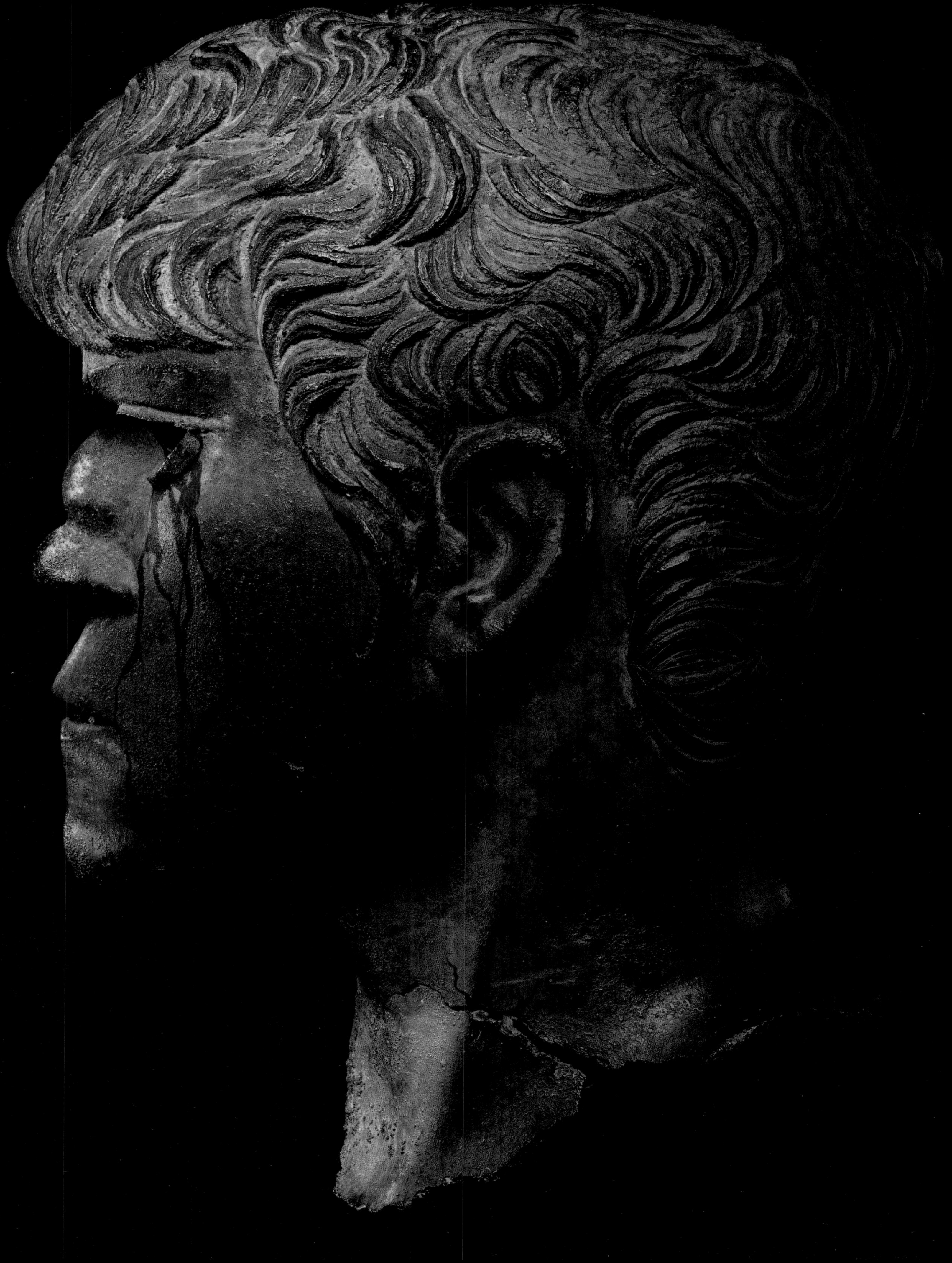

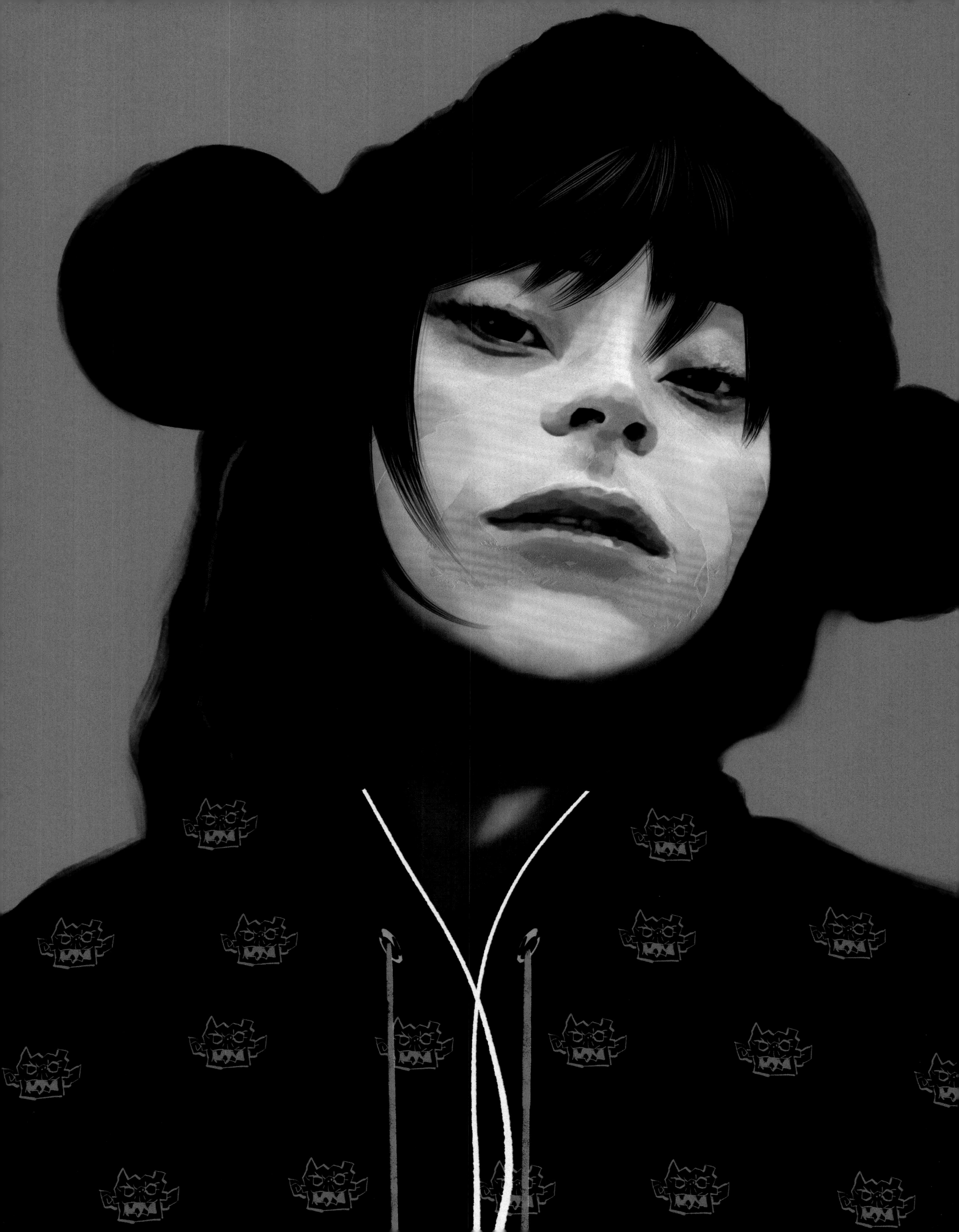

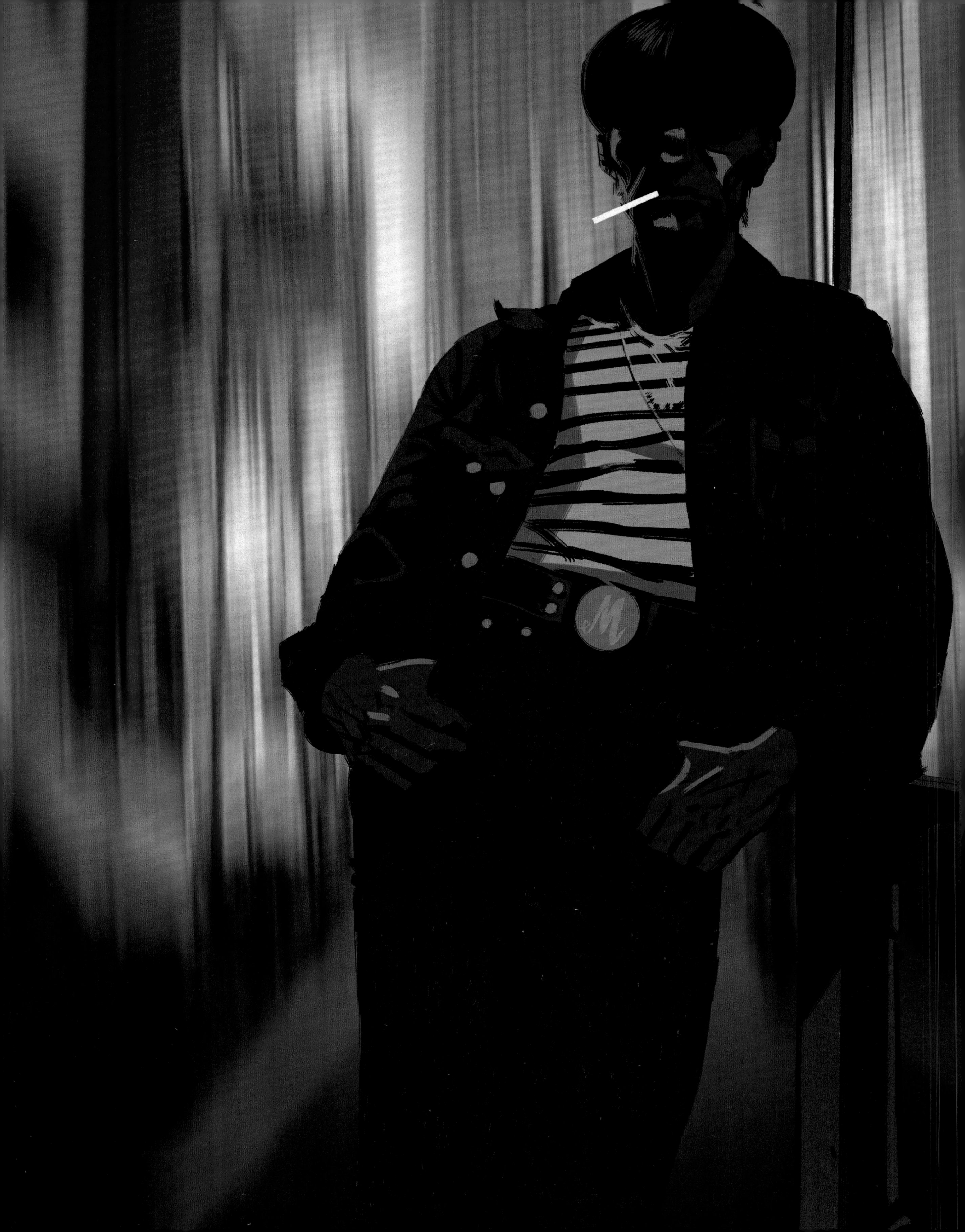

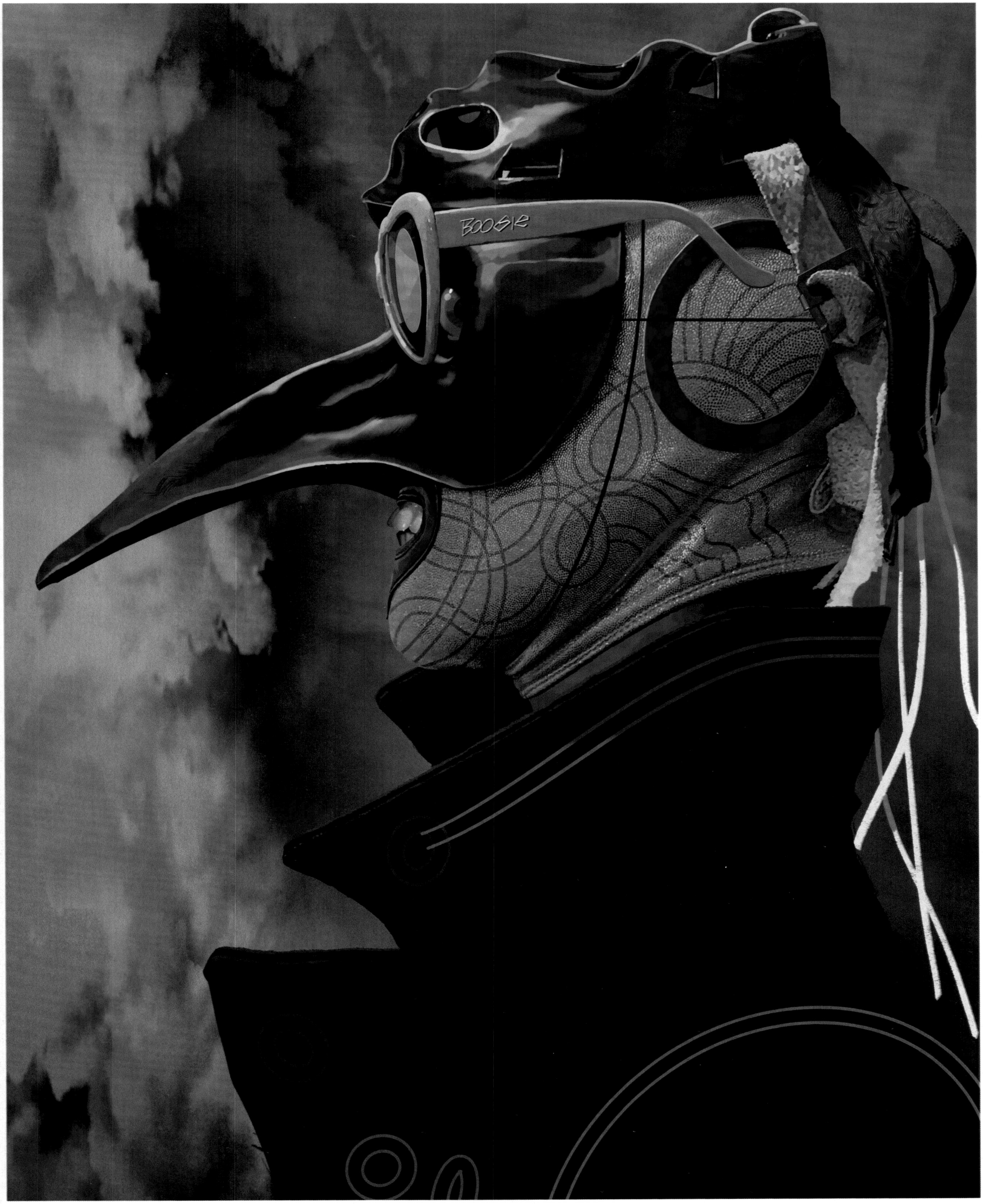
Boosie

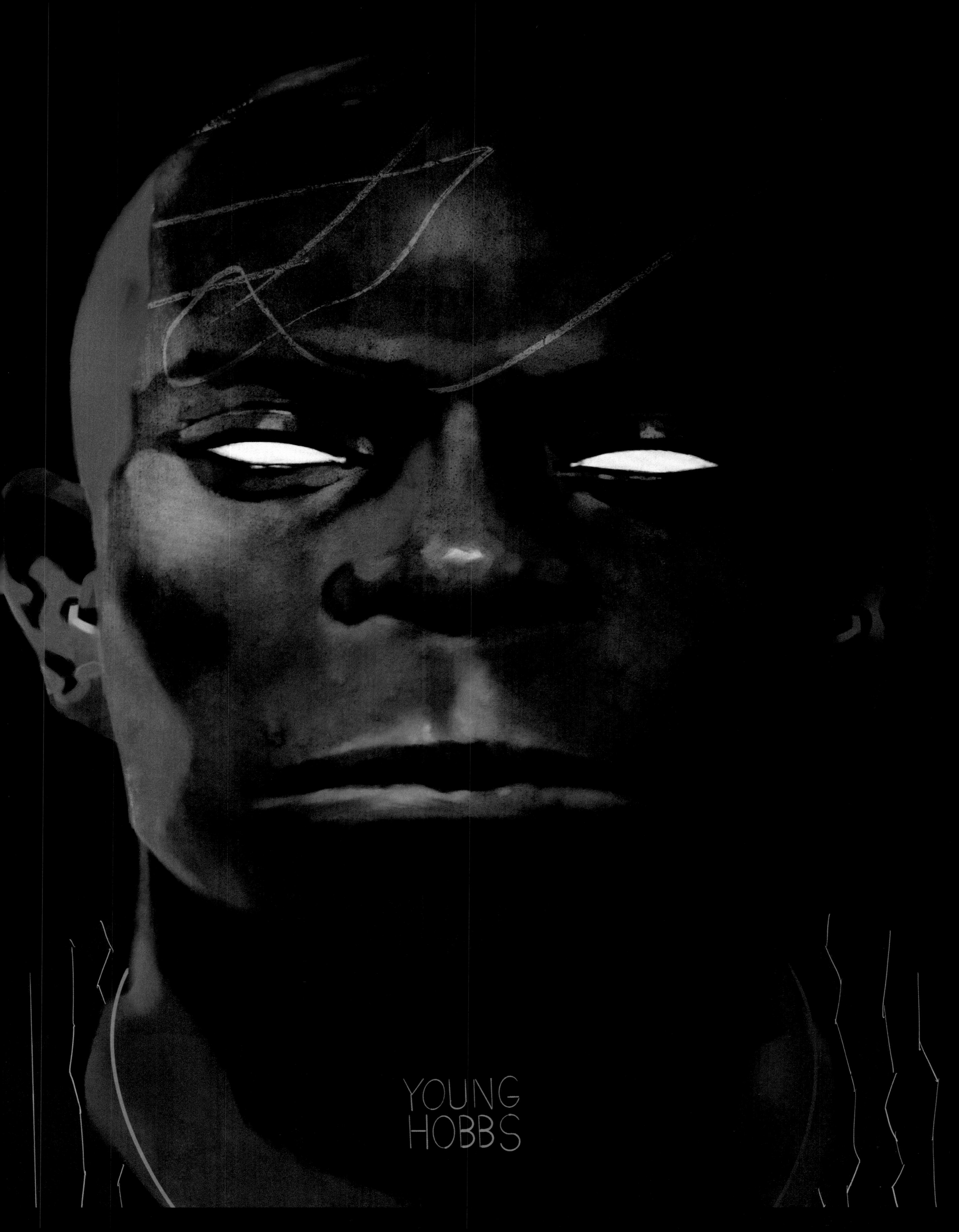
YOUNG
HOBBS

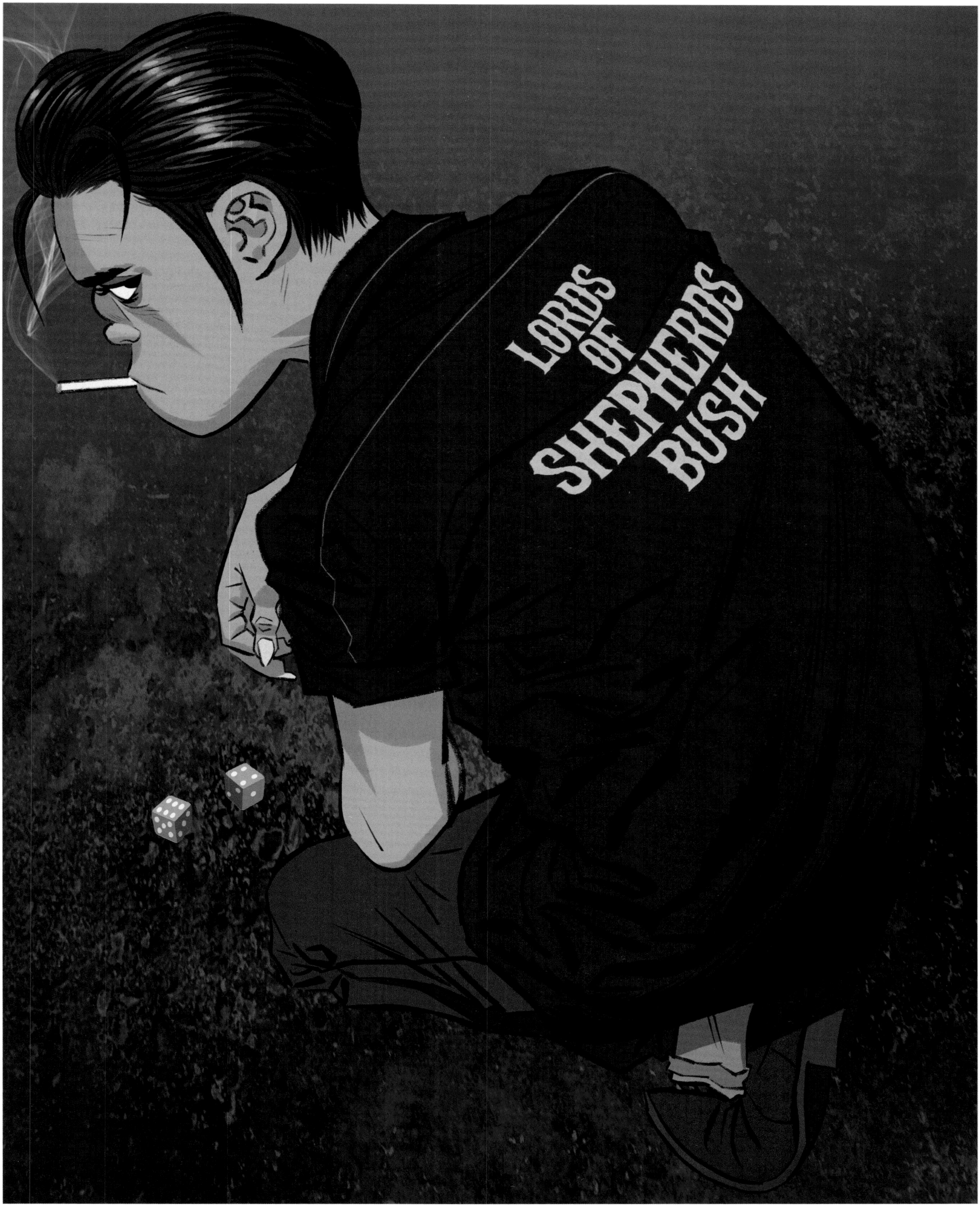
LORDS
OF
SHEPHERDS
BUSH

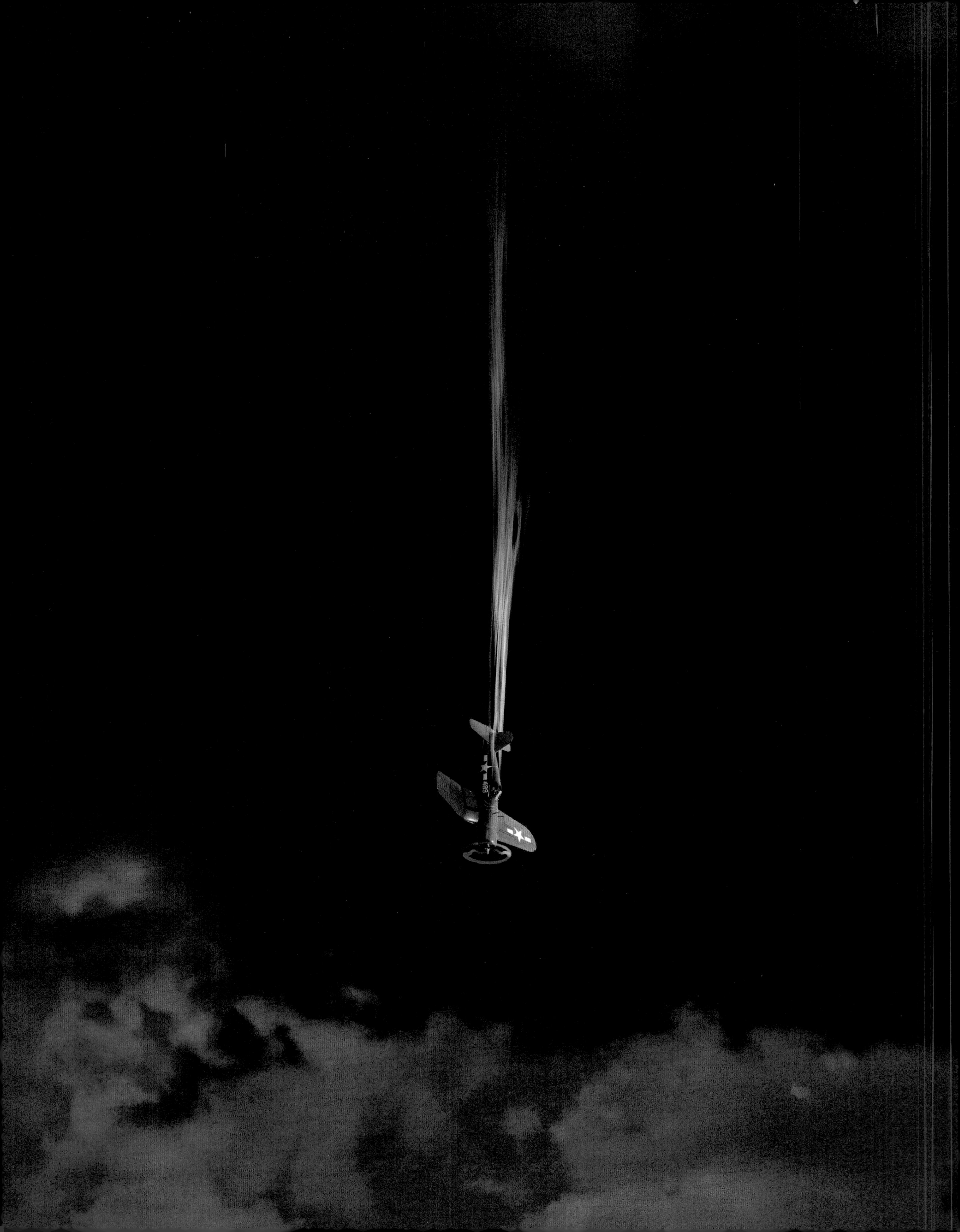

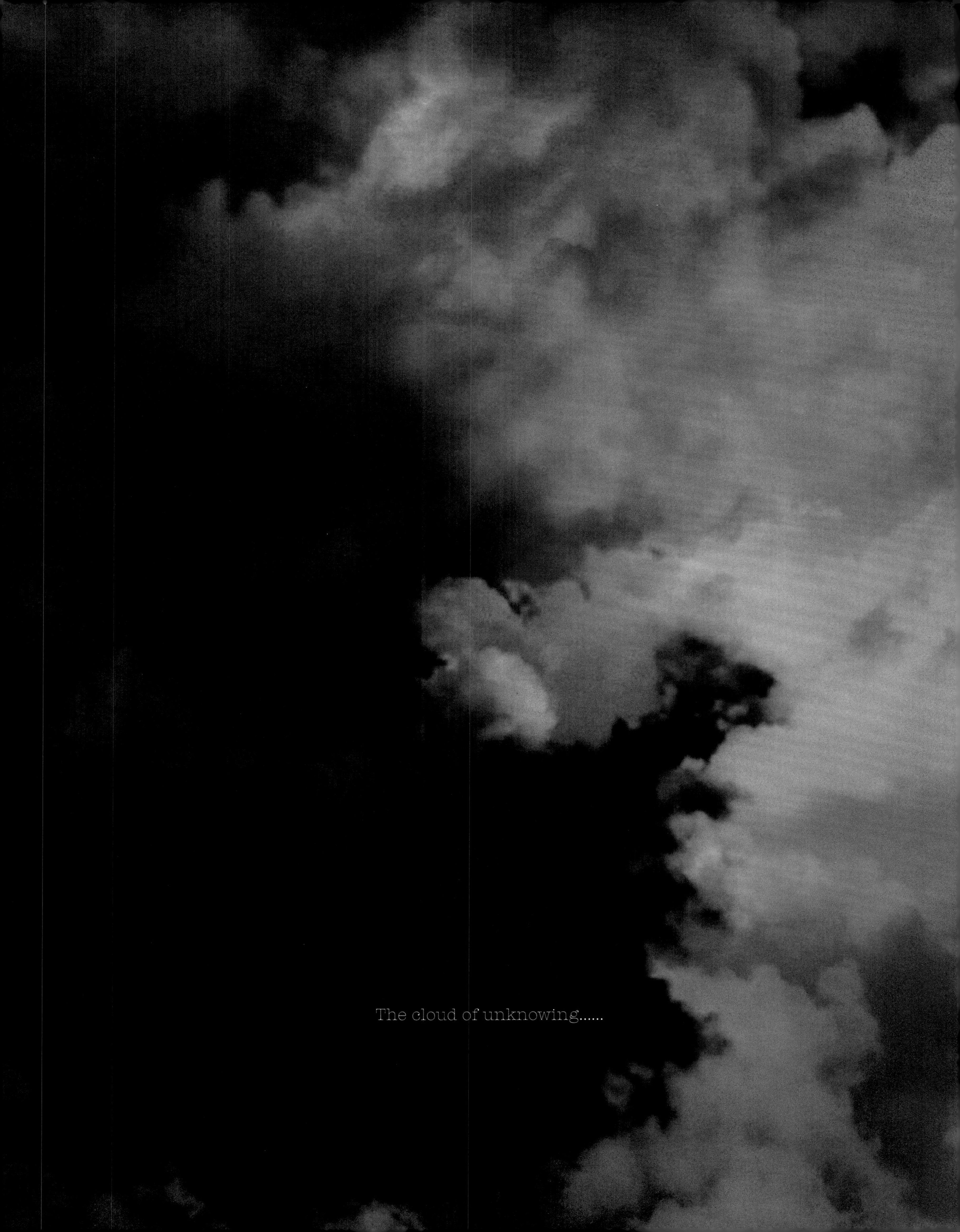
The cloud of unknowing......

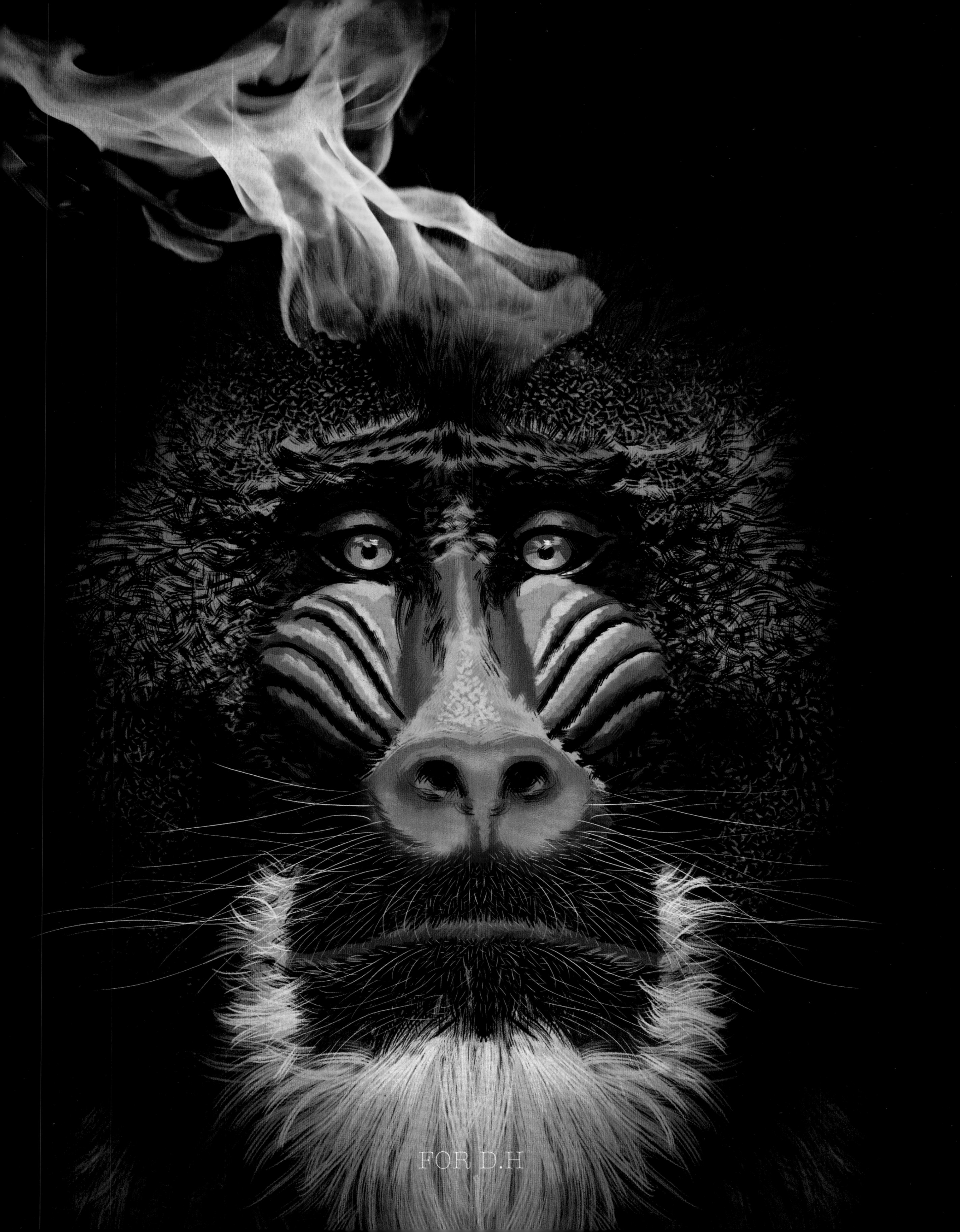
FOR D.H

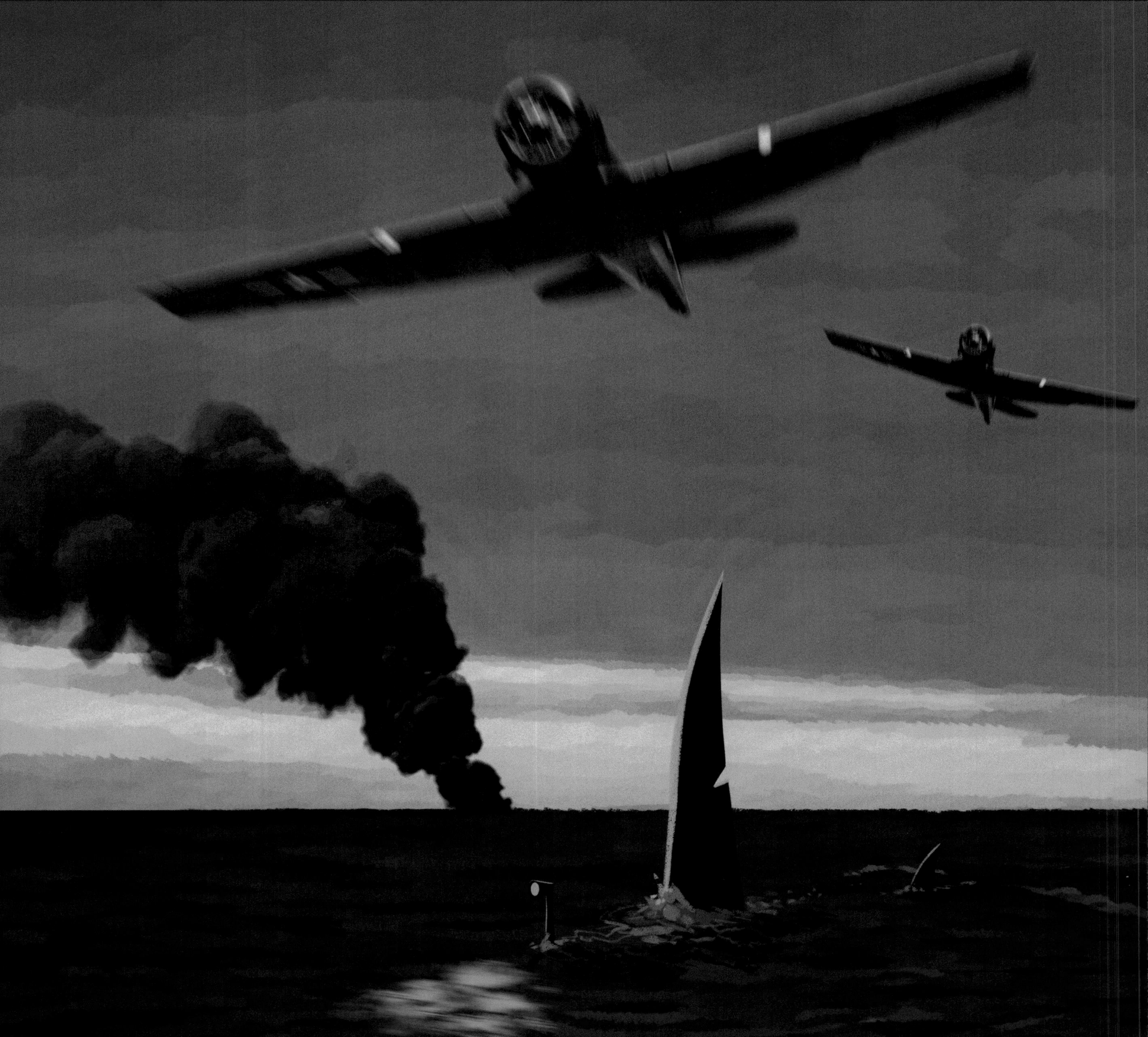

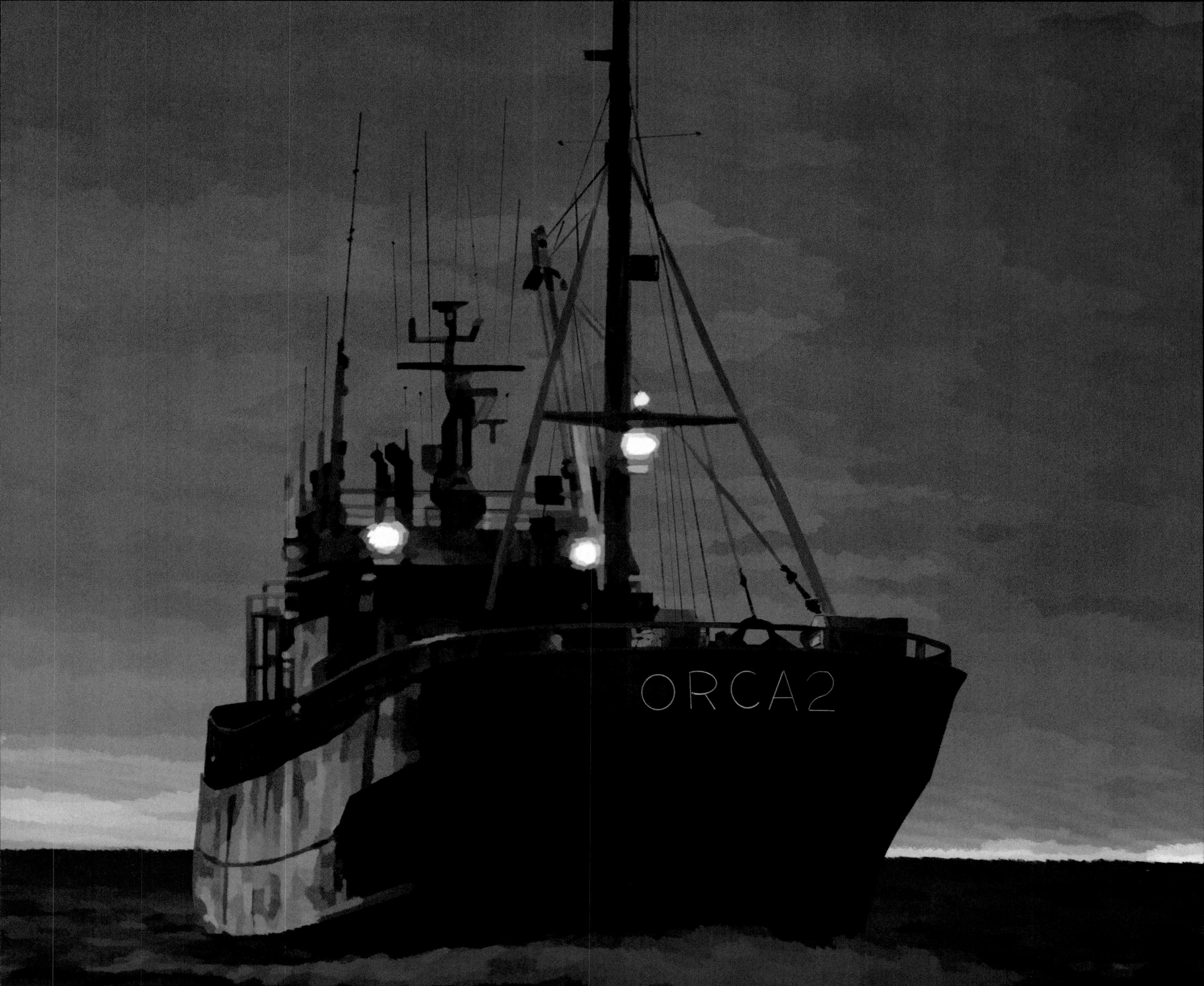
ORCA2

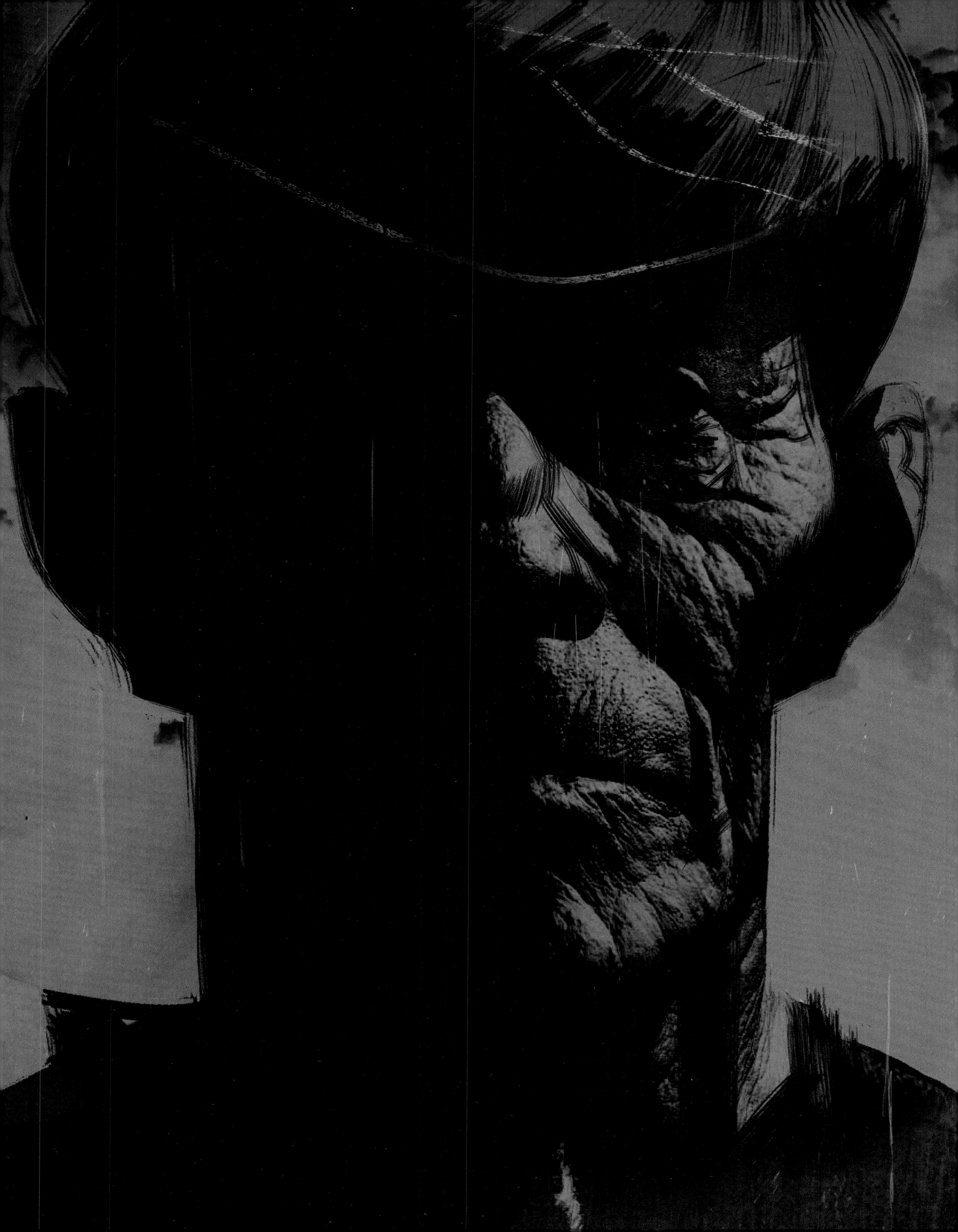

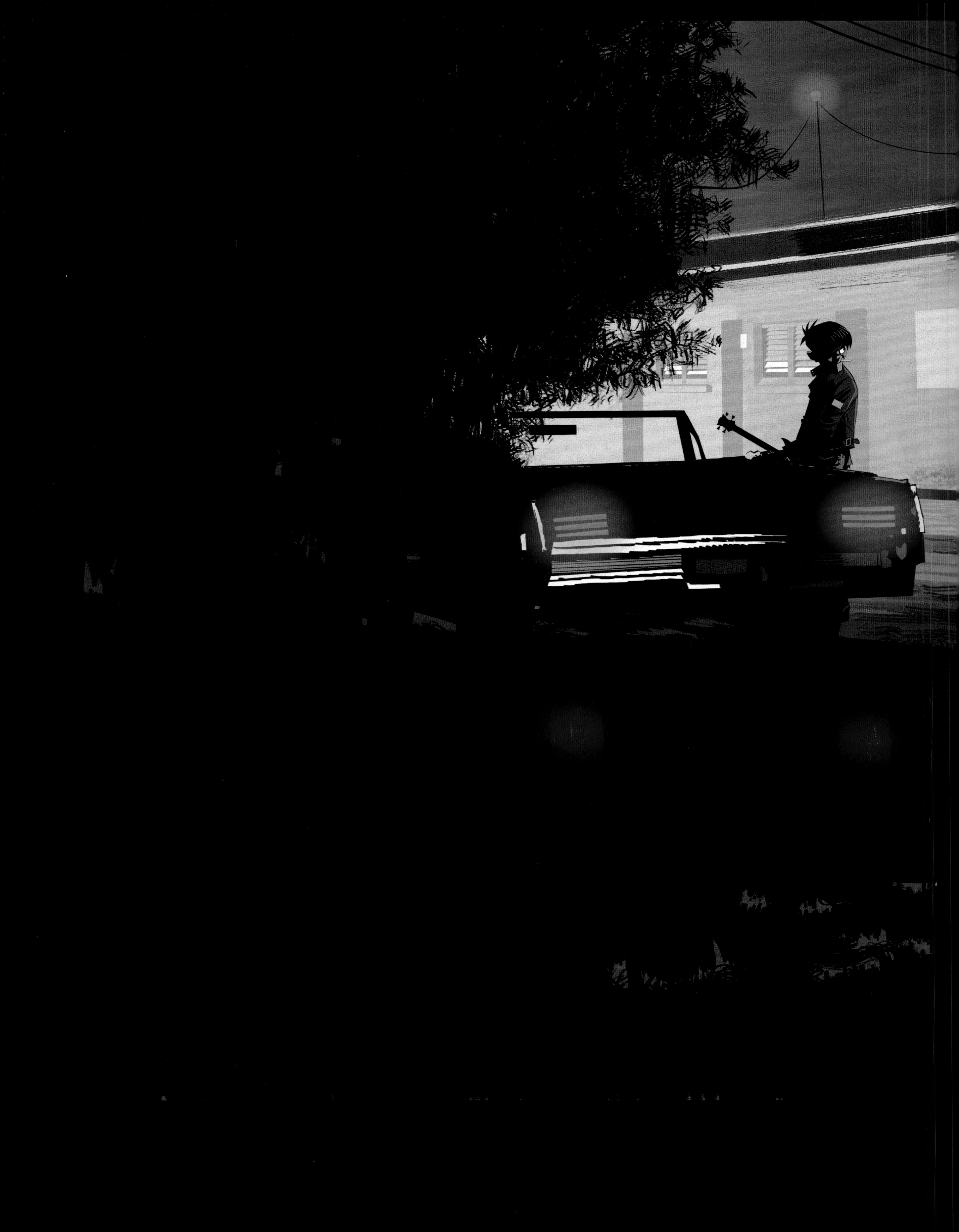

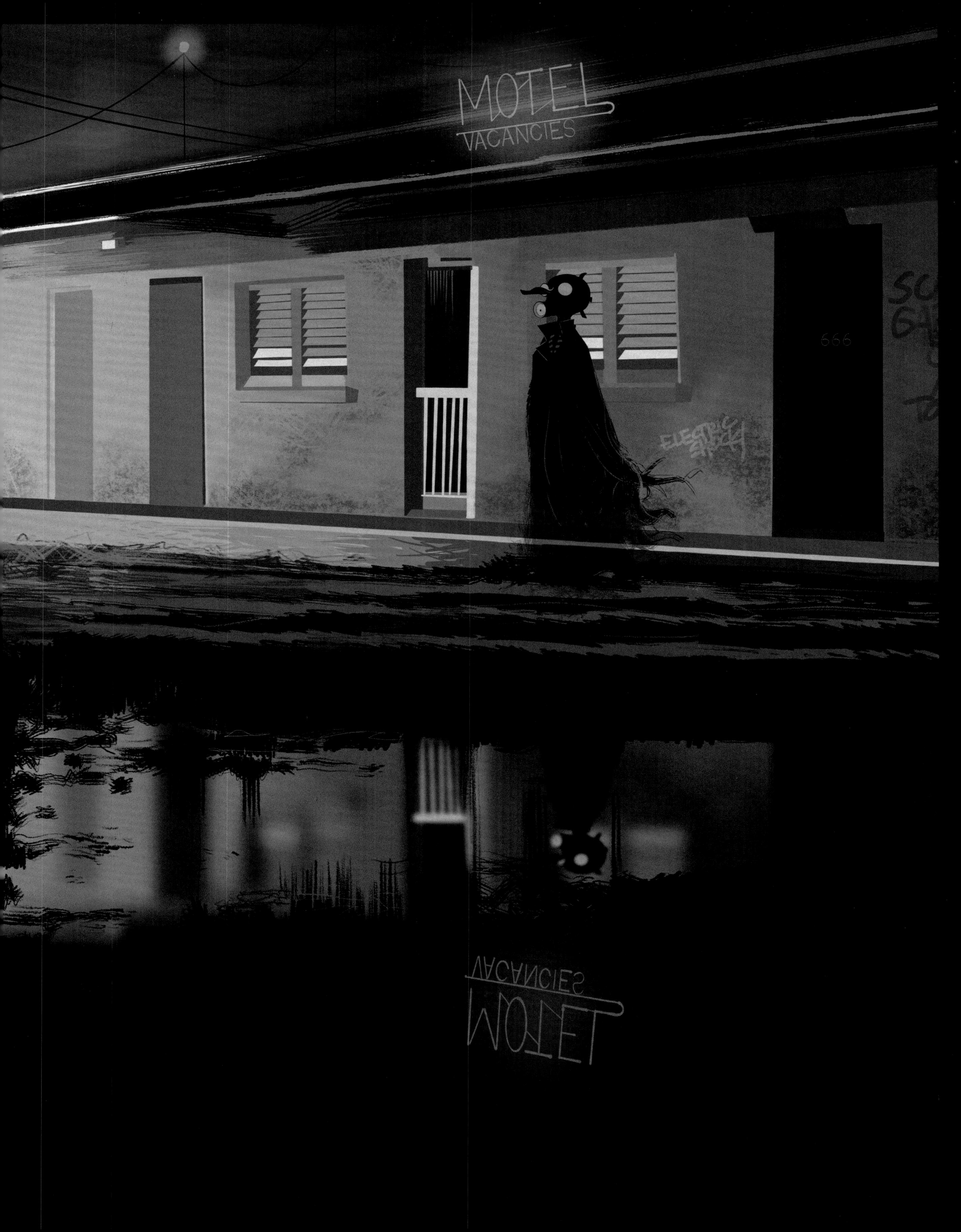
MOTEL
VACANCIES
666
ELECTRIC

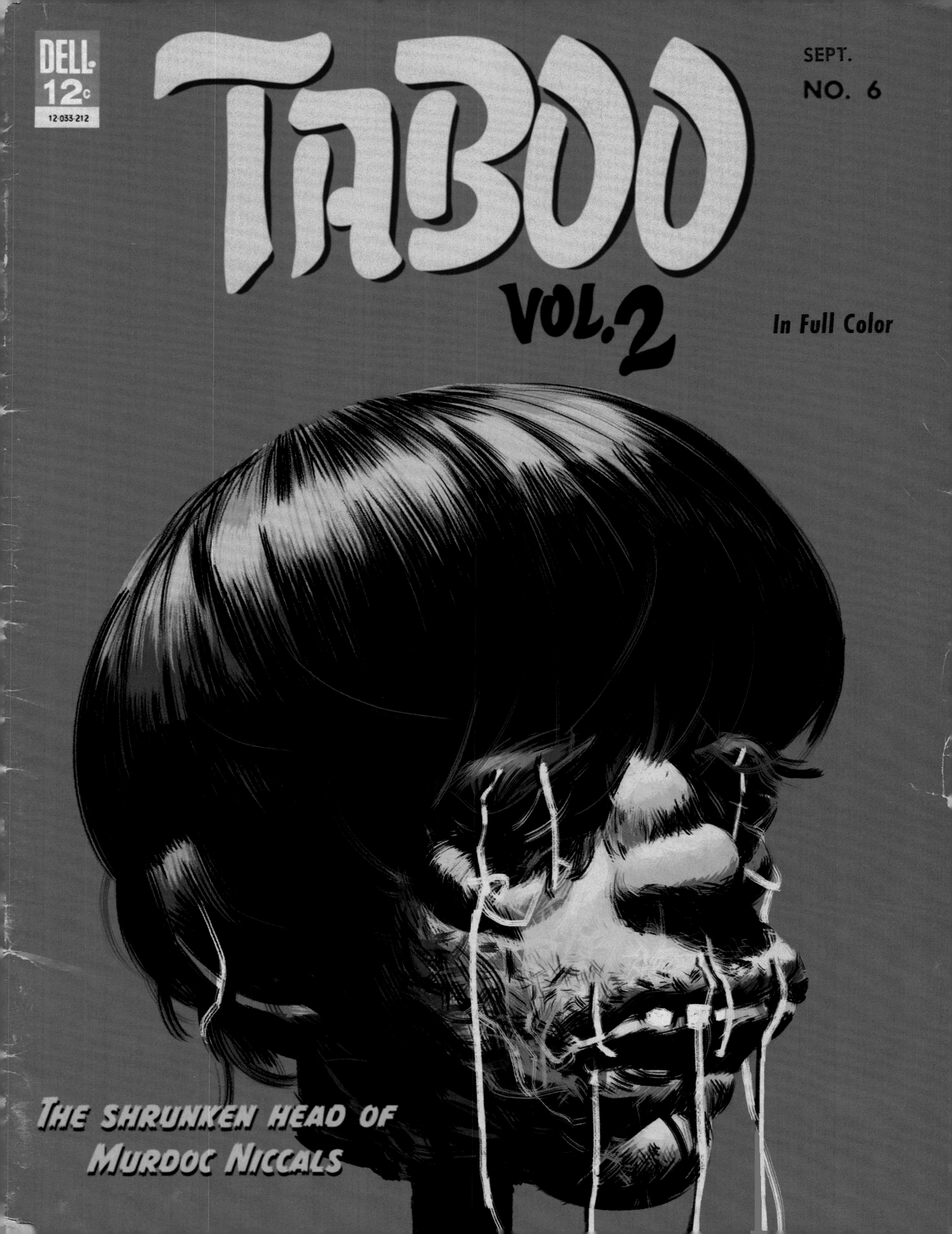
DELL
12¢
12-033-212
TABOO
SEPT.
NO. 6
VOL. 2
In Full Color
THE SHRUNKEN HEAD OF
MURDOC NICCALS

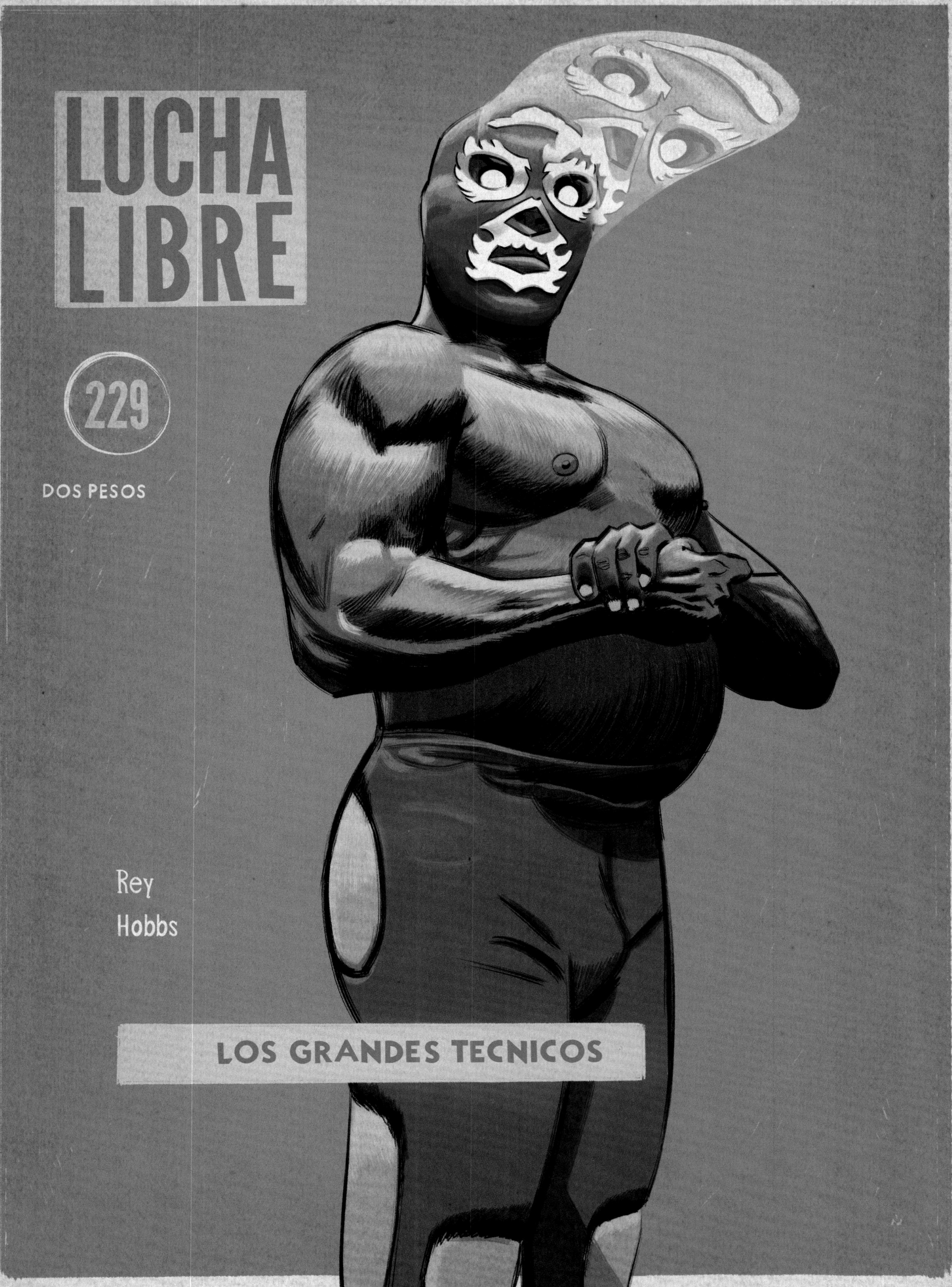
LUCHA
LIBRE
229
DOS PESOS
Rey
Hobbs
LOS GRANDES TECNICOS

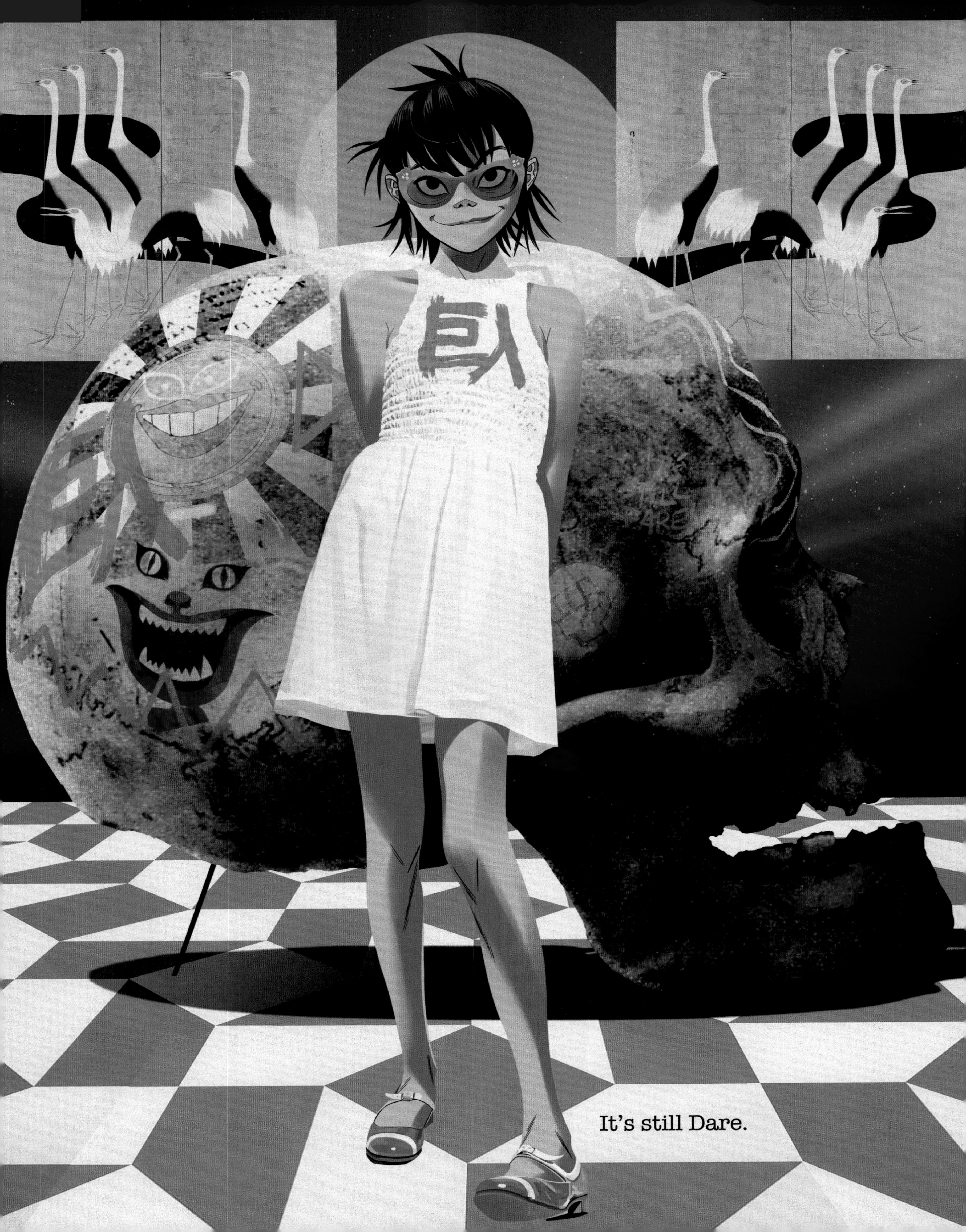
It's still Dare.

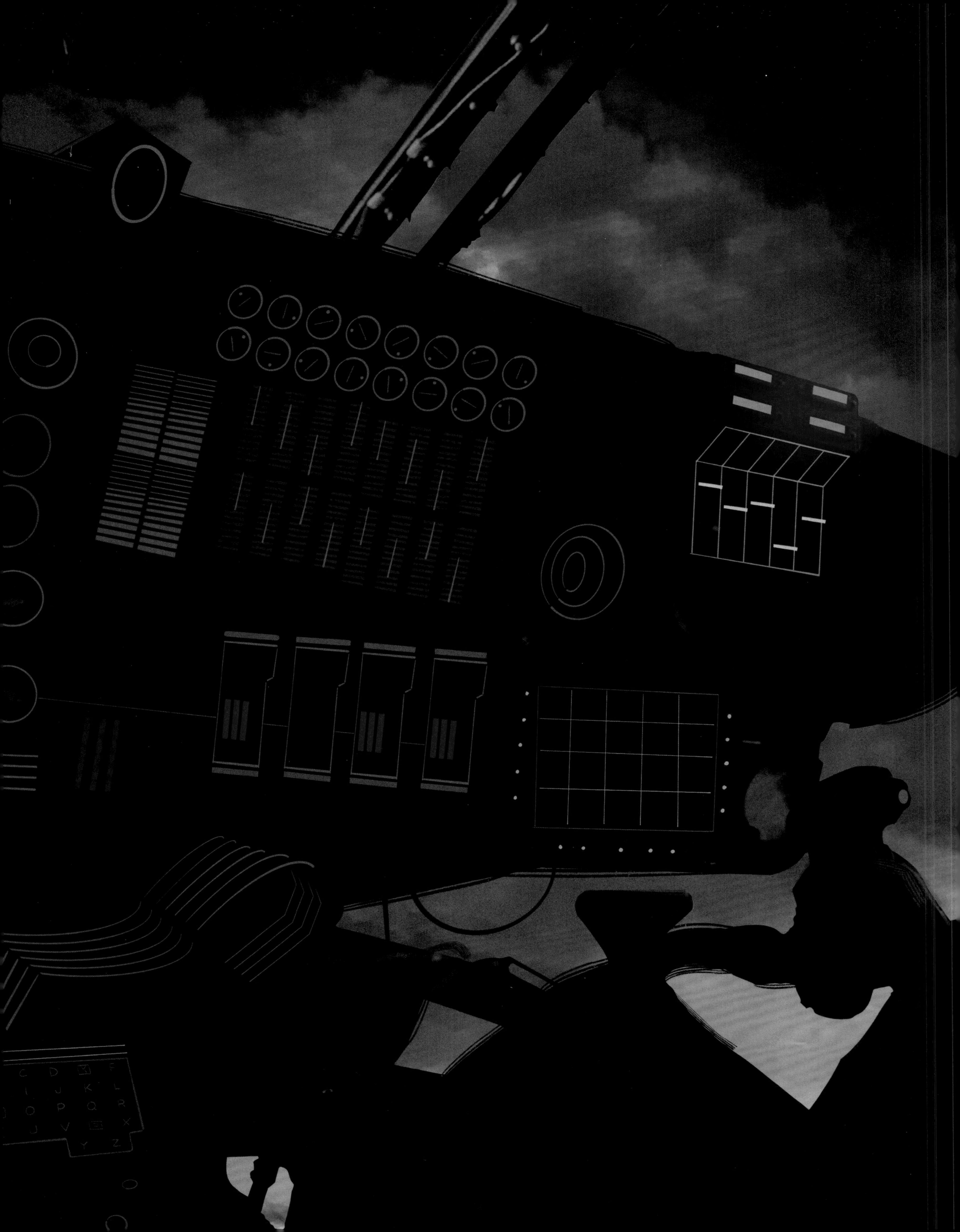

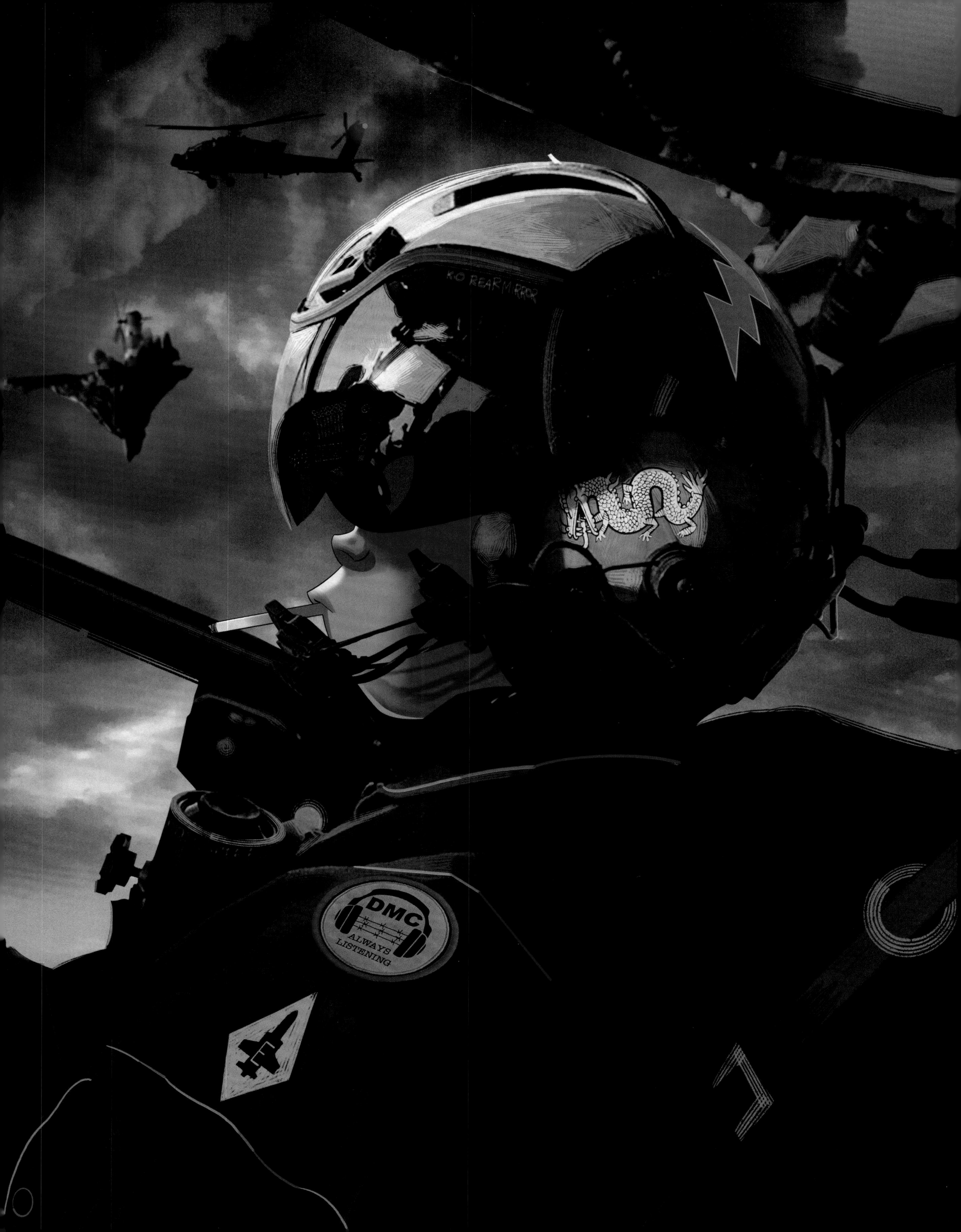
DMC
ALWAYS
LISTENING

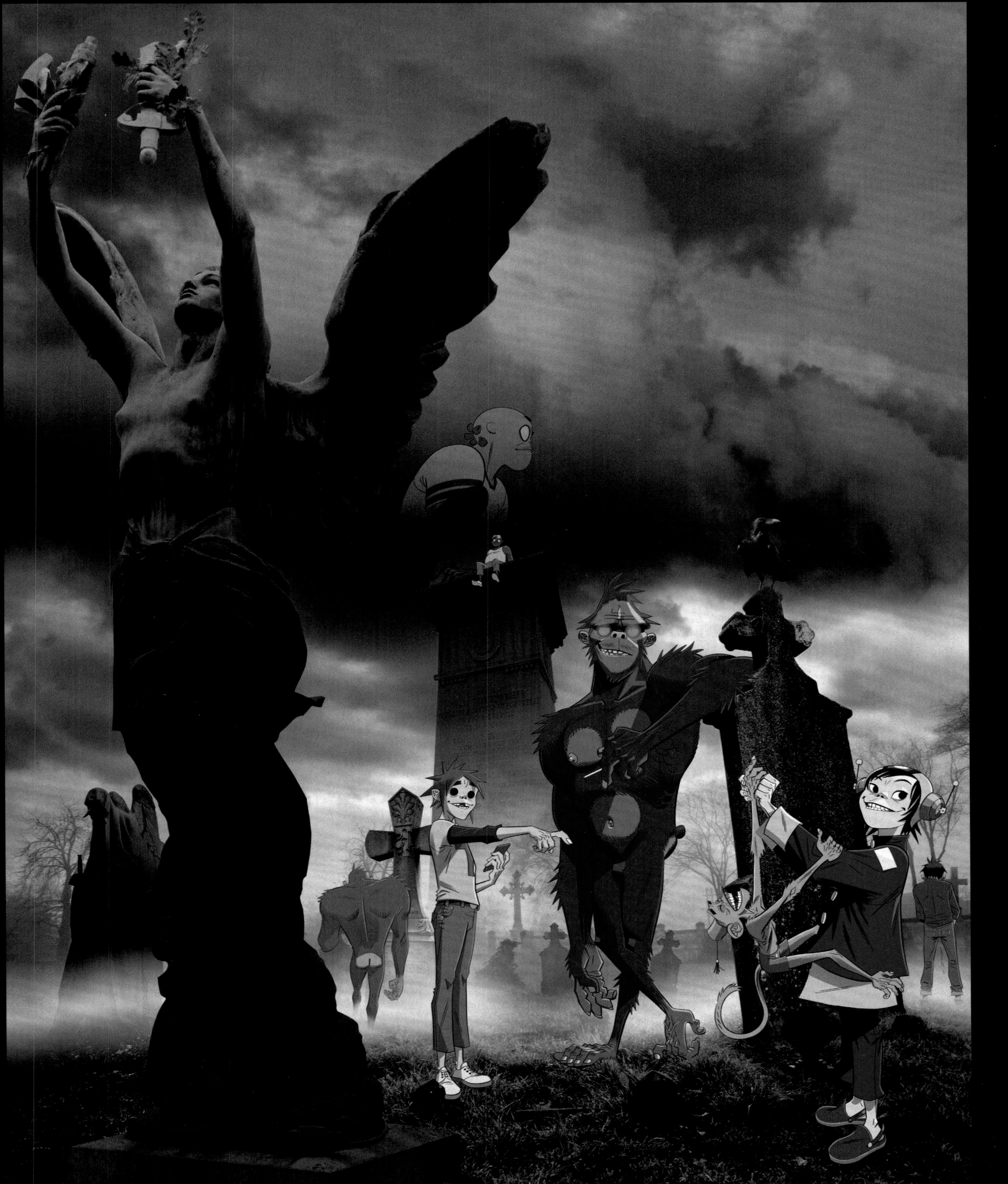

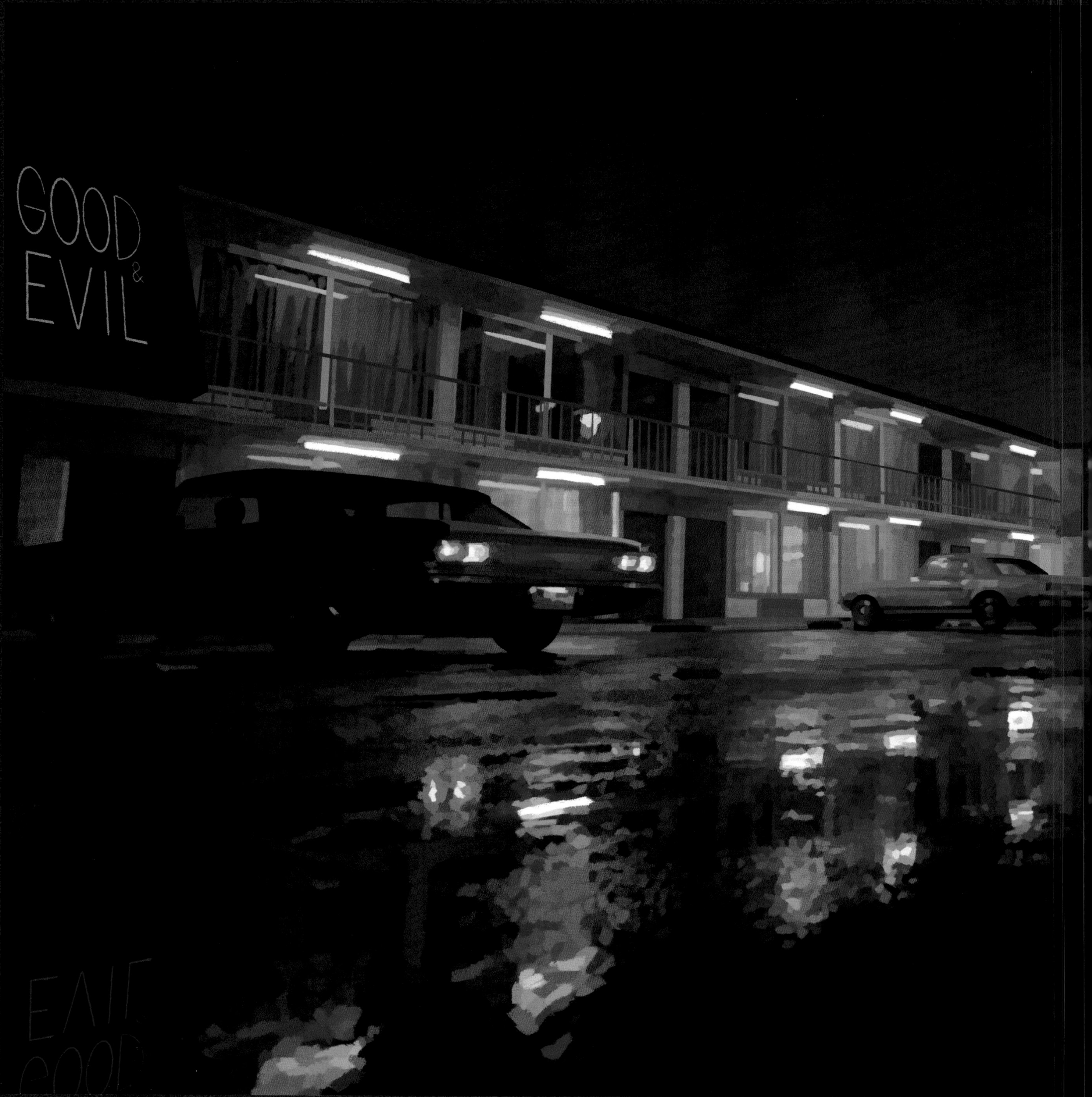
GOOD & EVIL

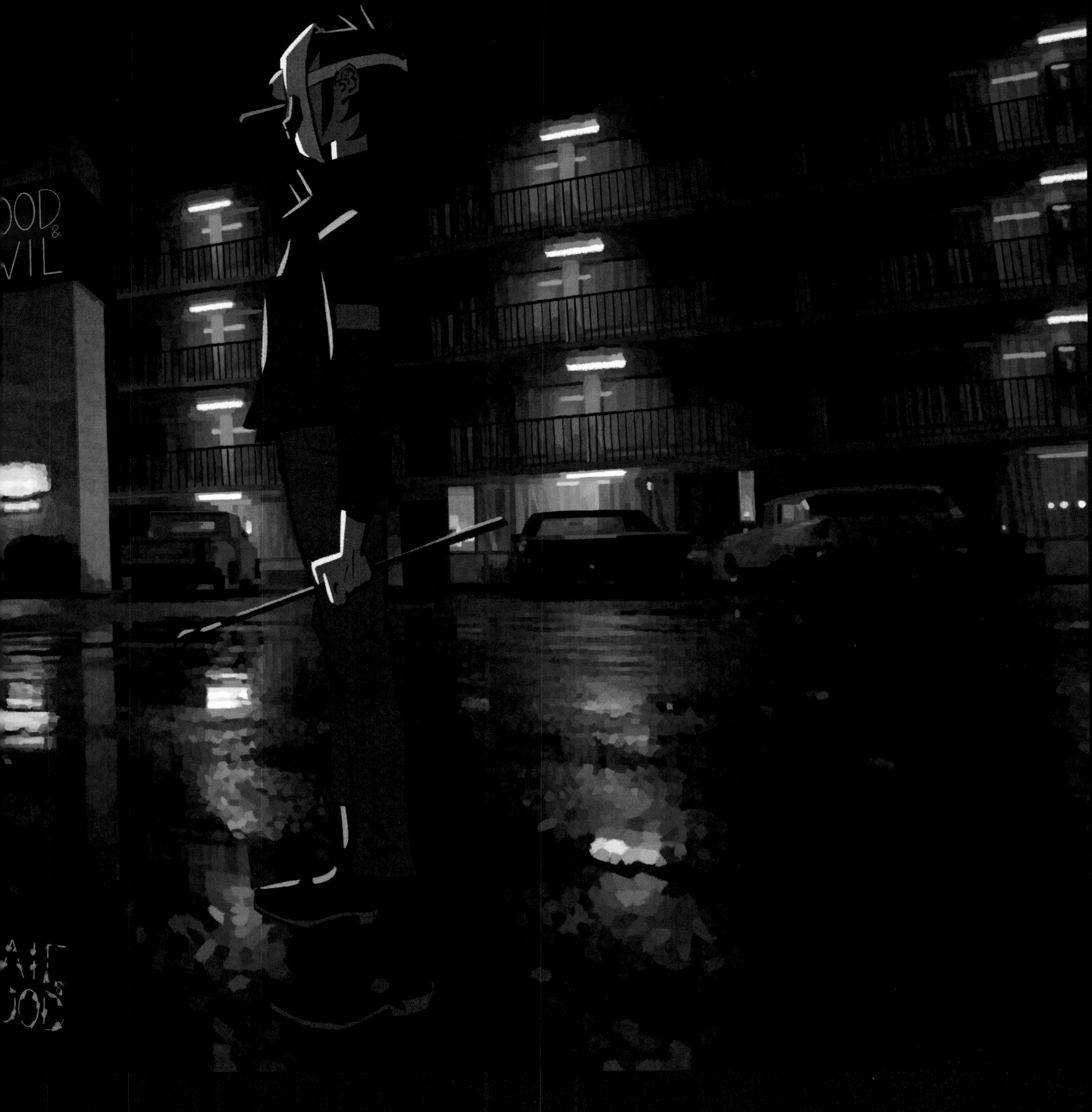

Midnight in the carpark of Good & Evil.

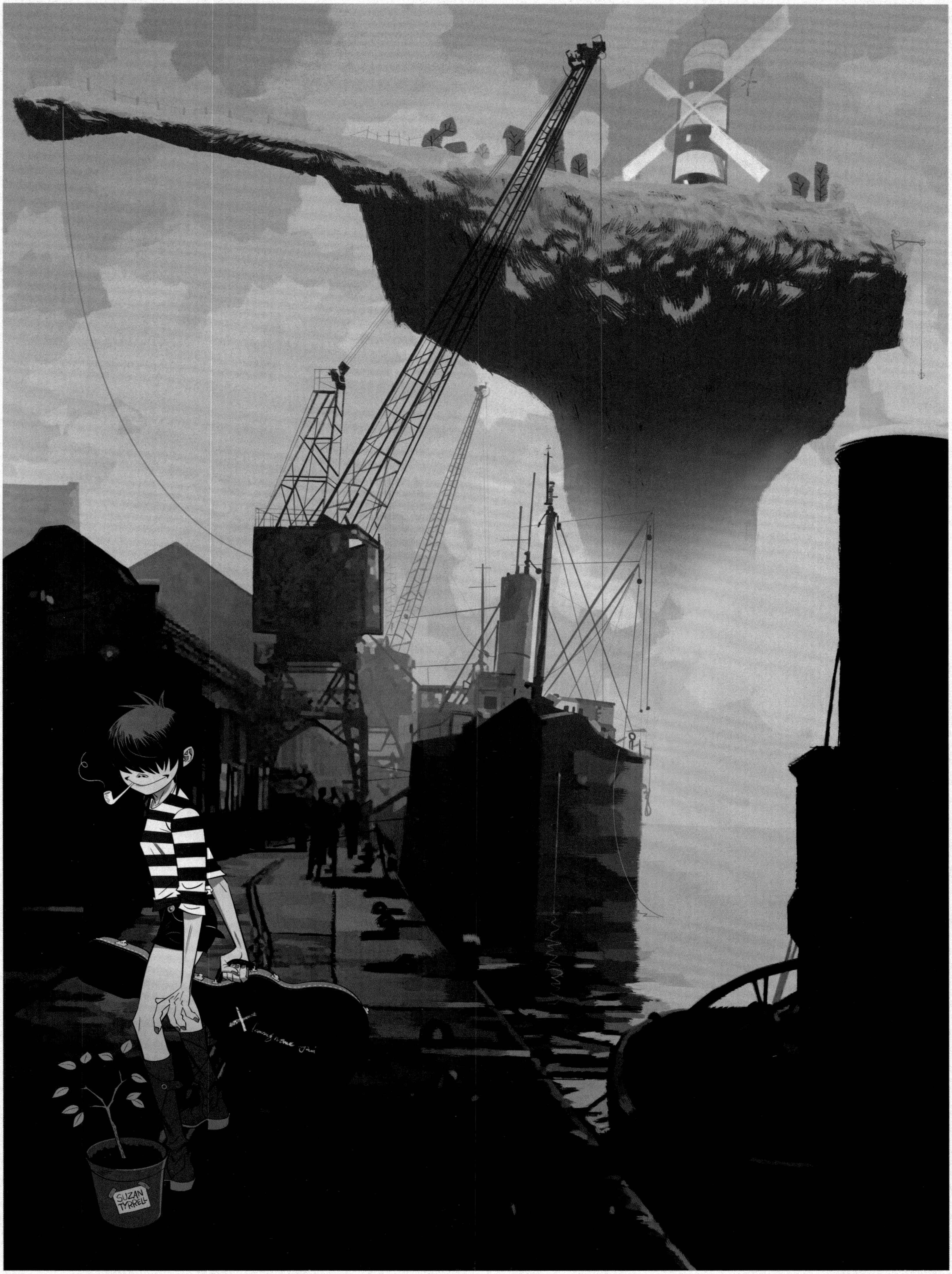
SUZAN
TYRRELL

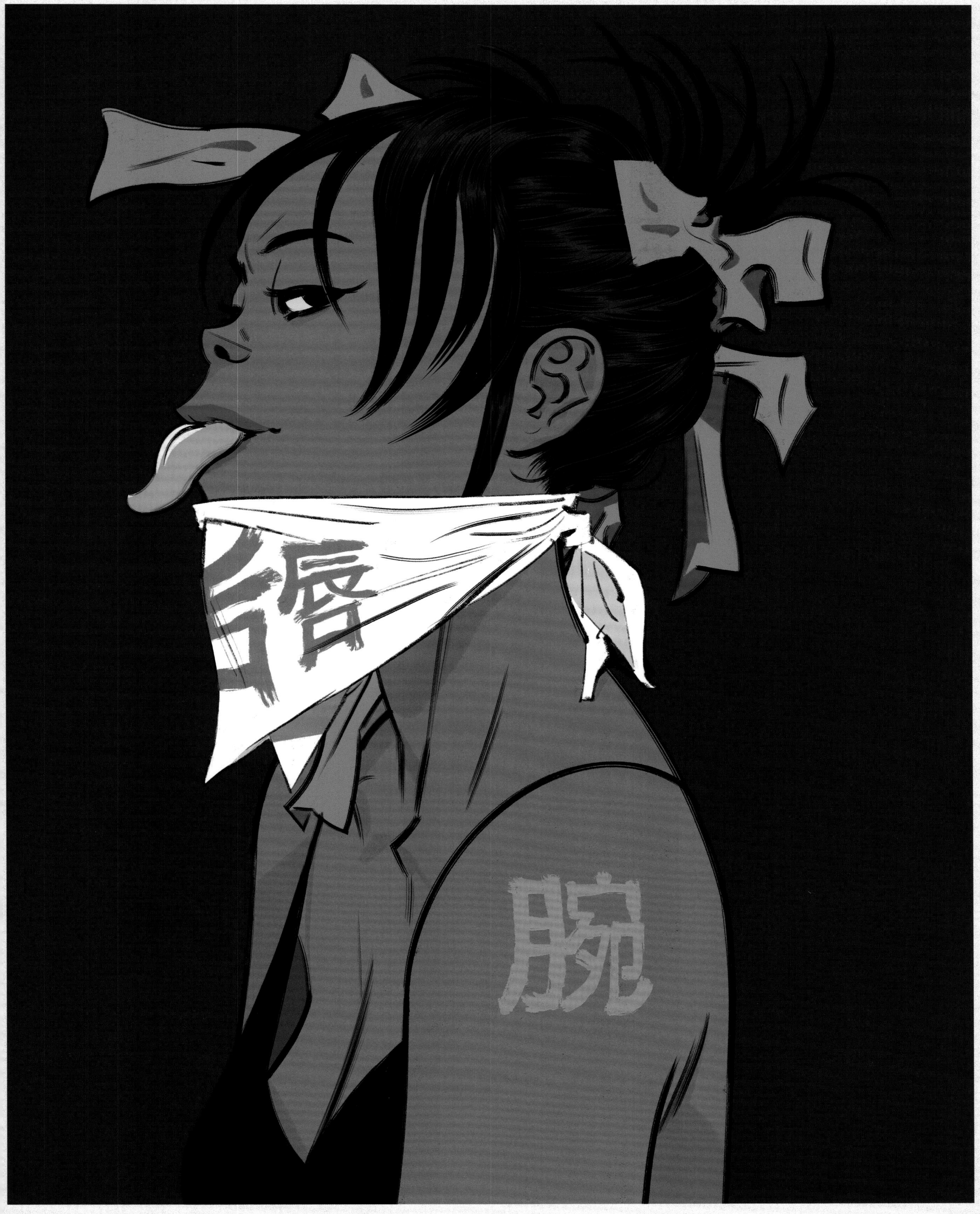
唇
腕

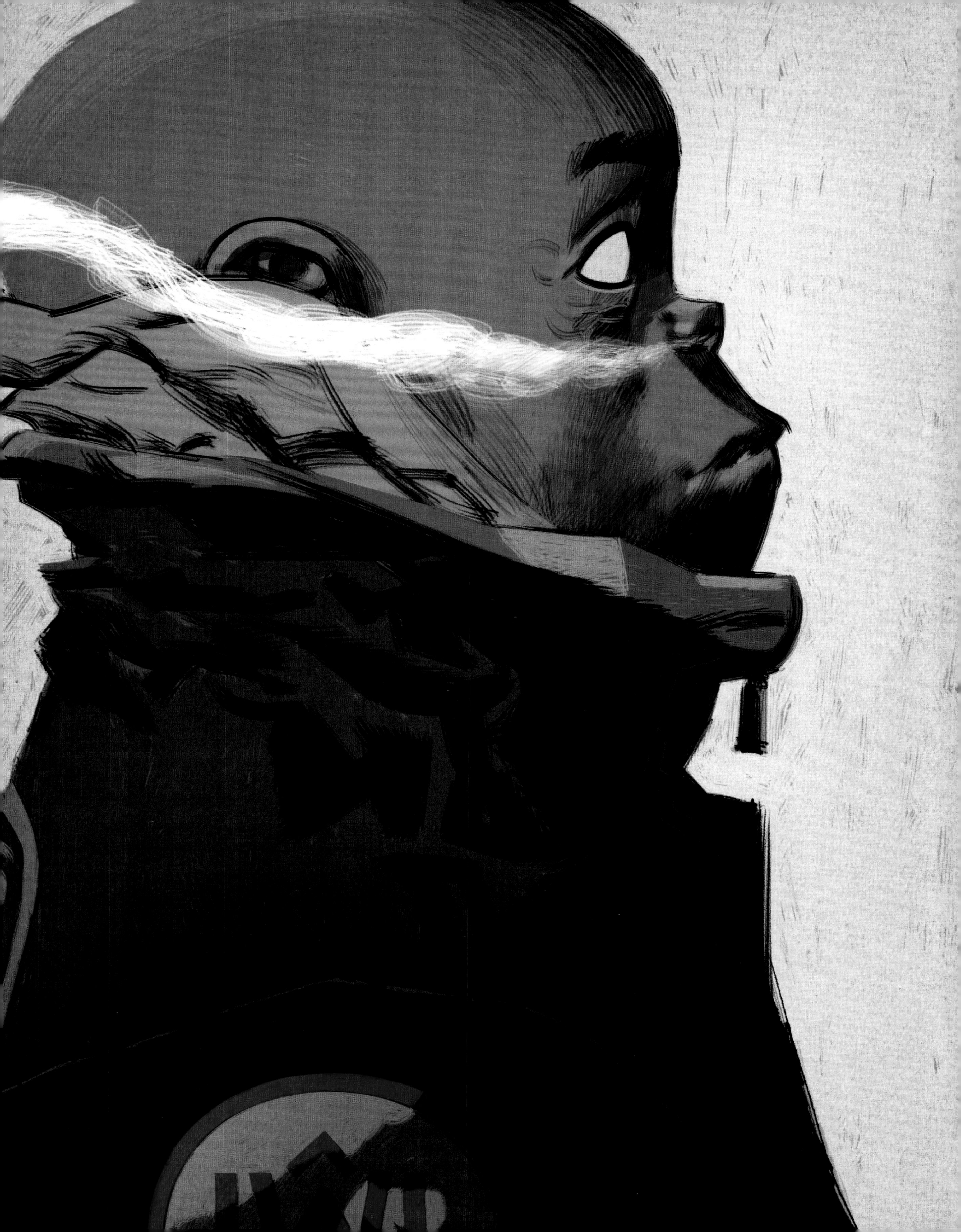

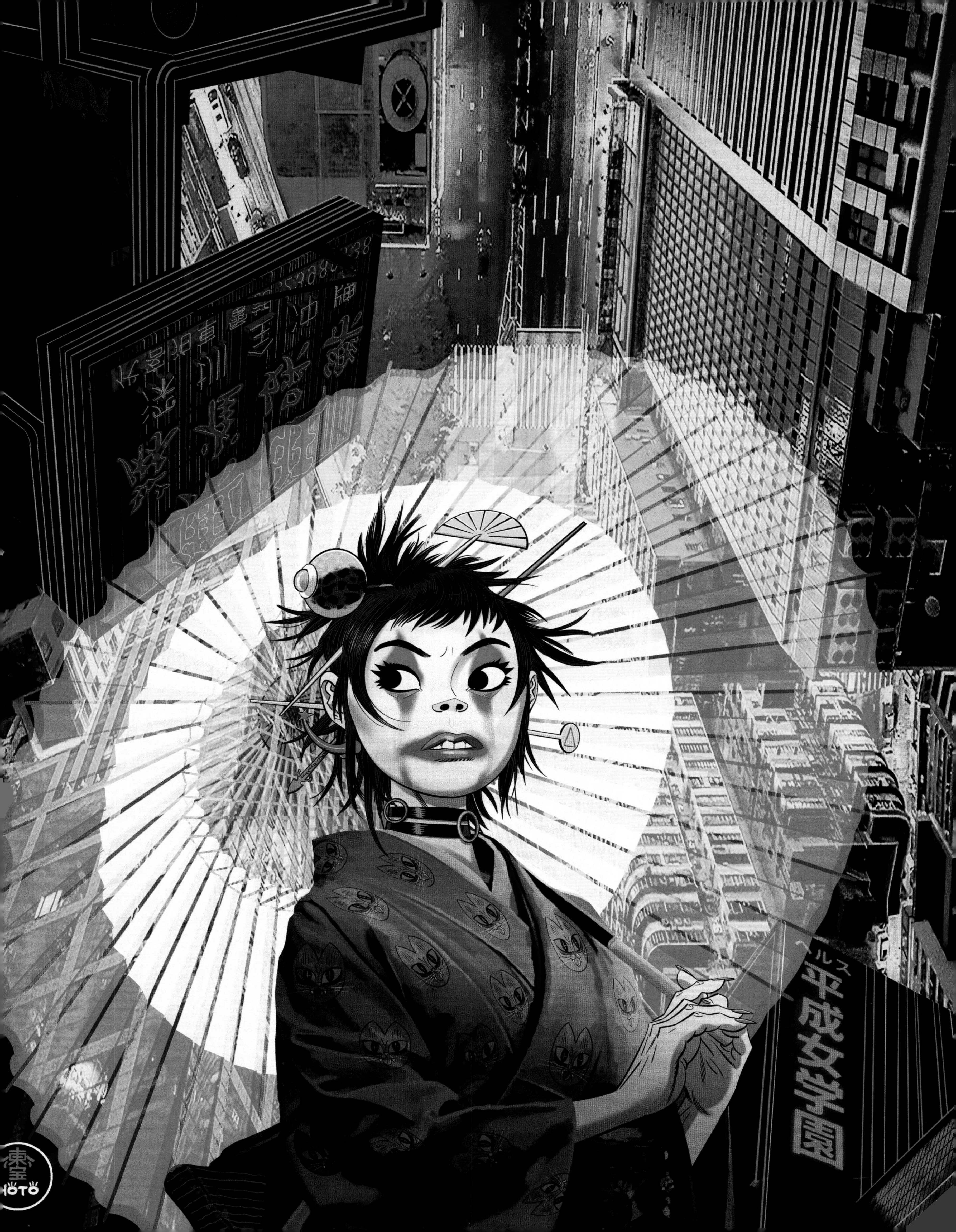
平成女学園

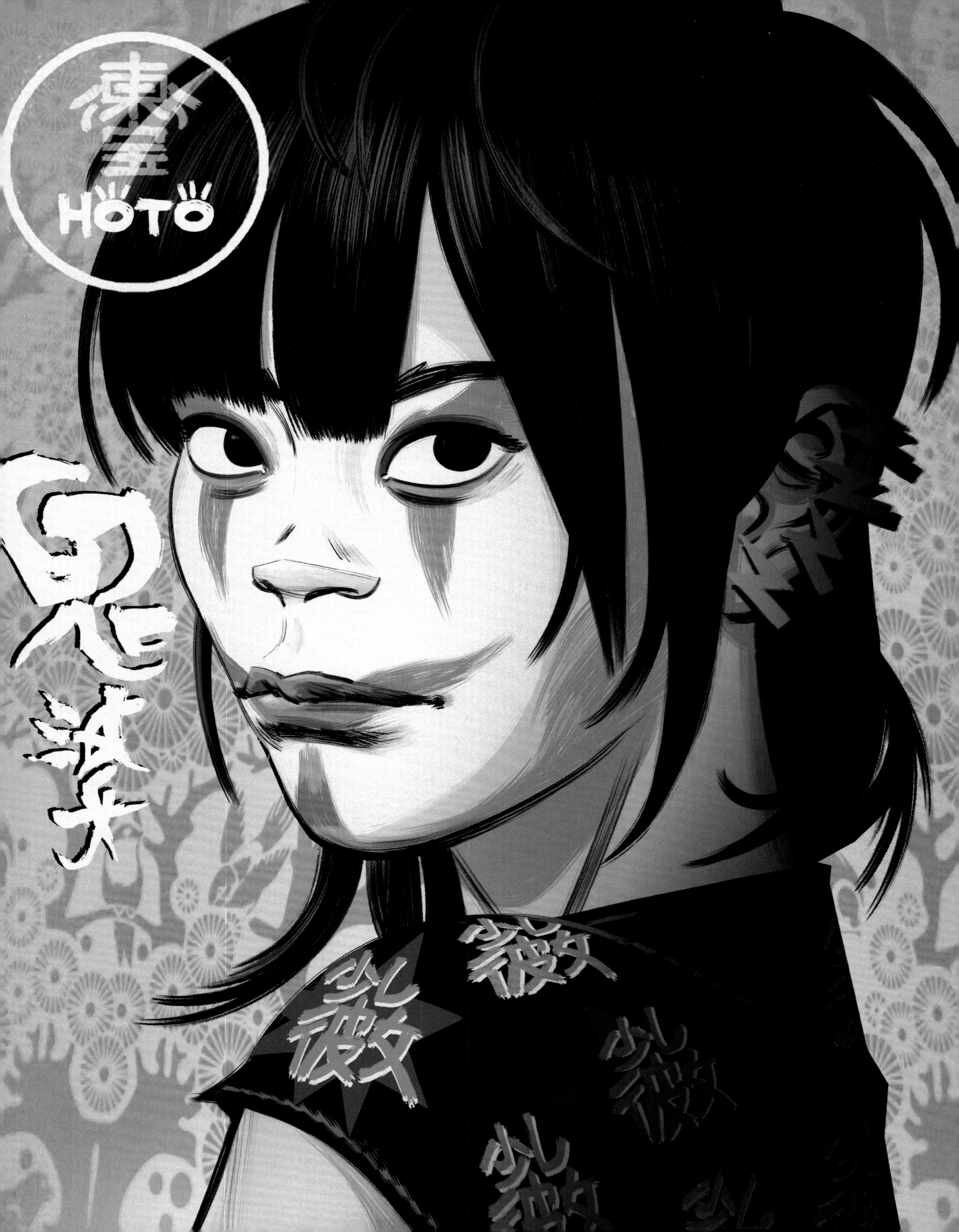
HOTO

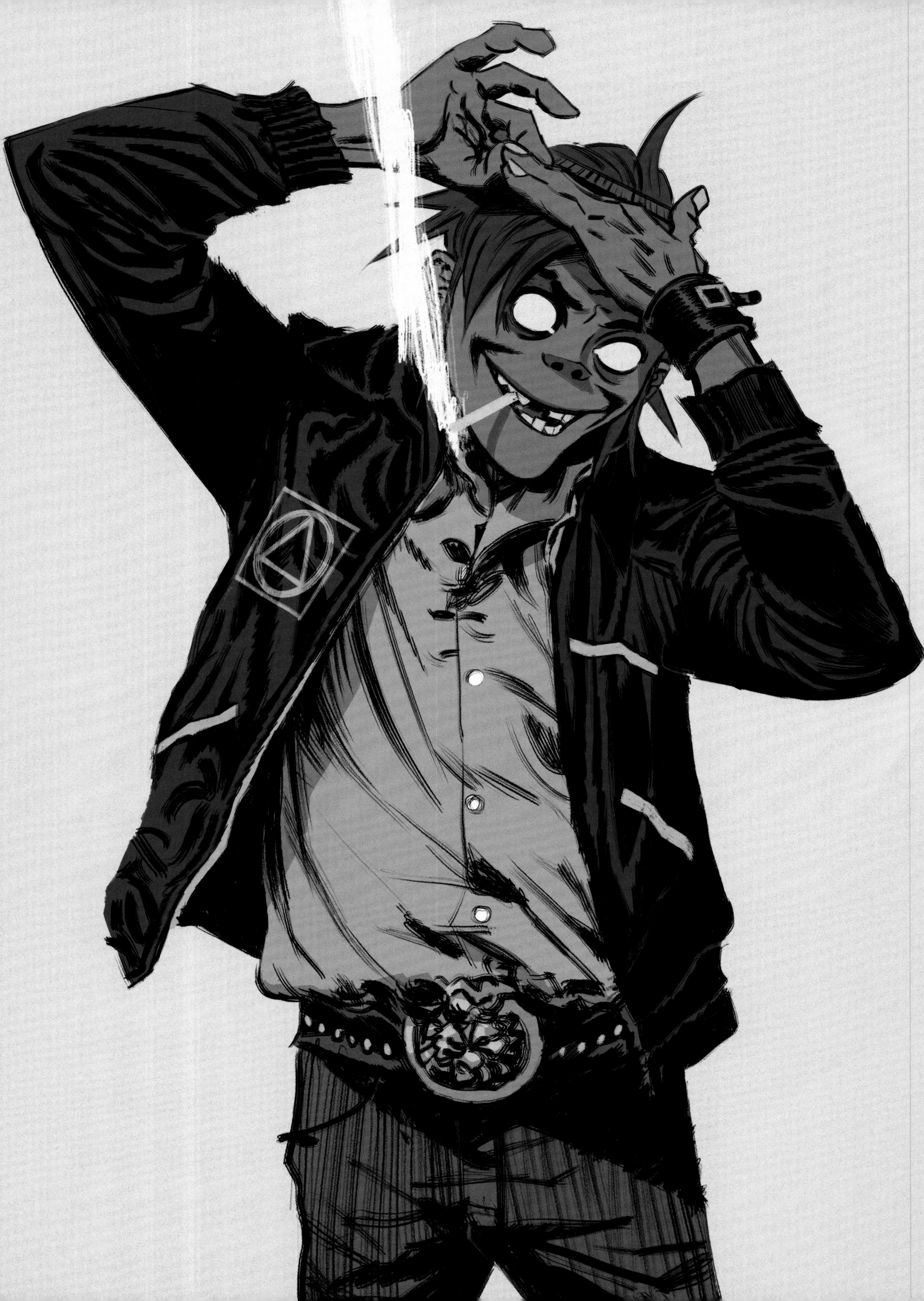

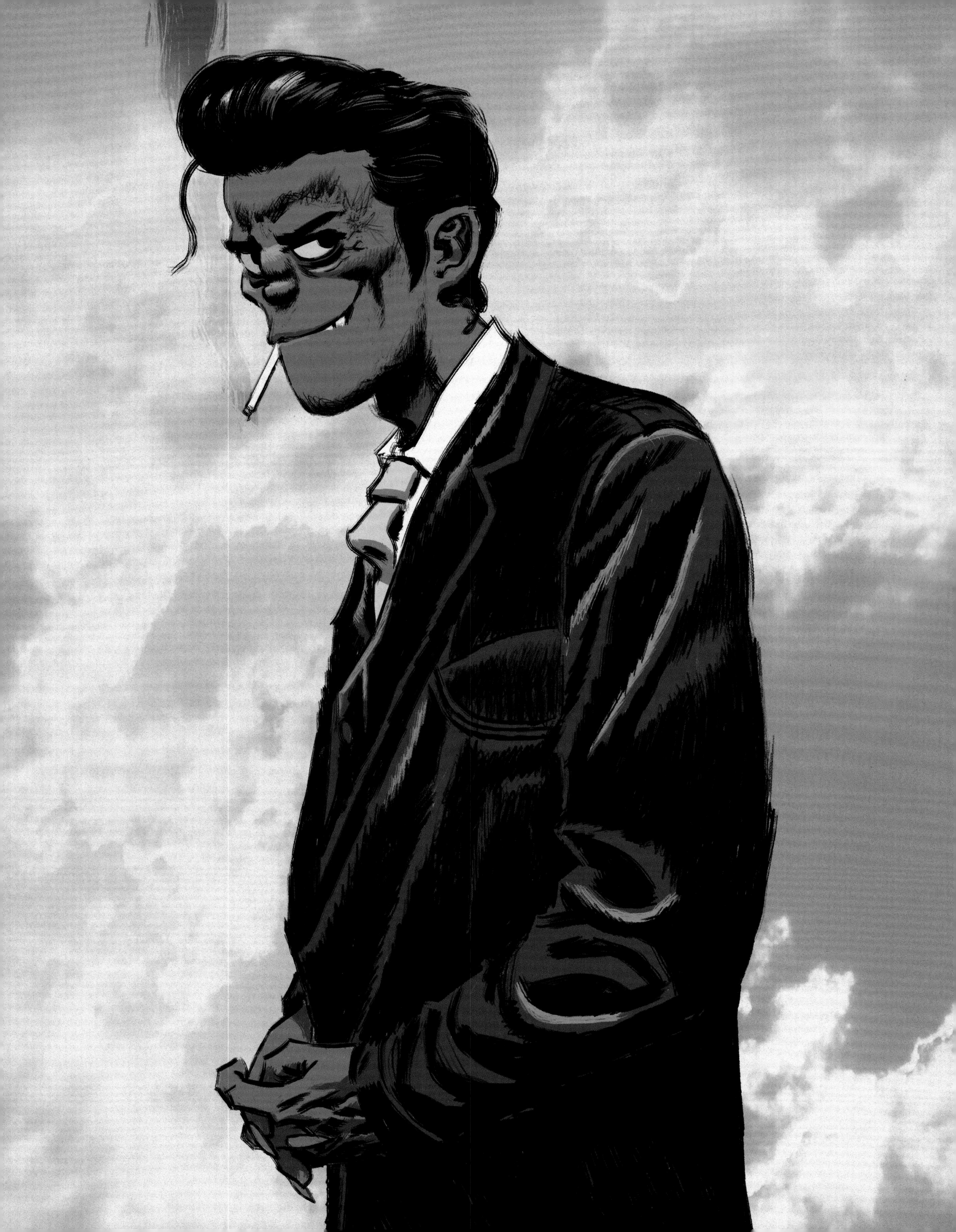

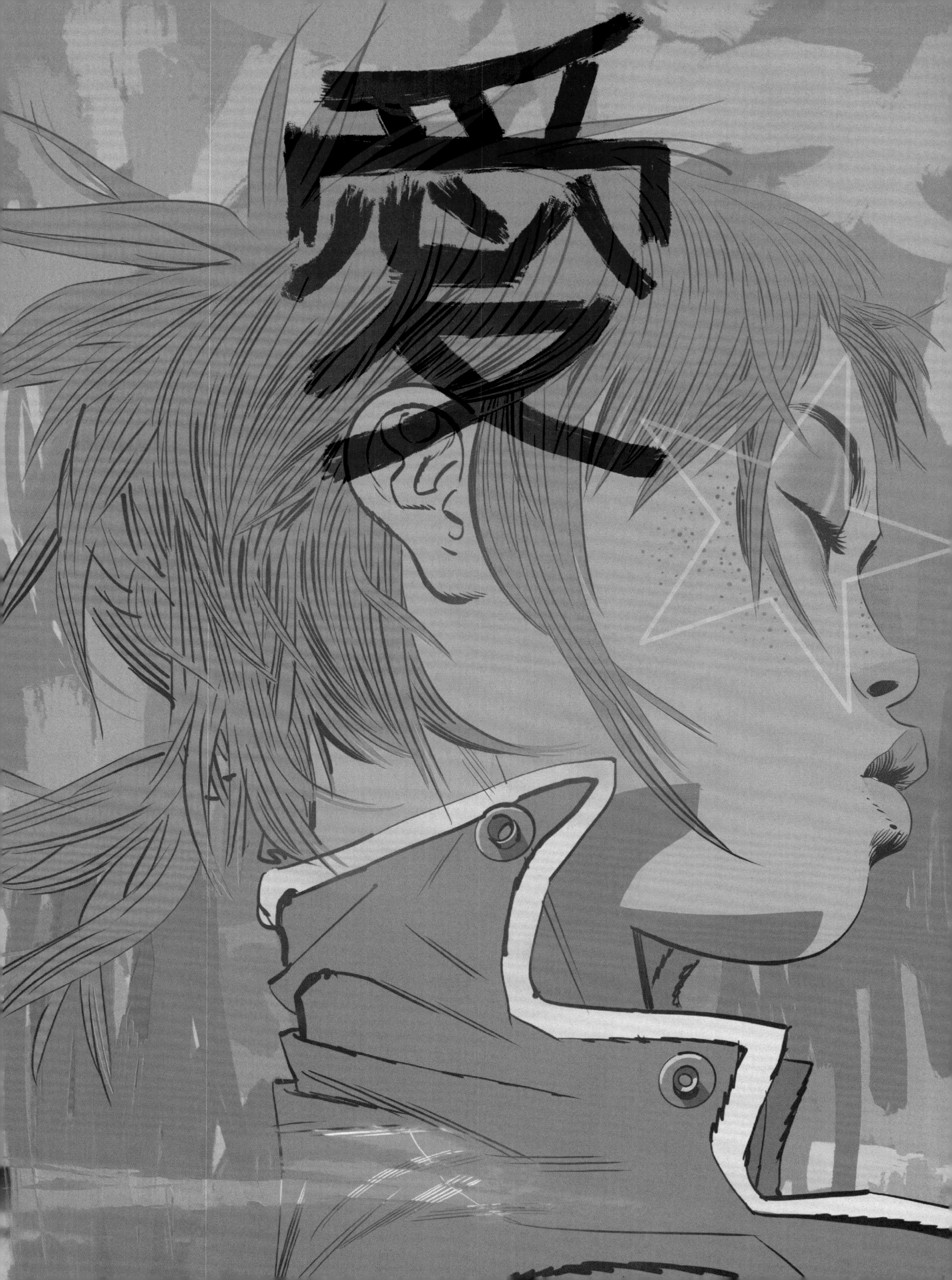
愛

東
ドバシカメ

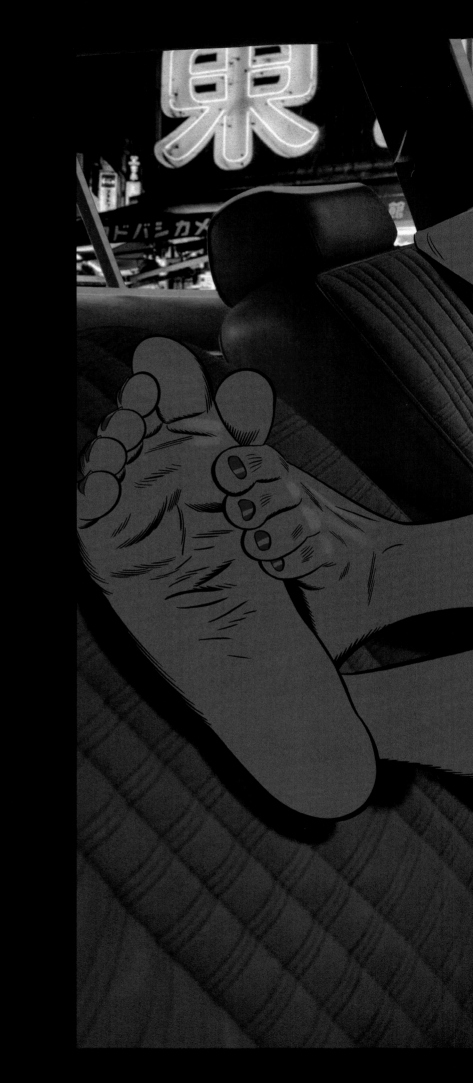

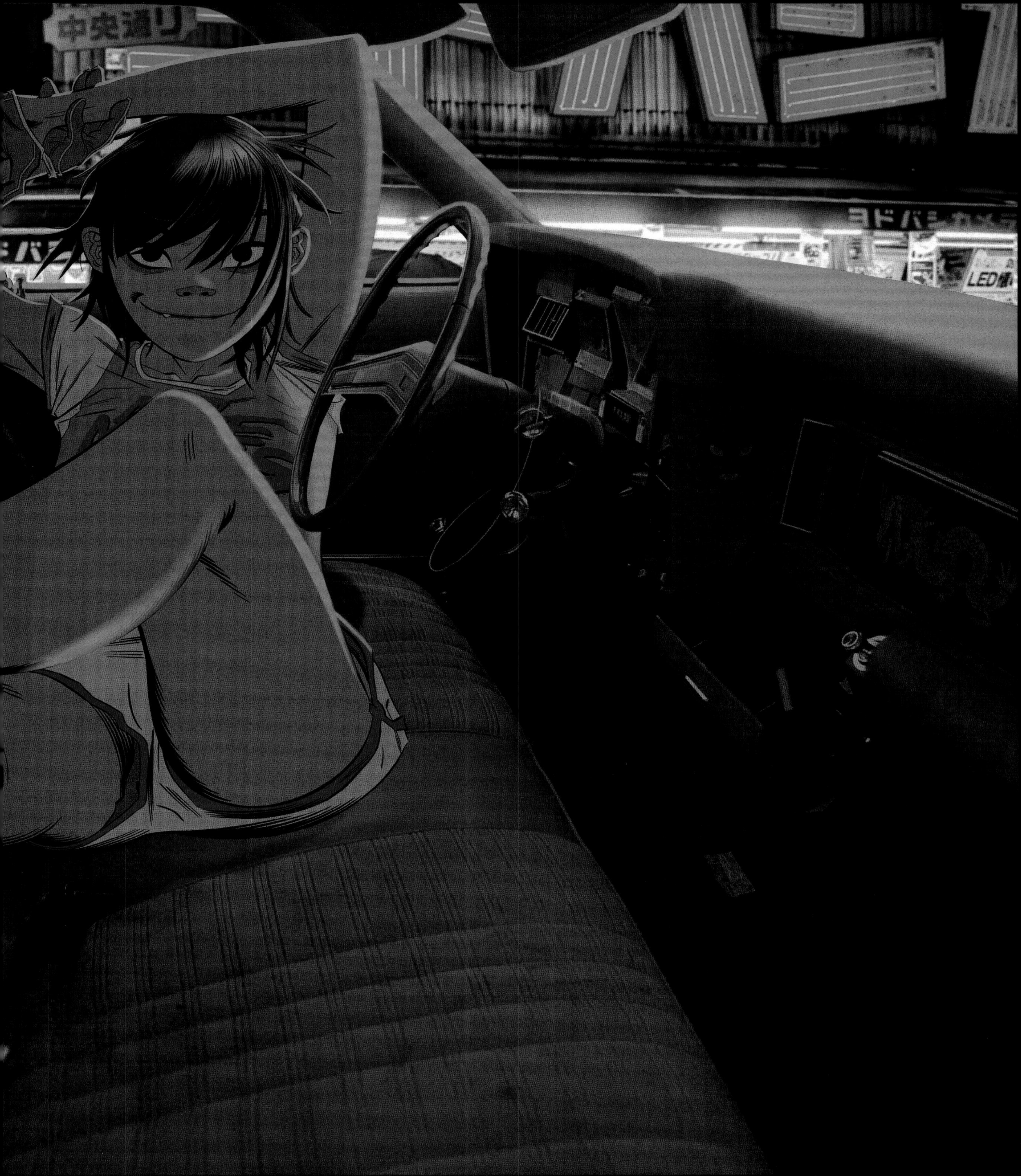
中央通り
LED

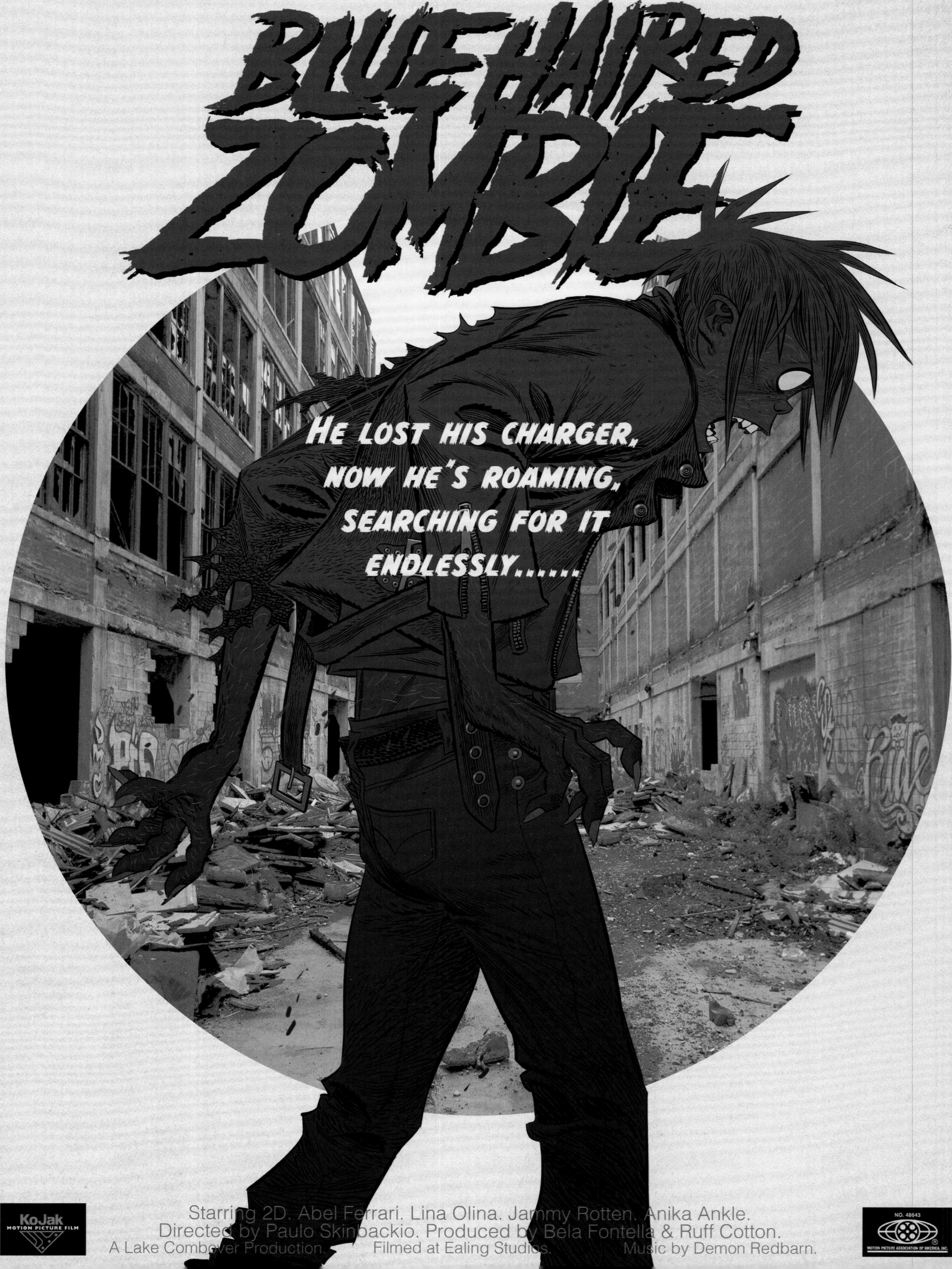
BLUE HAIRED ZOMBIE
HE LOST HIS CHARGER, NOW HE'S ROAMING, SEARCHING FOR IT ENDLESSLY......
KoJak MOTION PICTURE FILM
Starring 2D. Abel Ferrari. Lina Olina. Jammy Rotten. Anika Ankle.
Directed by Paulo Skinbackio. Produced by Bela Fontella & Ruff Cotton.
A Lake Combover Production. Filmed at Ealing Studios. Music by Demon Redbarn.
NO. 48643
MOTION PICTURE ASSOCIATION OF AMERICA, INC.

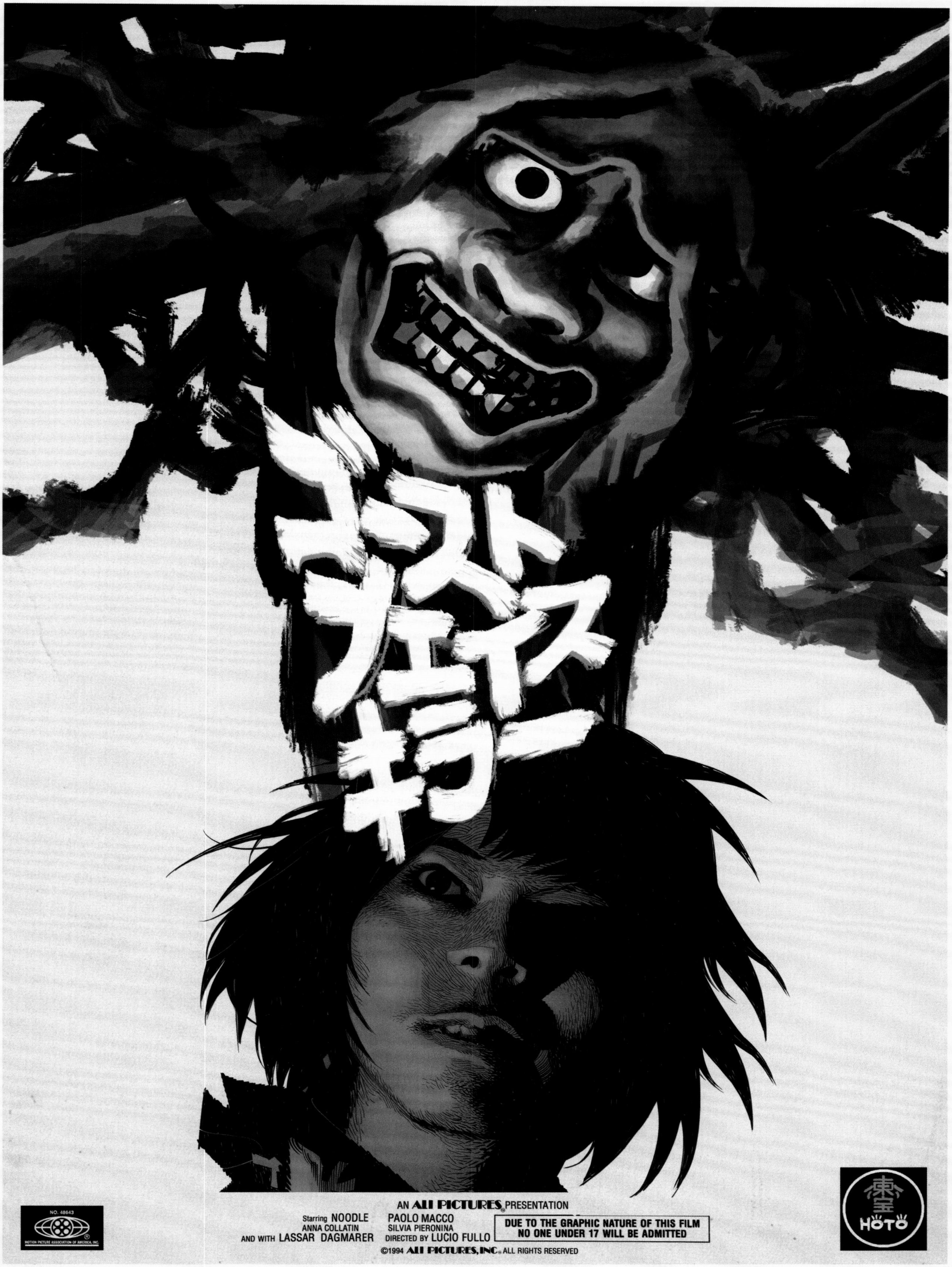

AN ALI PICTURES® PRESENTATION
Starring NOODLE PAOLO MACCO
ANNA COLLATIN SILVIA PIERONINA
AND WITH LASSAR DAGMARER DIRECTED BY LUCIO FULLO
DUE TO THE GRAPHIC NATURE OF THIS FILM
NO ONE UNDER 17 WILL BE ADMITTED
©1994 ALI PICTURES, INC.® ALL RIGHTS RESERVED
NO. 48643
MOTION PICTURE ASSOCIATION OF AMERICA, INC.
HOTO

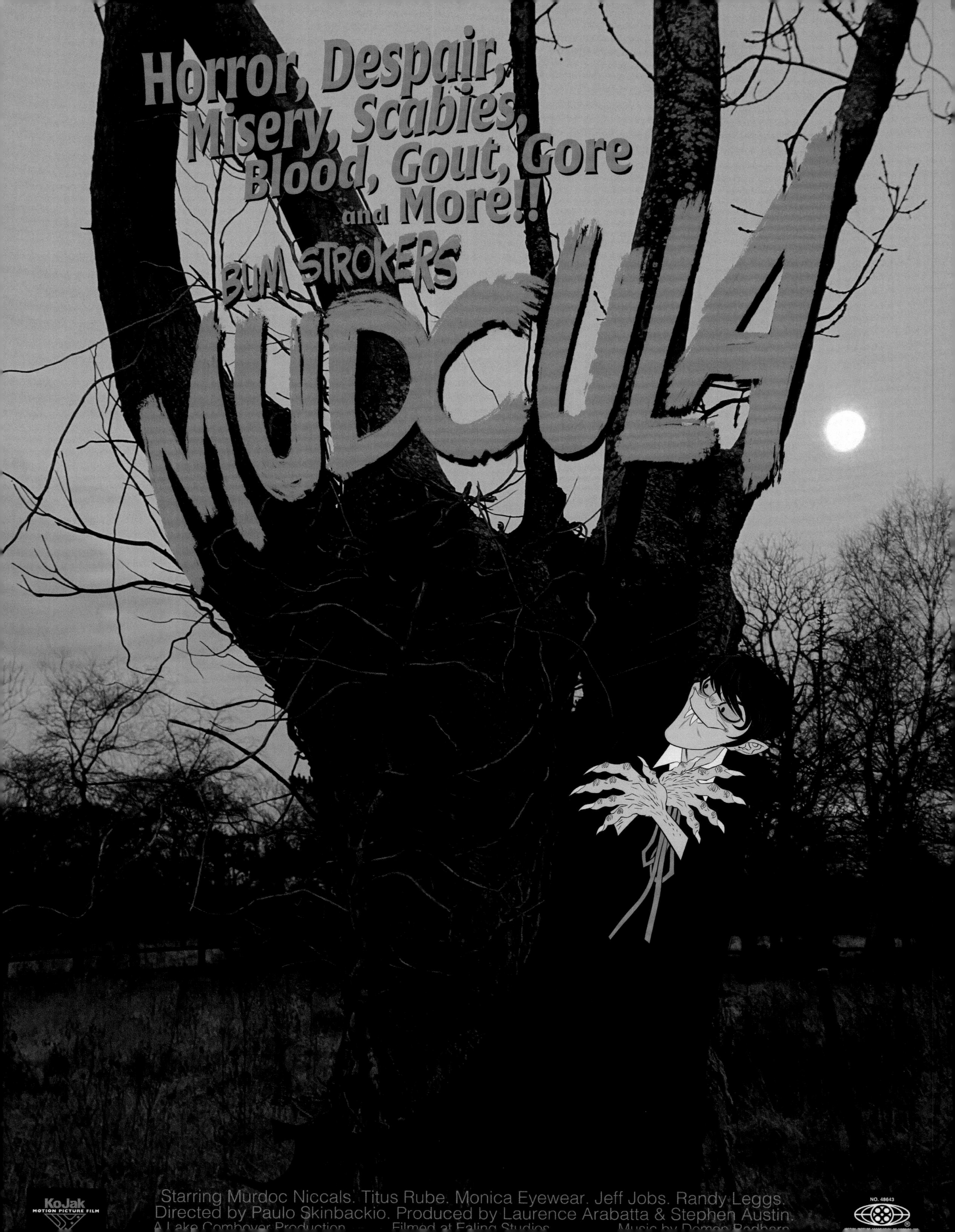
Horror, Despair, Misery, Scabies, Blood, Gout, Gore and More!!
BUM STROKERS
MUDCULA
KoJak
MOTION PICTURE FILM
Starring Murdoc Niccals. Titus Rube. Monica Eyewear. Jeff Jobs. Randy Leggs.
Directed by Paulo Skinbackio. Produced by Laurence Arabatta & Stephen Austin.
A Lake Combover Production
Filmed at Ealing Studios

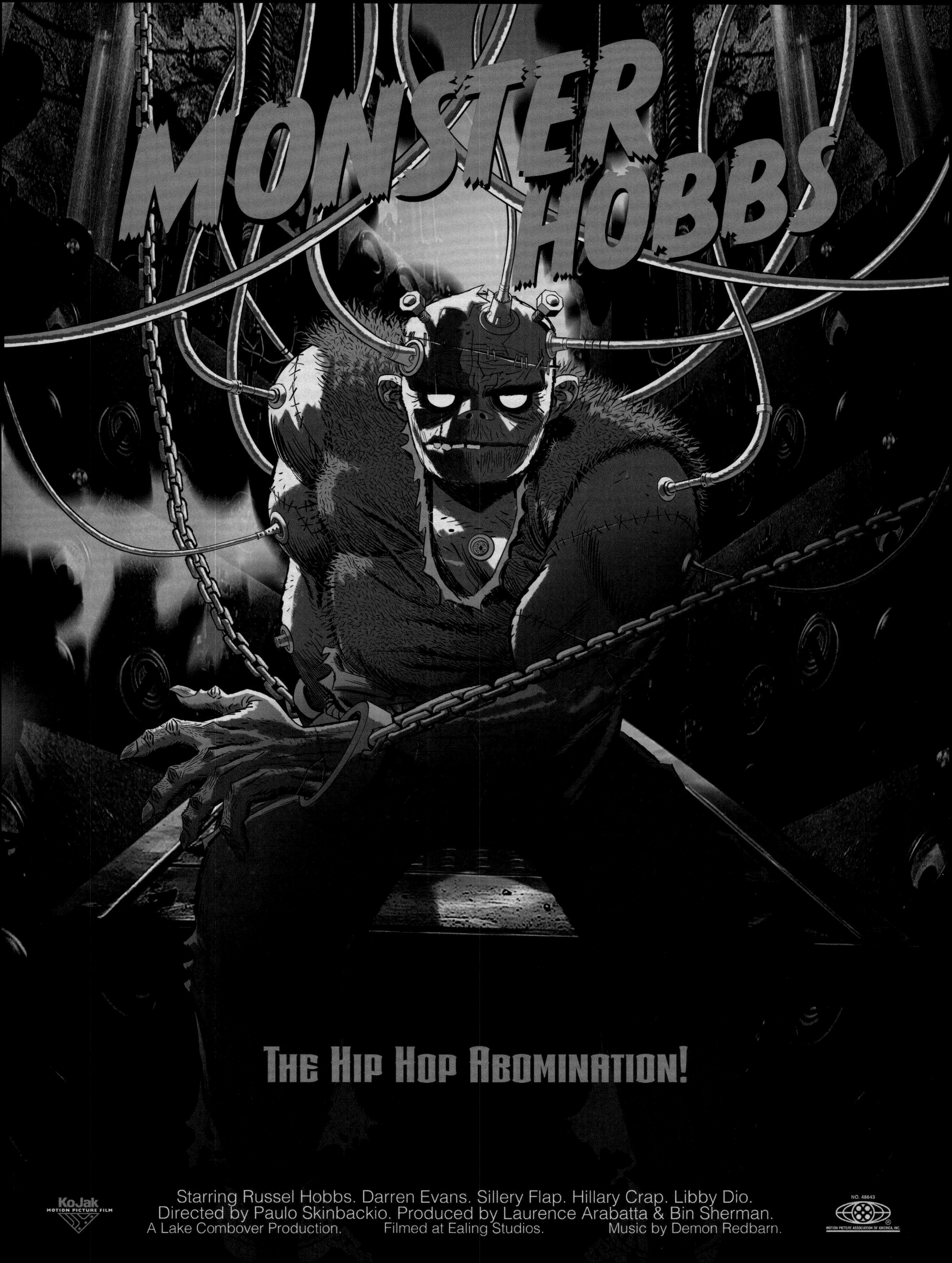
MONSTER HOBBS
THE HIP HOP ABOMINATION!
KoJak
MOTION PICTURE FILM
Starring Russel Hobbs. Darren Evans. Sillery Flap. Hillary Crap. Libby Dio.
Directed by Paulo Skinbackio. Produced by Laurence Arabatta & Bin Sherman.
A Lake Combover Production.
Filmed at Ealing Studios.
Music by Demon Redbarn.
NO. 48643
MOTION PICTURE ASSOCIATION OF AMERICA, INC.

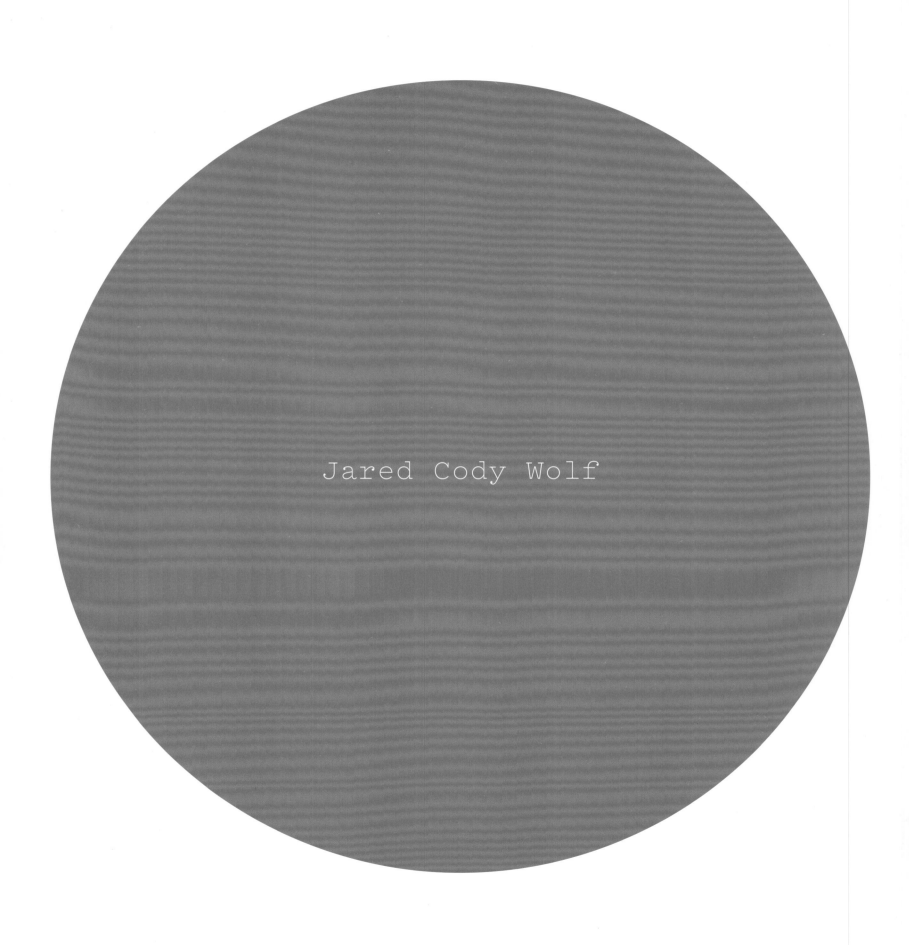

Jared Cody Wolf

NOODLE
+ the
gorillaz
84
APR 1968
noodle
FRESH
Murdoc
Russel
+ − % ÷
e=mc
other weapons
C
3
N40
The hand of Fâṭimah.
Stuart
2D
ferring power

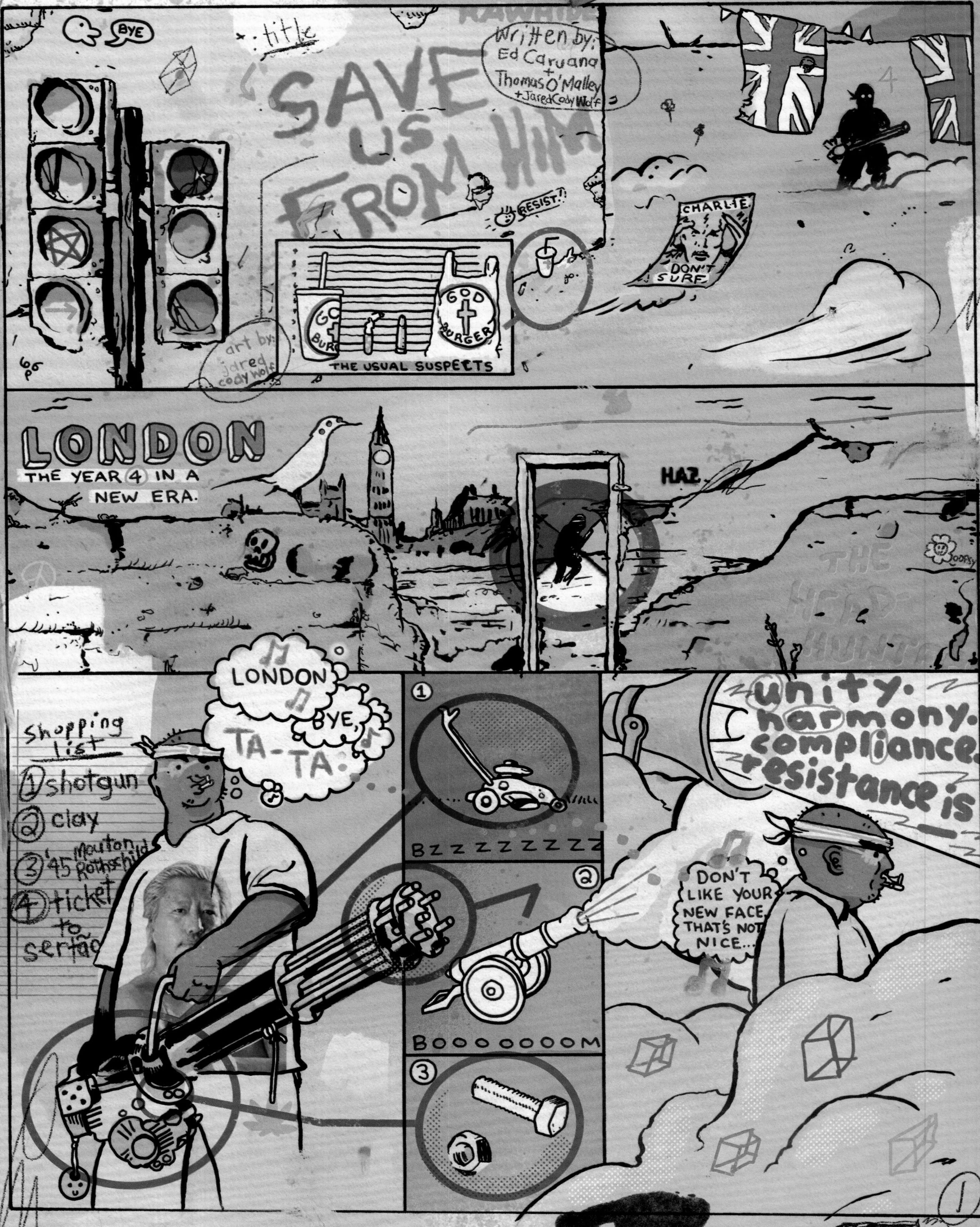
BYE
title
Written by:
Ed Caruana + Thomas O'Malley + Jared Cody Wolf
SAVE US FROM HIM
RESIST.?!
CHARLIE DON'T SURF.
GOD BURGER
THE USUAL SUSPECTS
art by: jared cody wolf
4
LONDON
THE YEAR 4 IN A NEW ERA.
HAZ.
OOPSY
LONDON BYE, TA-TA.
Shopping list
1 shotgun
2 clay
3 '45 mouton Rothschild
4 ticket to sertão
1
BZZZZZZZZZ
2
BOOOOOOOOM
3
unity. harmony. compliance. resistance is —
DON'T LIKE YOUR NEW FACE. THAT'S NOT NICE...
1

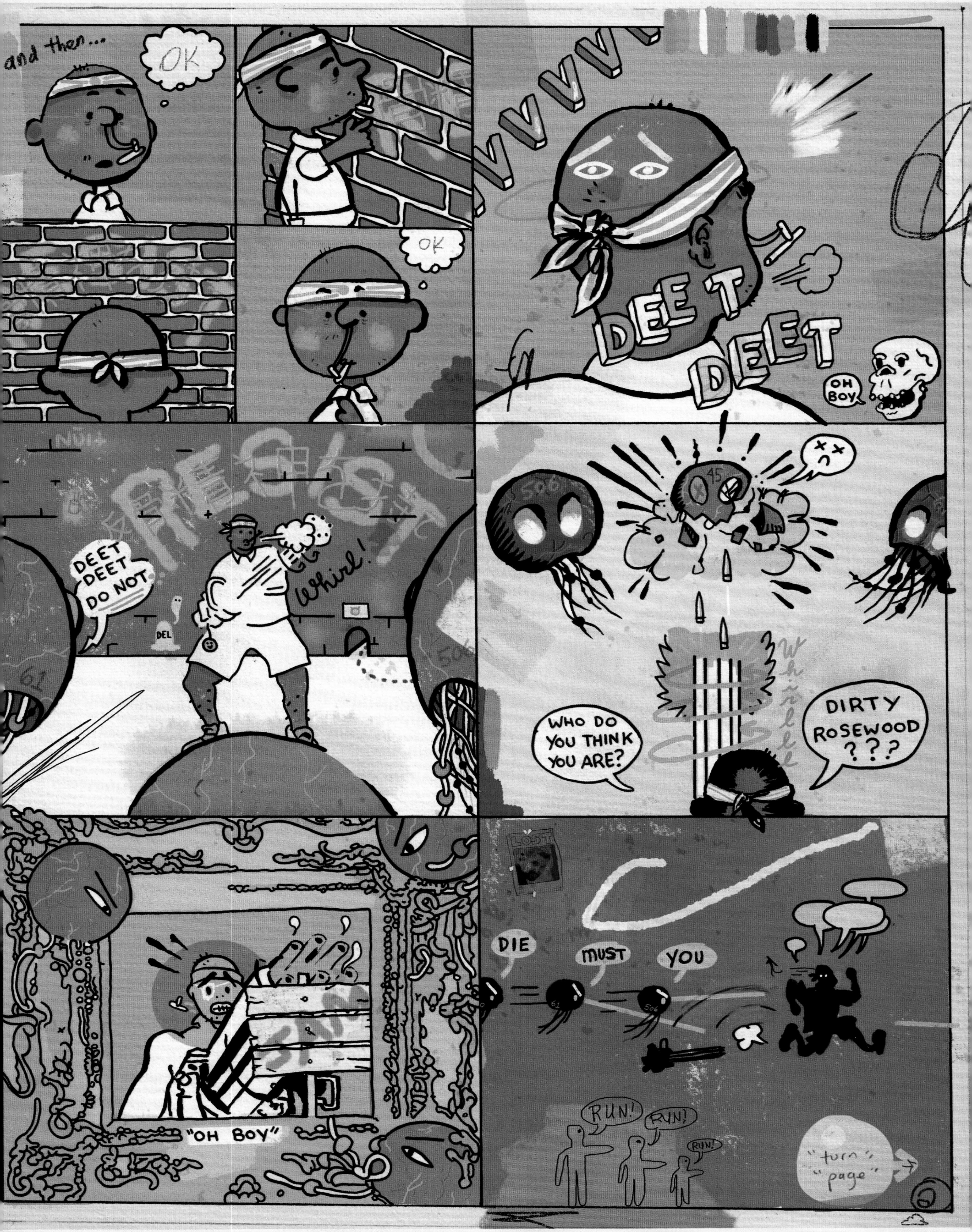
and then...
OK
OK
VVVVVV
DEE T
DEET
OH BOY
DEET DEET DO NOT
Whirl!
DEL
WHO DO YOU THINK YOU ARE?
DIRTY ROSEWOOD ???
"OH BOY"
LOST
DIE
MUST
YOU
RUN!
RUN!
RUN!
"turn" "page"

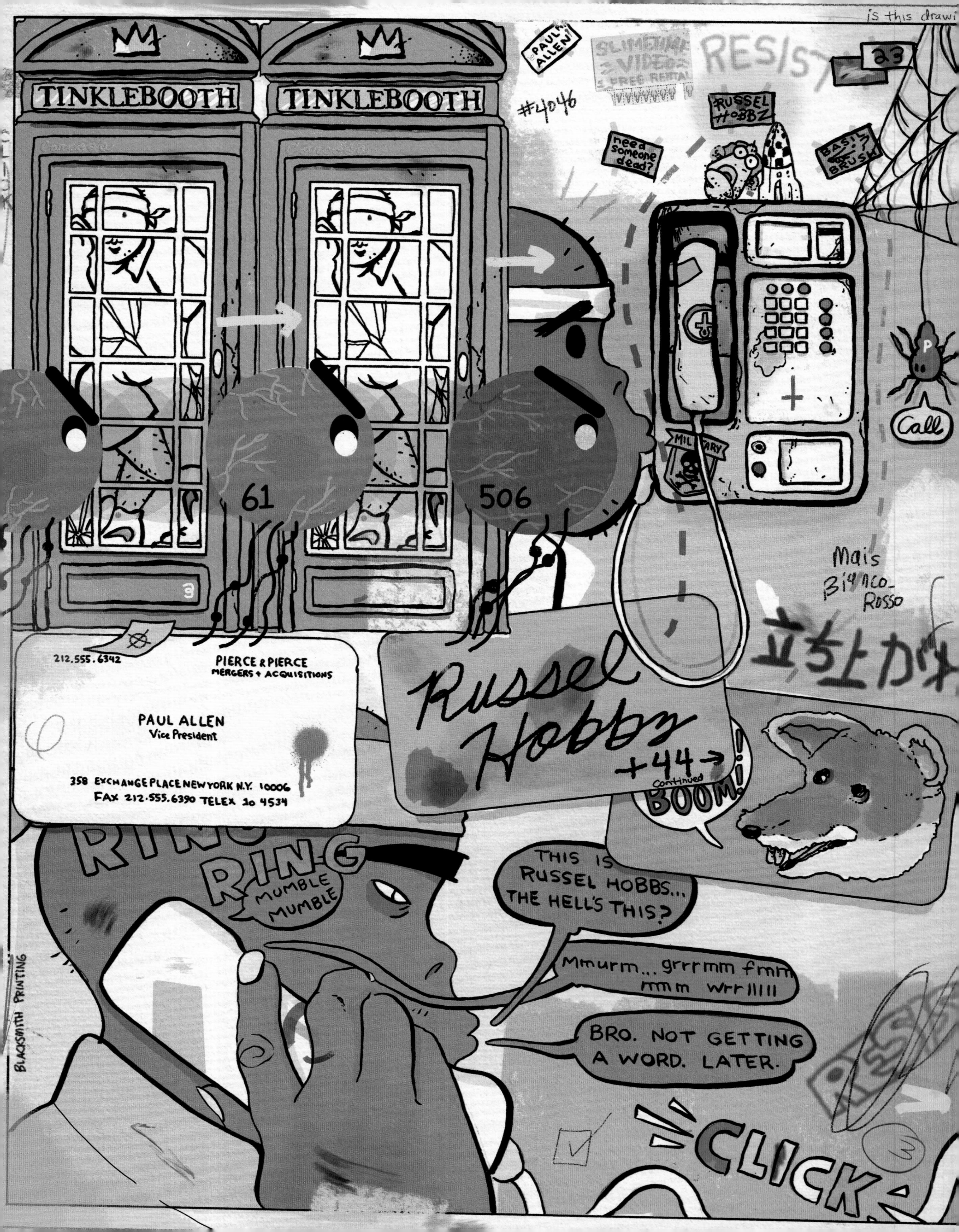
is this drawi
TINKLEBOOTH
TINKLEBOOTH
PAUL ALLEN
SLIMETIME VIDEO FREE RENTAL
RESIST
23
#4046
RUSSEL HOBBZ
need someone dead?
BASIL BRUSH
MILITARY
Call
61
506
Mais Bianco Rosso
212.555.6342
PIERCE & PIERCE
MERGERS + ACQUISITIONS
PAUL ALLEN
Vice President
358 EXCHANGE PLACE NEW YORK N.Y. 10006
FAX 212.555.6390 TELEX 10 4534
Russel Hobbz
+44→
Continued
BOOM!
RING
RING
MUMBLE MUMBLE
THIS IS RUSSEL HOBBS... THE HELL'S THIS?
Mmurm... grrrmm fmm rmm wrrlllll
BRO. NOT GETTING A WORD. LATER.
CLICK
BLACKSMITH PRINTING

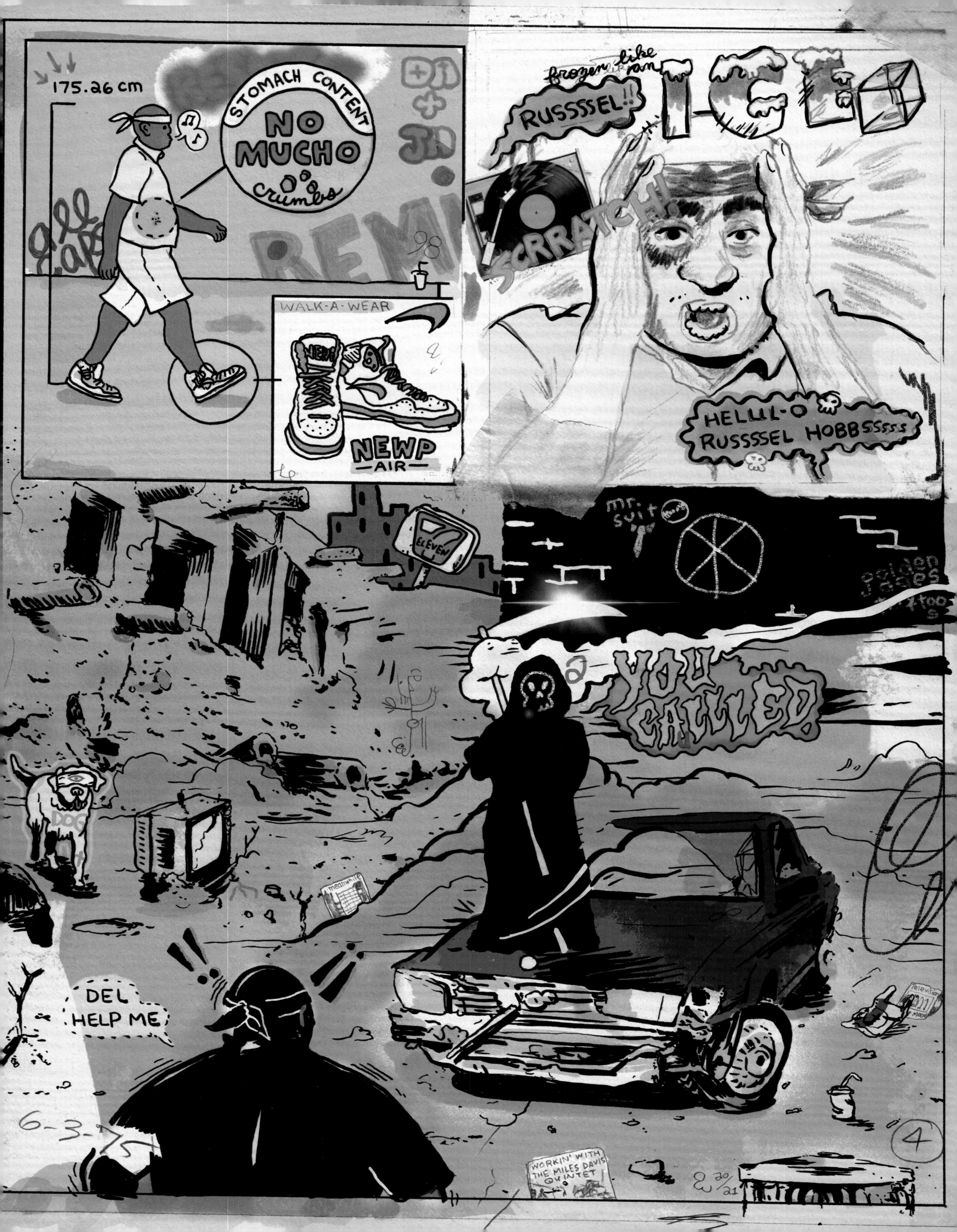

175.26 cm
STOMACH CONTENT
NO MUCHO
crumbs
WALK-A-WEAR
NEWP
NEWP AIR
frozen like an
RUSSSSEL!!
I-C-E
SCRRATCH!
HELUL-O RUSSSSEL HOBBSSSSS
ELEVEN
mr. suit
YOU CALLED.
DOG
DEL HELP ME
WORKIN' WITH THE MILES DAVIS QUINTET
6-3-75
4

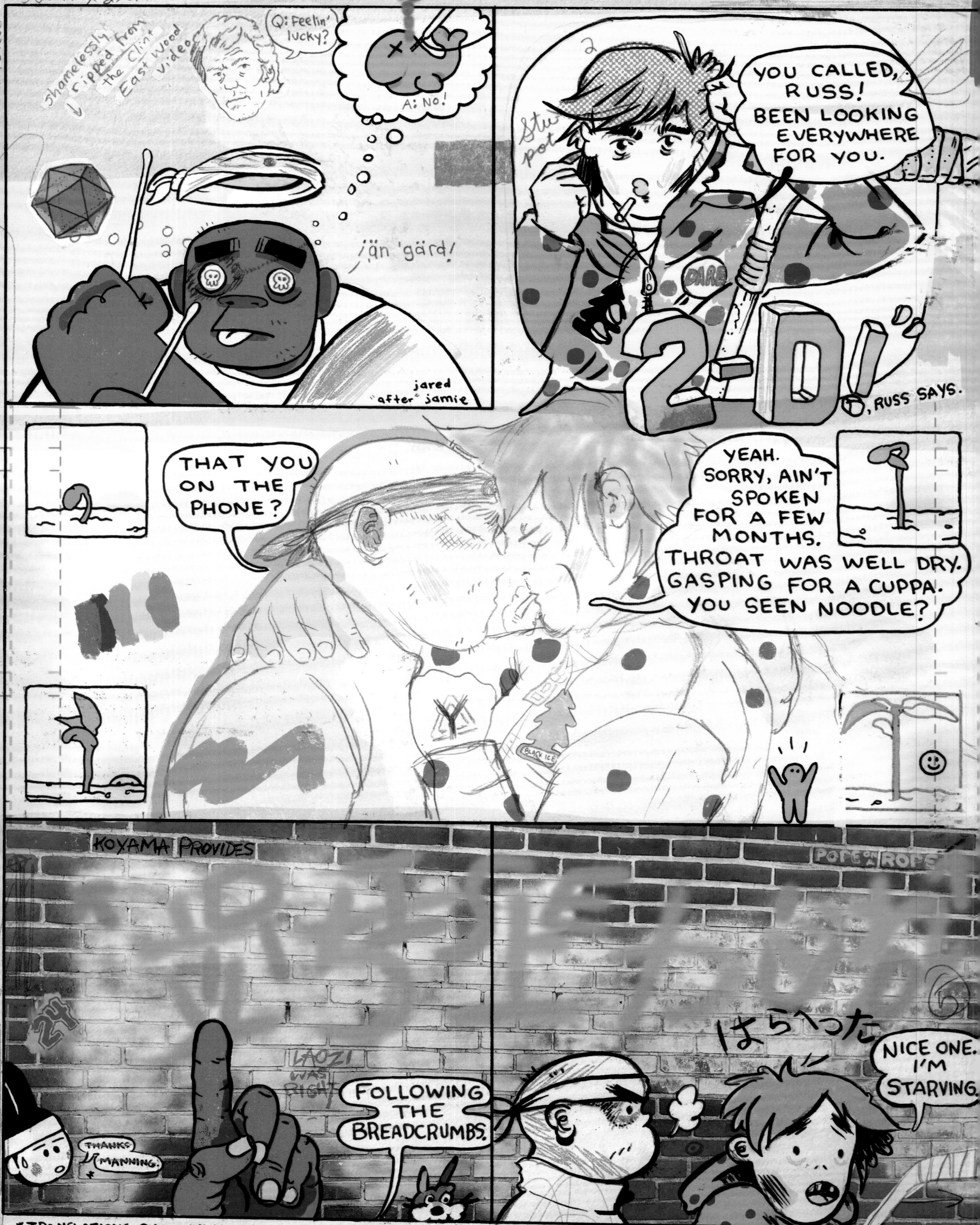
shamelessly ripped from the Clint East Wood video
Q: Feelin' lucky?
A: No!
¡än 'gärd!
jared "after" jamie
Stu pot
YOU CALLED, RUSS! BEEN LOOKING EVERYWHERE FOR YOU.
DARE
2-D!, RUSS SAYS.
THAT YOU ON THE PHONE?
YEAH. SORRY, AIN'T SPOKEN FOR A FEW MONTHS. THROAT WAS WELL DRY. GASPING FOR A CUPPA. YOU SEEN NOODLE?
BLACK ICE
KOYAMA PROVIDES
POPE ON A ROPE
LAOZI WAS RIGHT
THANKS MANNING.
FOLLOWING THE BREADCRUMBS.
はらへった
NICE ONE. I'M STARVING.

*TRANSLATIONS BY MANNING COE

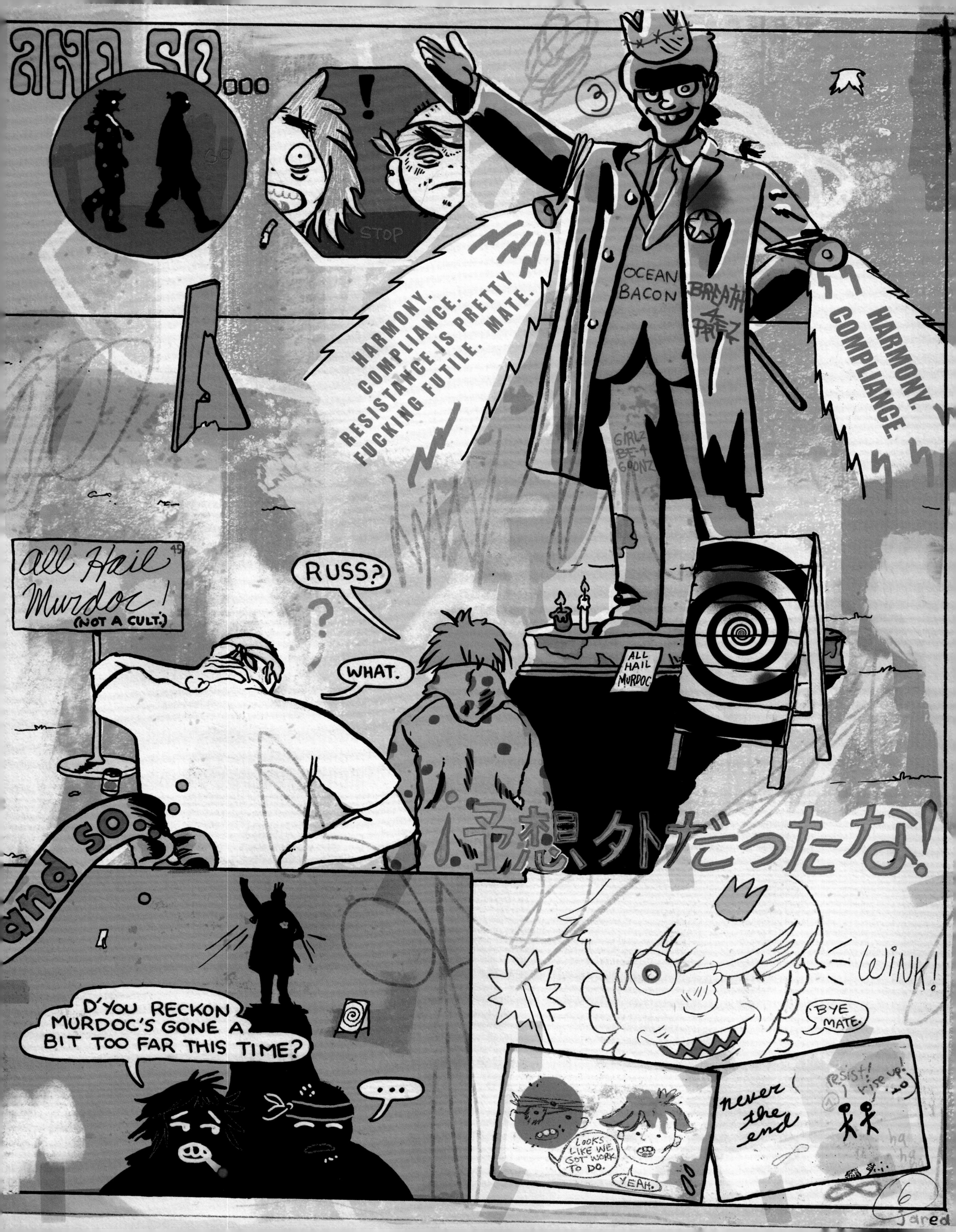
and so...
GO
!
STOP
HARMONY. COMPLIANCE. RESISTANCE IS PRETTY FUCKING FUTILE. MATE.
OCEAN BACON
HARMONY. COMPLIANCE.
GIRLZ BE-4 GOONZ
all Hail Murdoc! (NOT A CULT.)
RUSS?
?
WHAT.
ALL HAIL MURDOC
予想外だったな!
and so...
WINK!
BYE MATE.
D'YOU RECKON MURDOC'S GONE A BIT TOO FAR THIS TIME?
...
LOOKS LIKE WE GOT WORK TO DO.
YEAH.
never the end
RESIST! RISE UP!
6
Jared

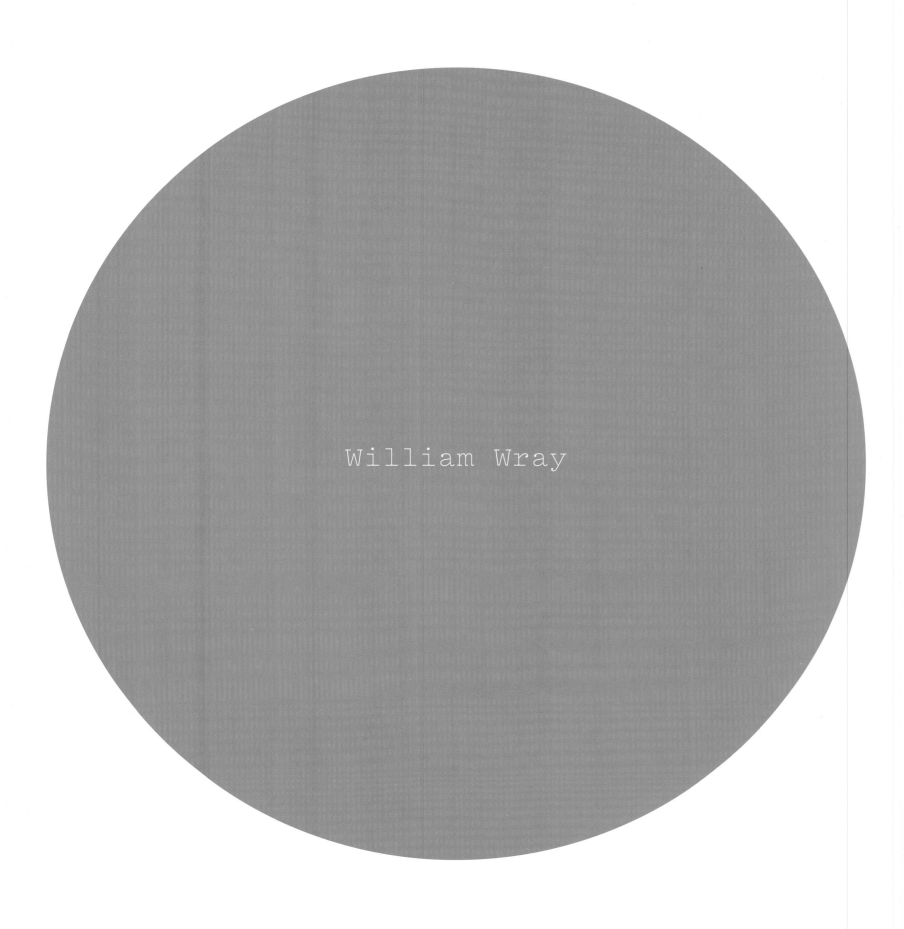

William Wray

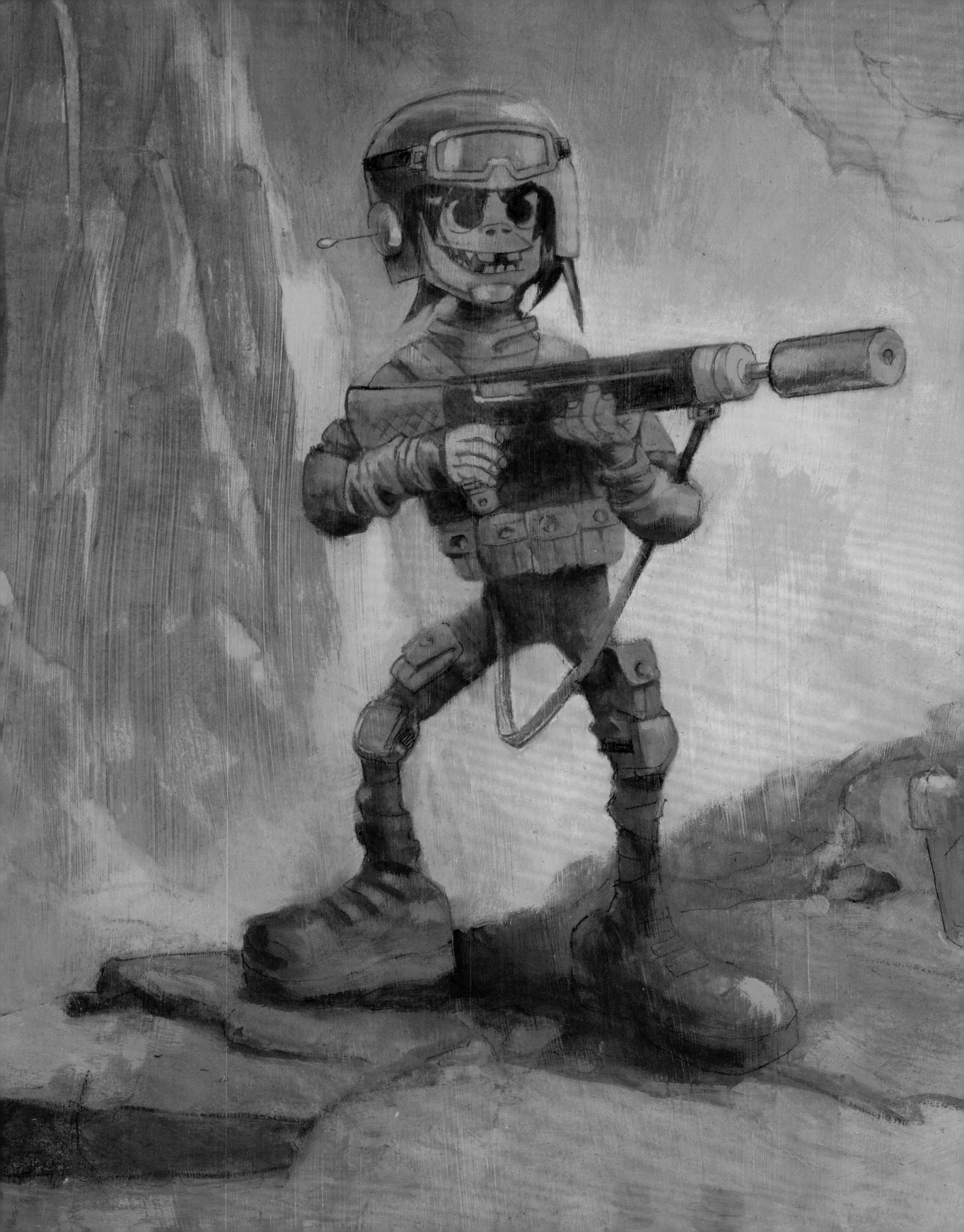

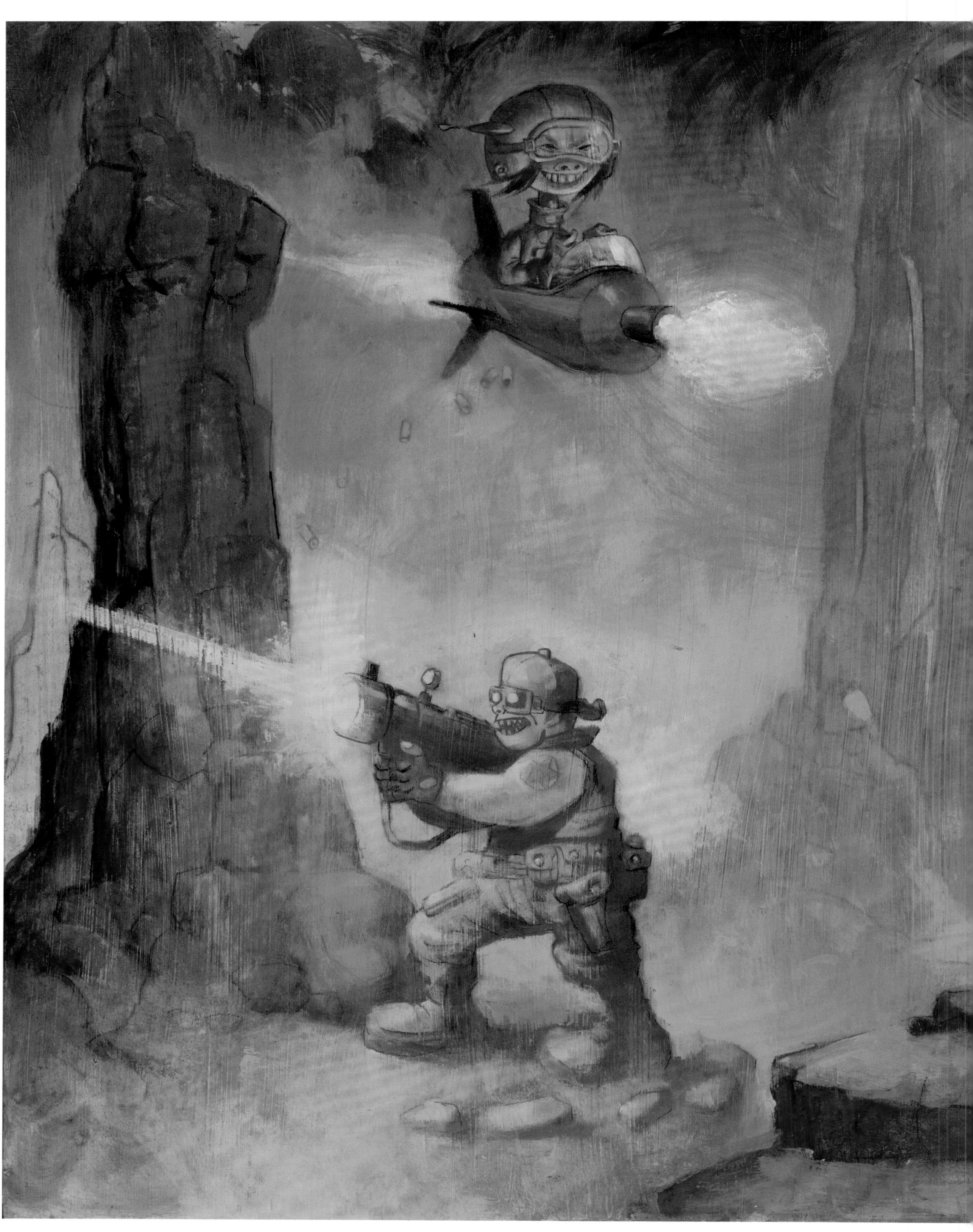

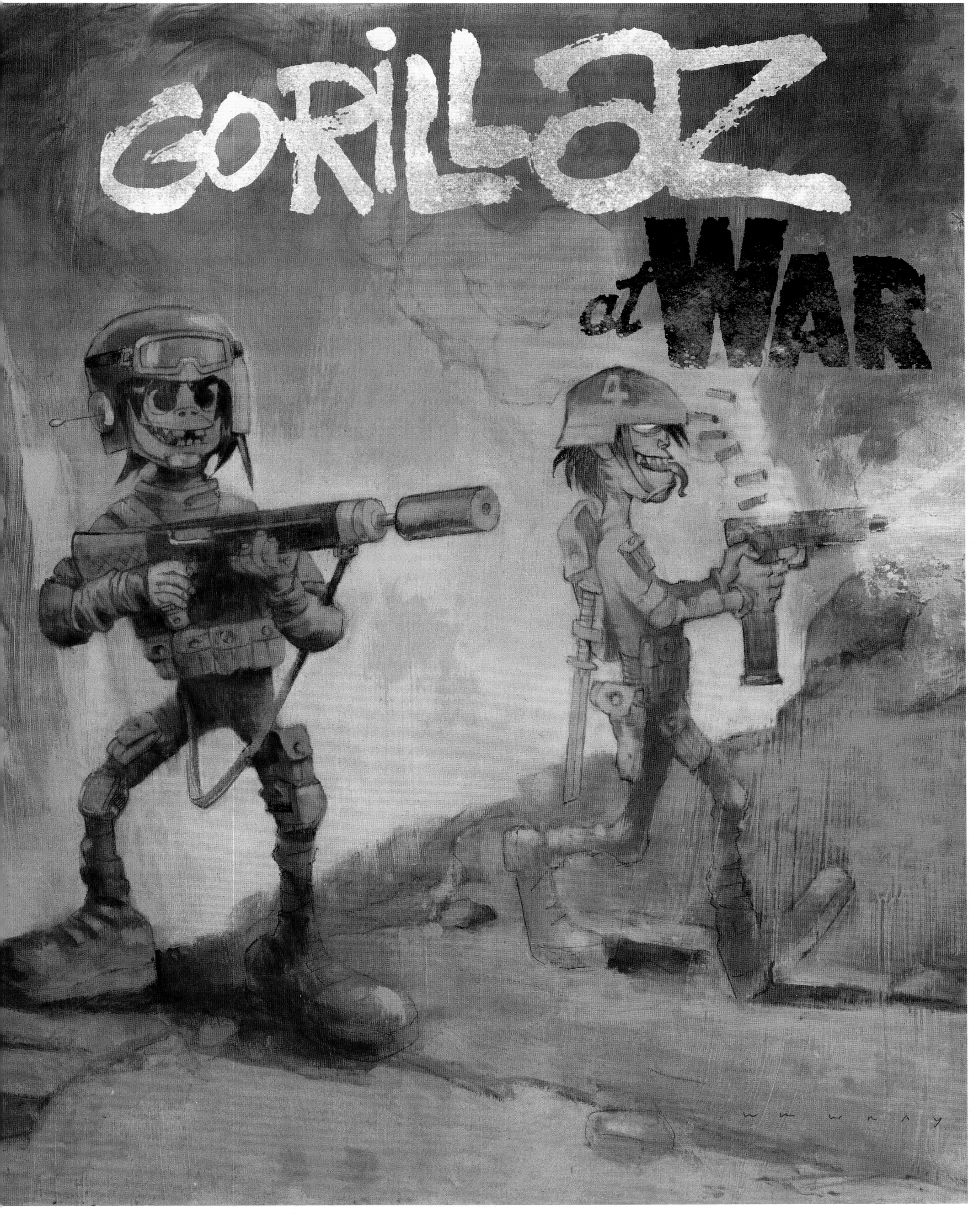
GORILLAZ
at WAR
4
WWWRAY

Craig McCracken

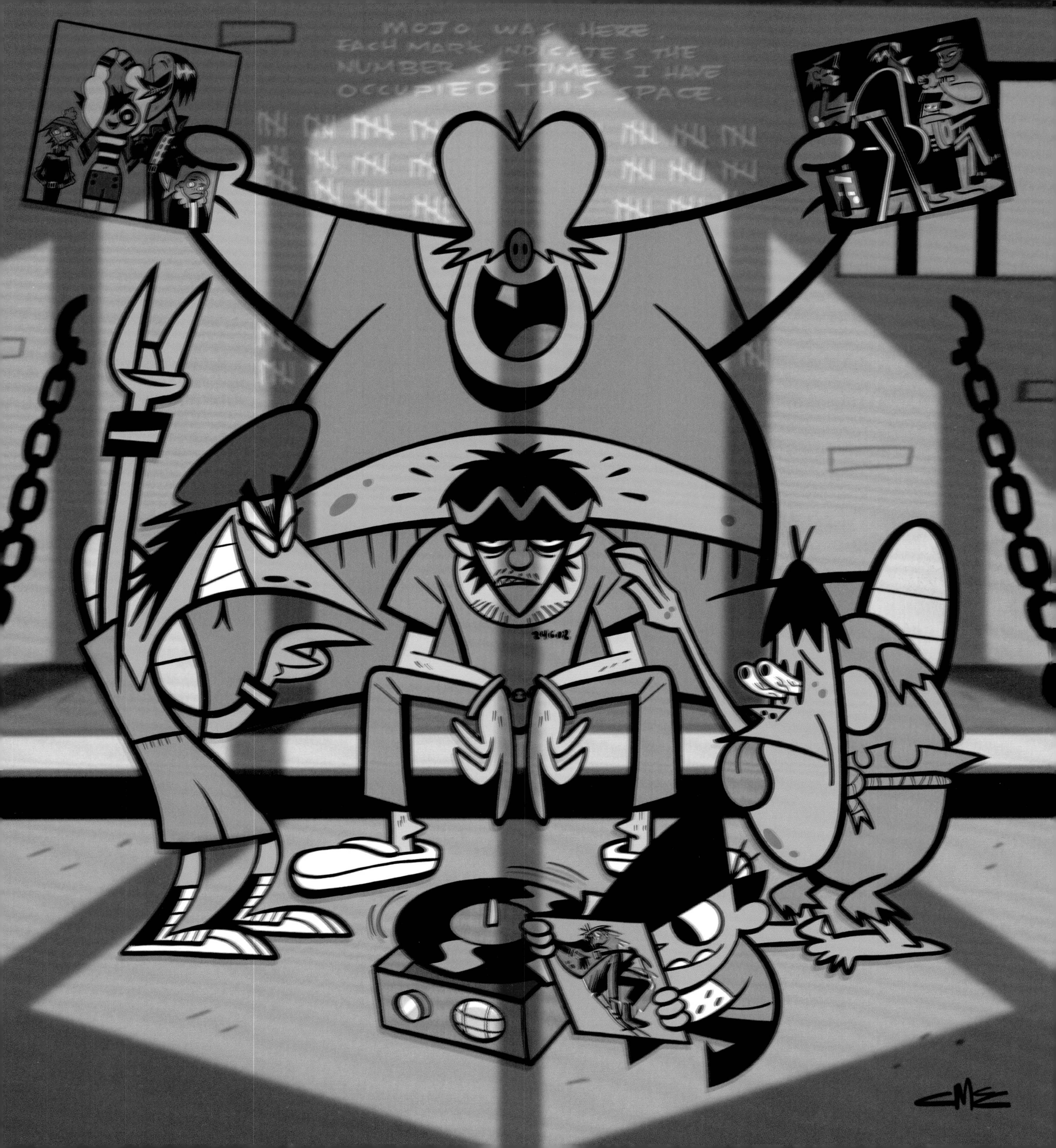
MOJO WAS HERE.
EACH MARK INDICATES THE
NUMBER OF TIMES I HAVE
OCCUPIED THIS SPACE.
2-14-6-02
CME

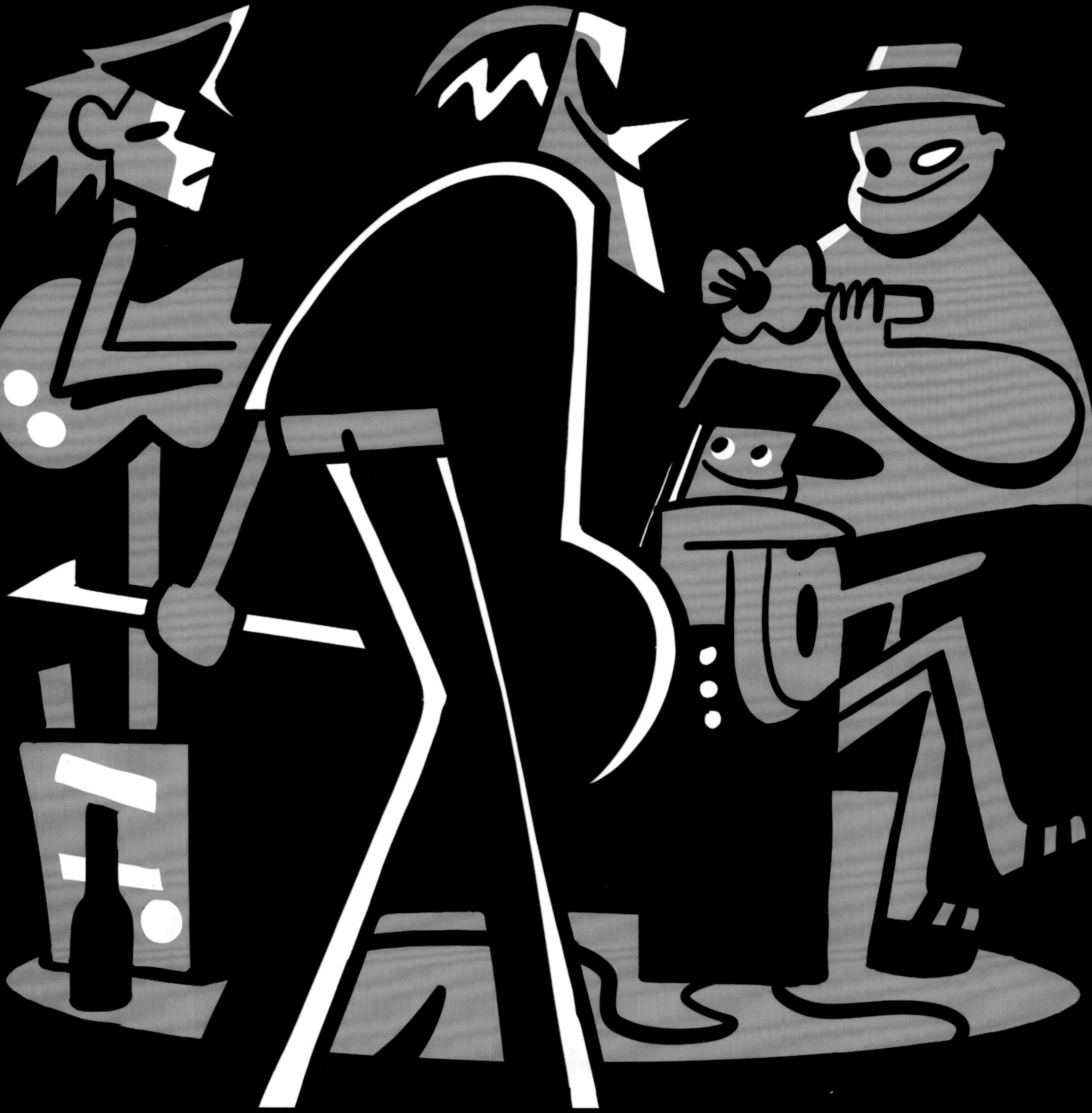

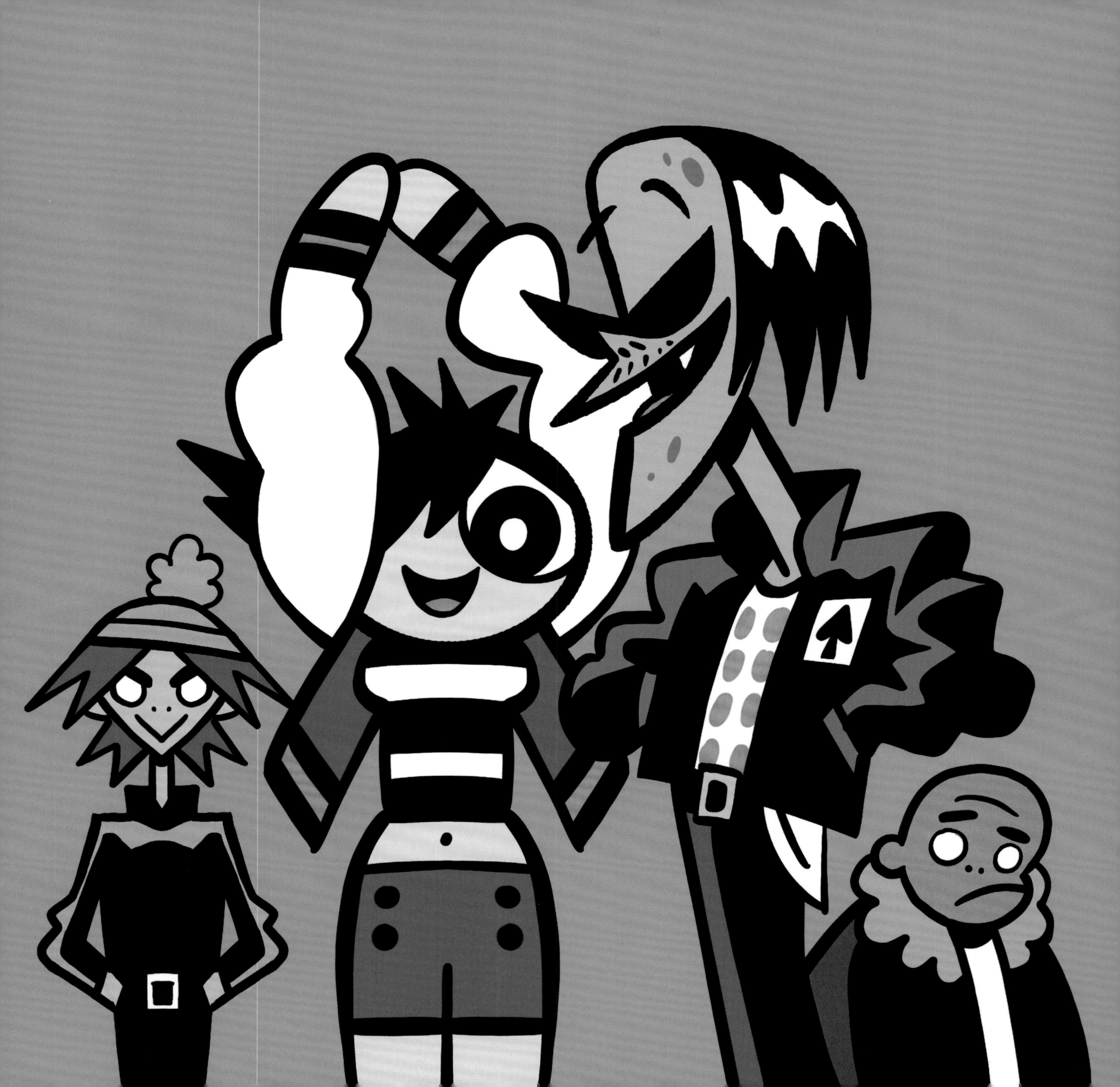

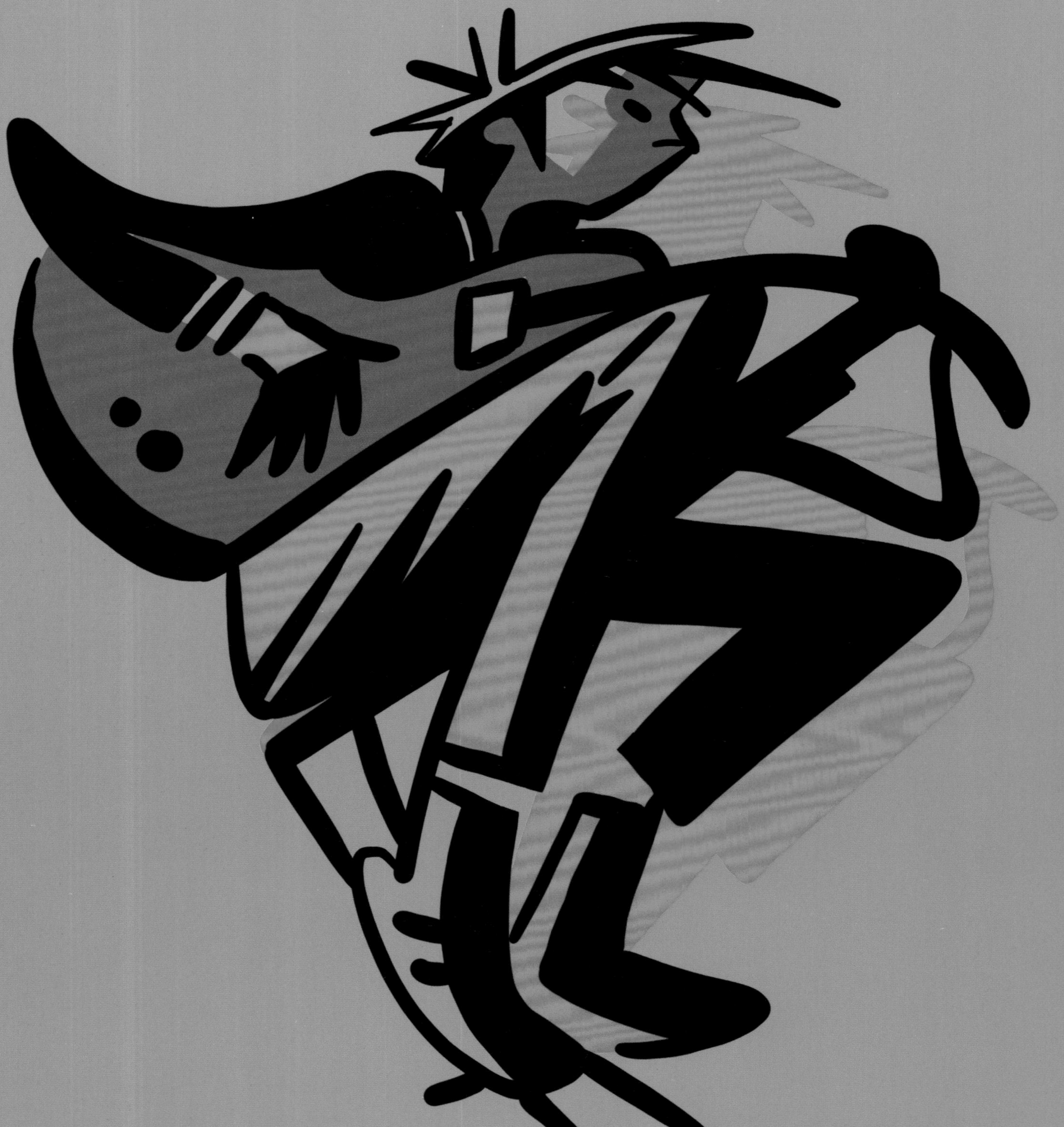

Glyn Dillon

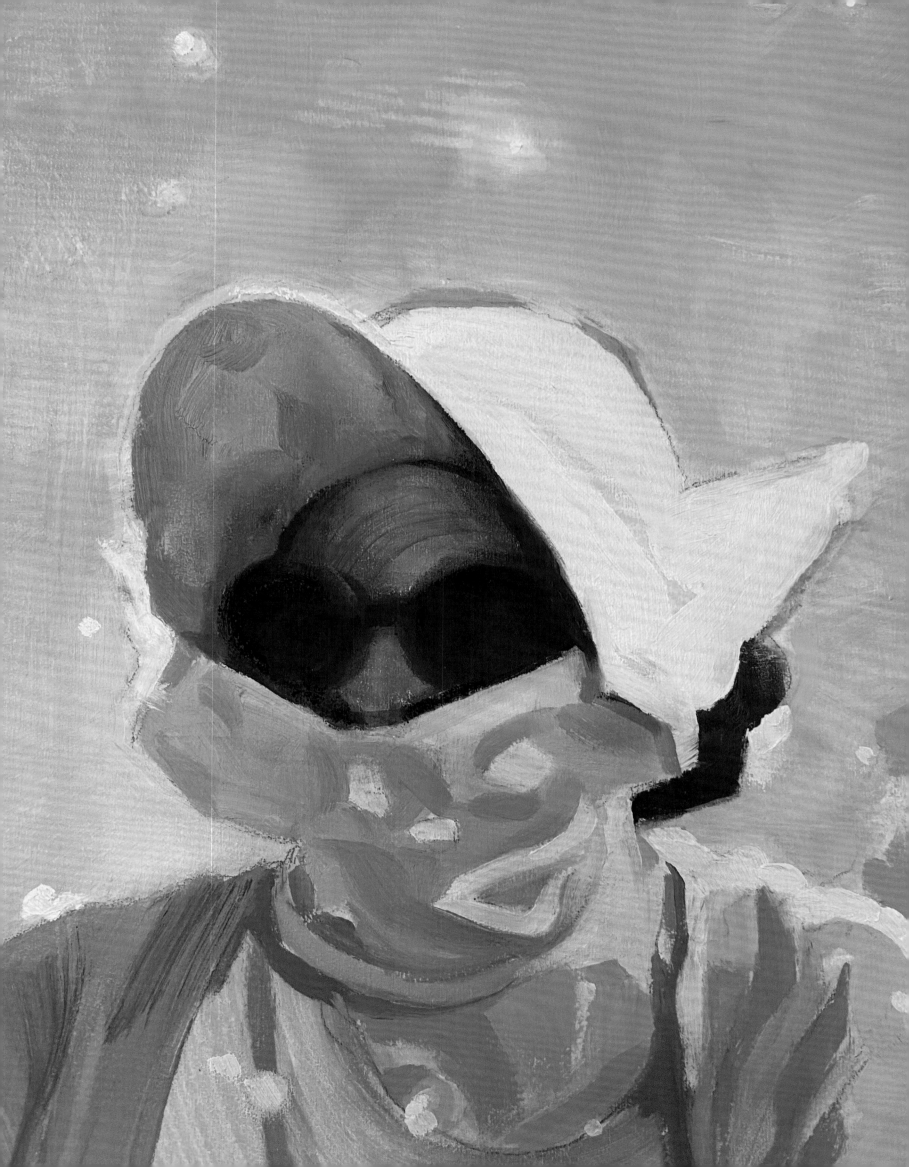

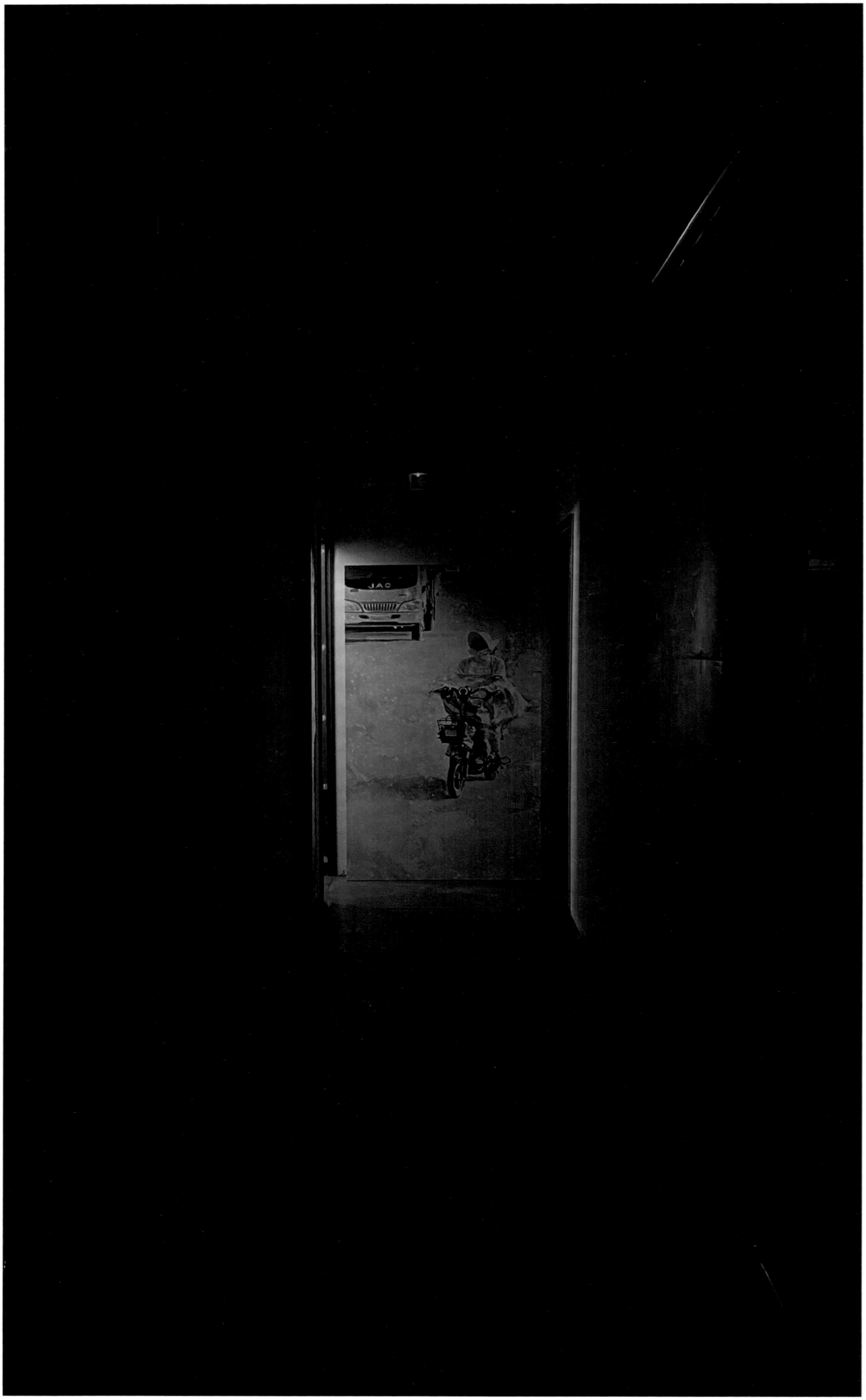
JAC

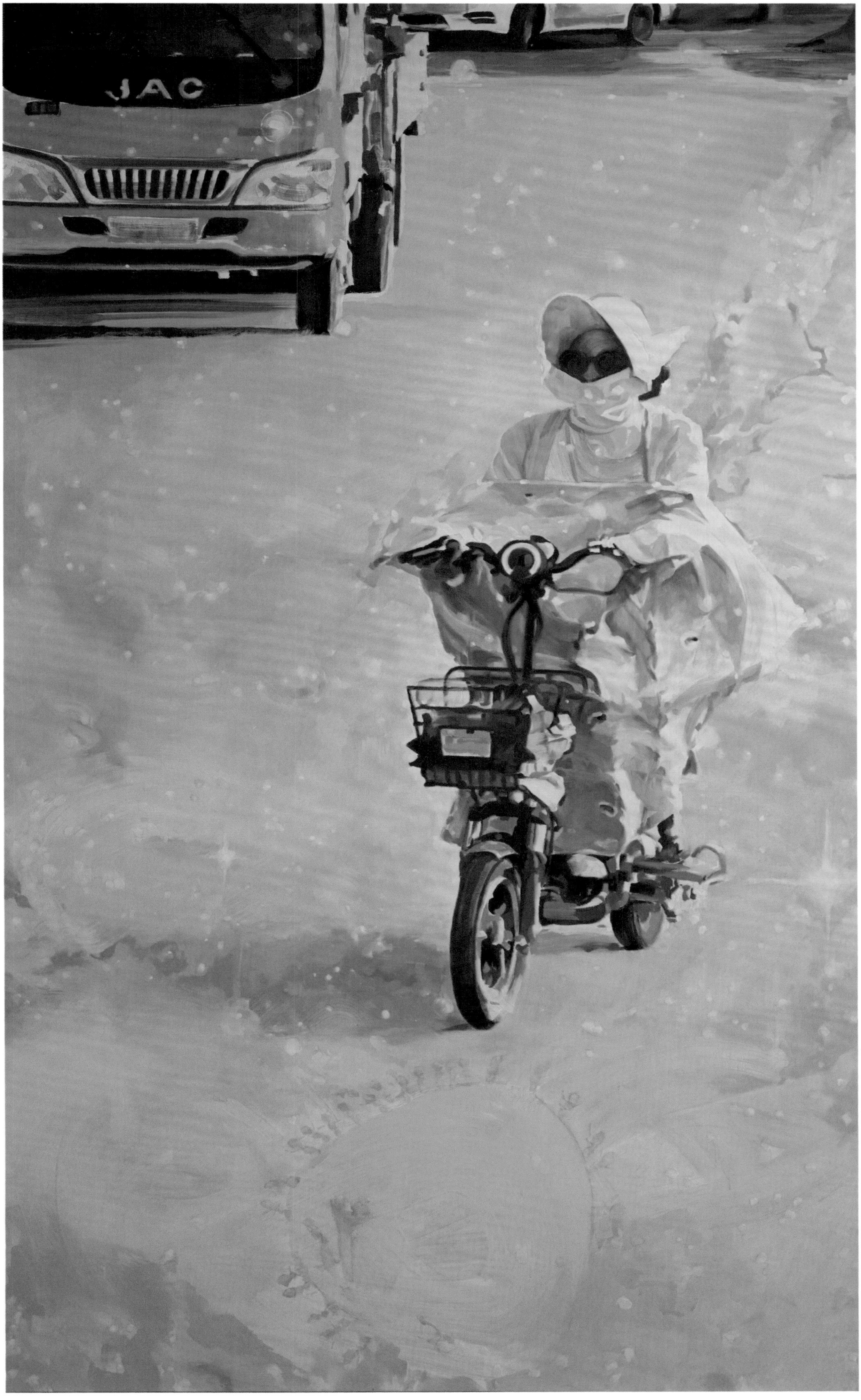
JAC

Soon, Like A Wave,
Empires Will Fall.
Glyn Dillon
110 × 184 cm
Oil and acrylic on board

EPHK

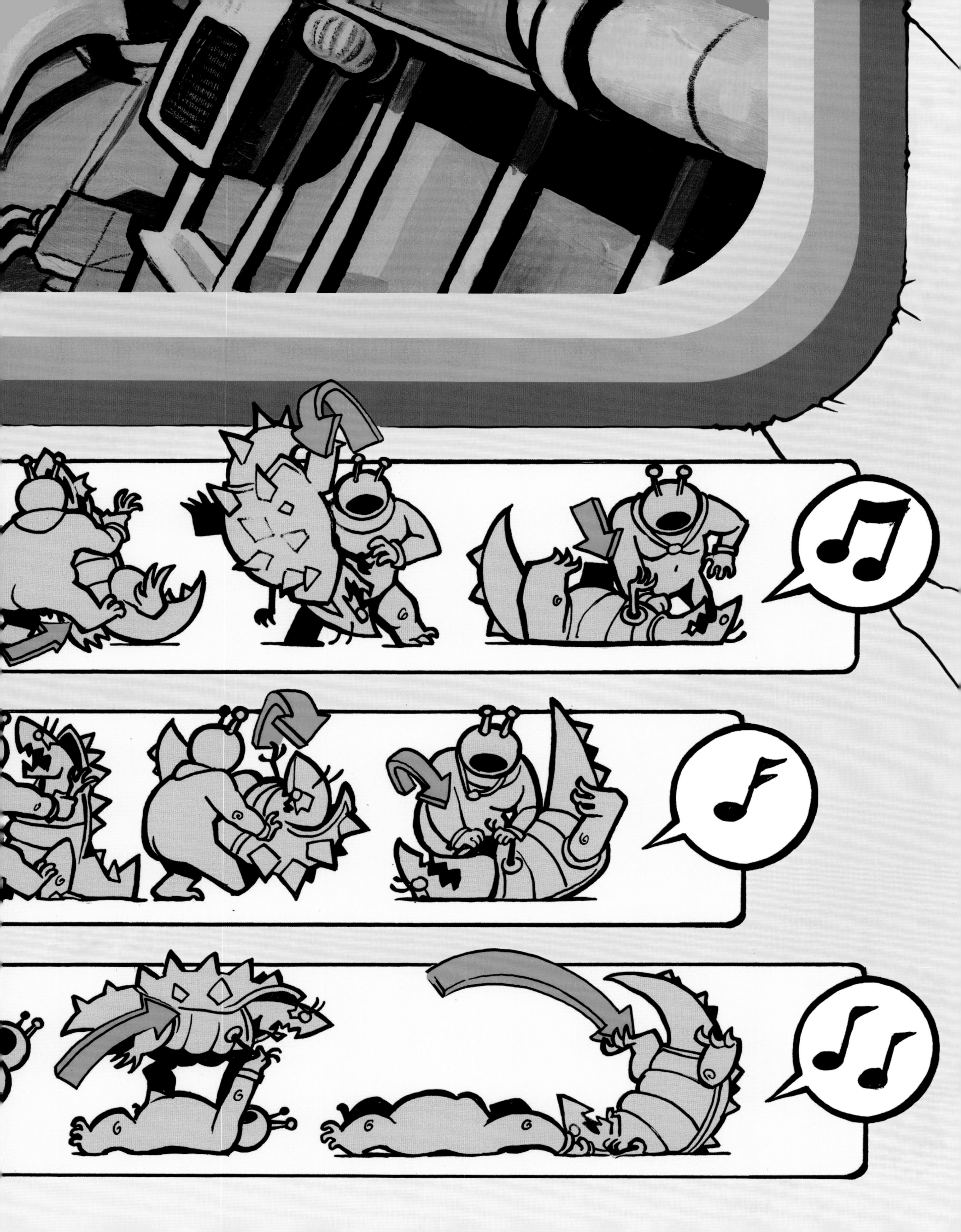

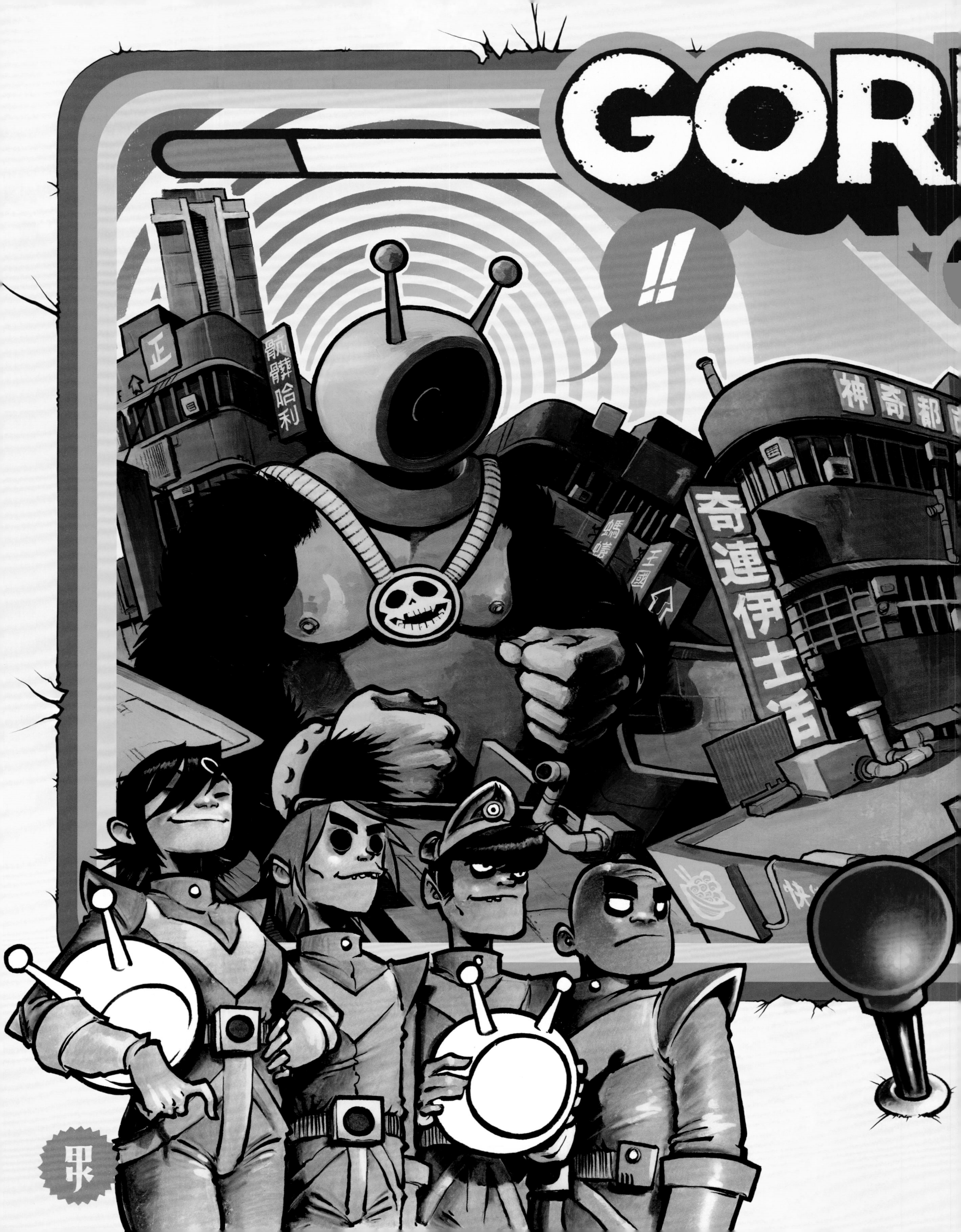

GOR
!!
神奇都
奇連伊士

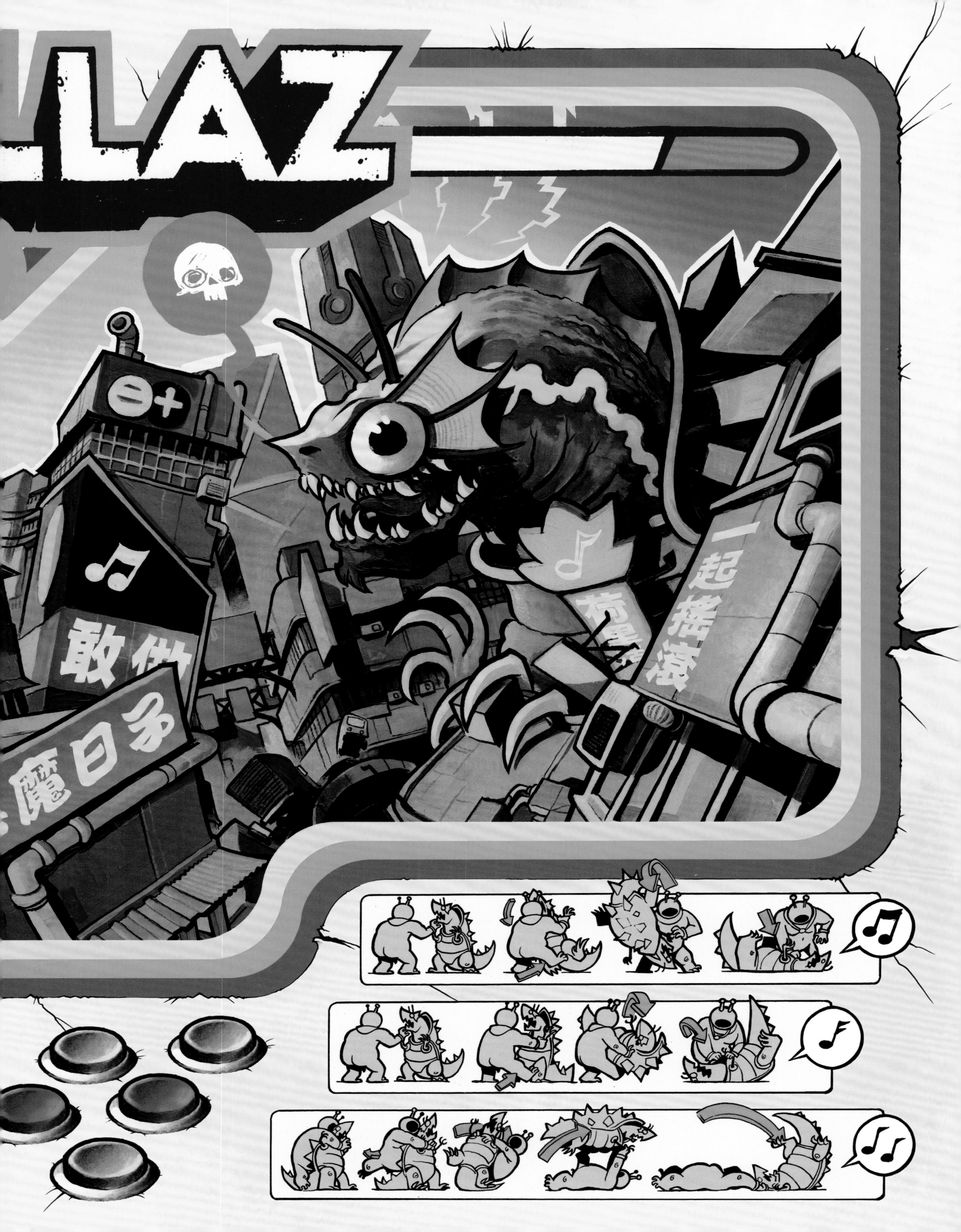
LAZ
一起搖滾

Jeremy Enecio

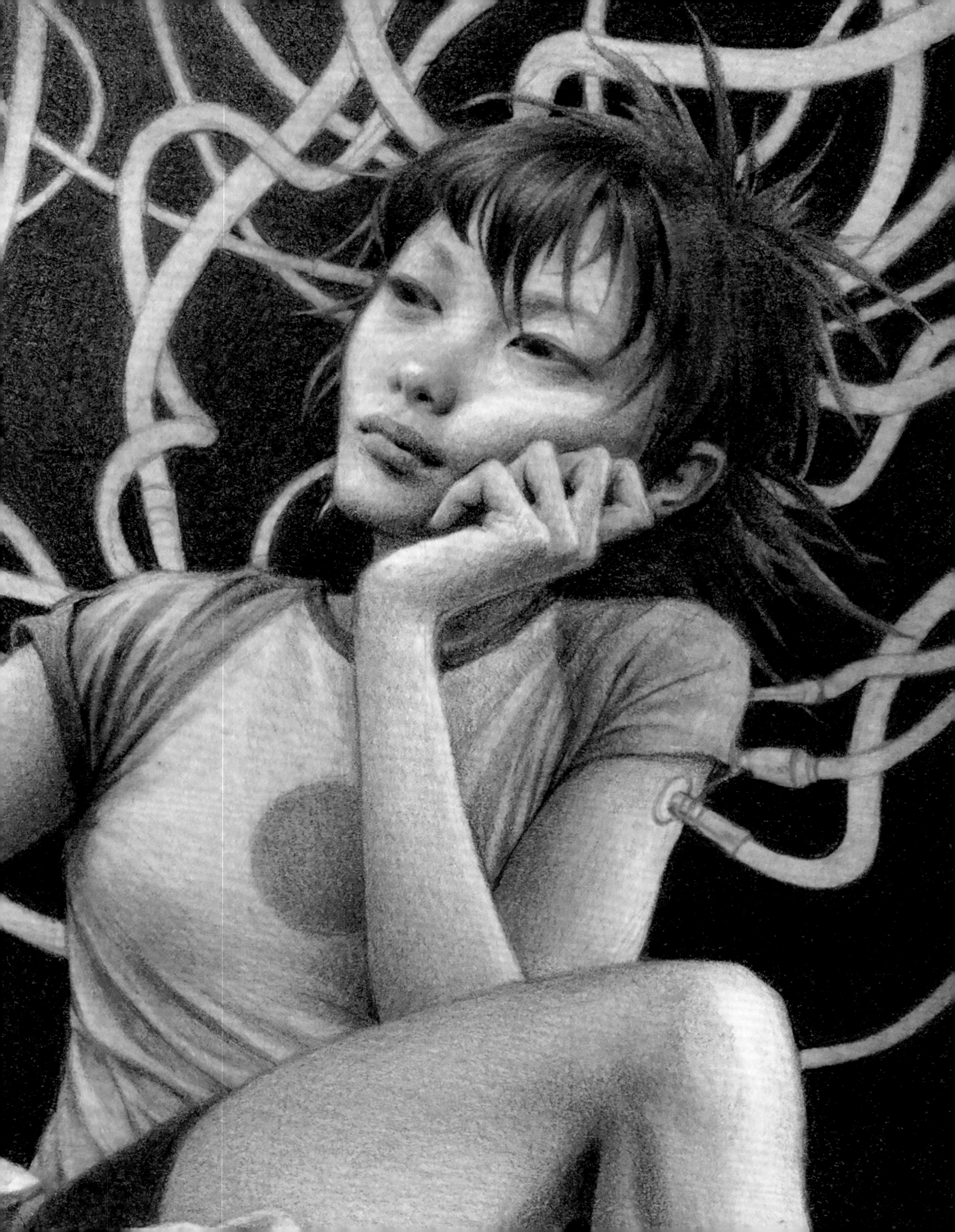

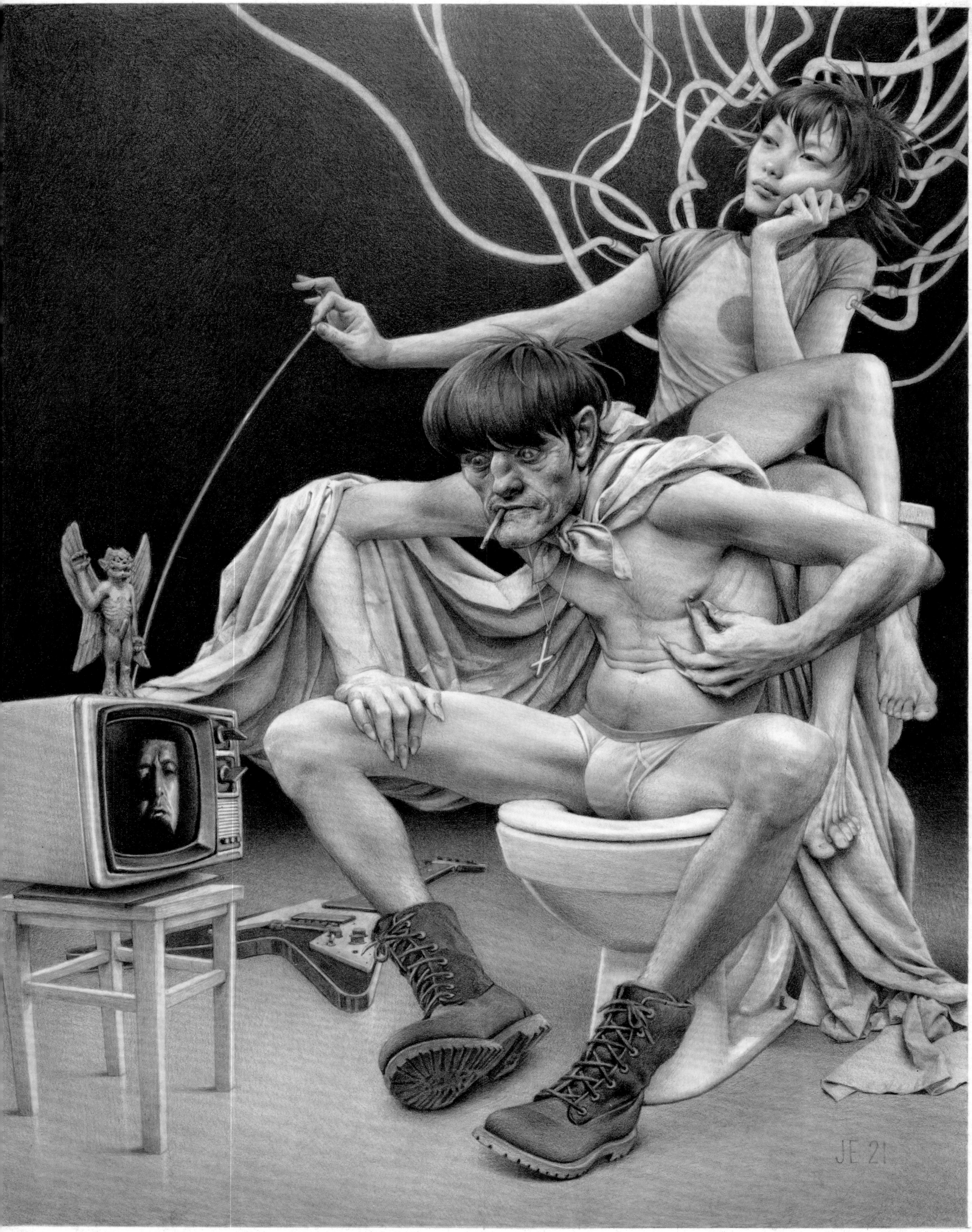
JE 21

Tara Billinger

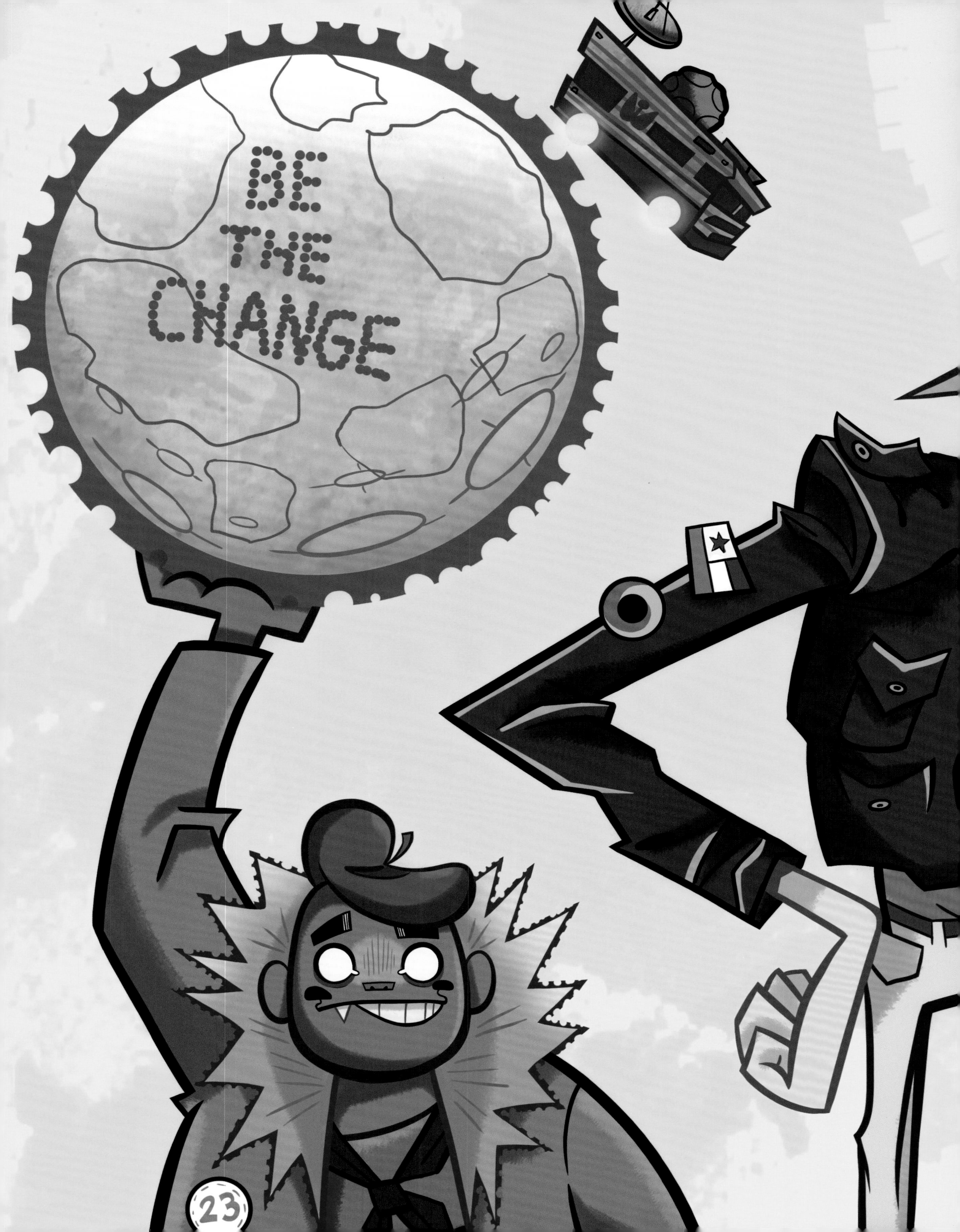
BE
THE
CHANGE

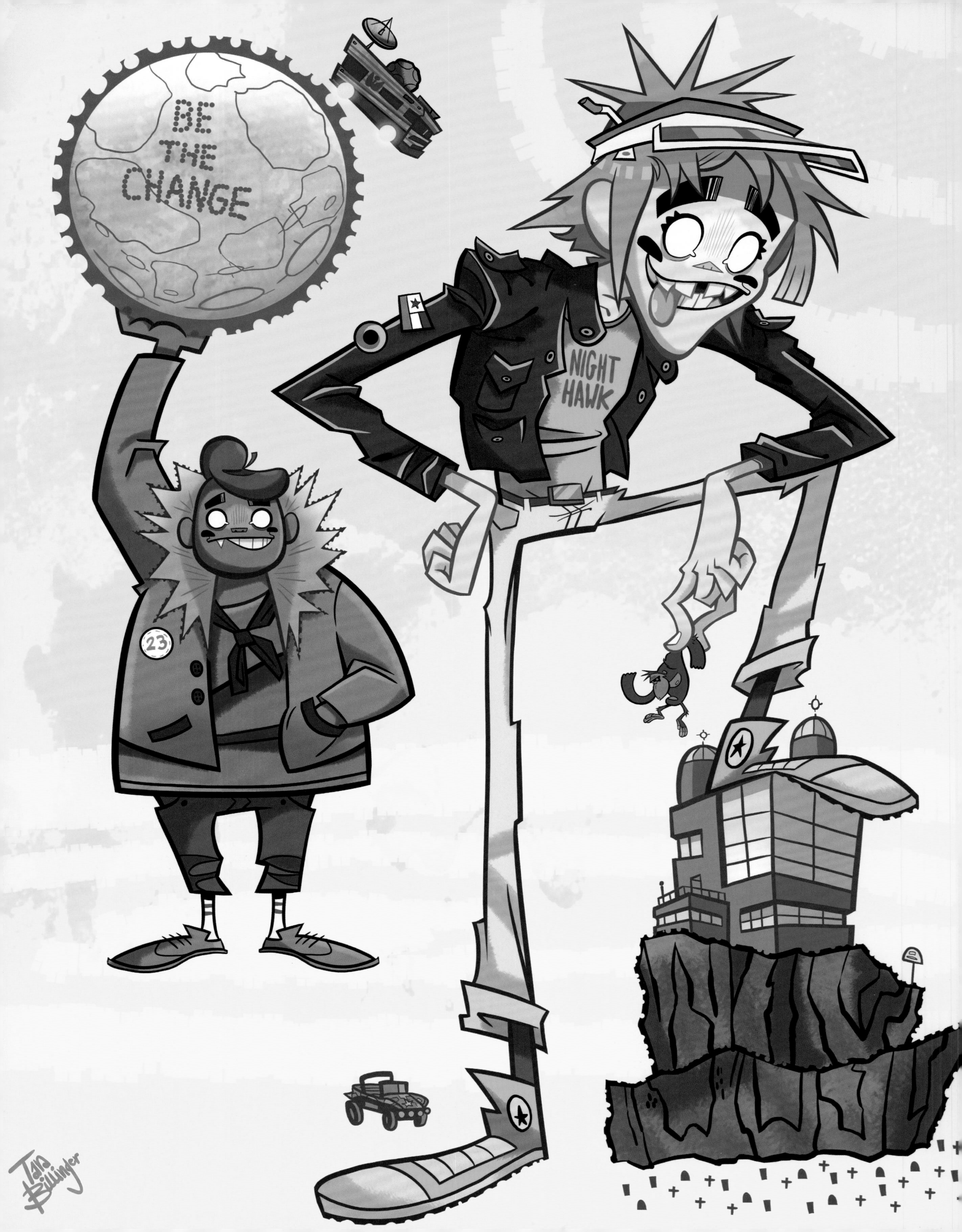
BE THE CHANGE
NIGHT HAWK
23
Tara Billinger

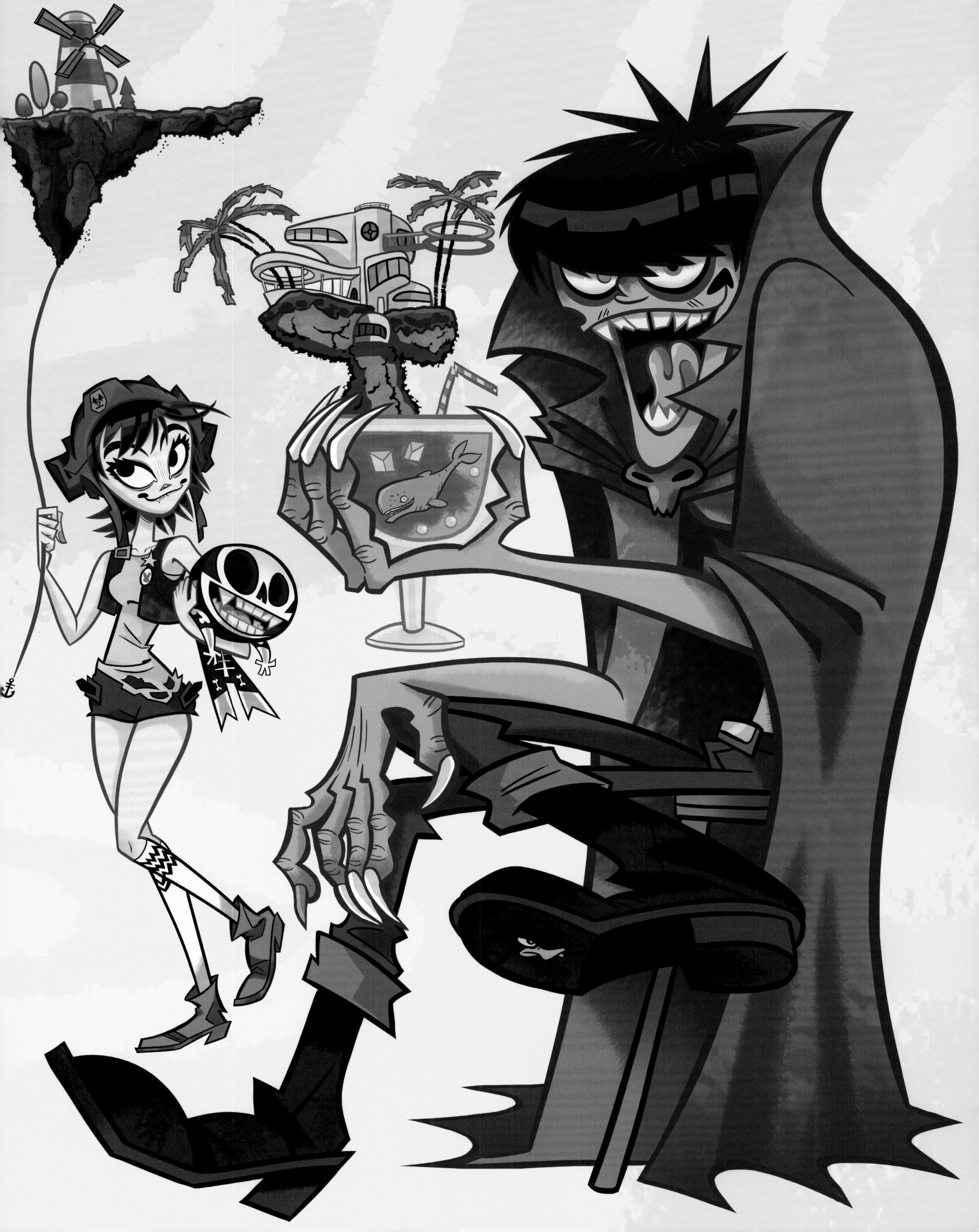

André Carrilho

2001

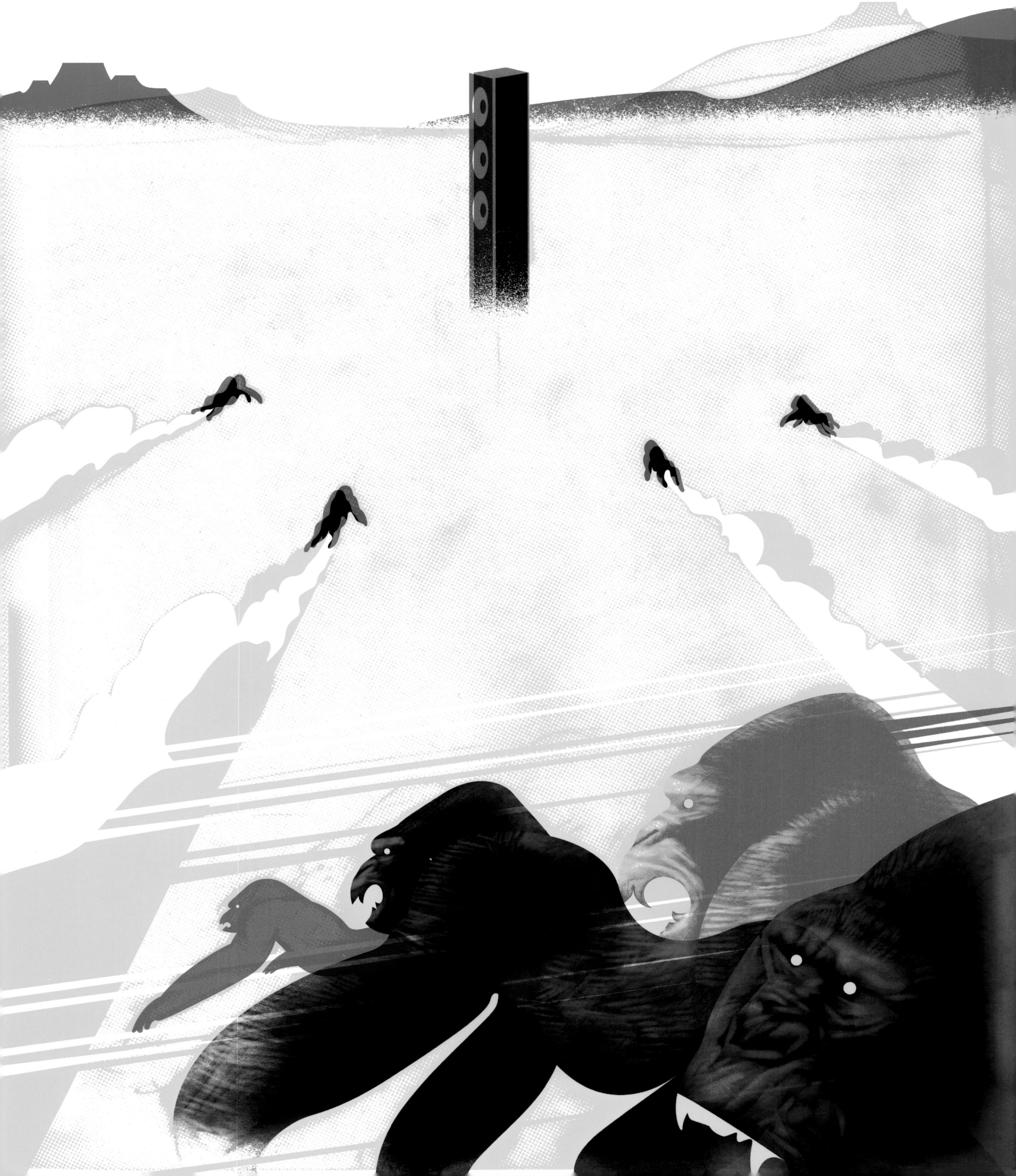

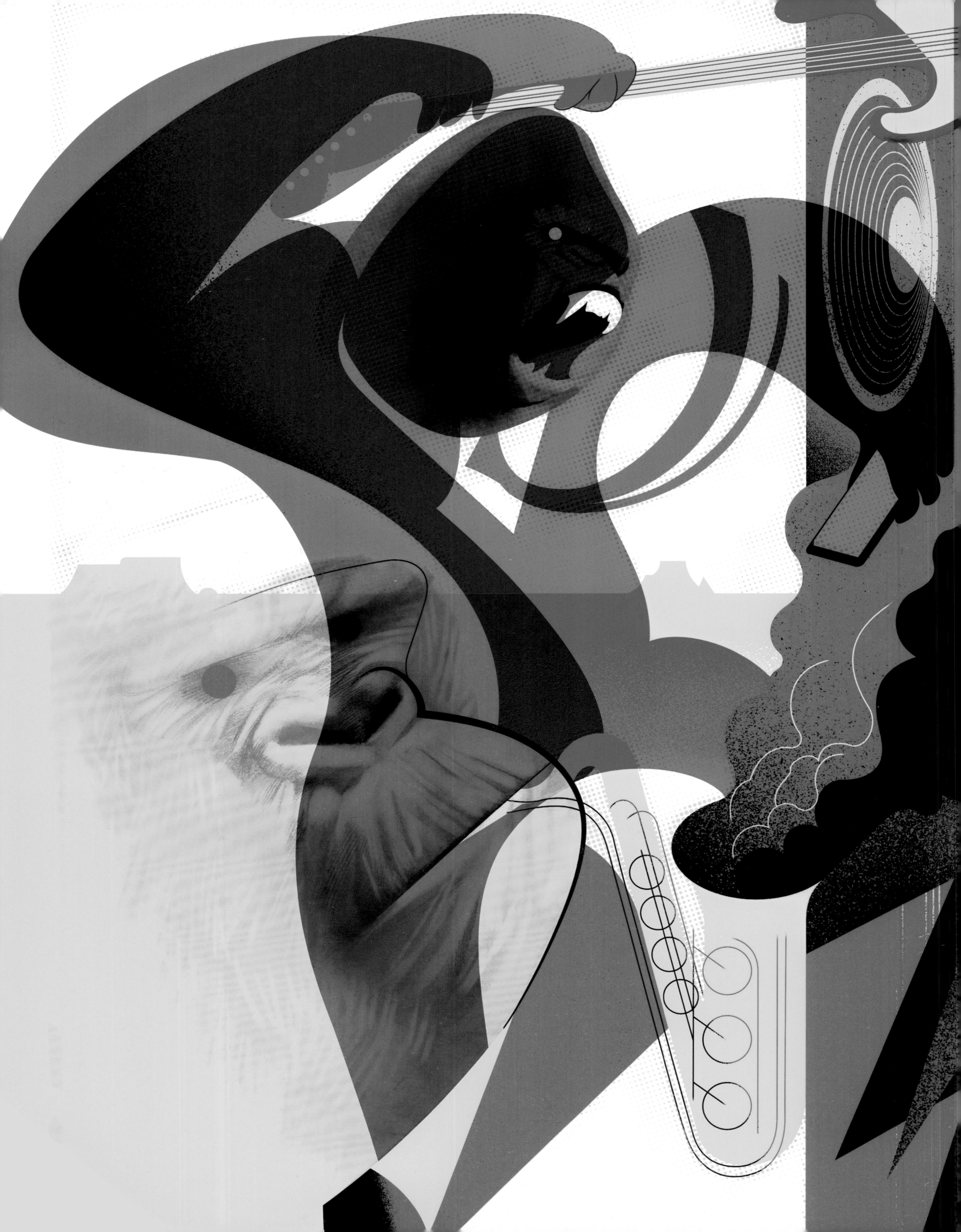

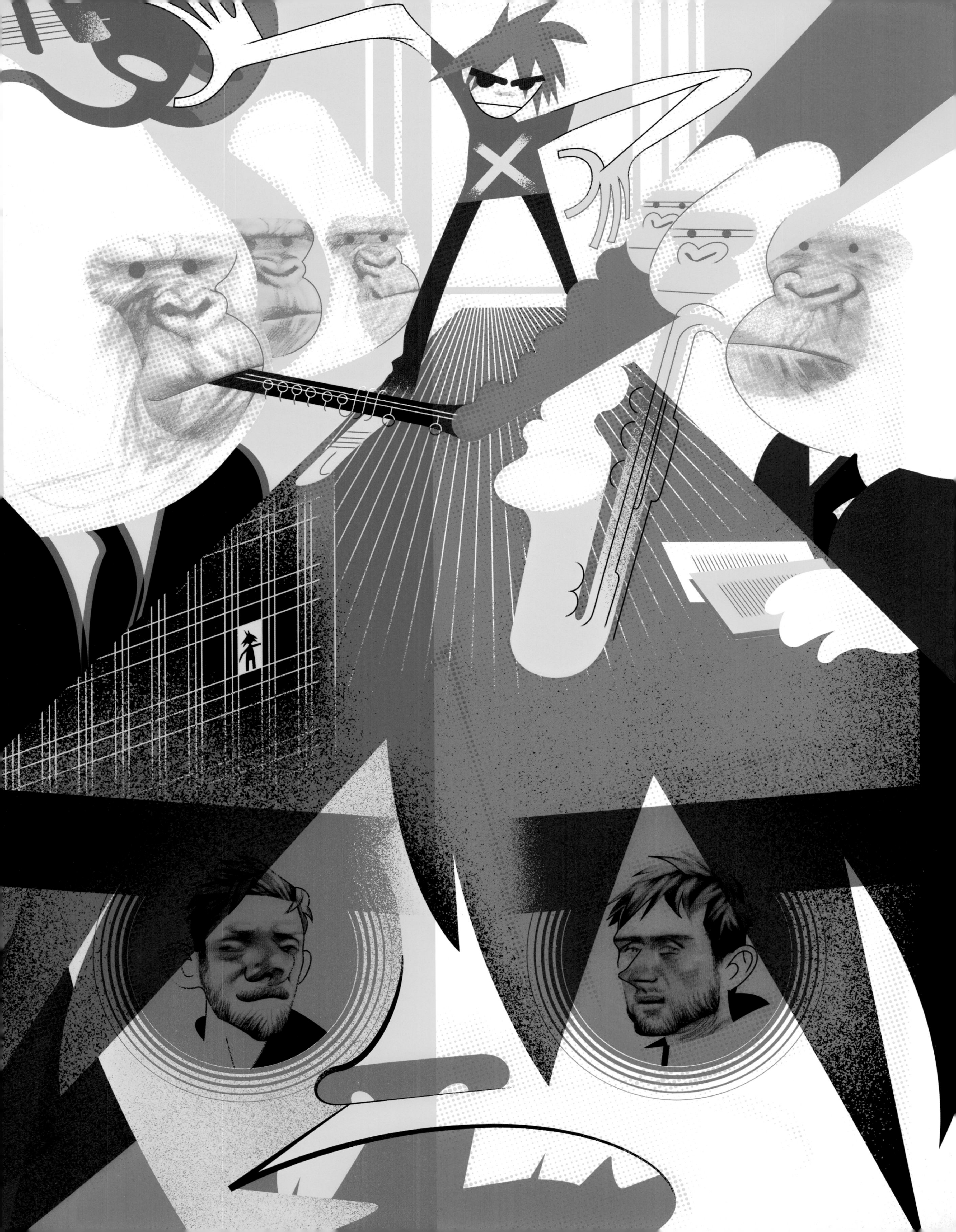

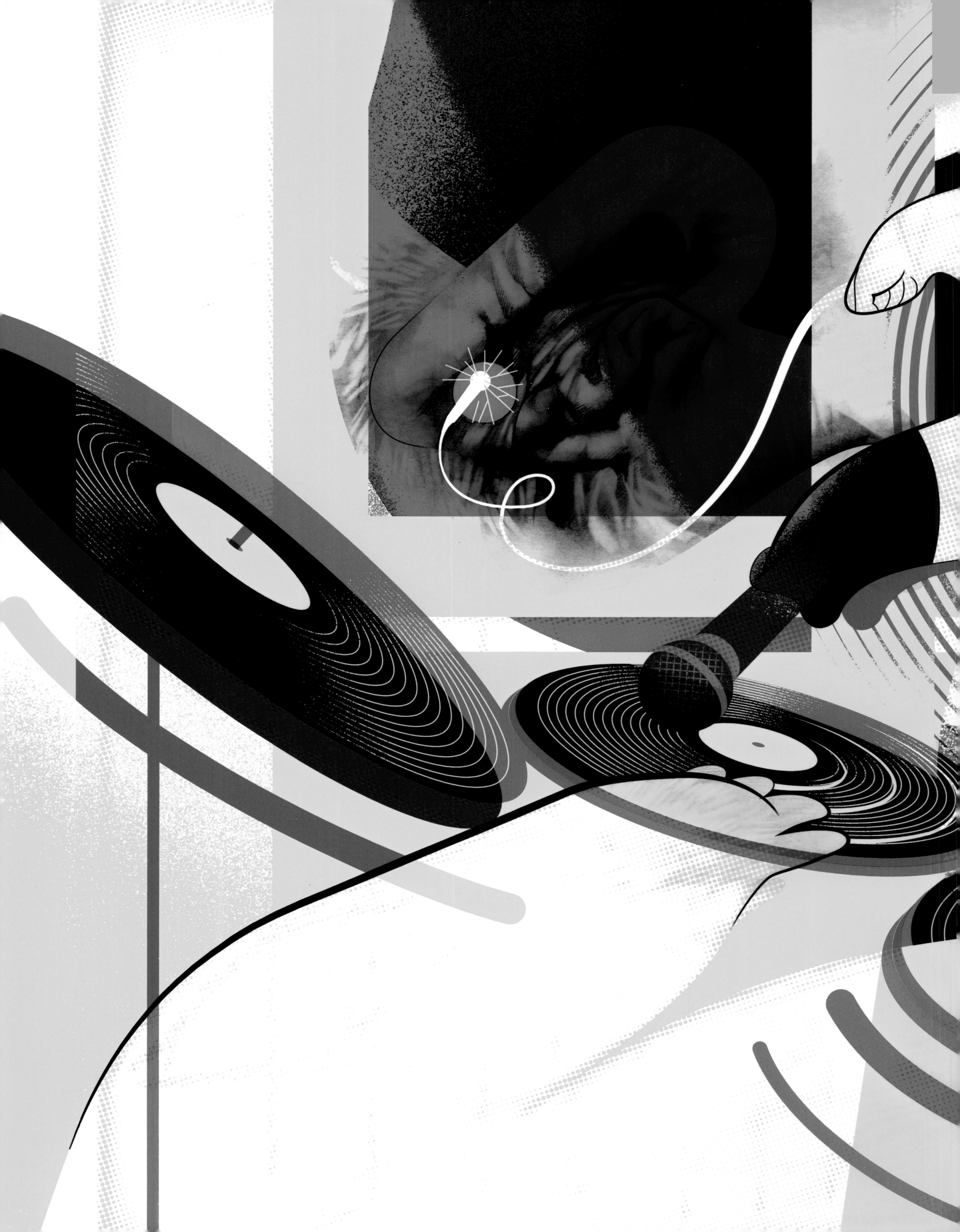

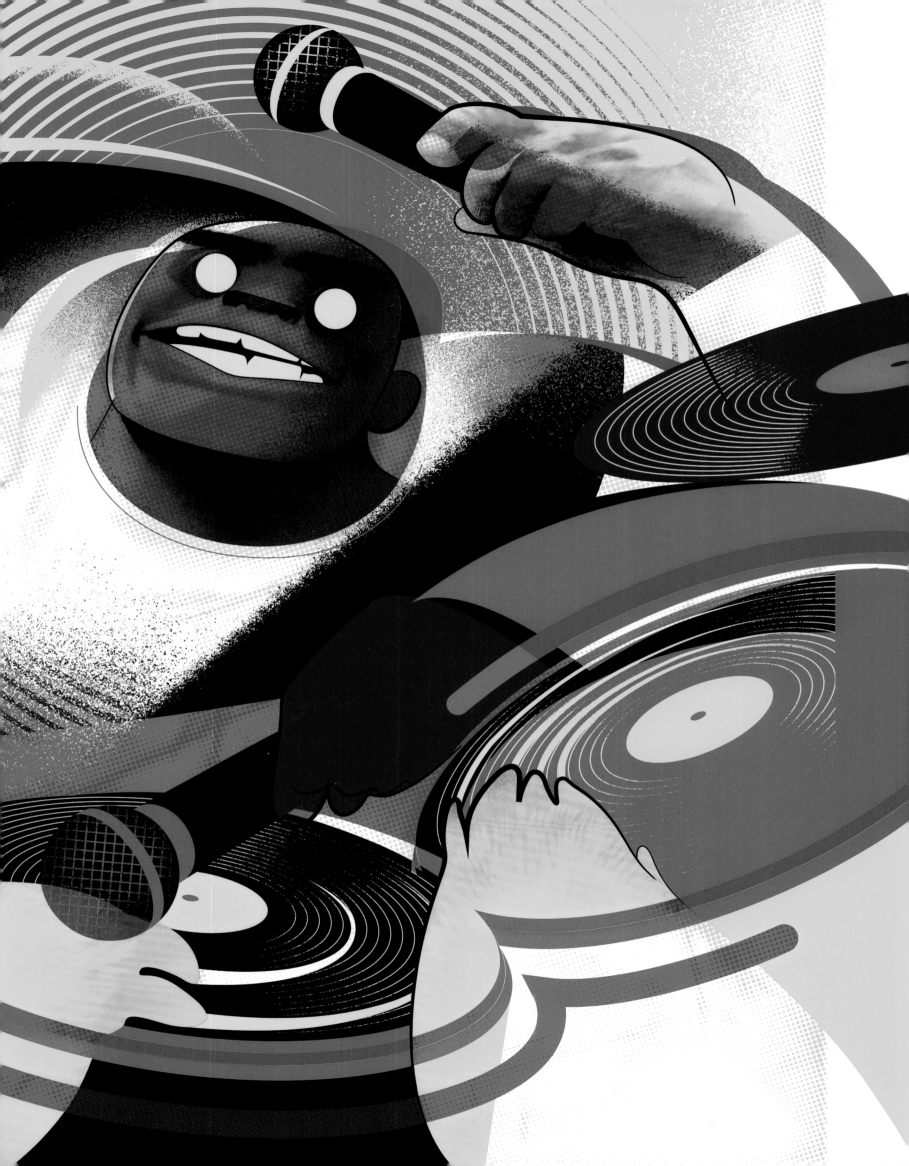

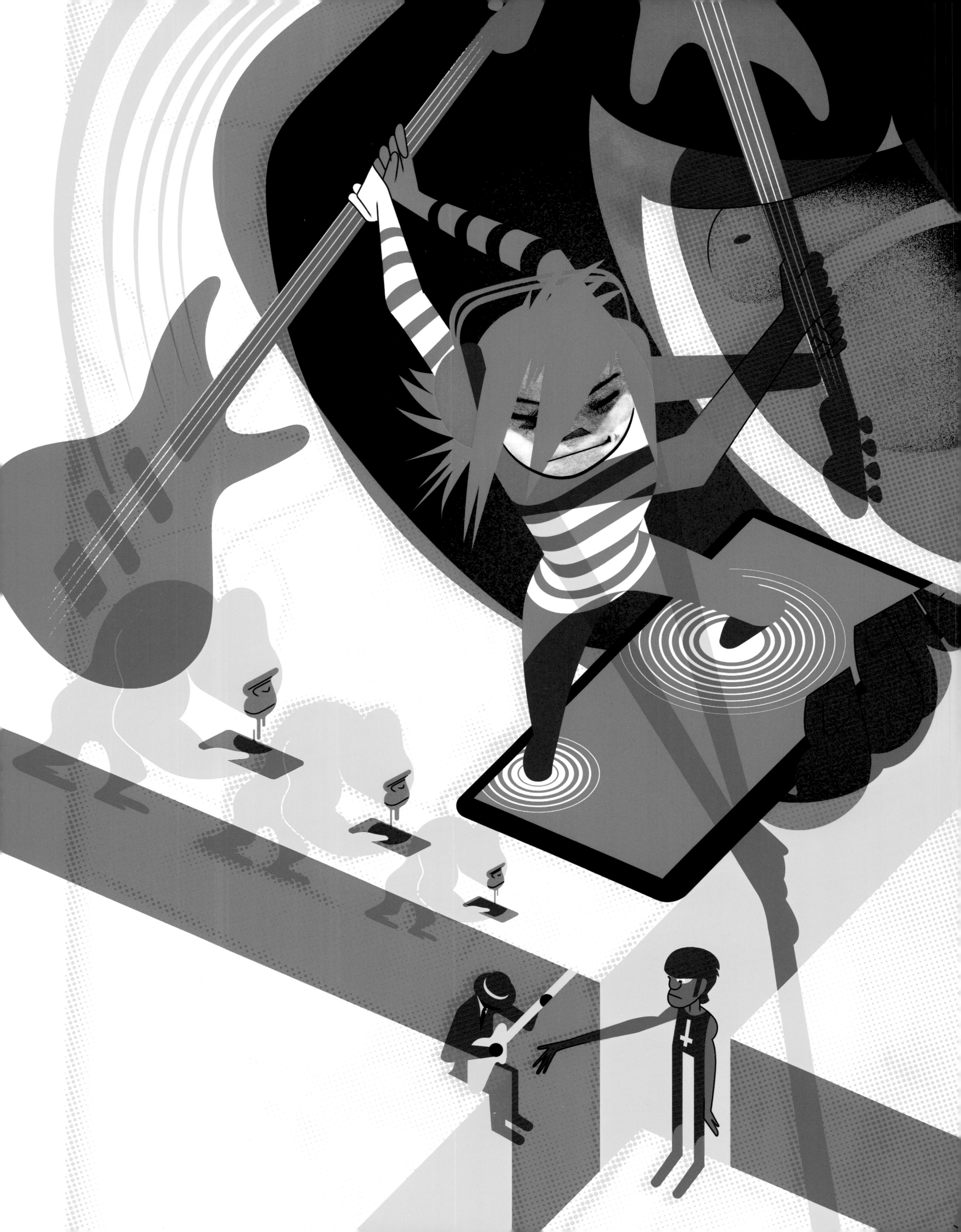

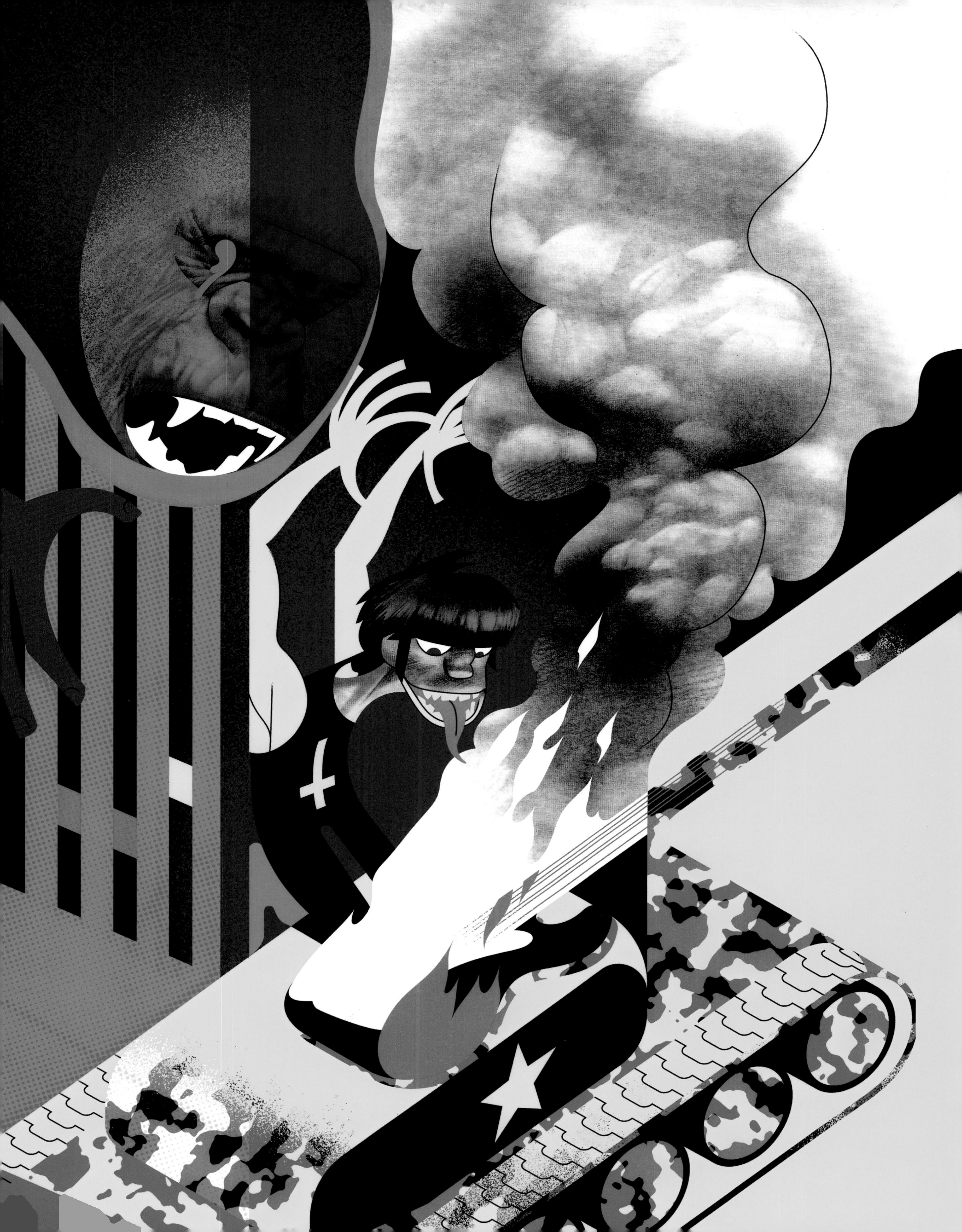

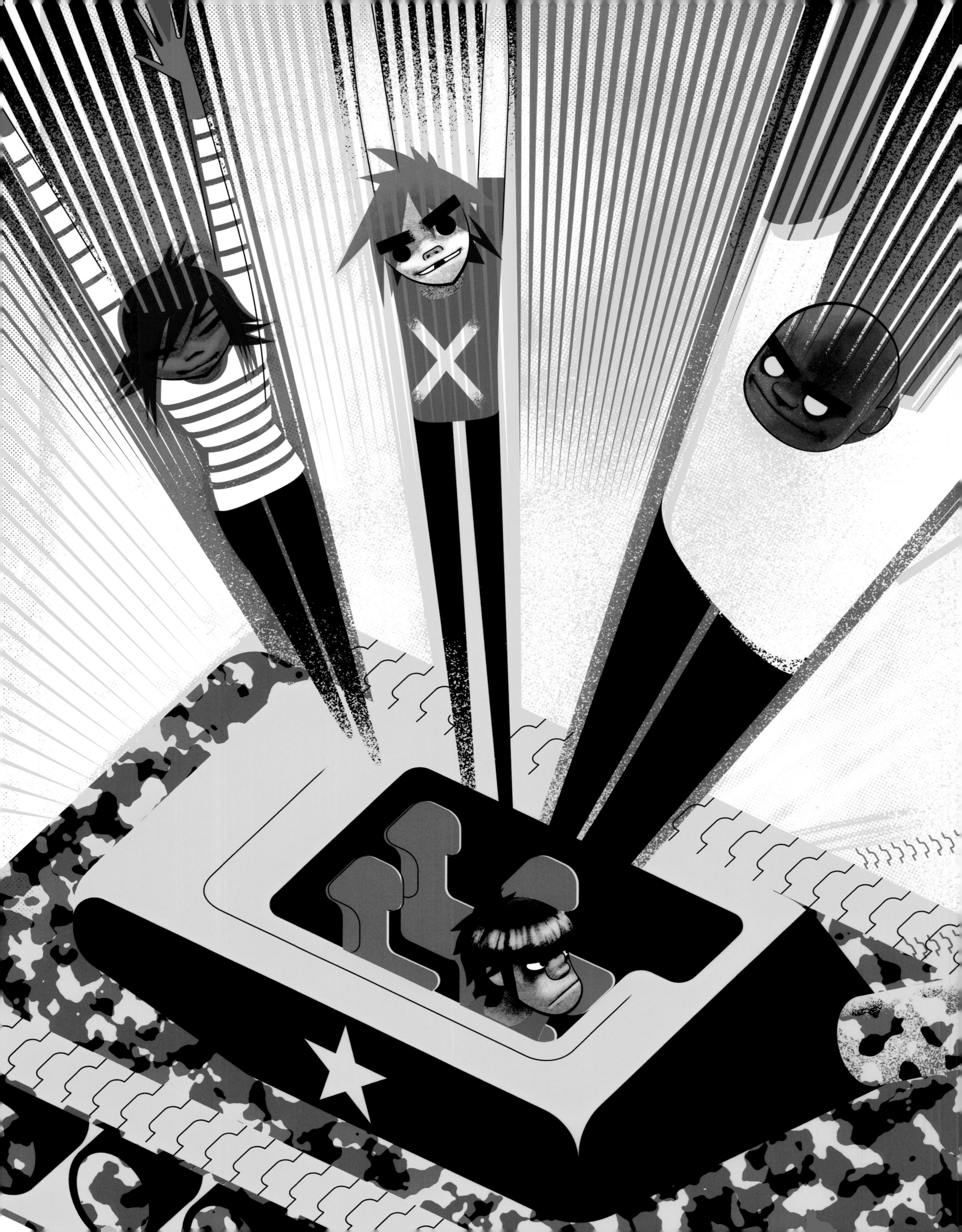

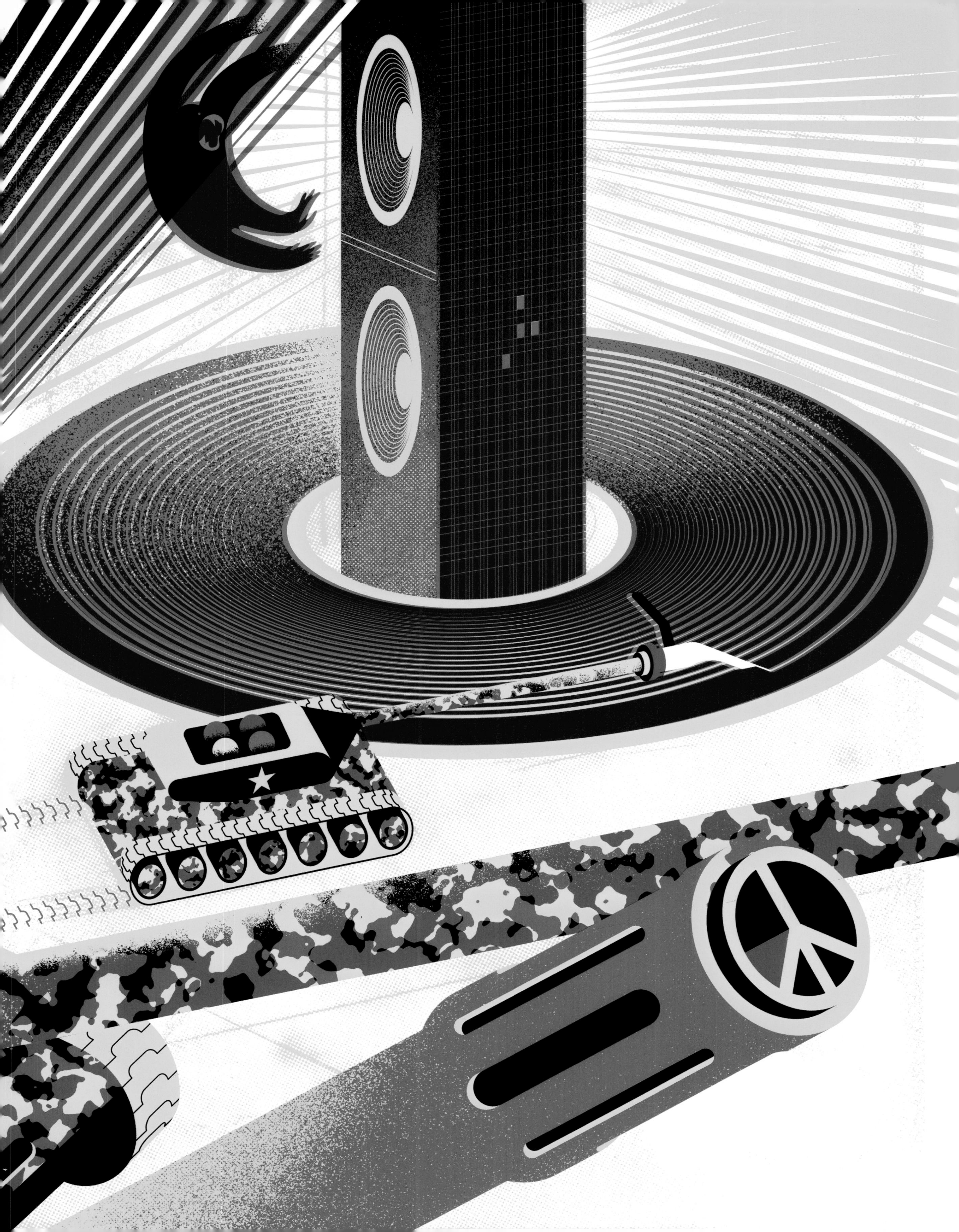

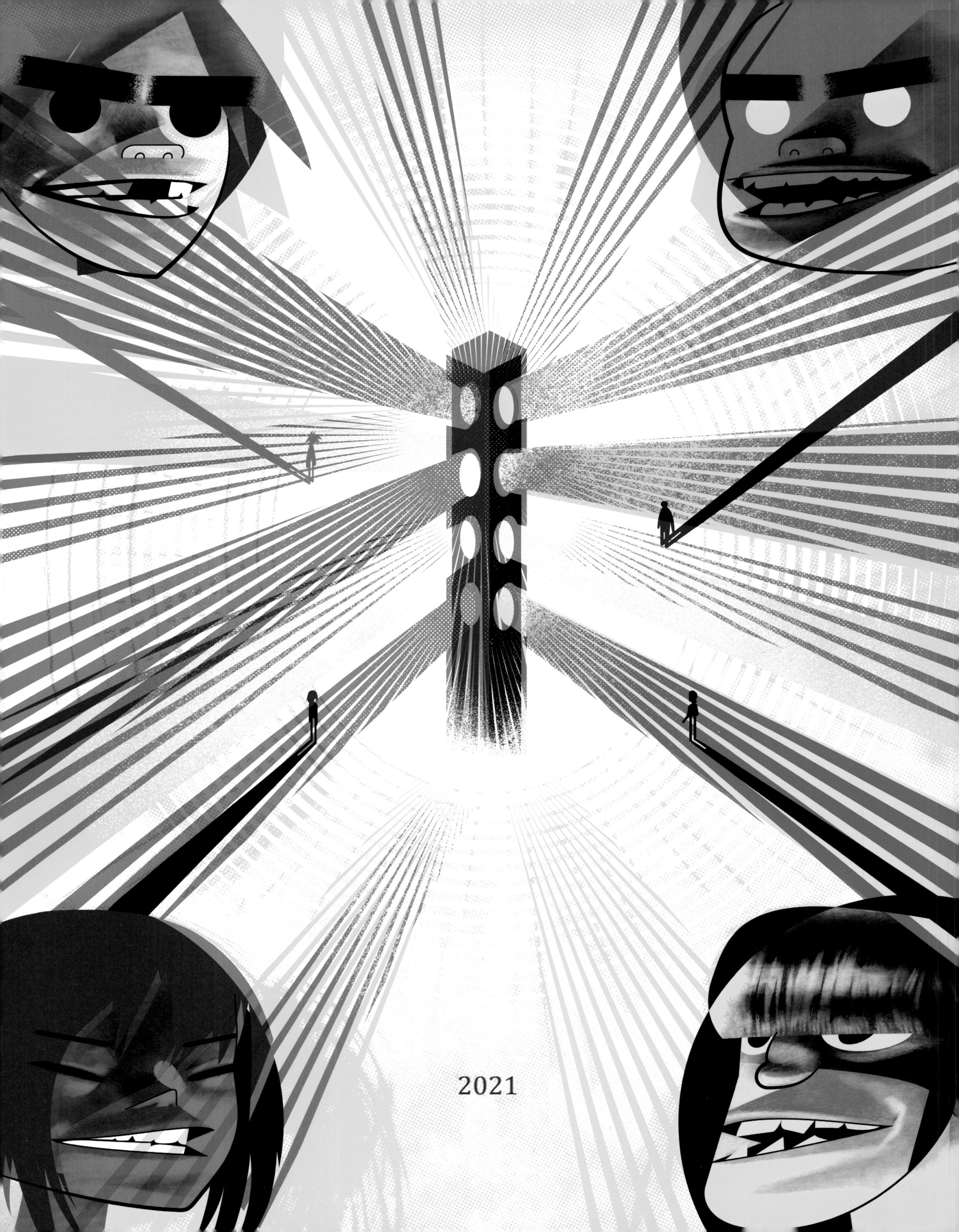
2021

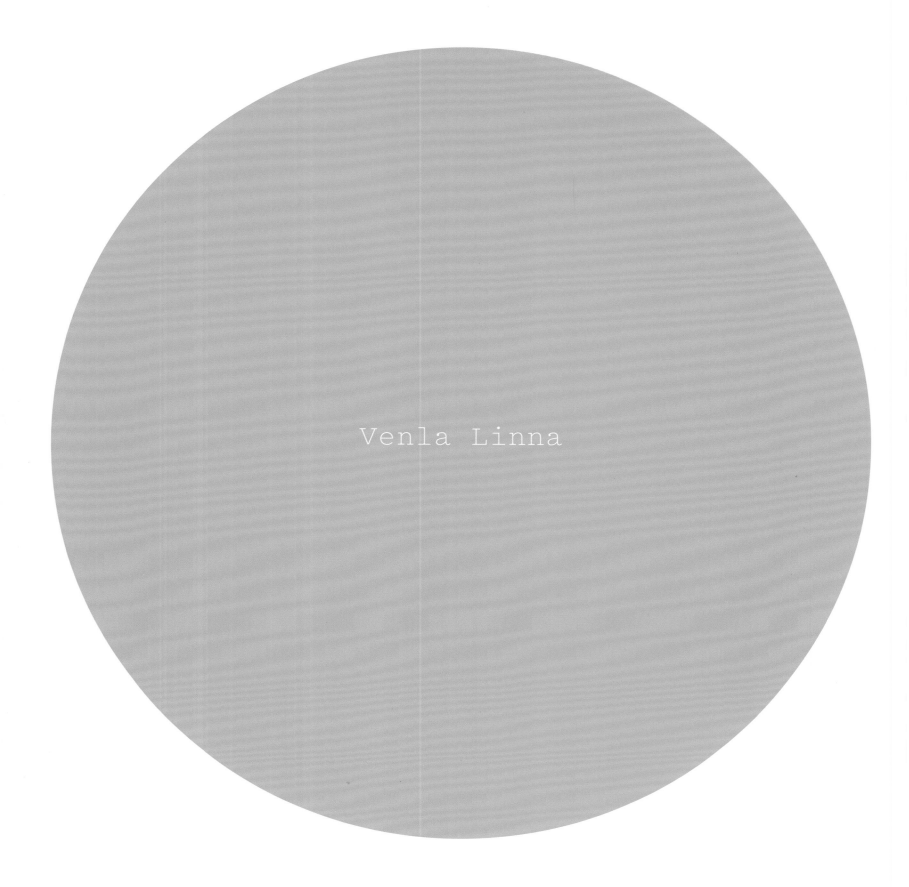

Venla Linna

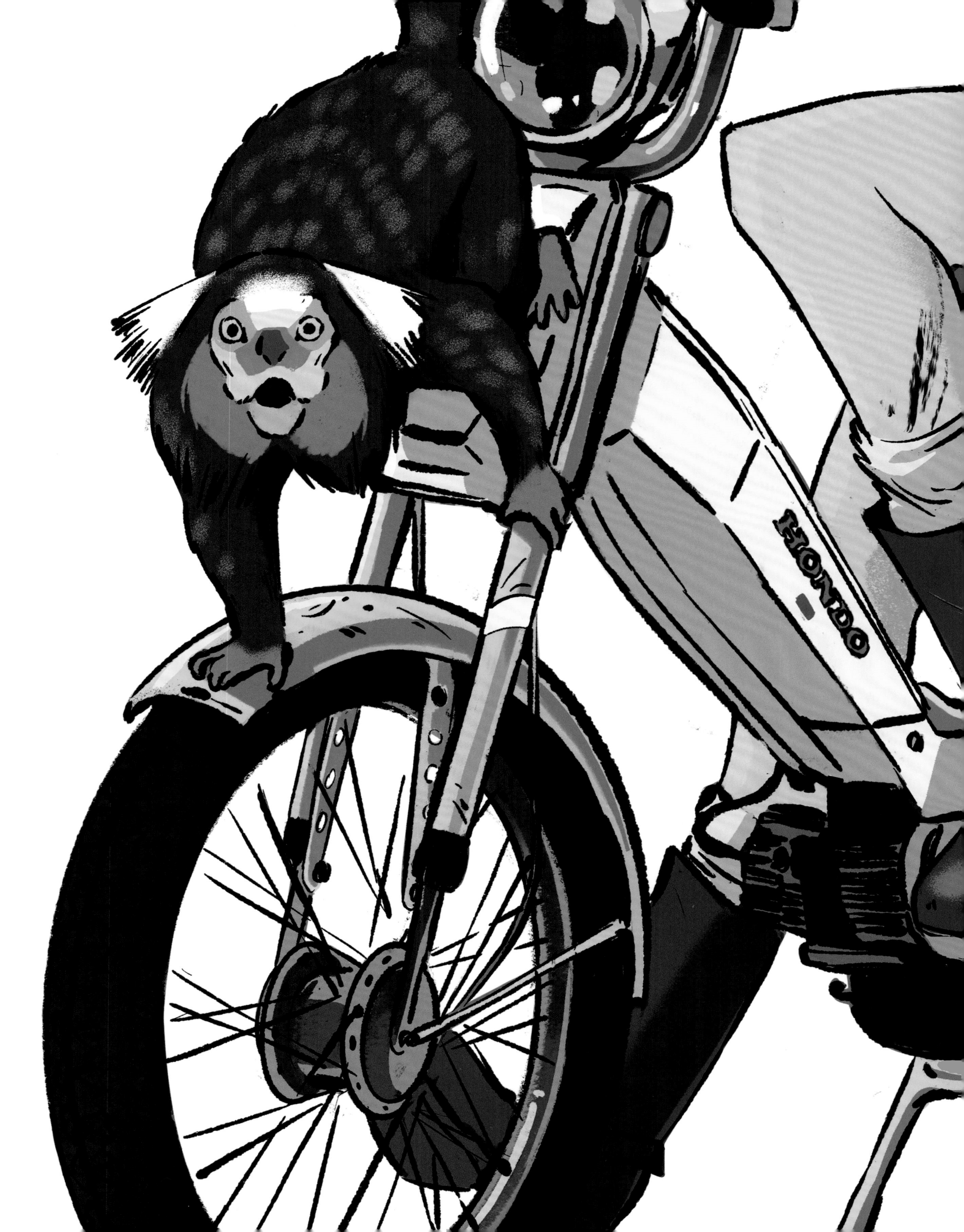
HONDO

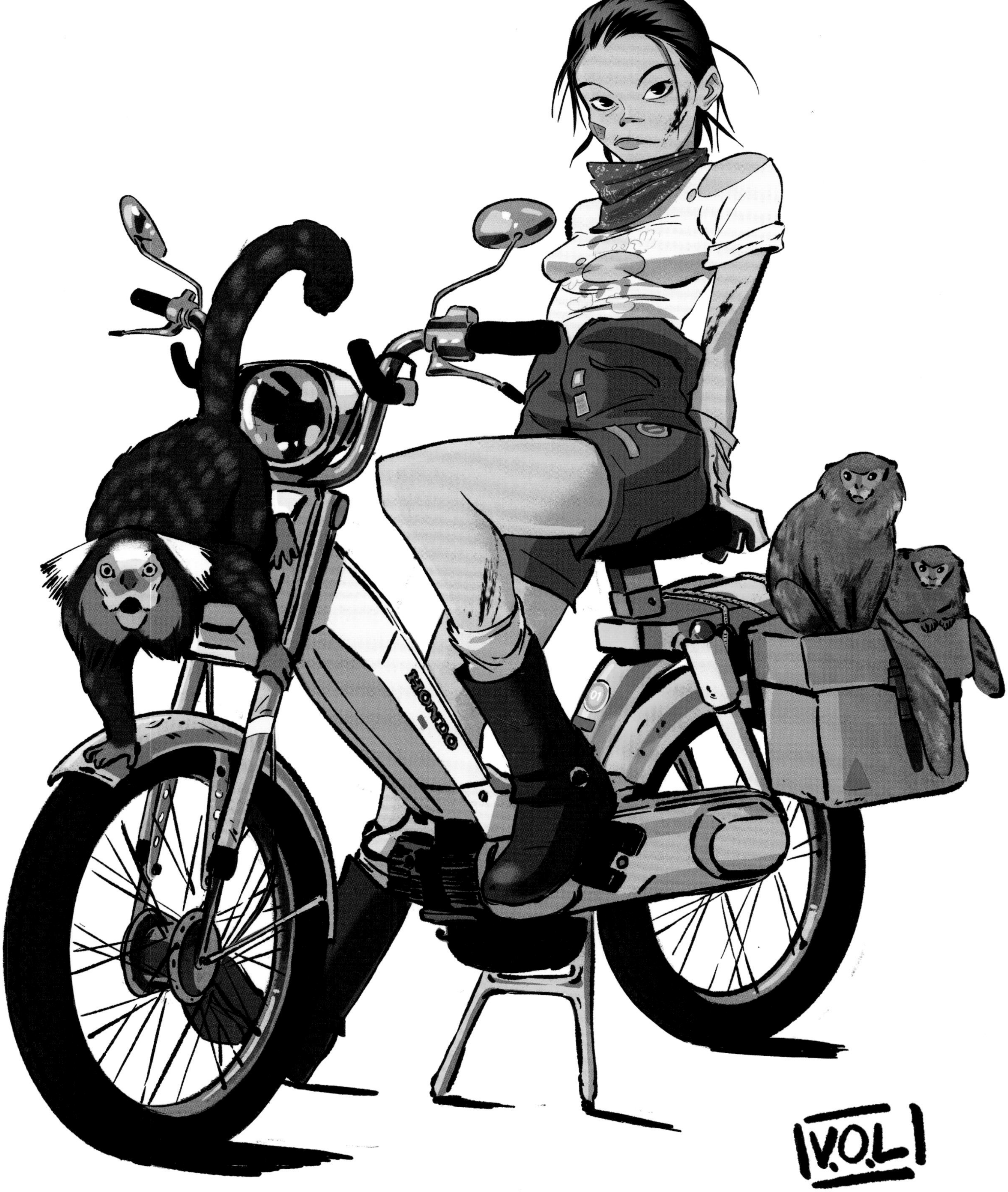
HONDO
V.O.L

Daniela Uhlig

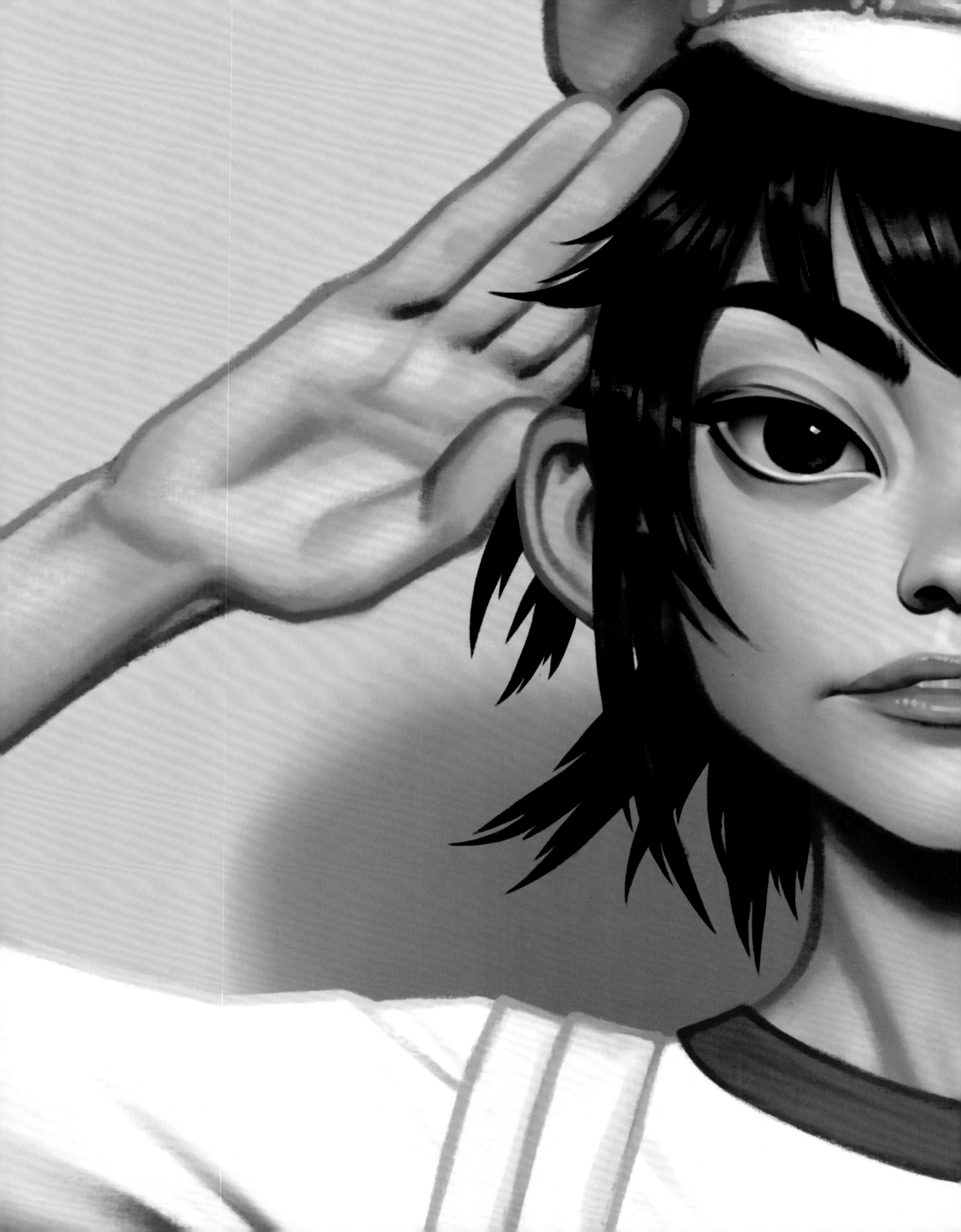

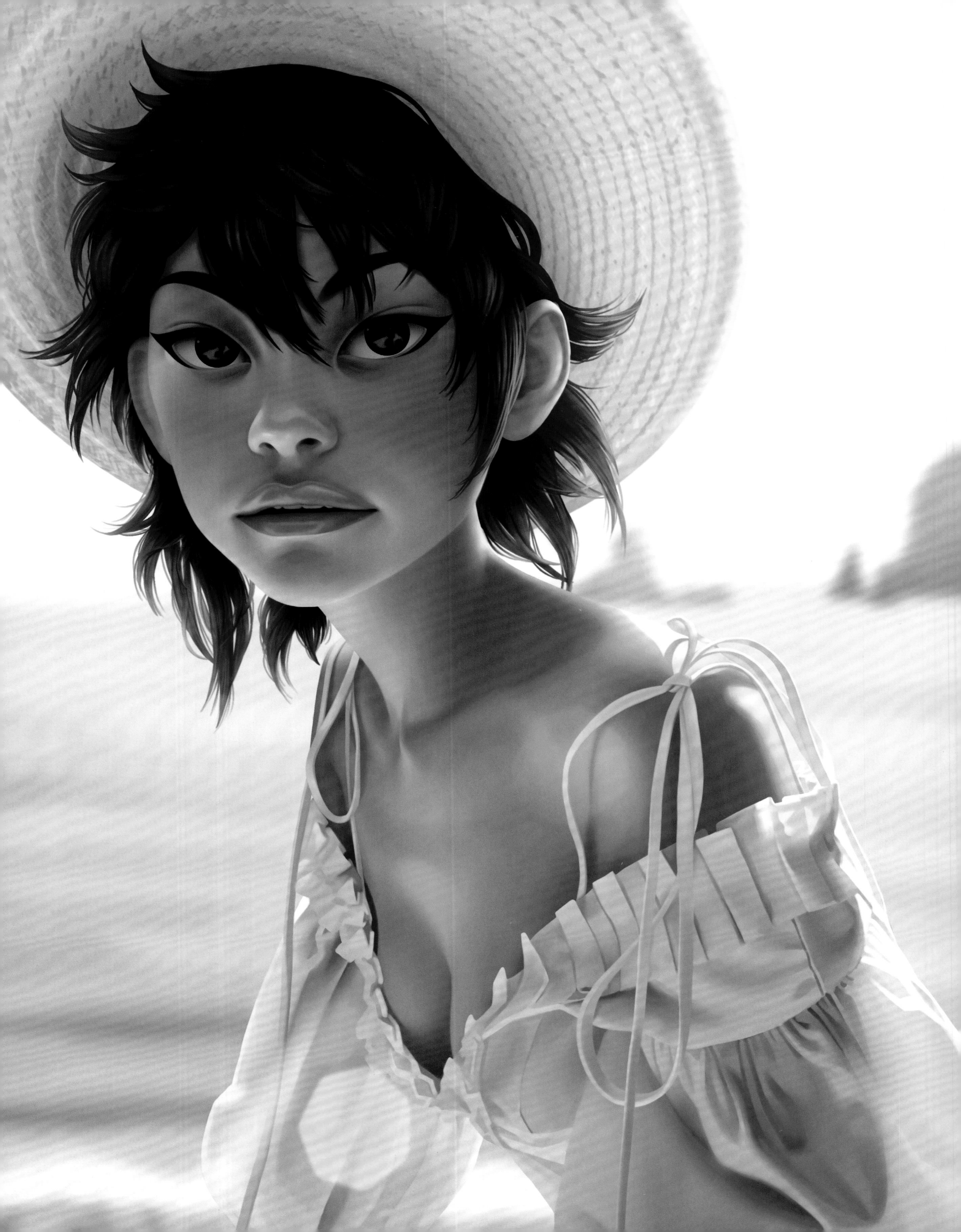

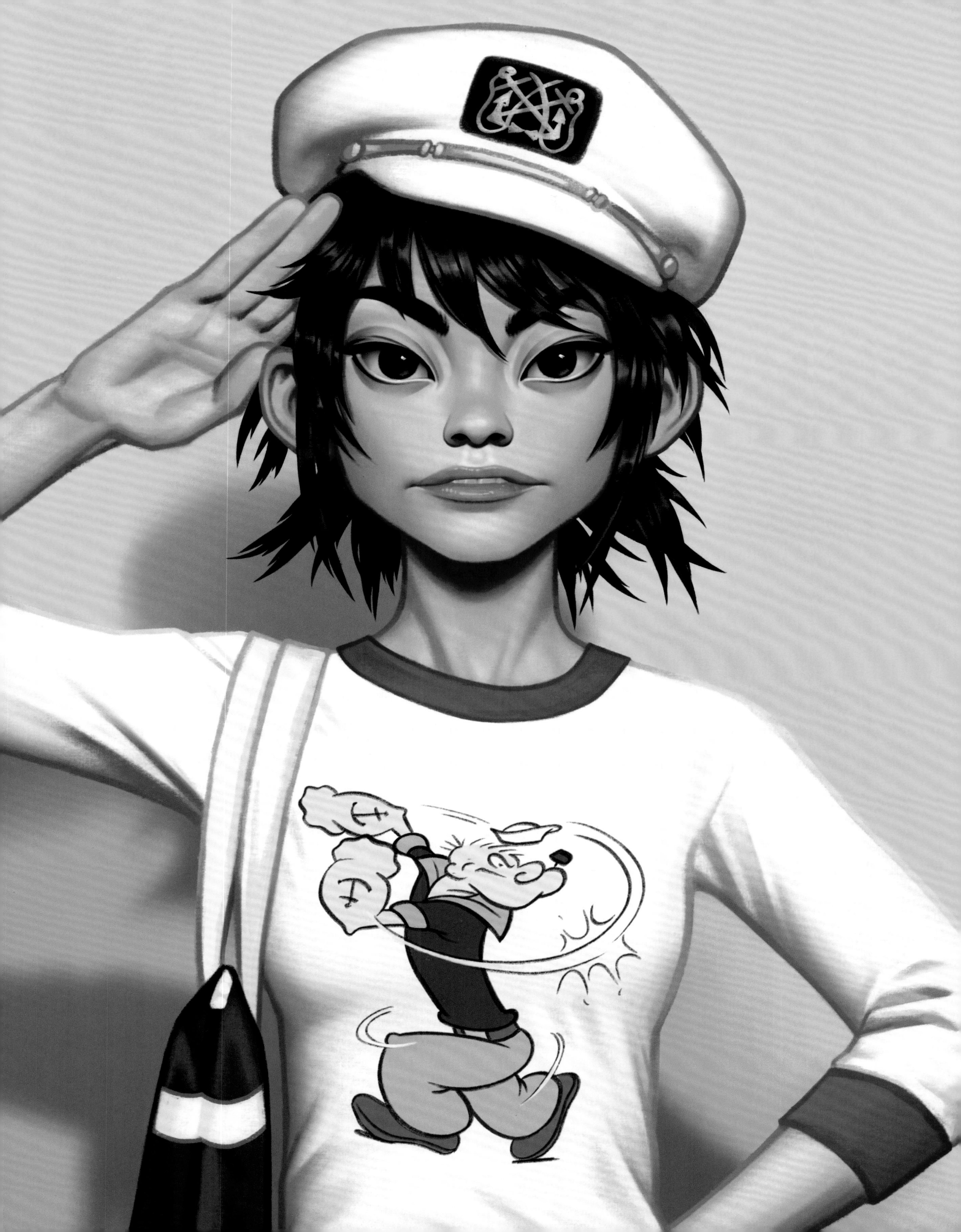

Sainer

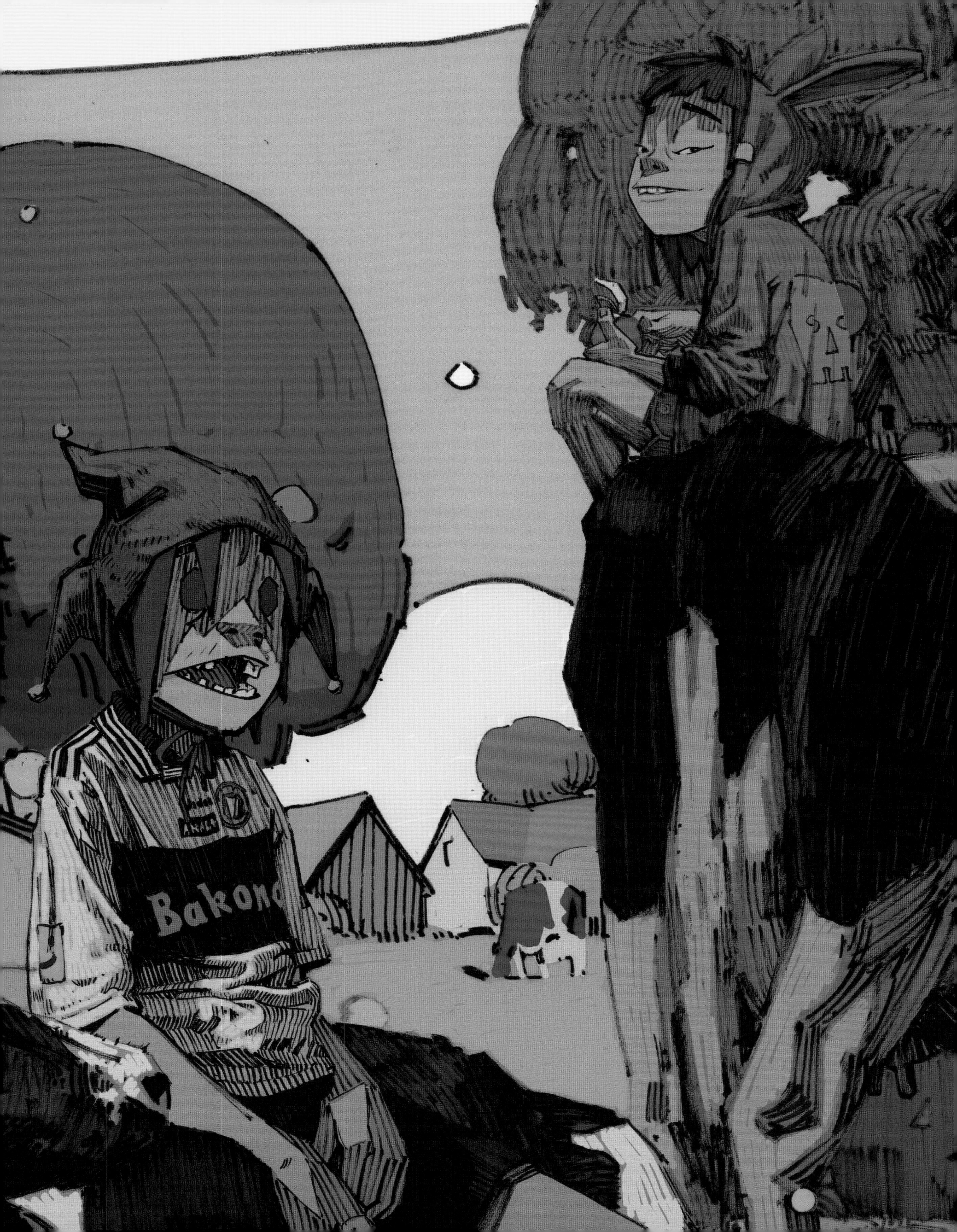

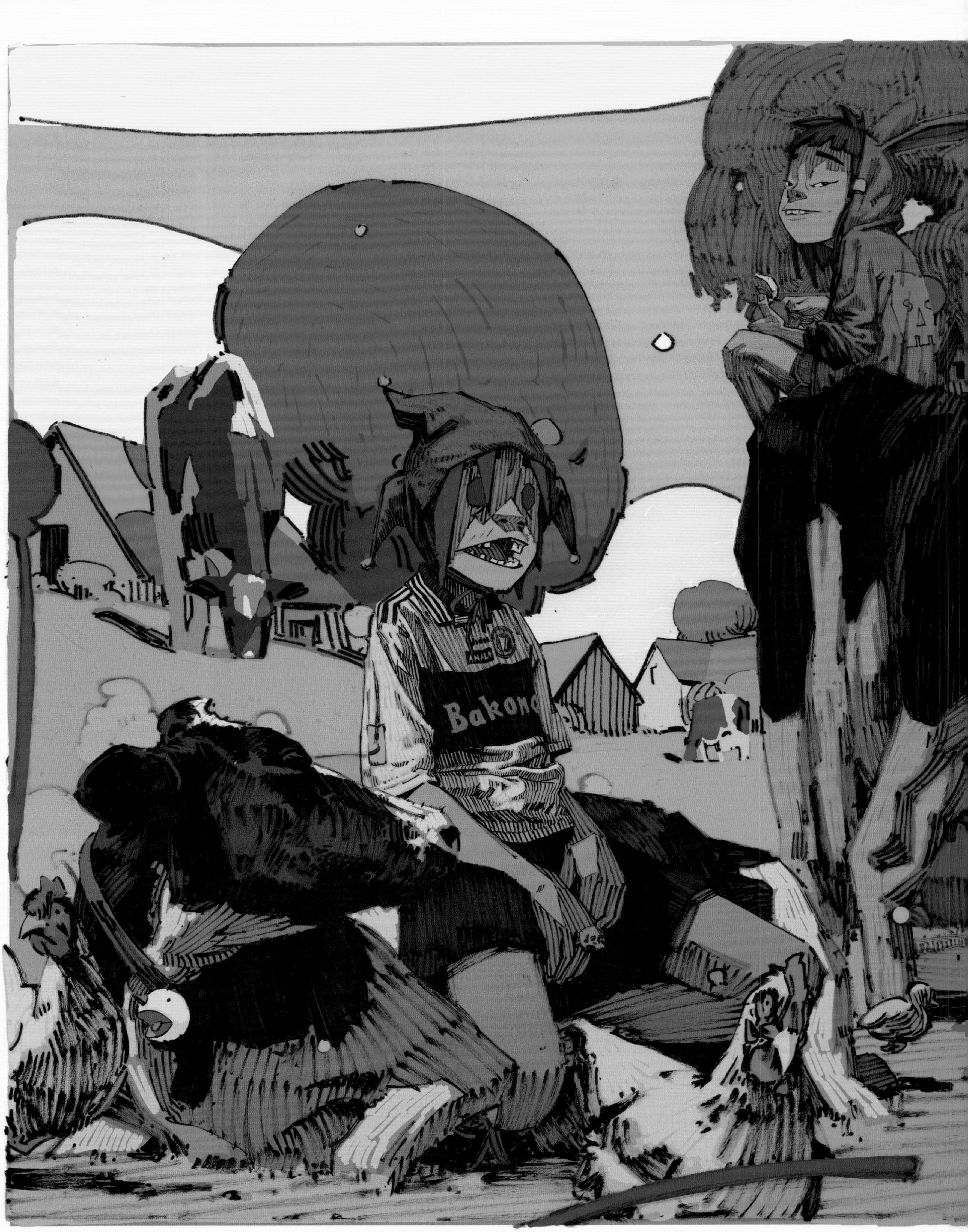
Bakona

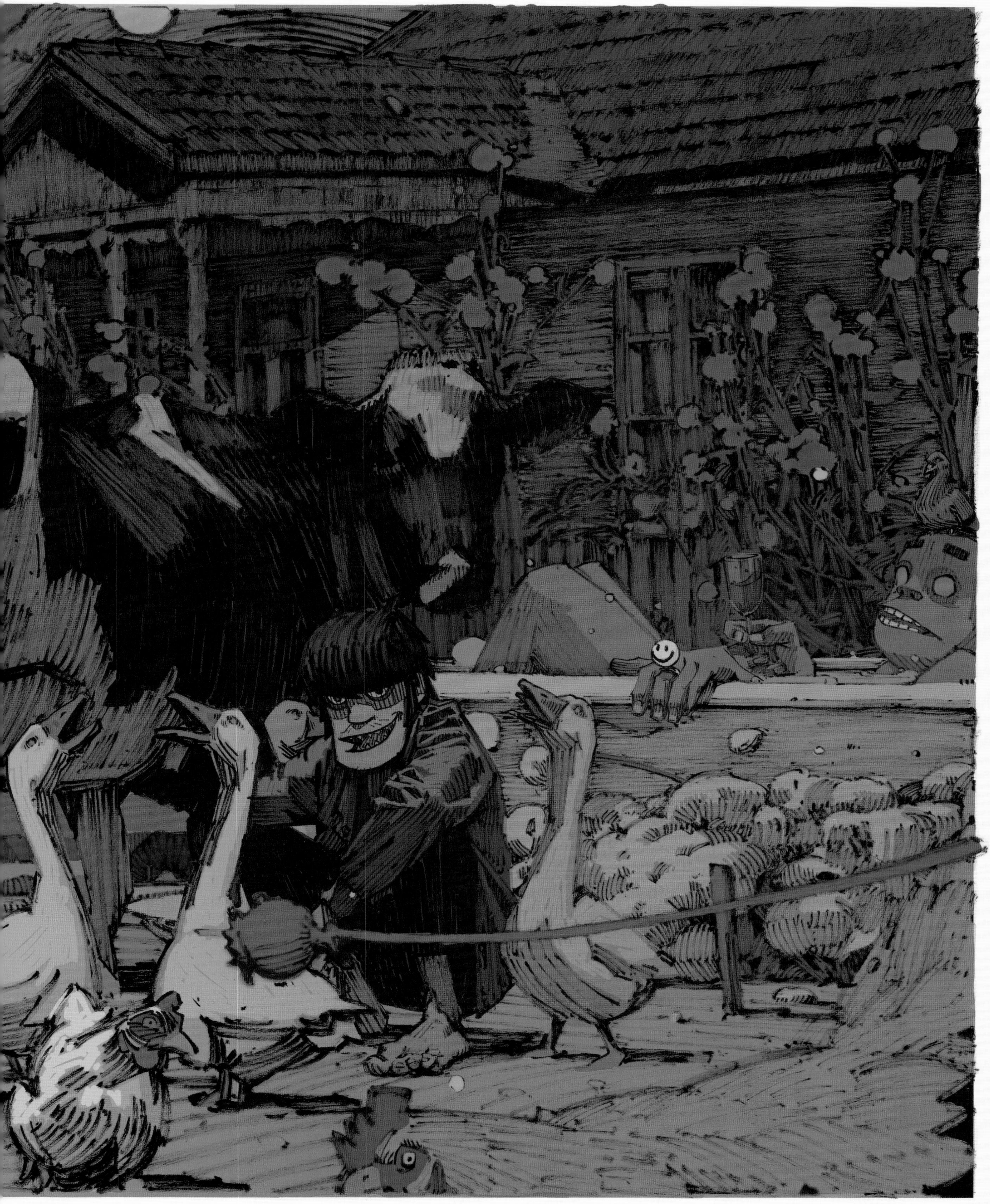

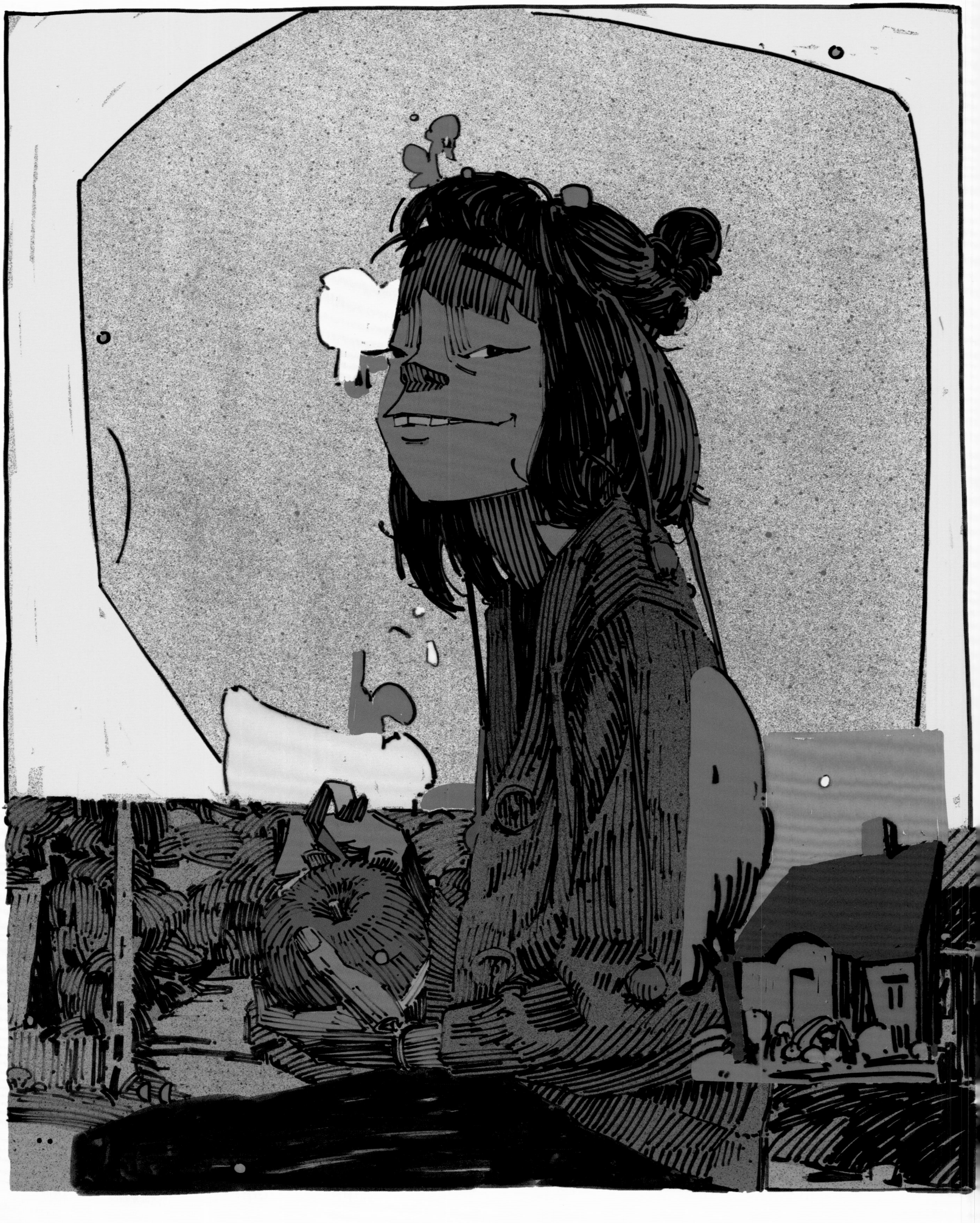

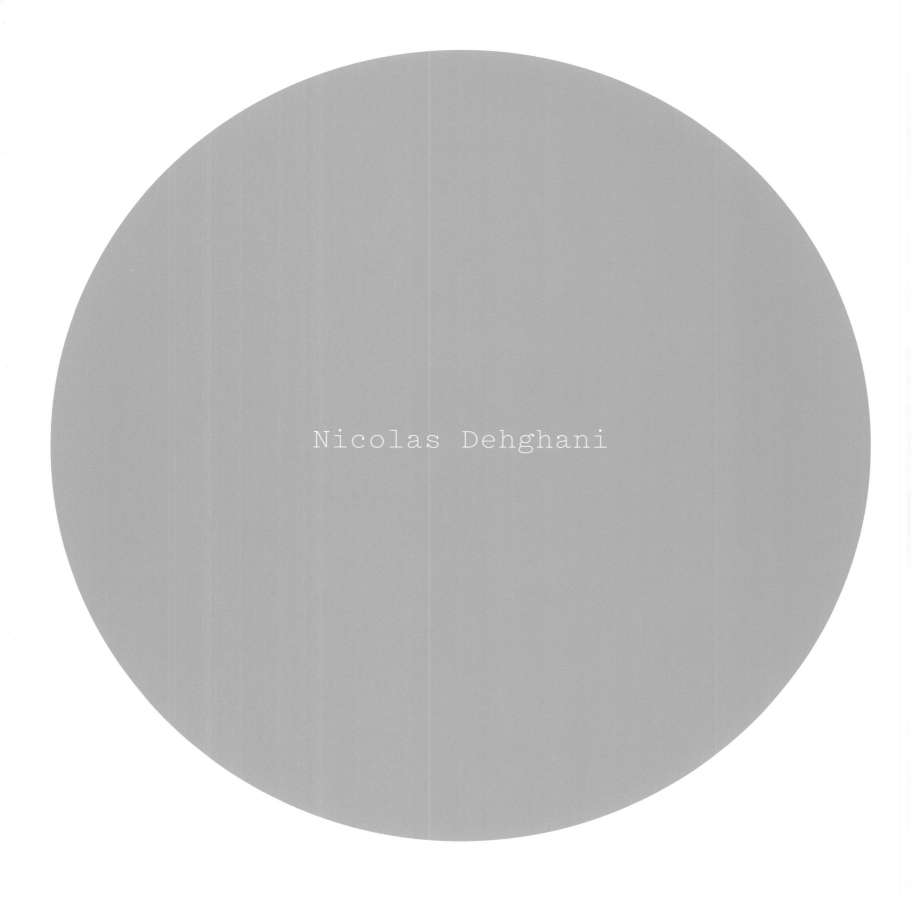

Nicolas Dehghani

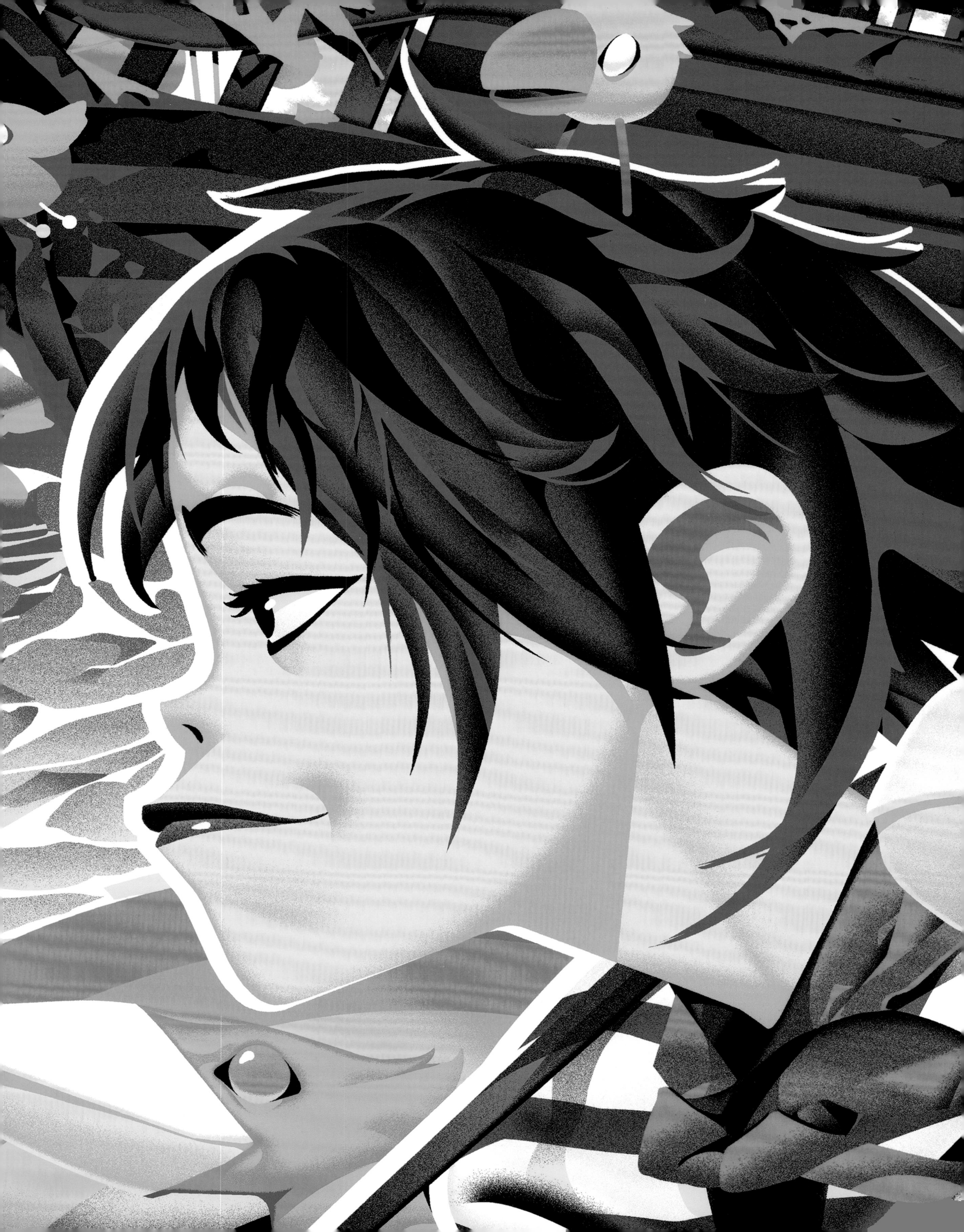

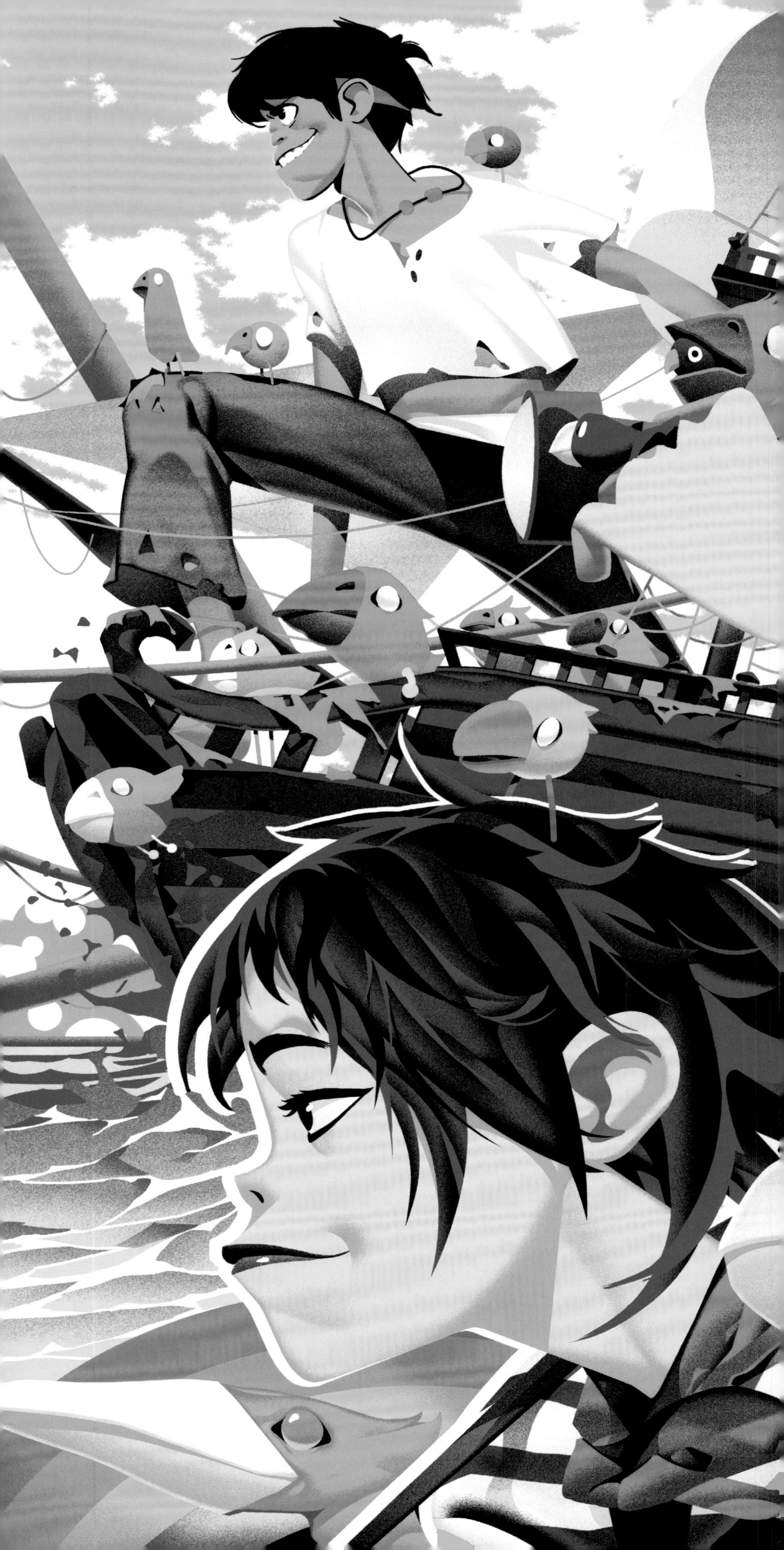

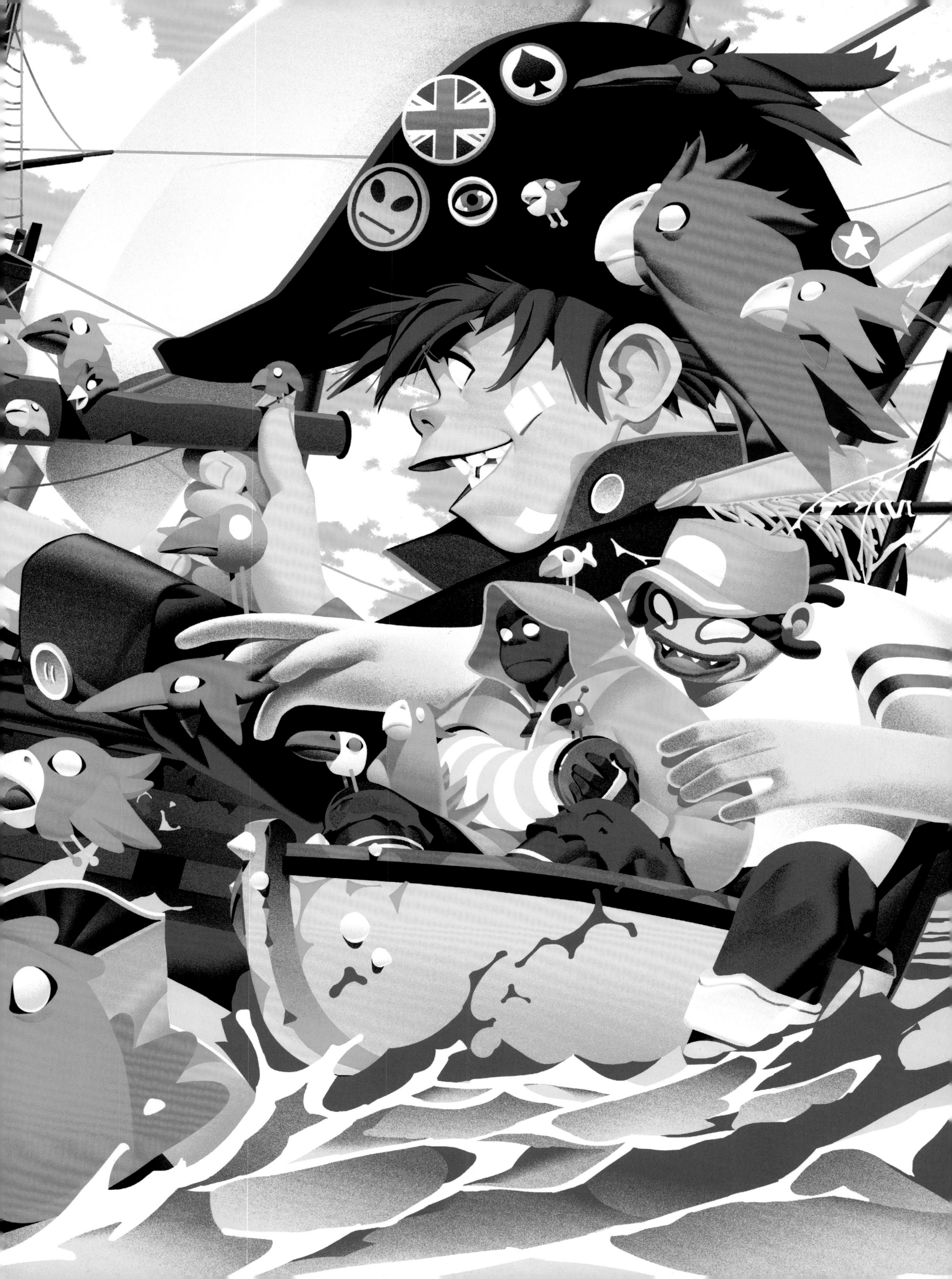

Marella Moon Albanese

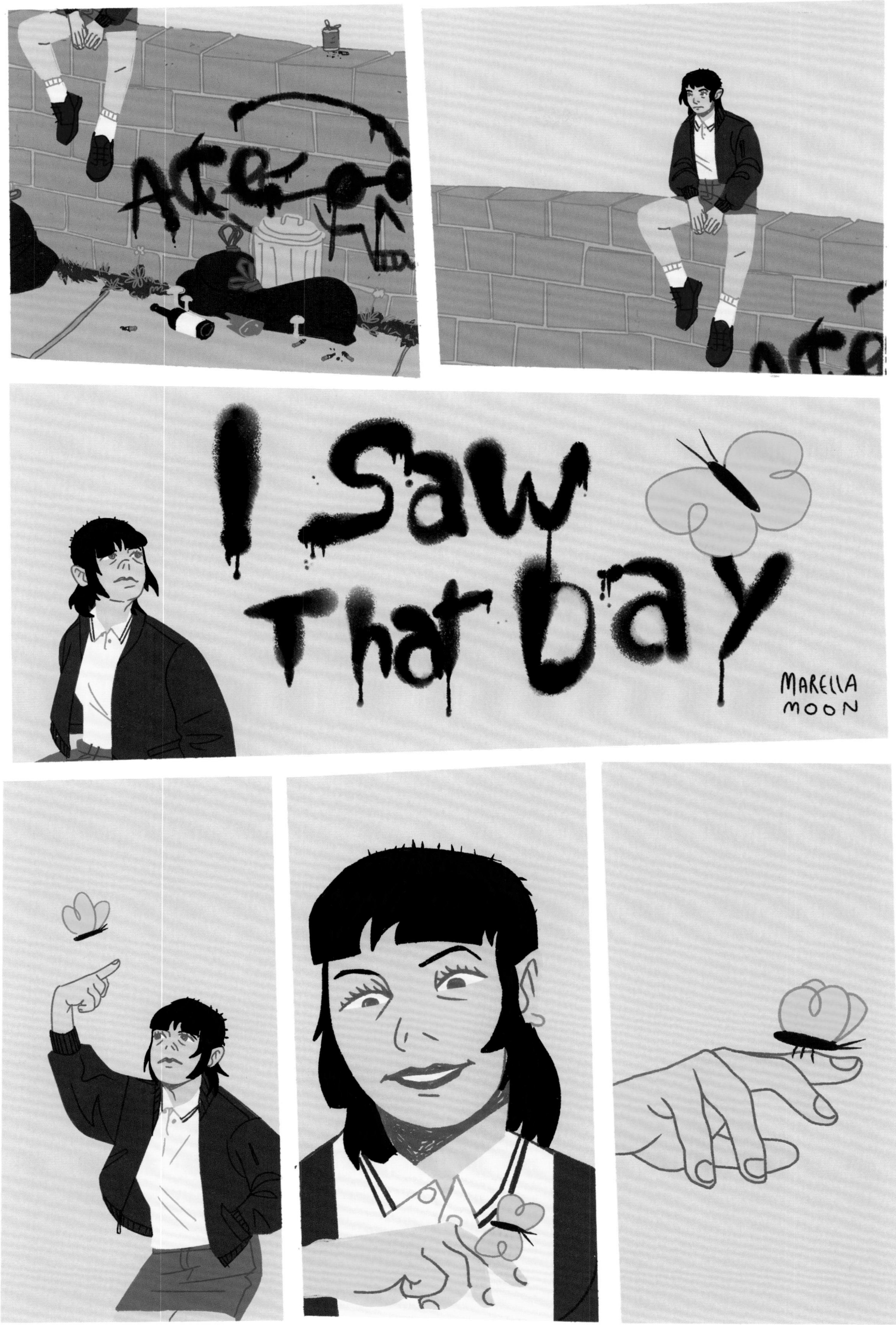
I Saw That Day
MARELLA MOON

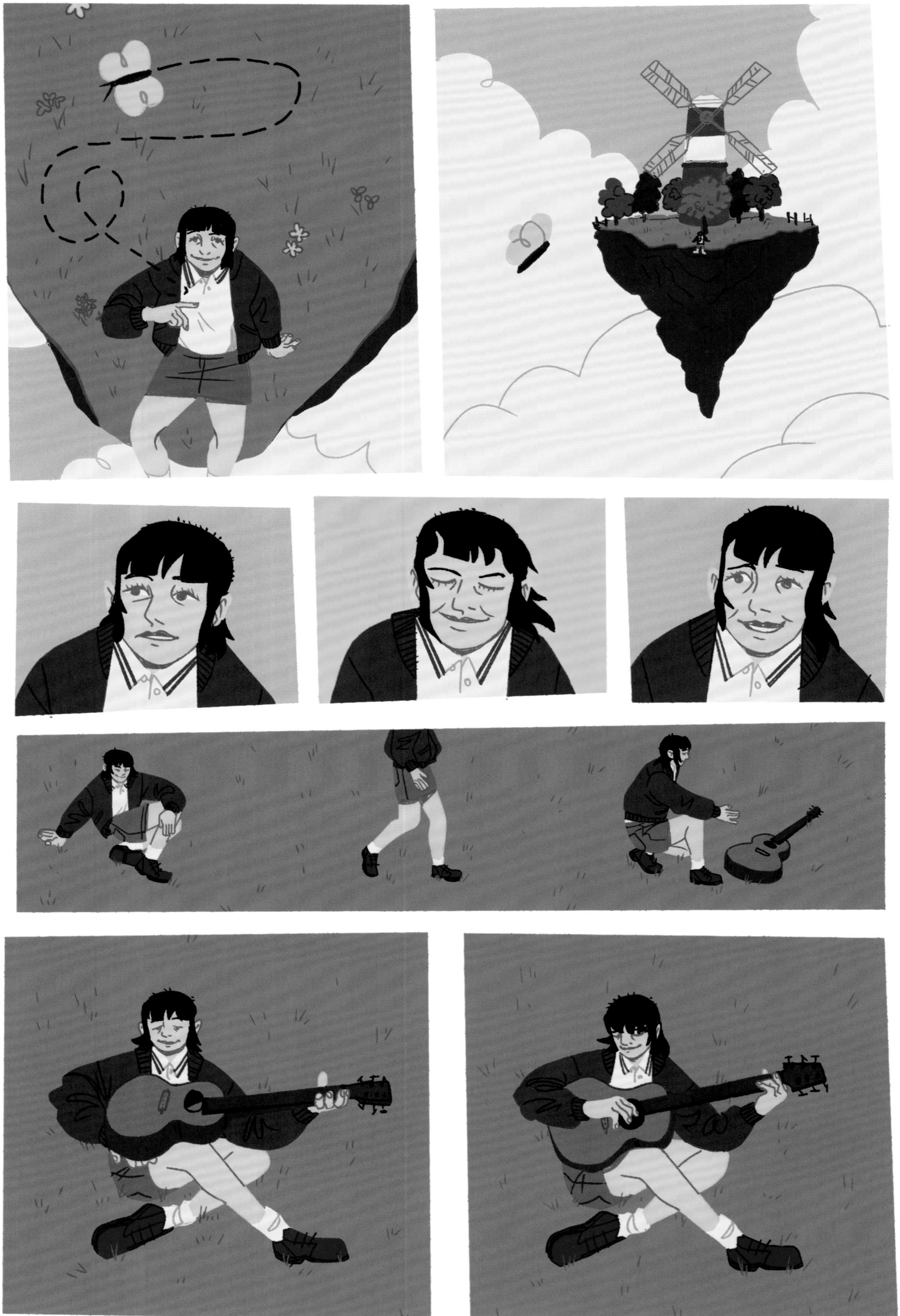

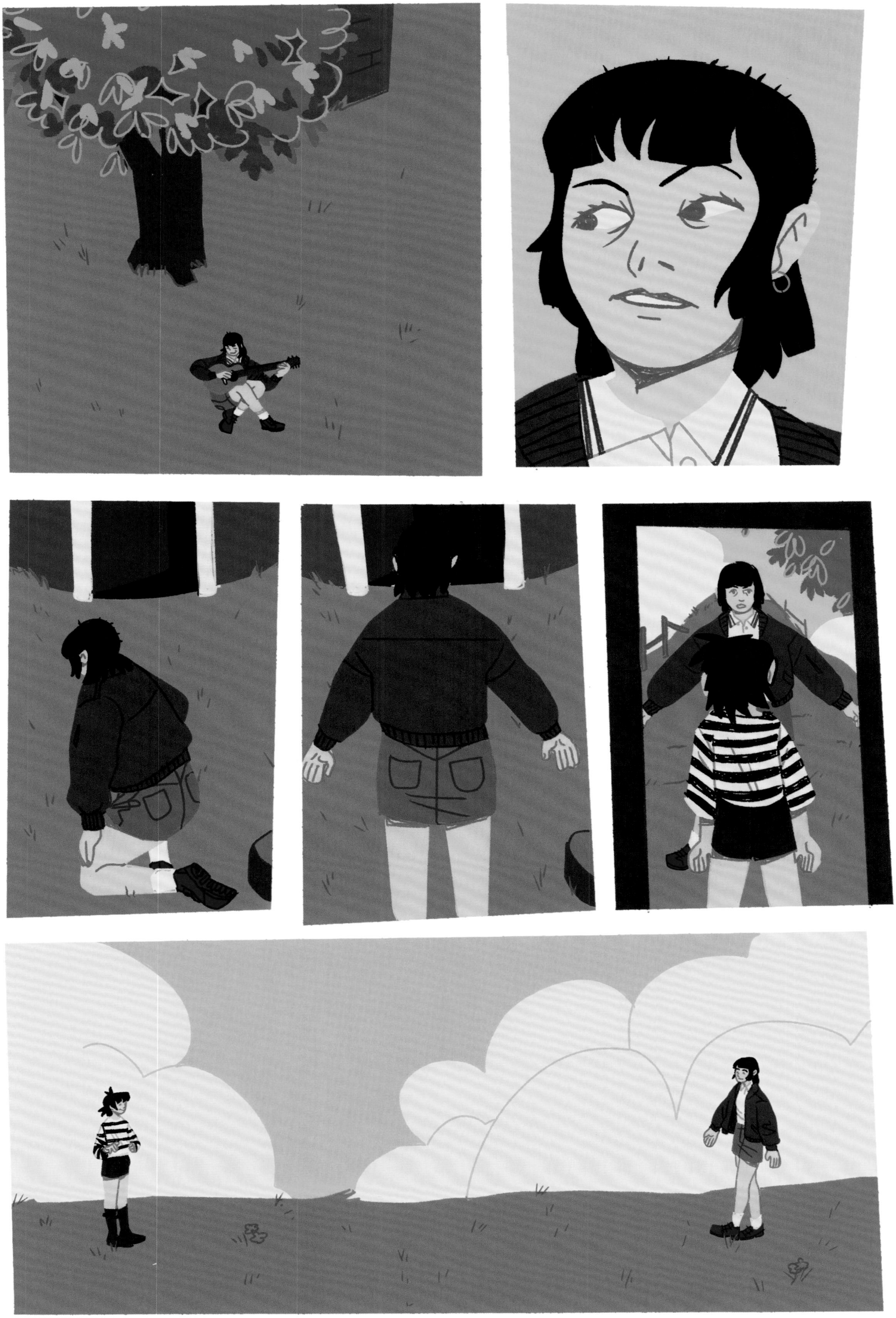

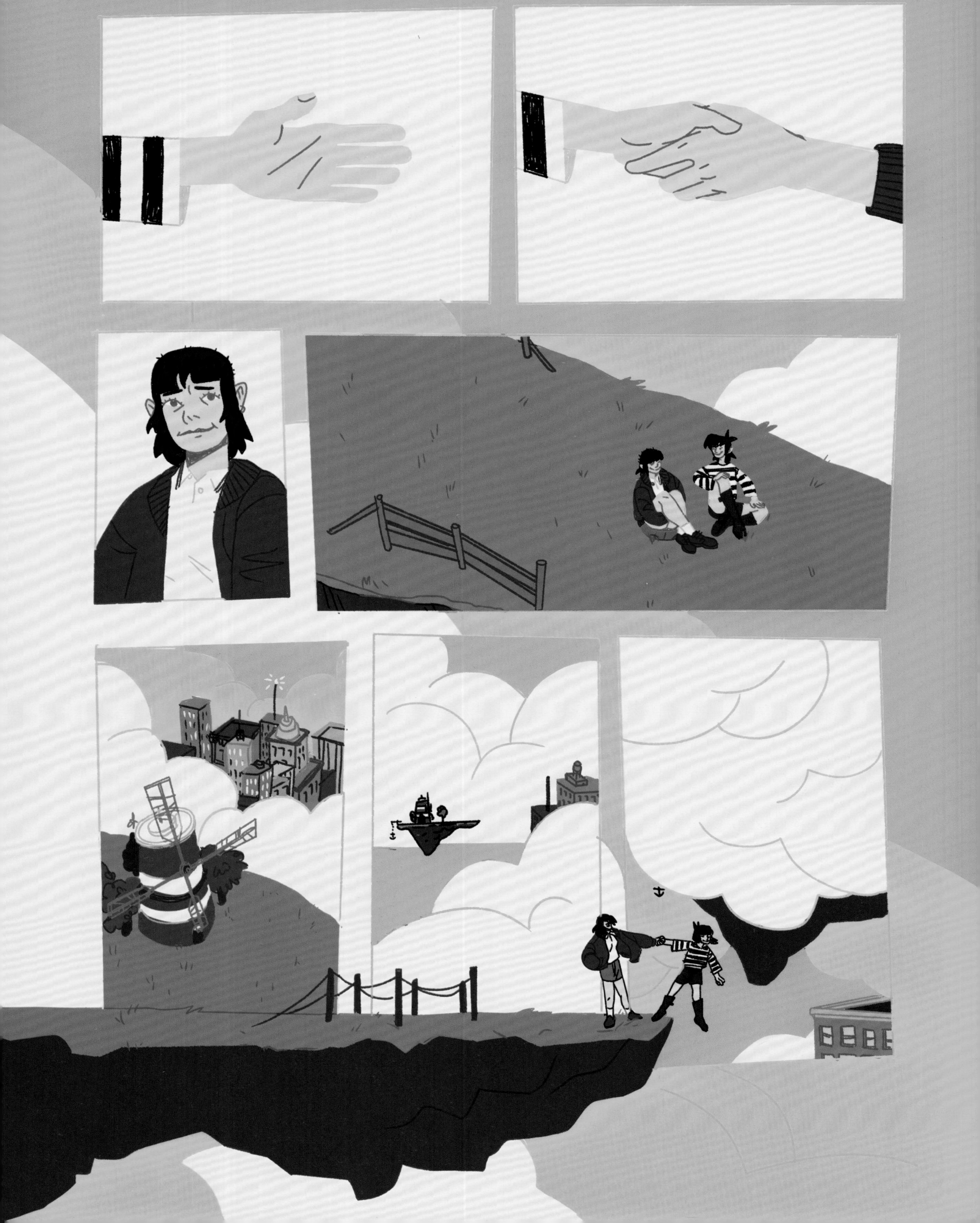

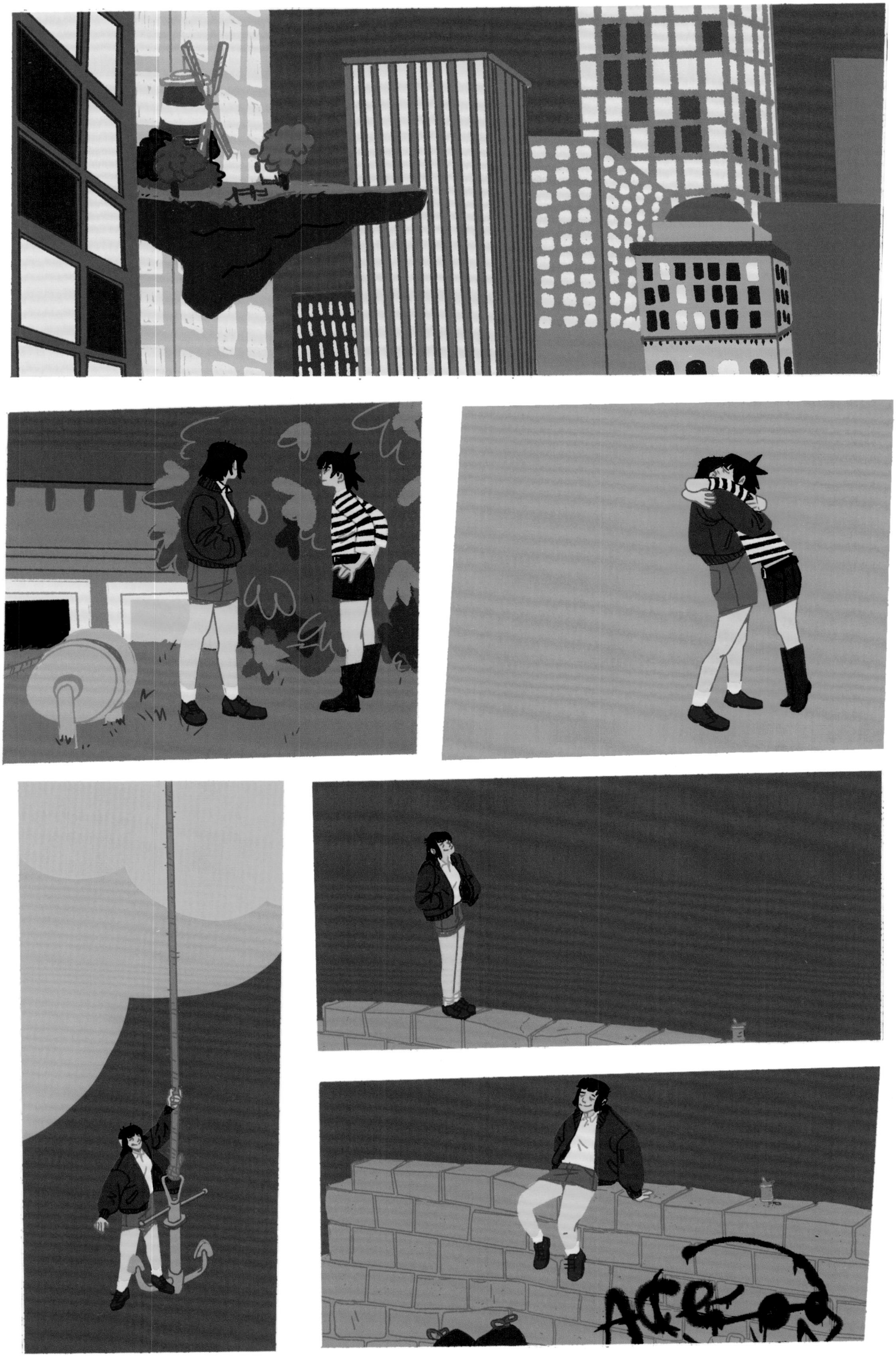
ACE

Tim McCourt & Max Taylor

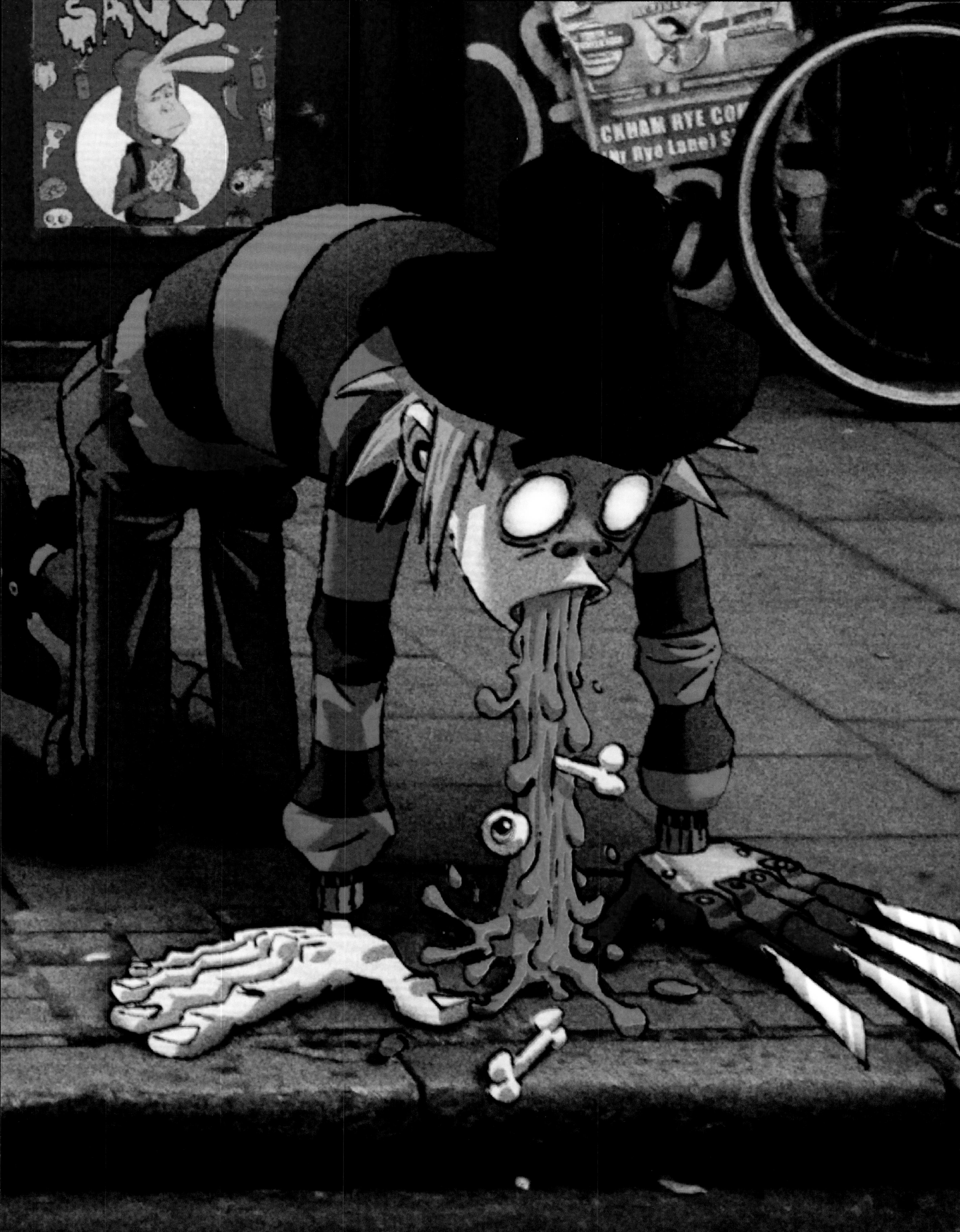

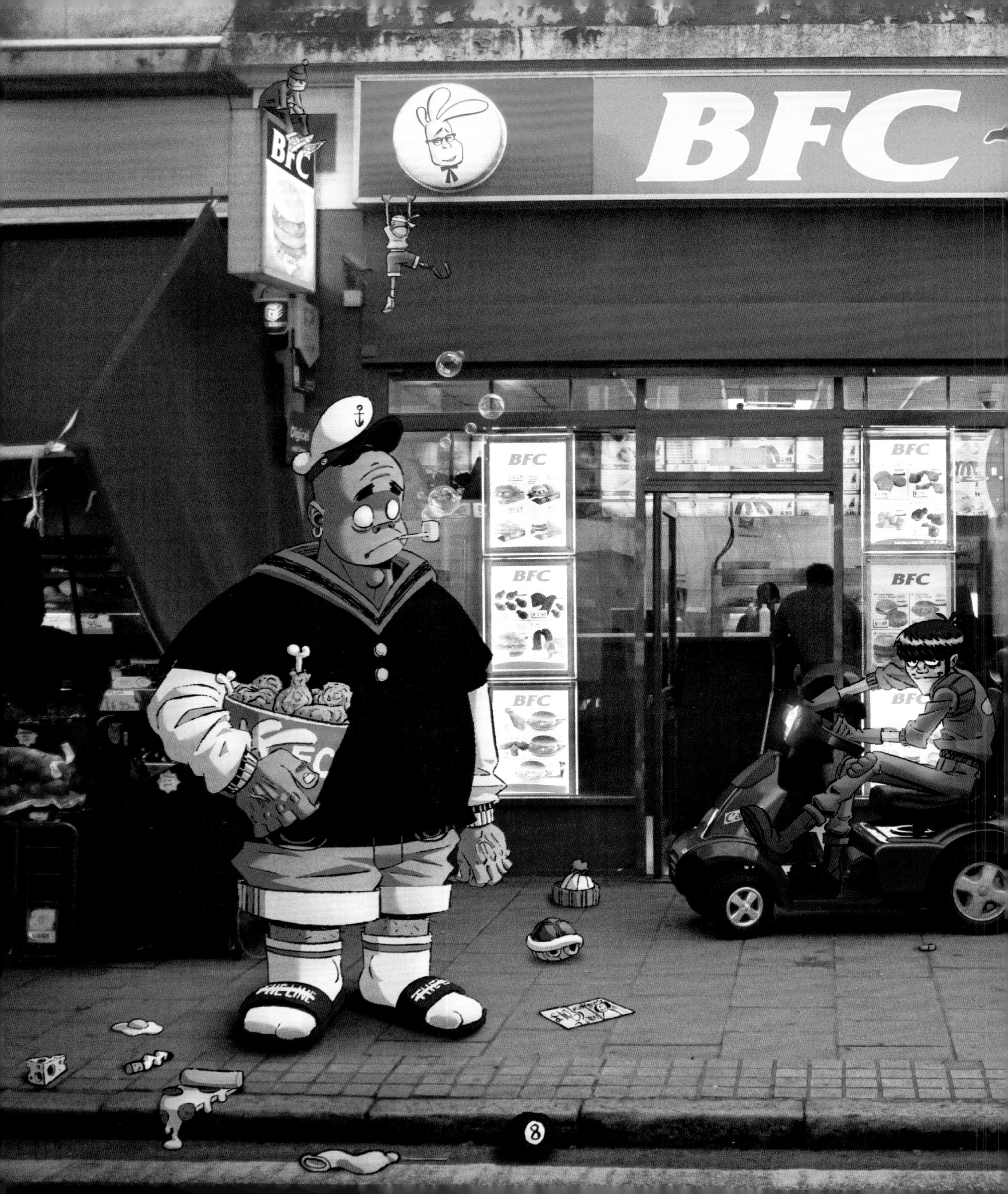
BFC
BFC
Digicel
BFC
BFC
BFC
BFC
BFC
BFC

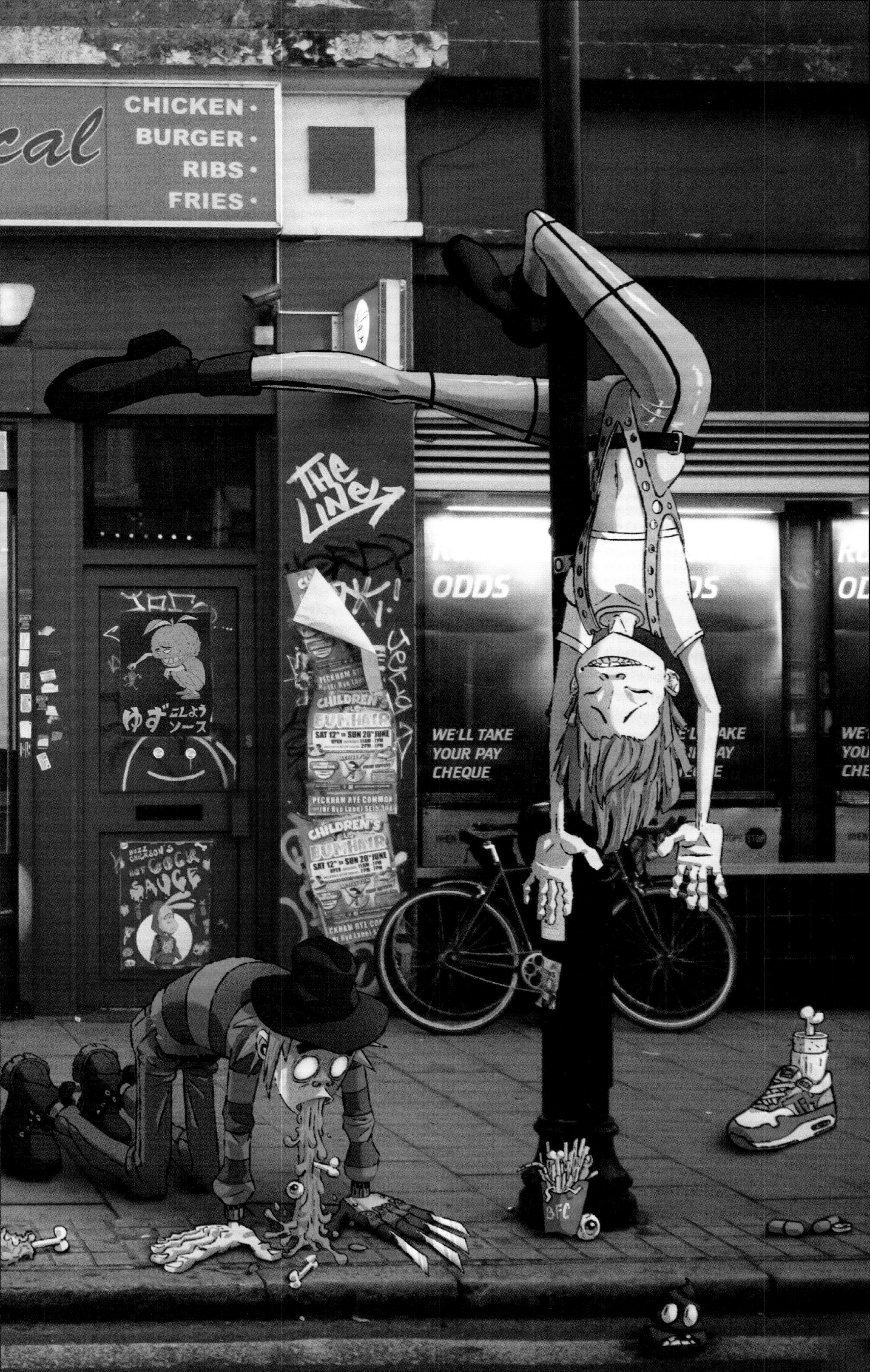

CHICKEN •
BURGER •
RIBS •
FRIES •
THE LINE
ODDS
WE'LL TAKE
YOUR PAY
CHEQUE
ゆずこしょう
ソース
CHILDREN'S
BUMHAIR
SAT 12th to SUN 20th JUNE
PECKHAM RYE COMMON
SAUCE
BFC

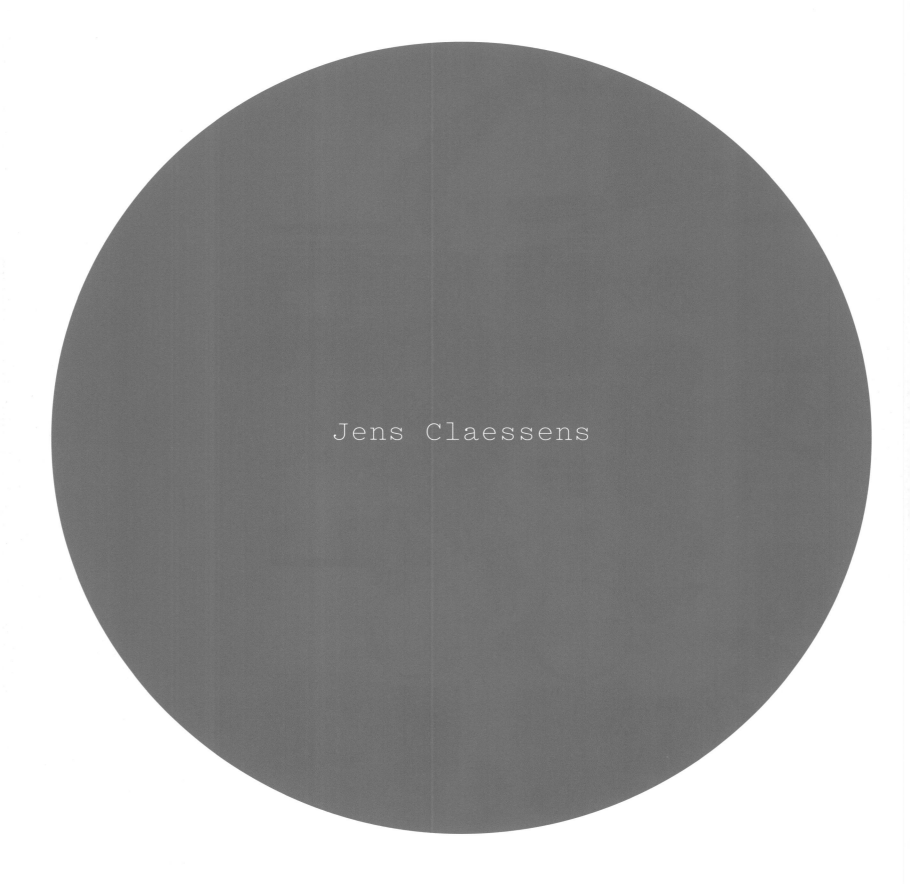

Jens Claessens

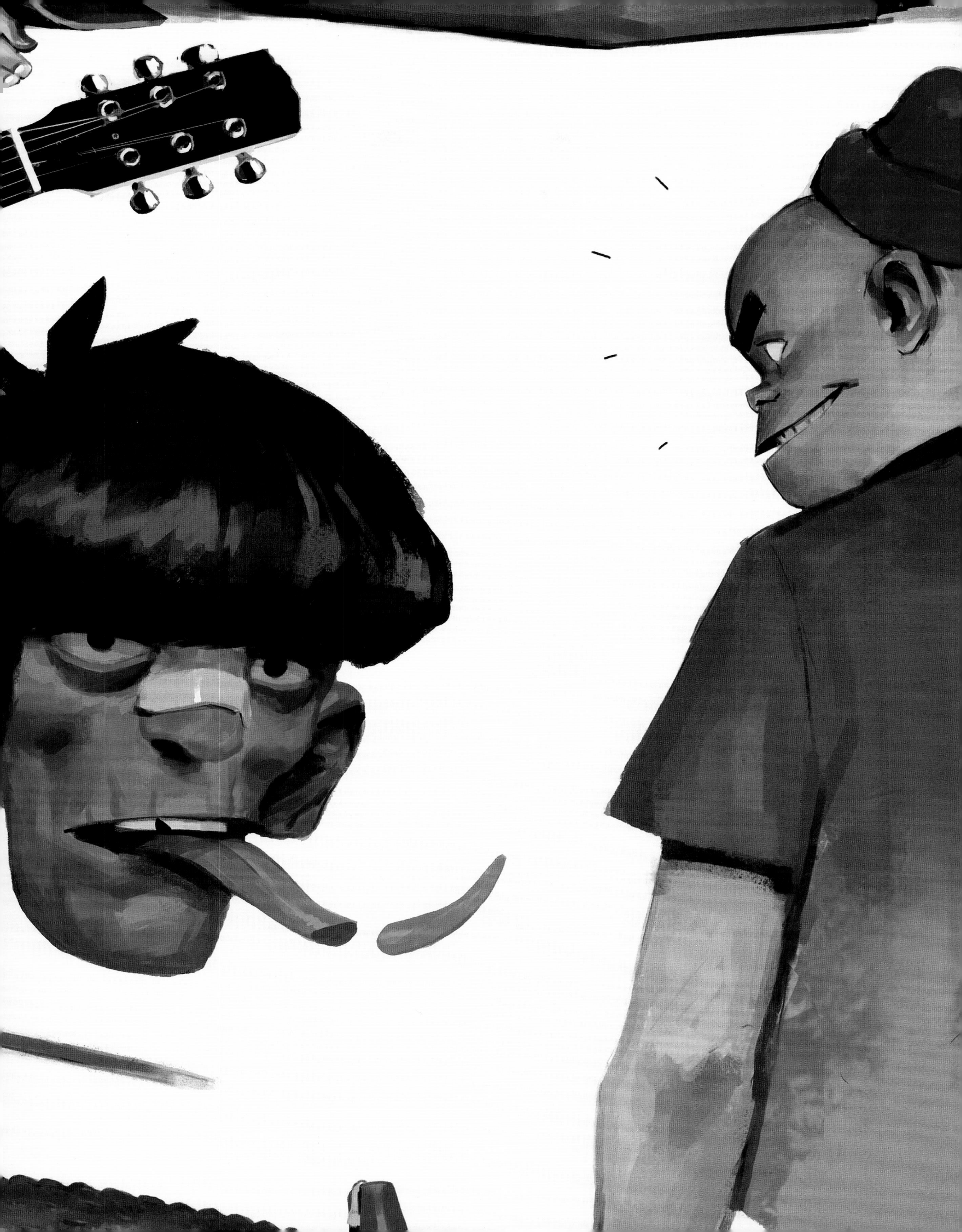

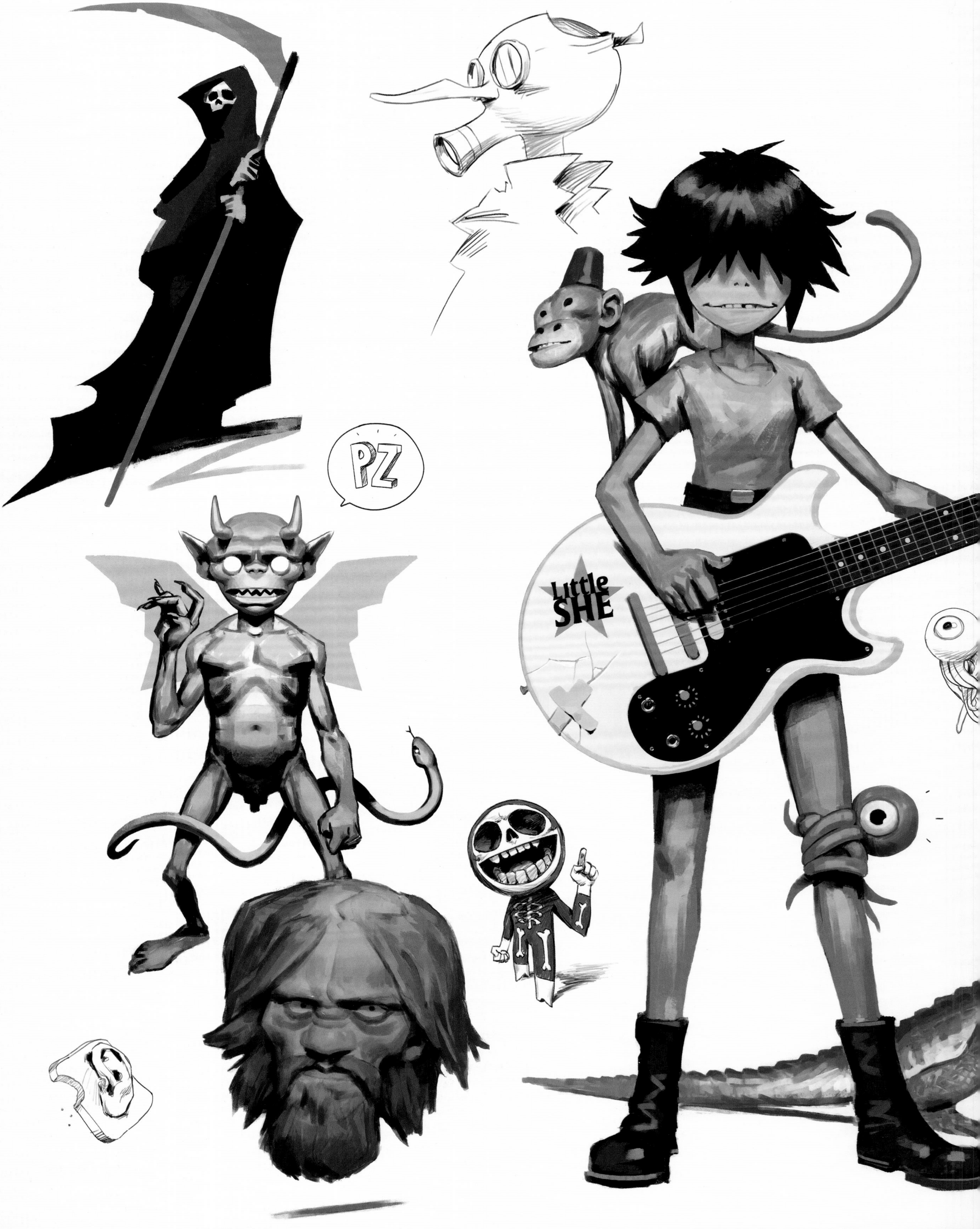
PZ
Little
SHE

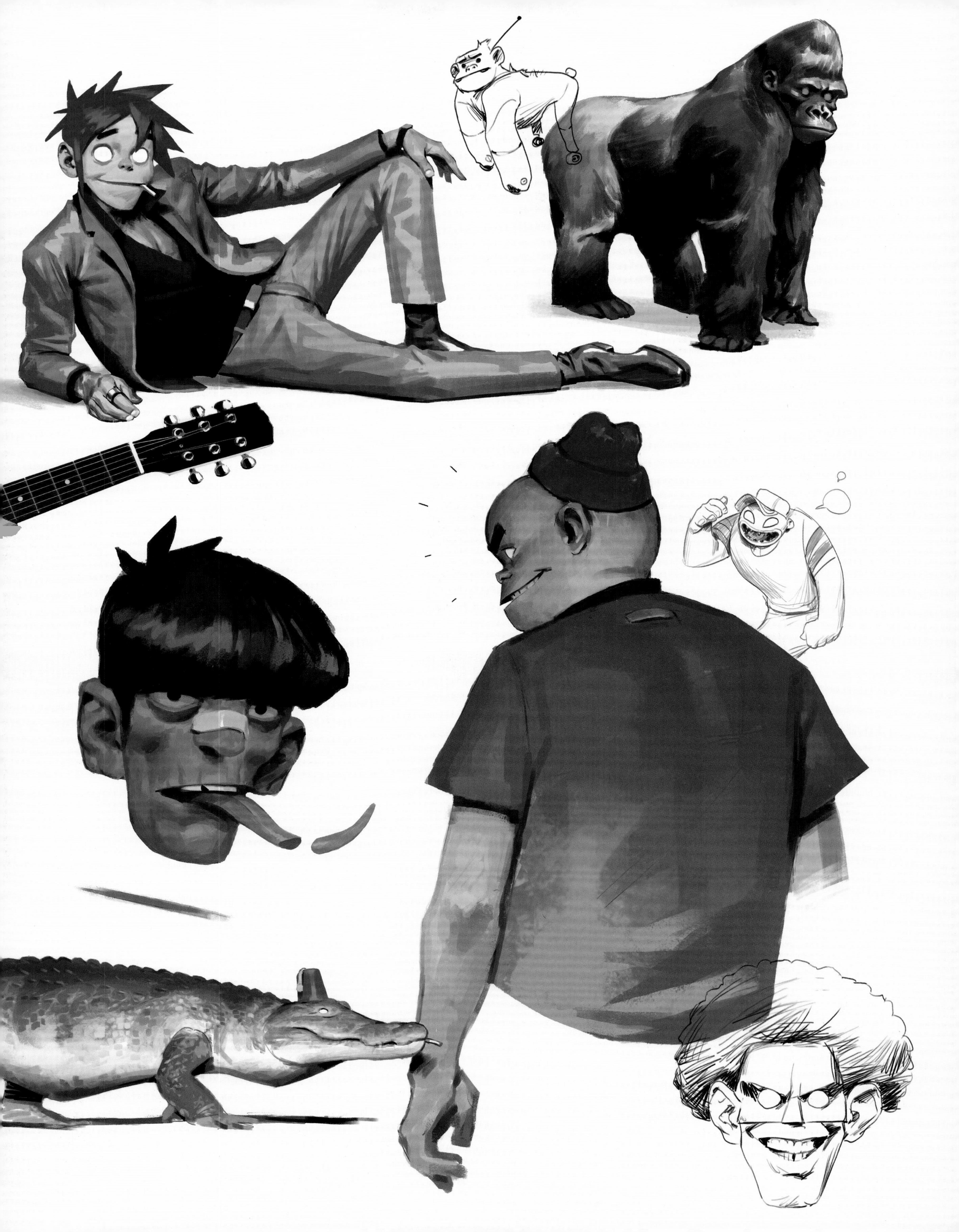

Jack Black

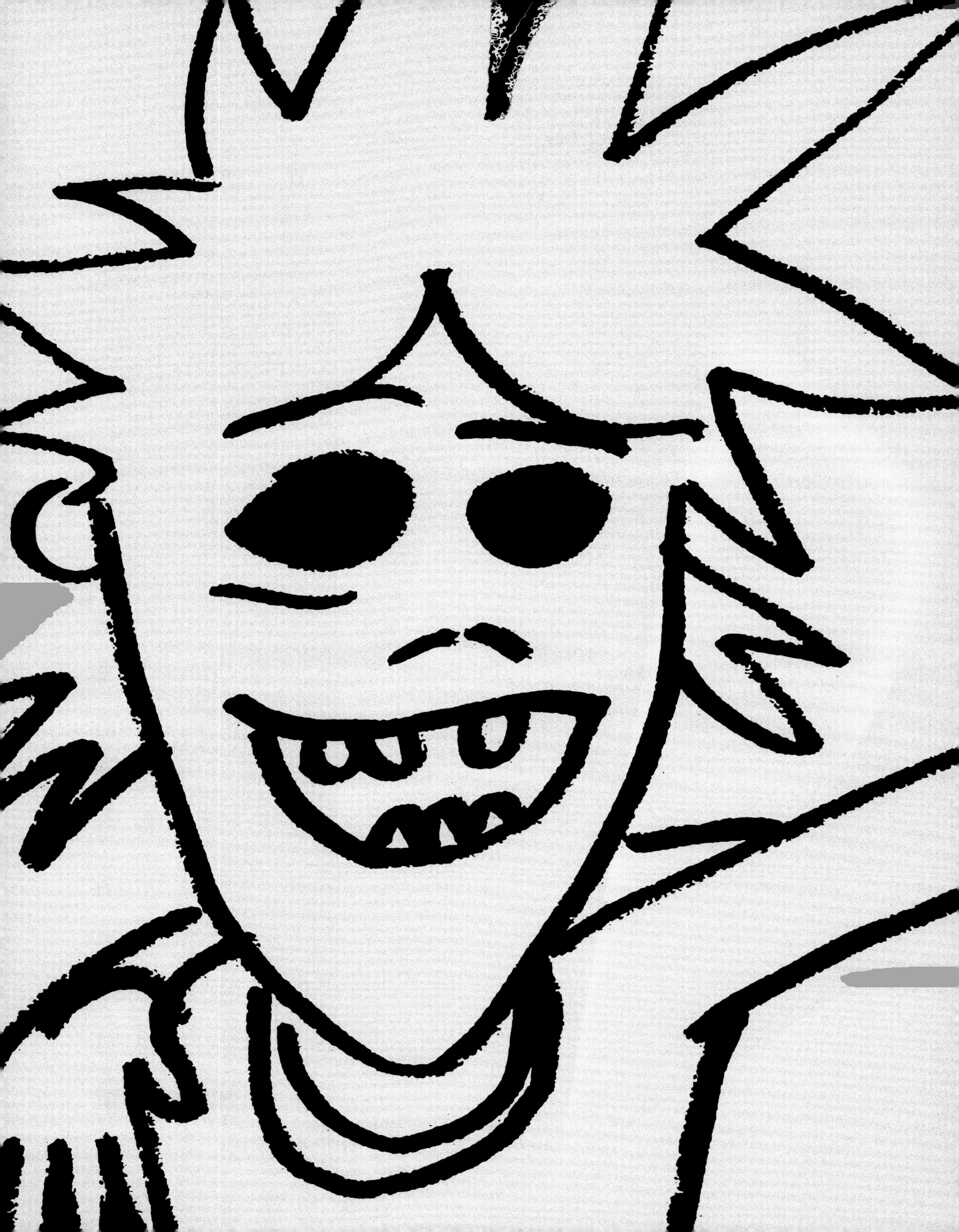

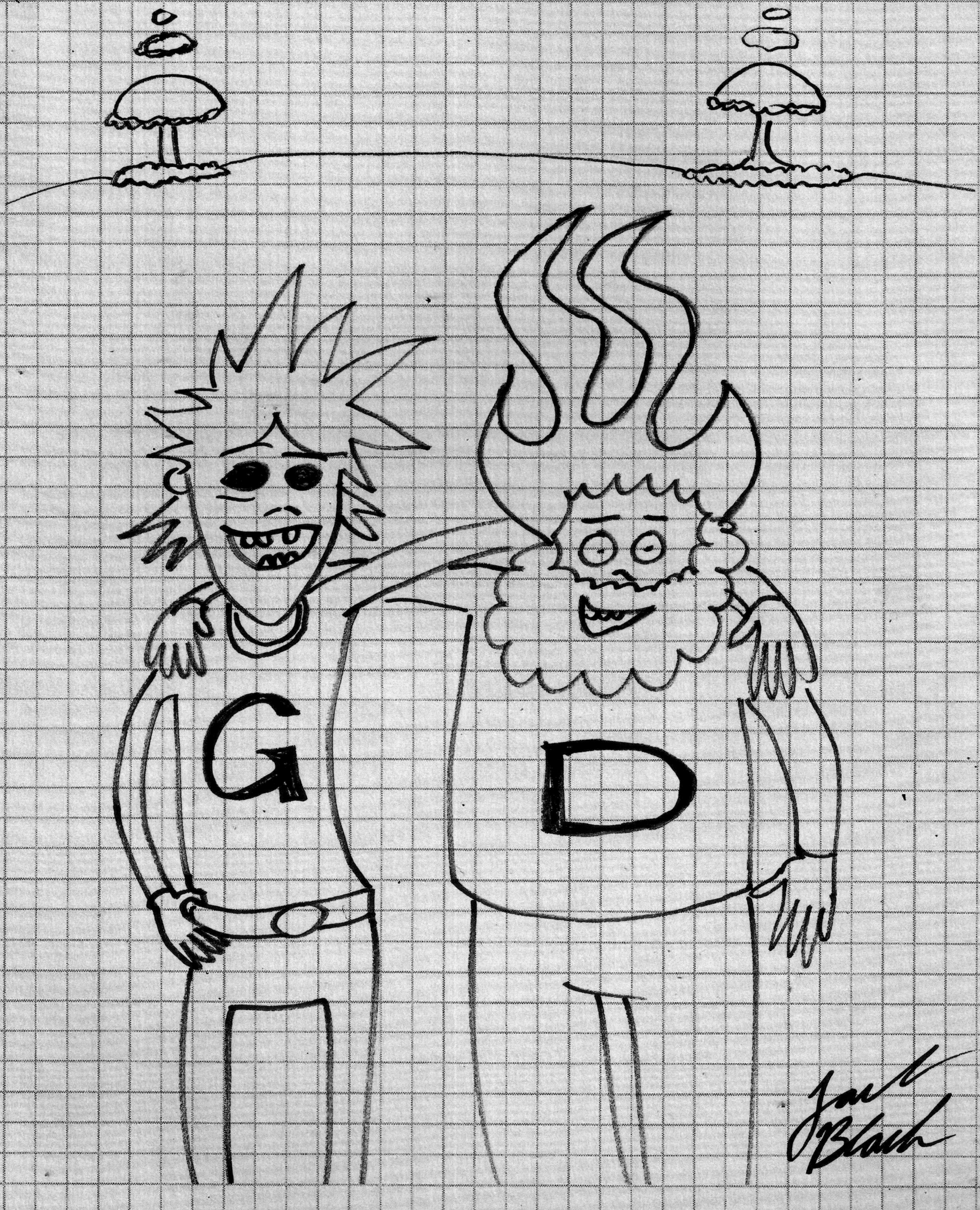
G
D
Jack Black

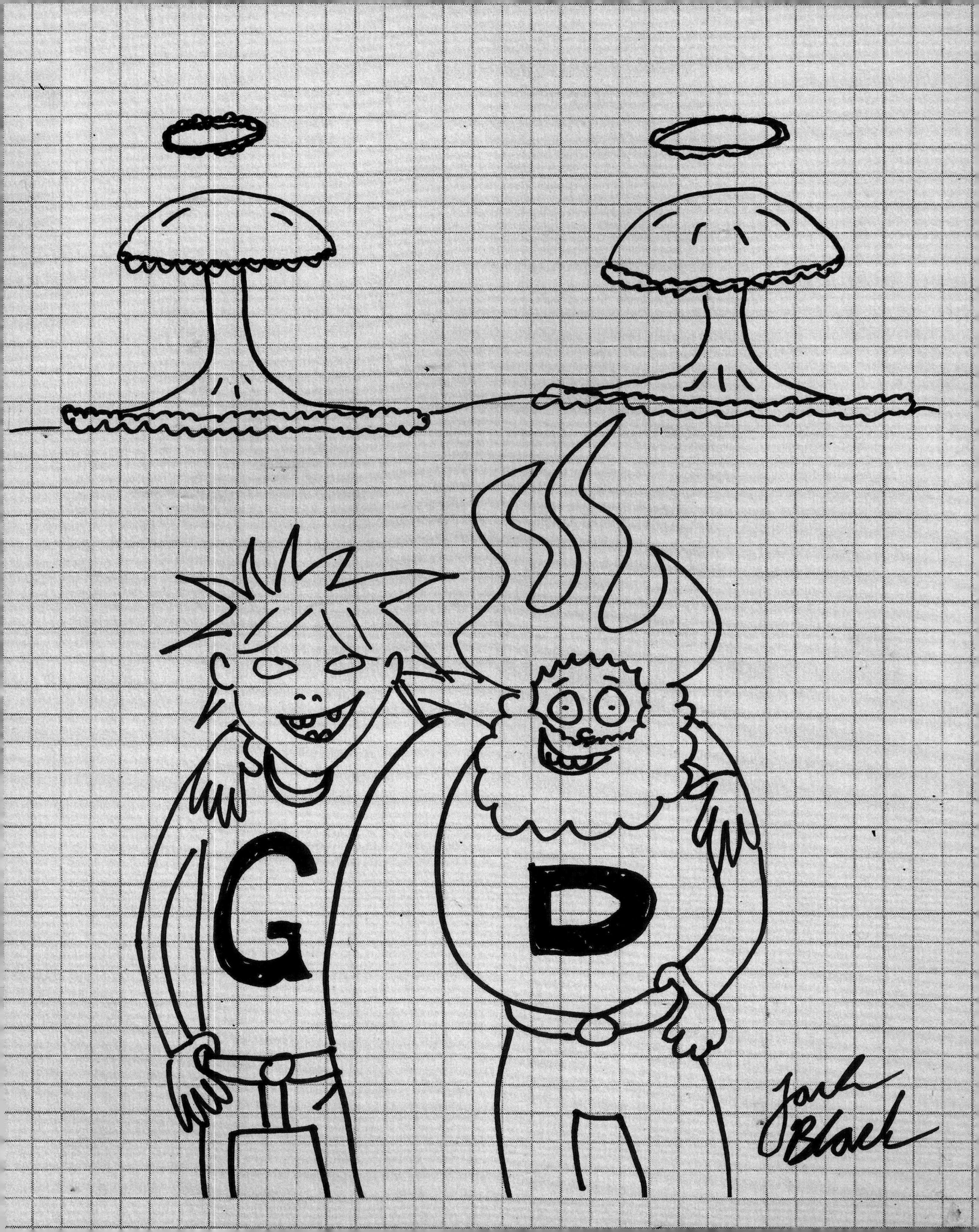
G
D
Jack Black

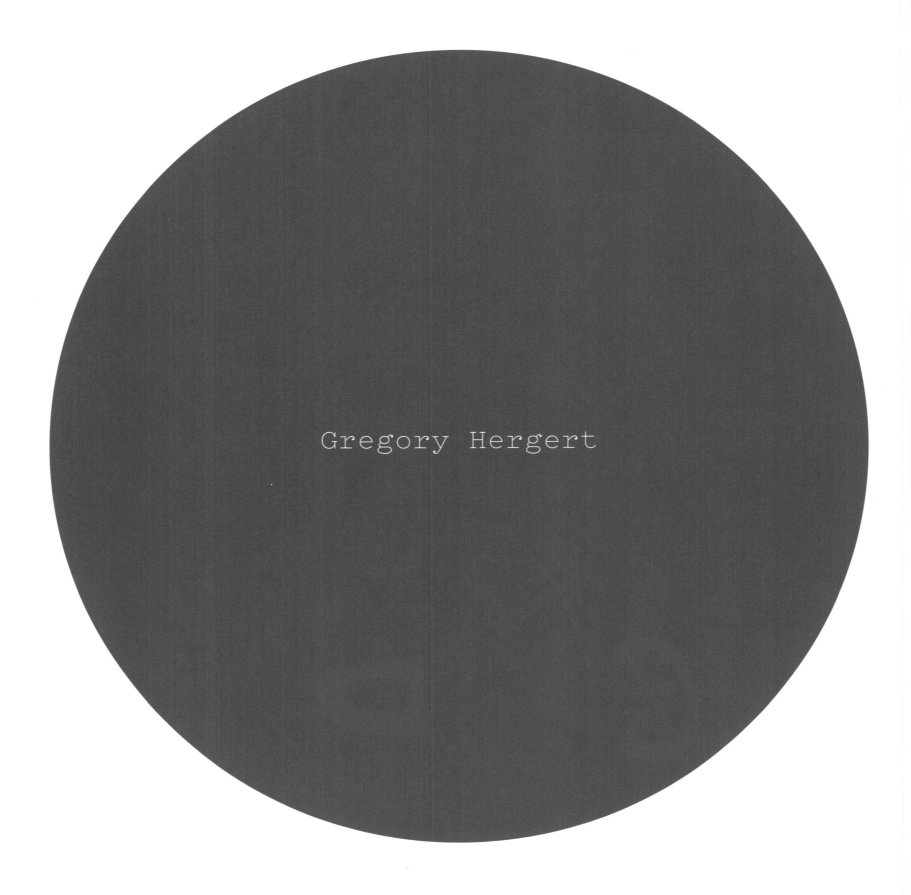

Gregory Hergert

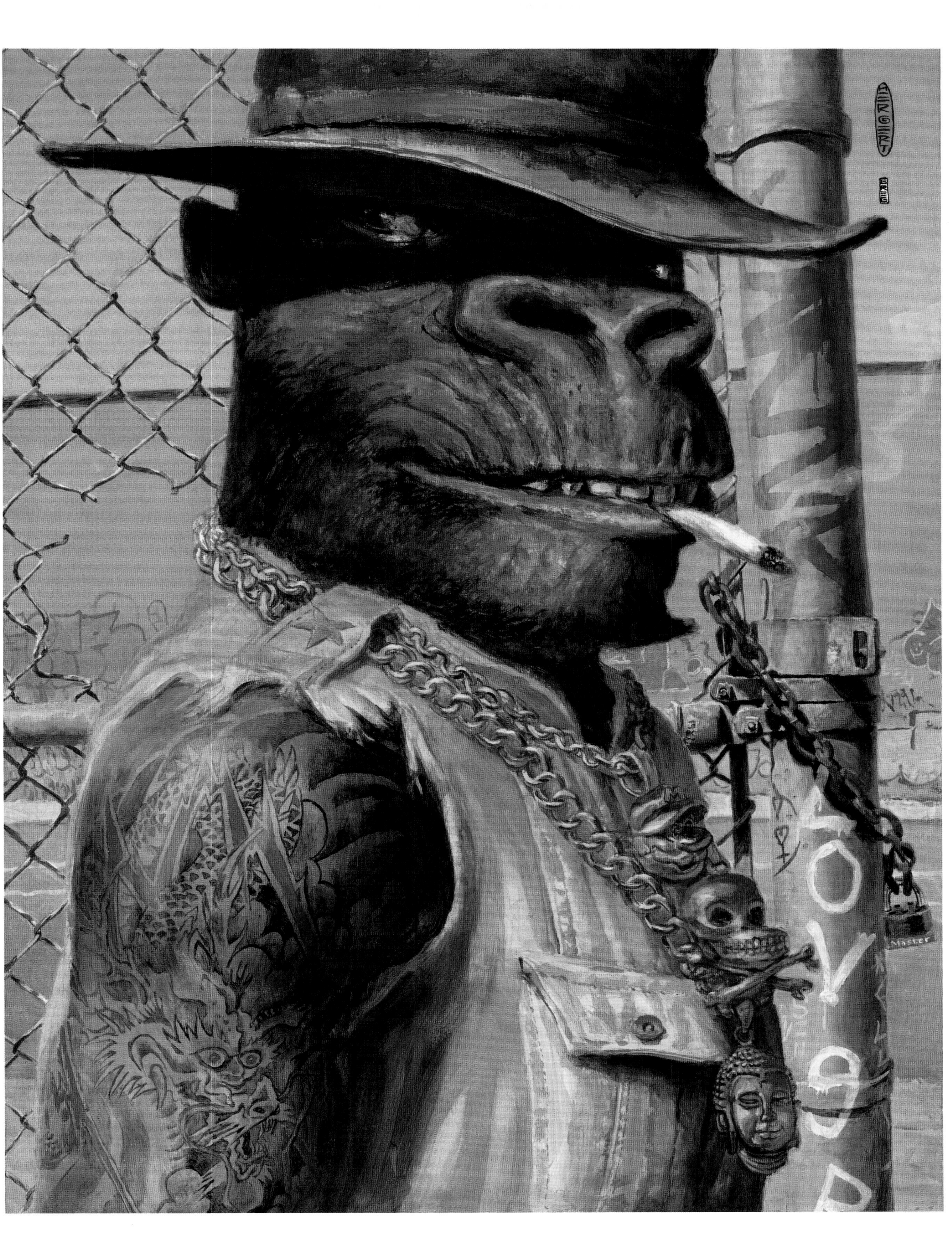
Master

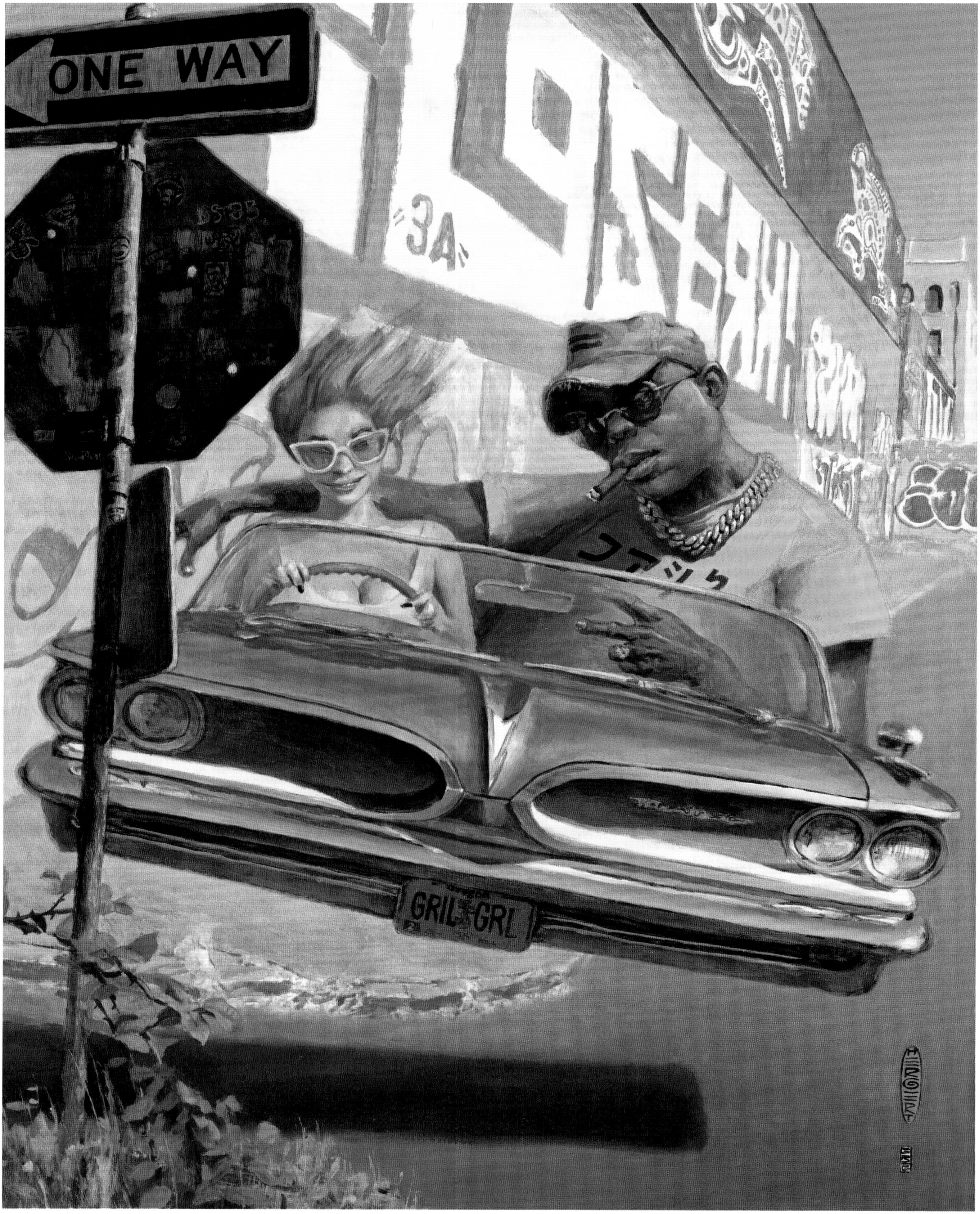
ONE WAY
3A
GRIL GRL

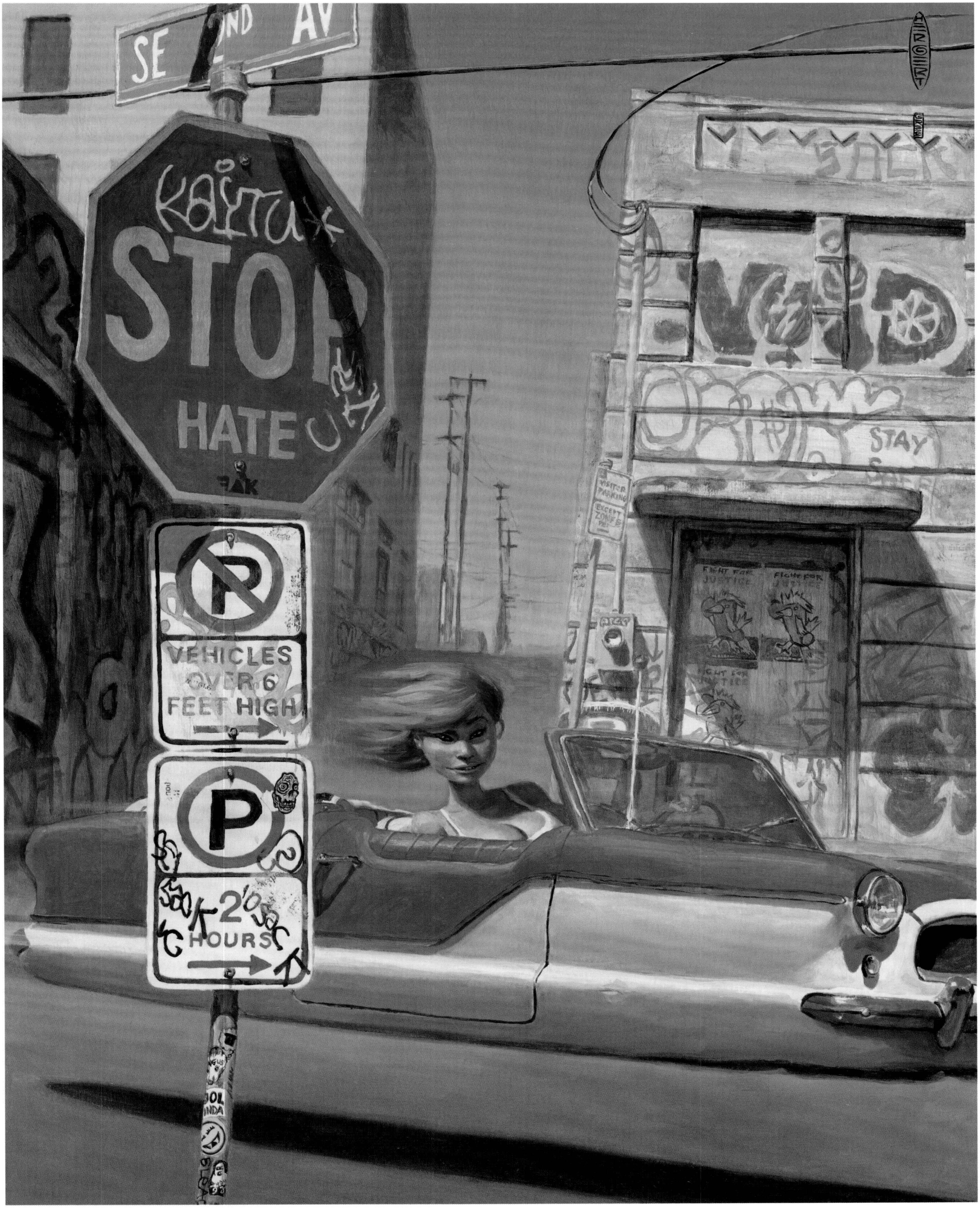
SE 2ND AV
STOP
HATE
VEHICLES OVER 6 FEET HIGH
P
2 HOURS
STAY
FIGHT FOR JUSTICE

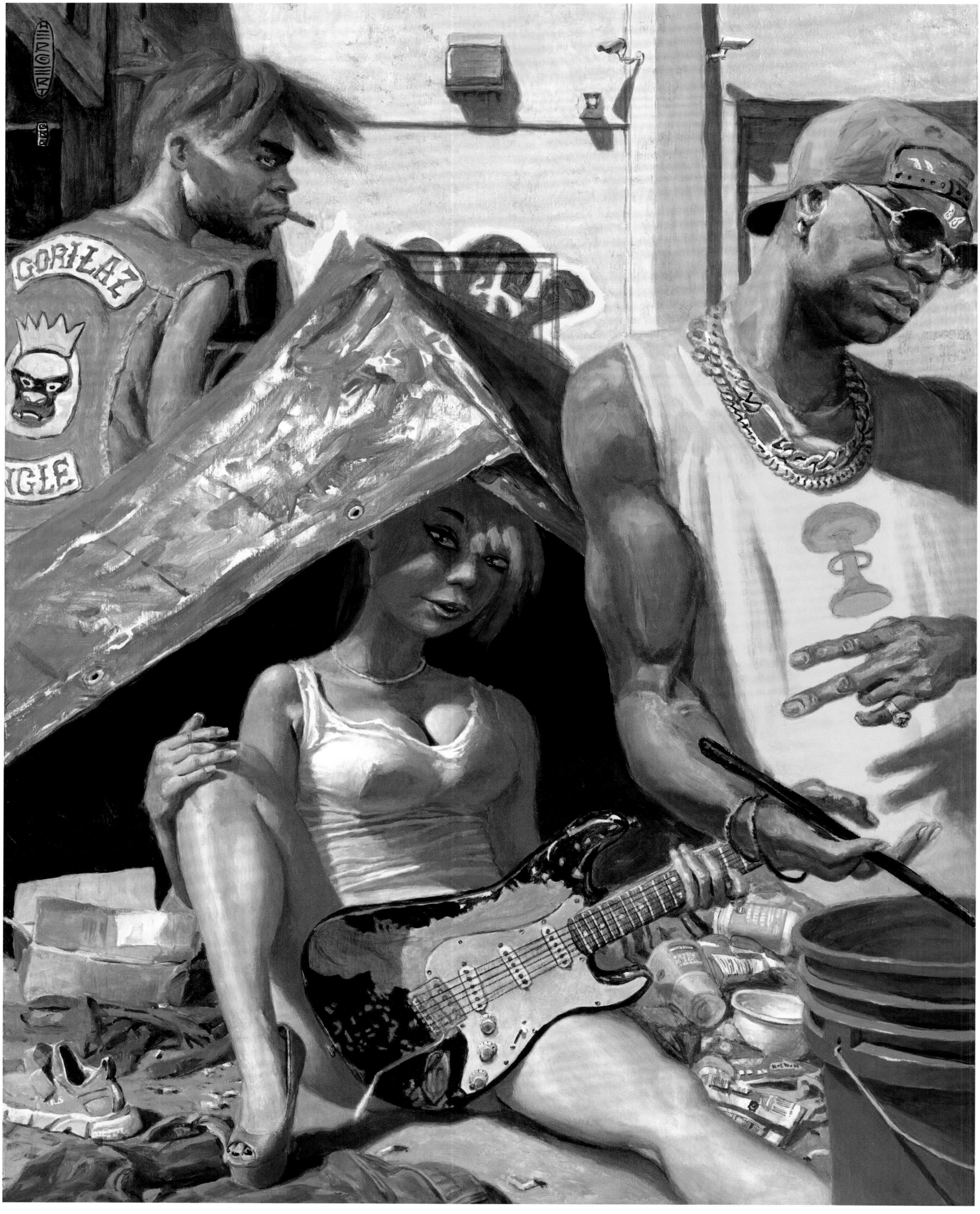
GORILAZ
NGLE

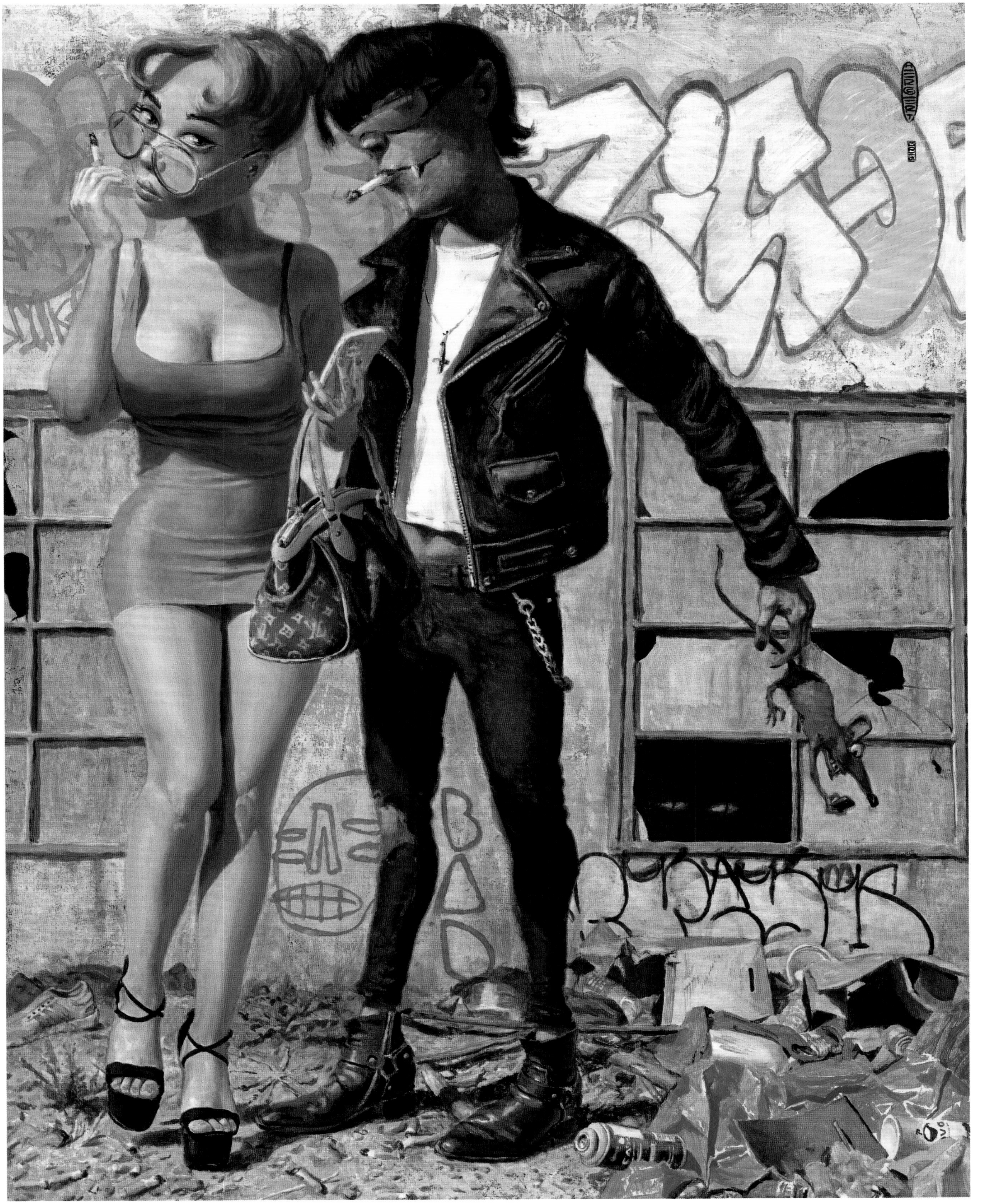
BAD

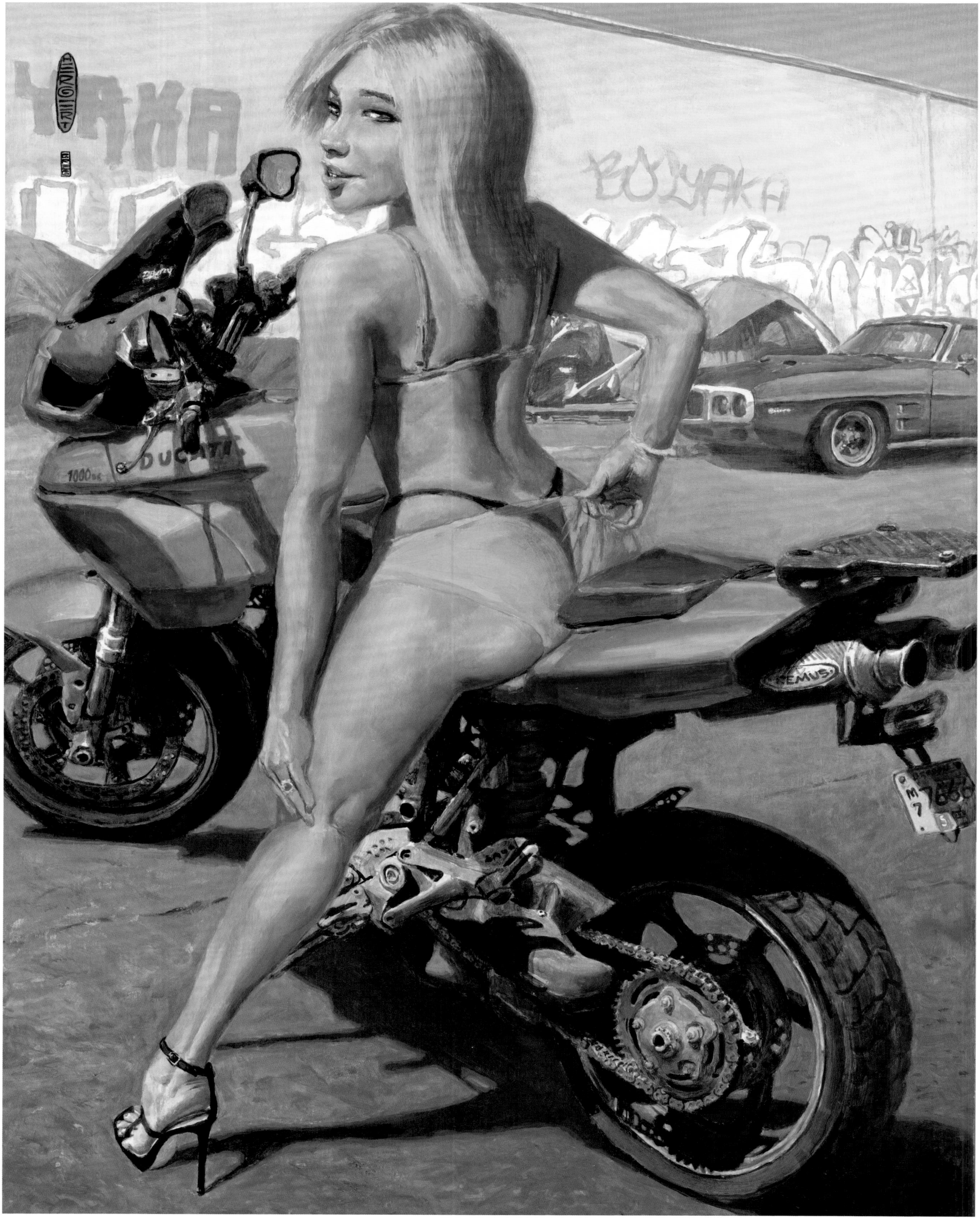
YAKA
DUCATI

Robert Valley

August 15th 1997 'D-Day'

*RETOLD BY ROBERT VALLEY SEPT. 29 2021

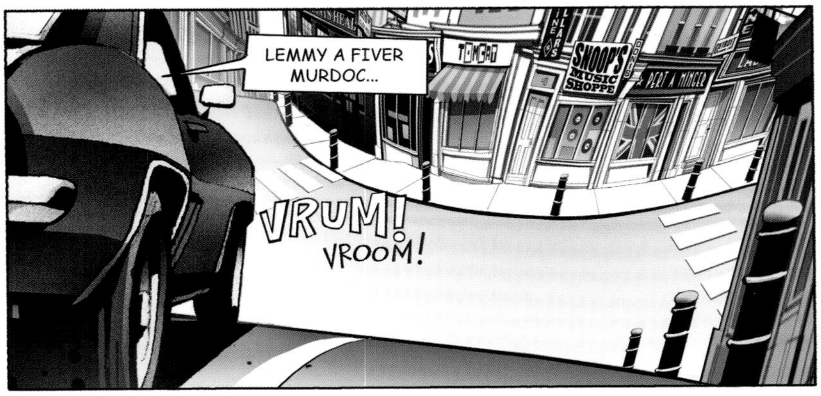
LEMMY A FIVER MURDOC...
SNOOP'S MUSIC SHOPPE
VRUM!
VROOM!

Robert: Hey Jamie, can you tell me the story of how Mudoc first met 2D again?

Jamie: Errr.... yeah... (lights a smoke) that's a bit of a sordid tale but here goes...

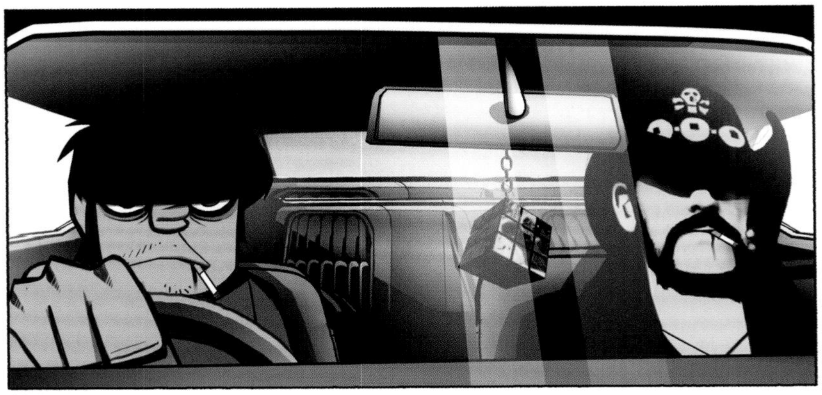

Back in the early days, Murdoc and his crew of snaggle tooth hard-nuts had dreams of making it big, but they were a little short on equipment. So they decided to do what any hard working band would do.

They were going to steal it.

Robert: Naturally.

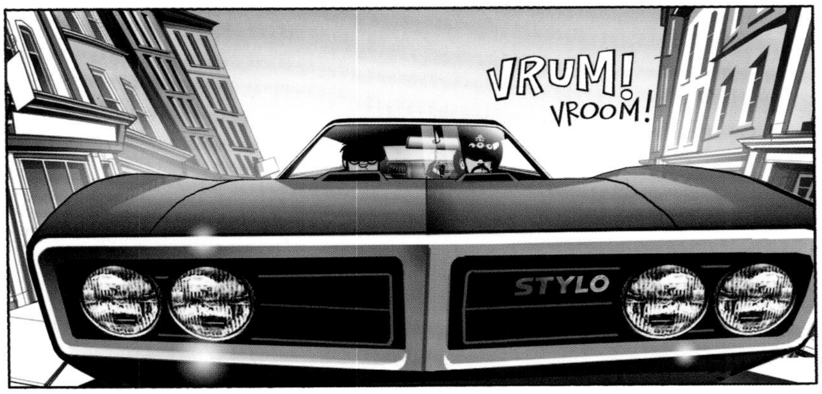
VRUM!
VROOM!
STYLO

Jamie: Errr.... anyways... (cracks a can of PBR)... so Murdoc and his crew weren't just going to steal the gear they needed, they were going to nick a car and ram-raid the local music store like any hard working band.

Robert: That sounds perfectly logical.

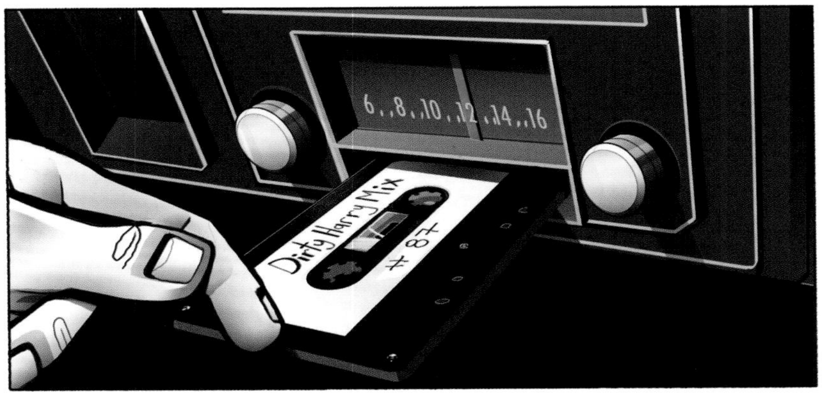
6 . . 8 . . 10 . . 12 . . 14 . . 16
Dirty Harry Mix

Jamie: (Takes a deep drag and ashes into his beer can, takes a big sip) ... anyways... so they put on their favorite music mix...

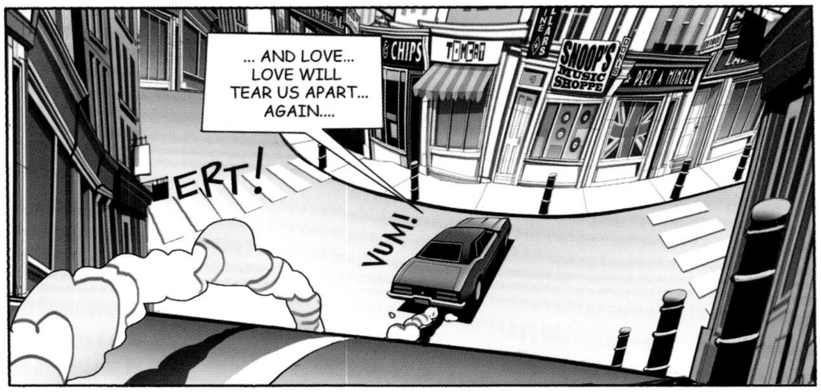
... AND LOVE... LOVE WILL TEAR US APART... AGAIN....
CHIPS
SNOOP'S MUSIC SHOPPE
ERT!
VUM!

Jamie: (Picking ashes from his teeth) ... now they were ready to roll.

Robert: Oh boy...

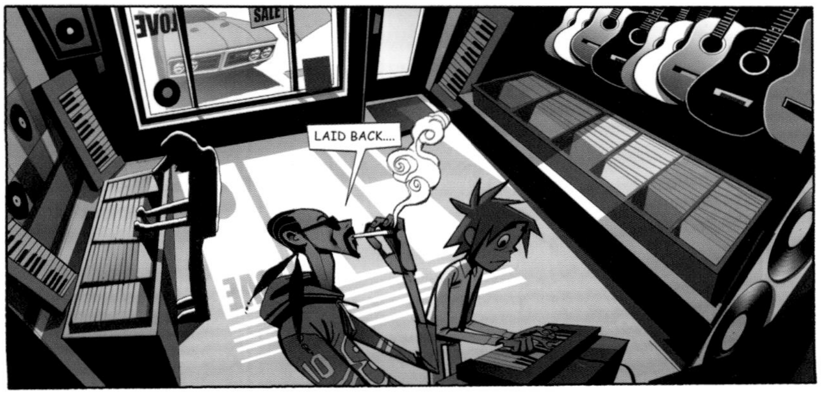
LAID BACK...

Jamie: (fumbling around for his lighter).... now where was I...?

Robert: Now they were ready to roll...

Jamie: Oh yeah.... (lights another smoke)... meanwhile inside the music store 2D and Snoop were unaware of the imminent danger they were in.

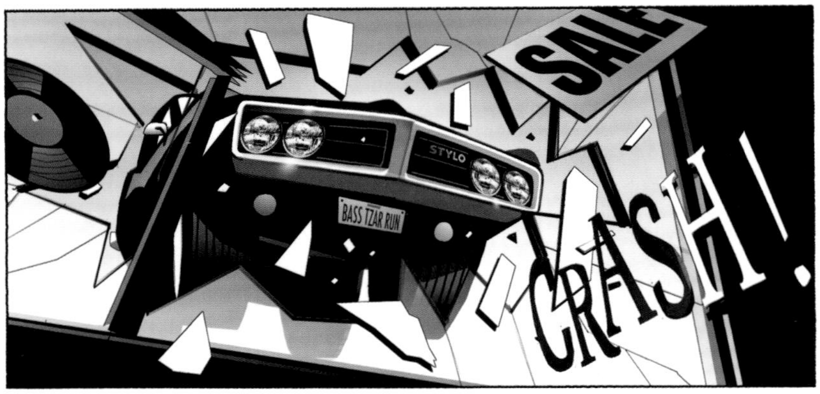
SALE
STYLO
BASS TZAR RUN
CRASH!

... suddenly imminent danger came smashing through the front window.

Robert: Jayus... F...

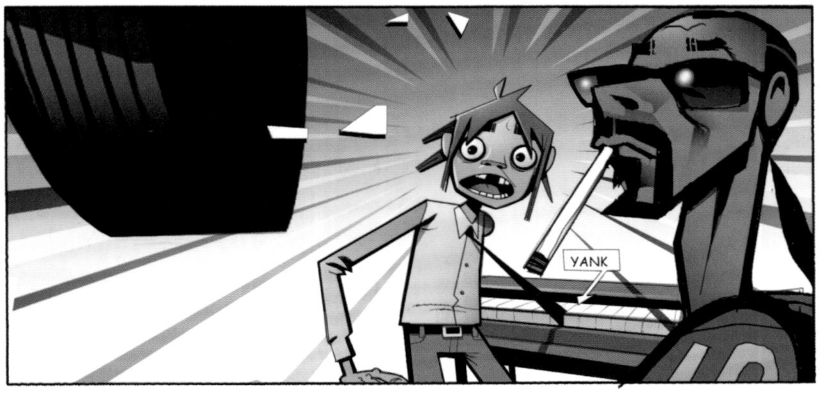
YANK

Jamie: Snoop was fortunate enough to avoid getting crushed on that fateful day...

... but 2D's necktie had other plans for him.

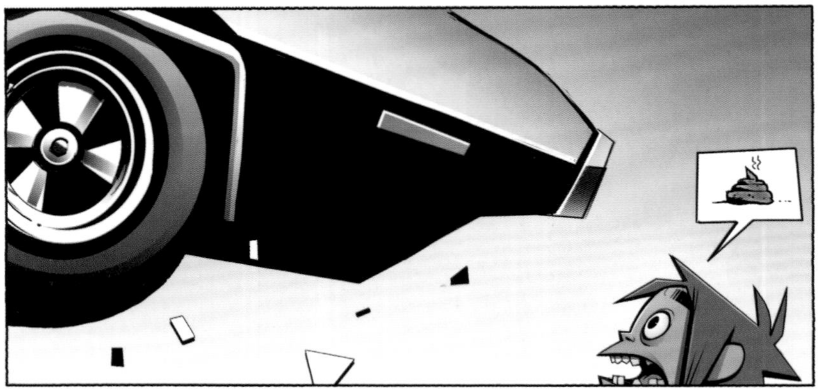

Robert: Damn neckties.

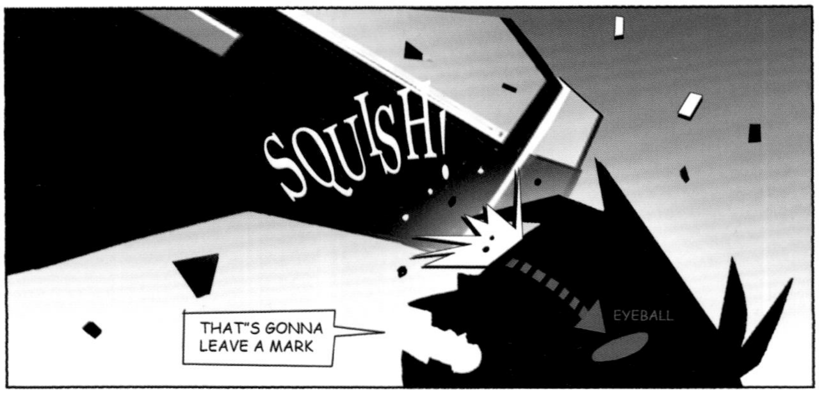
SQUISH!
EYEBALL
THAT'S GONNA LEAVE A MARK

Jamie: Murdoc drove that car bumper-first right into 2D's right eyeball.

Robert: Is that when 2D's eyeball came out?

Jamie: No, it wasn't knocked out it was pushed in, right near his damn prostate, causing his eye to go pitch black.

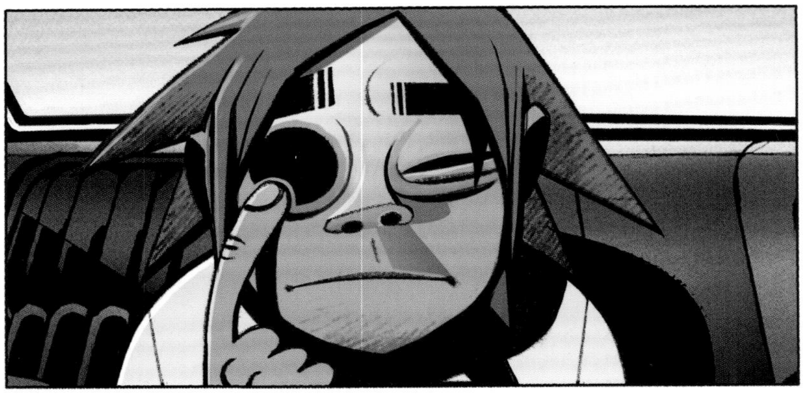

Jamie: black as night, black as coal, the light was permanently snuffed out of that right eye leaving 2D with an even more pronounced vacant expression.

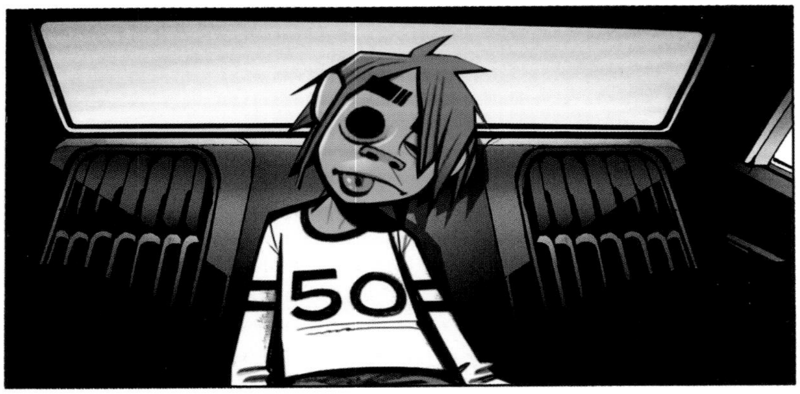
50

...and thus putting 2D into a deep catatonic state

Robert: Poor fella...

Jamie: (laughing) yeah he was a real f#cking vegetable...

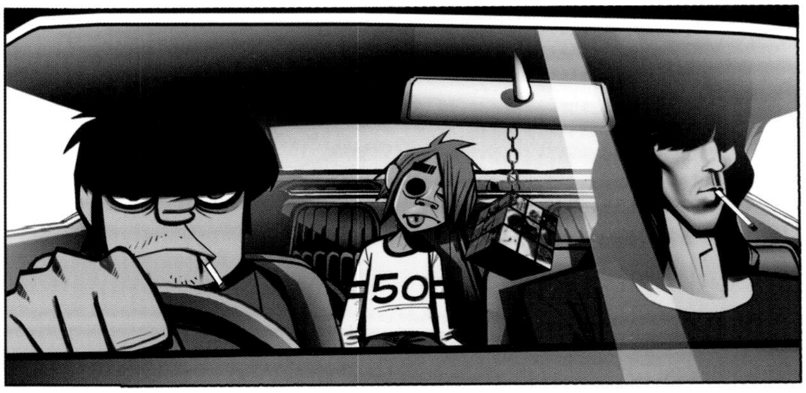
50

Murdoc opted not to take 2D directly to the hospital but instead thought it was wiser to just prop him up in the backseat like a bag of old laundry.

Robert: Keef !

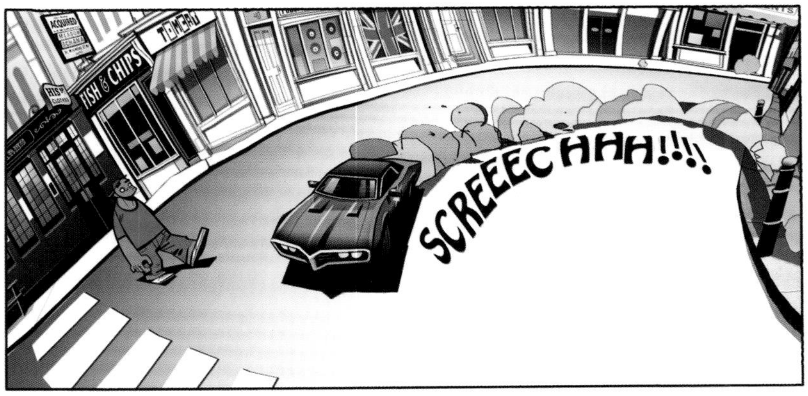
ACQUIRED
FISH & CHIPS
SCREEECHHH!!!!

Jamie: (Drops cigarette cherry on his shirt) then Murdoc proceeded to do the mother of all burn-outs.

Robert: Random...

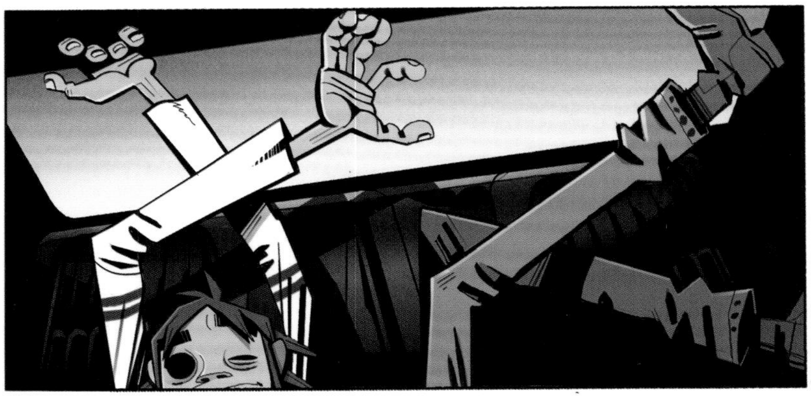

Jamie: (pouring beer on his smoldering shirt) yup... so poor 2D was getting knocked about in the back of the car like....

Robert: Like a bag of old laundry... ?

Jamie: (laughing) yeah.

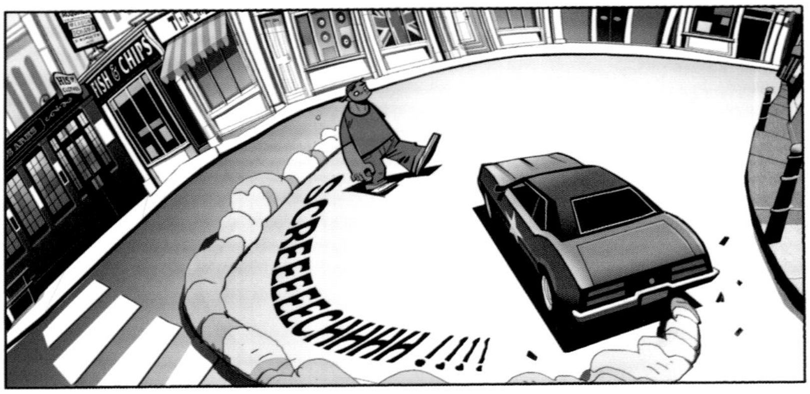
FISH & CHIPS
SCREEEEECHHHH!!!!

Jamie: (cracks another PBR)

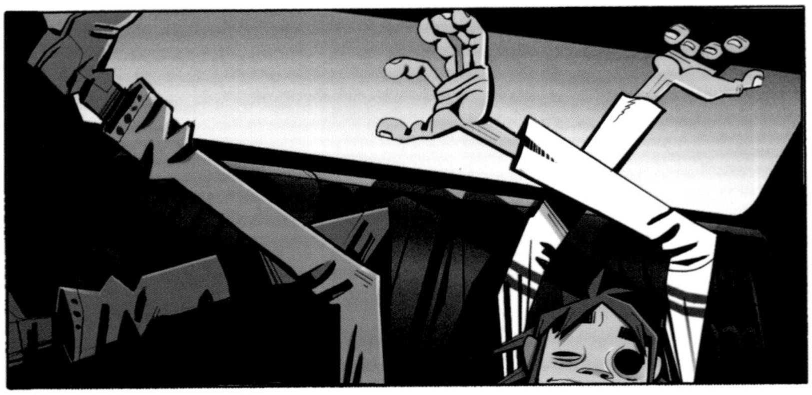

... anyways so the bag of laundry in the back seat was getting tossed about, that was a hell of a burn-out.

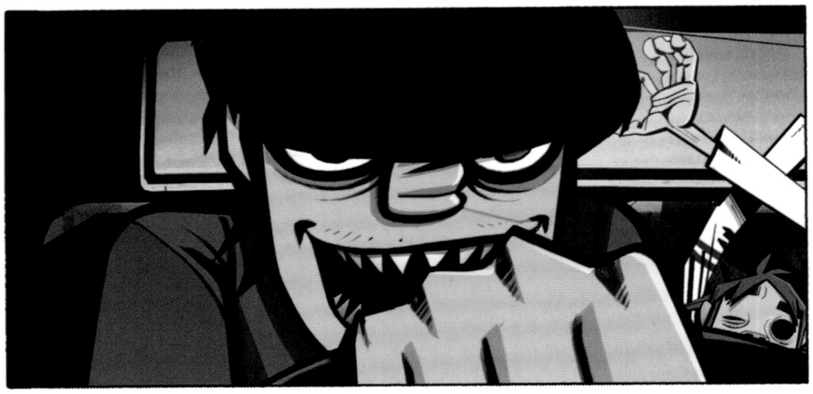

Jamie: Then for whatever reason Murdoc decided to take it to the next level.

Robert: As if things weren't bad enough.

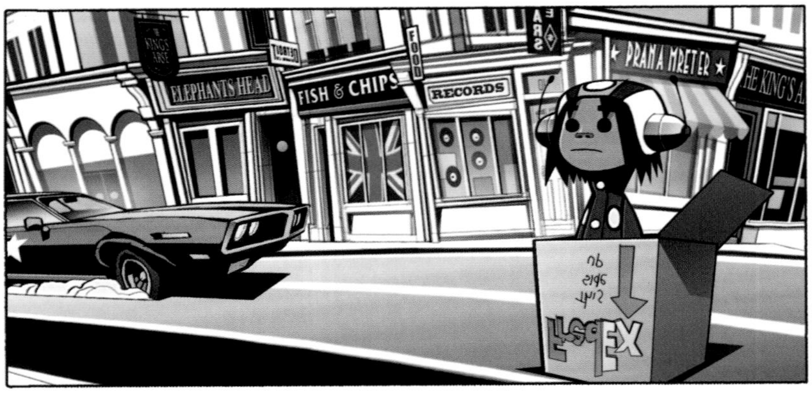
ELEPHANTS HEAD
FISH & CHIPS
RECORDS

Jamie: (burps loudly) so Murdoc gunned it down the high street.

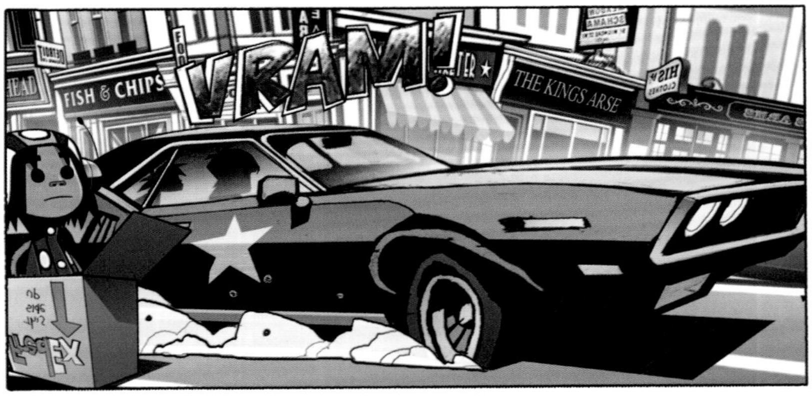
FISH & CHIPS
VRAM!
THE KINGS ARSE

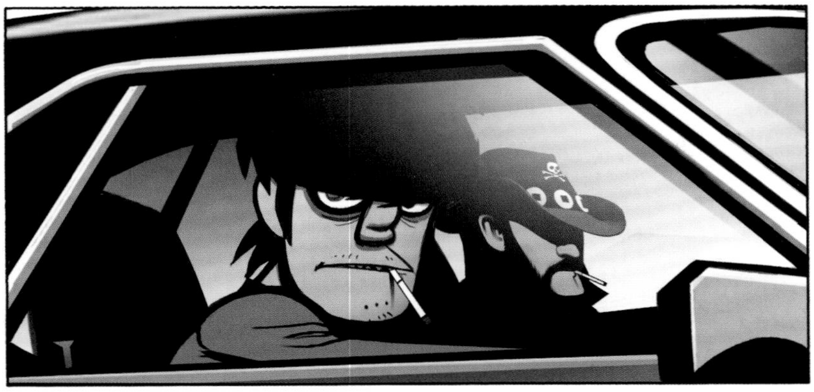

Robert: Whoa... what happened to Keef ?

Jamie: Never mind the continuity, I'm in the middle of a story here fer chrissakes.

Robert: Right...sorry.

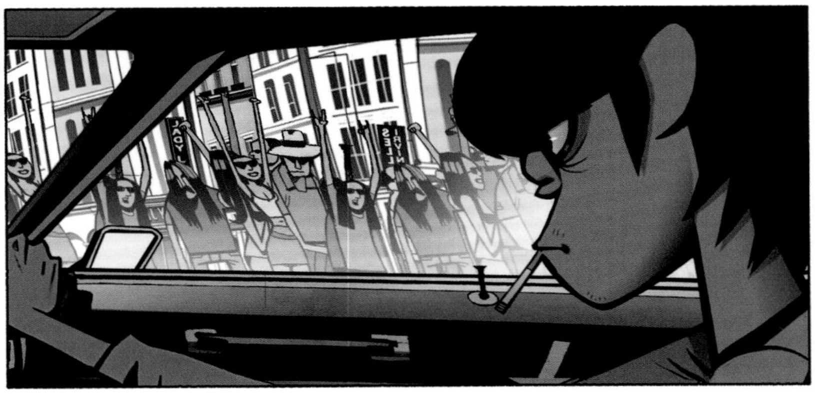

Jamie: (Belch!) by this time Murdoc's antics had caused a crowd of onlookers to gather.

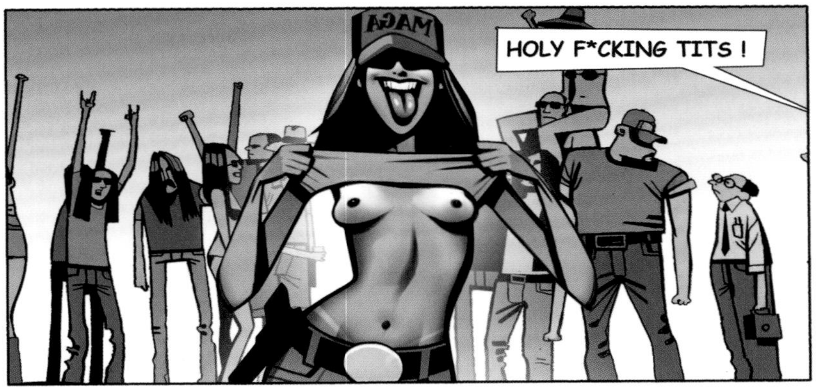
HOLY F*CKING TITS !

...Some of them were a little more enthusiastic than others...

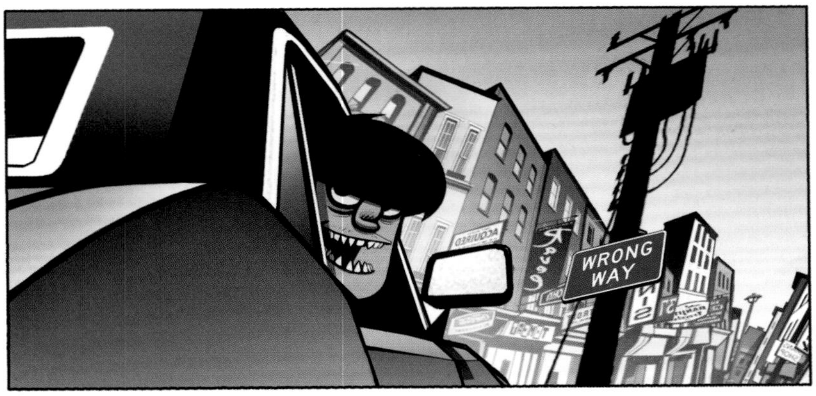
WRONG WAY

Jamie: I guess you could say Murdoc lost focus momentarily.

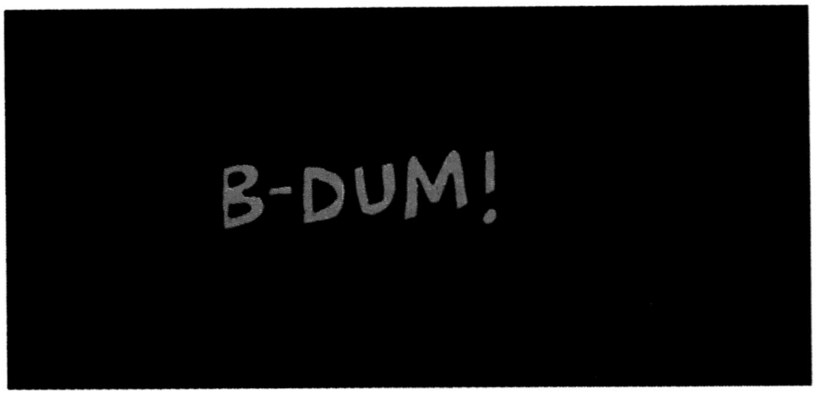
B-DUM!

... then what can I say...? Twisted wreckage.

Robert: oh dang!

Jamie: Murdoc and his crew did a runner, leaving a very broken 2D left to fend for himself.

Robert: That was cold.

Jamie: (Laughing and lighting another smoke) on the bright side, the impact of the accident had revived 2D from his catatonic state...

...but as he stood there in the darkness and rain, he knew that somehow his appearance had been altered...

... the transformation was complete...

...suddenly a burst of lightning flashed and revealed the extent of 2D's horrific injuries... now there were no eyes, just two black holes... a vacant stare.

2D

Next: The tale of Russel Hobbs Waking the Slumbering Giant...

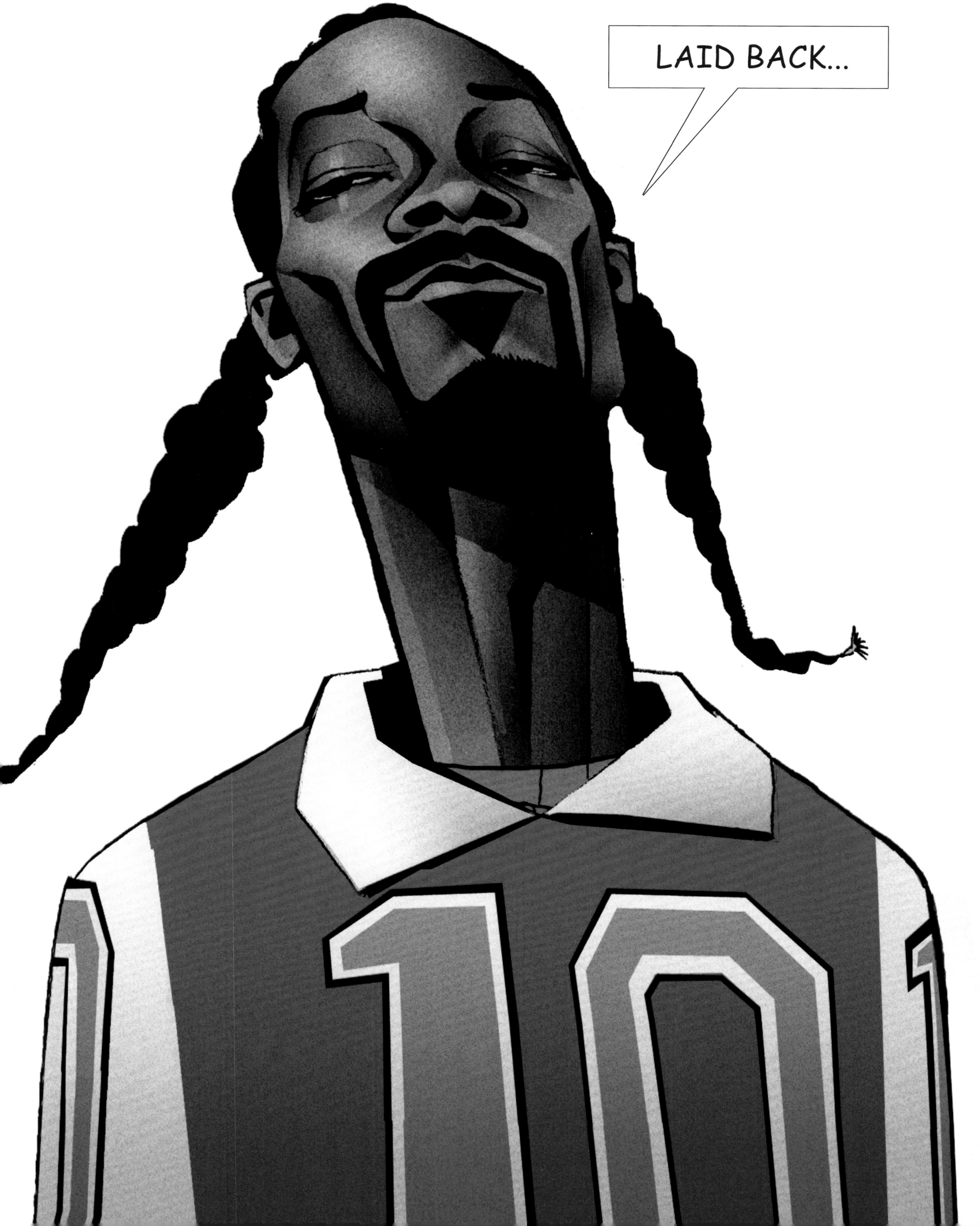
LAID BACK...

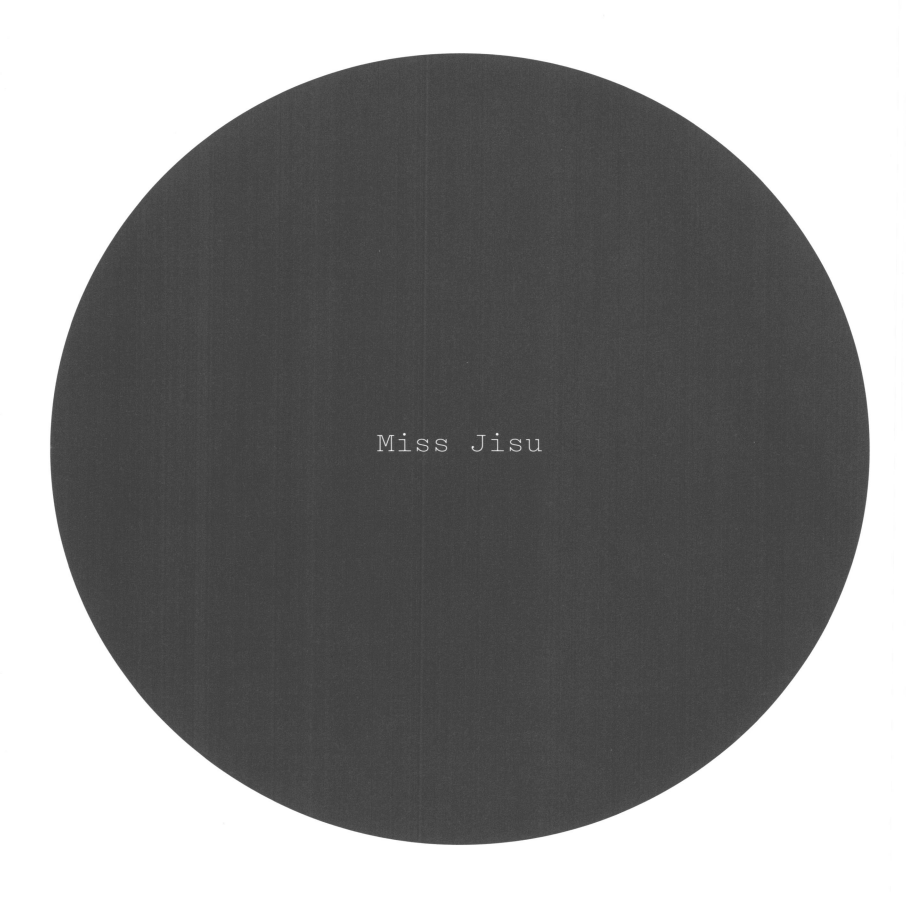

Miss Jisu

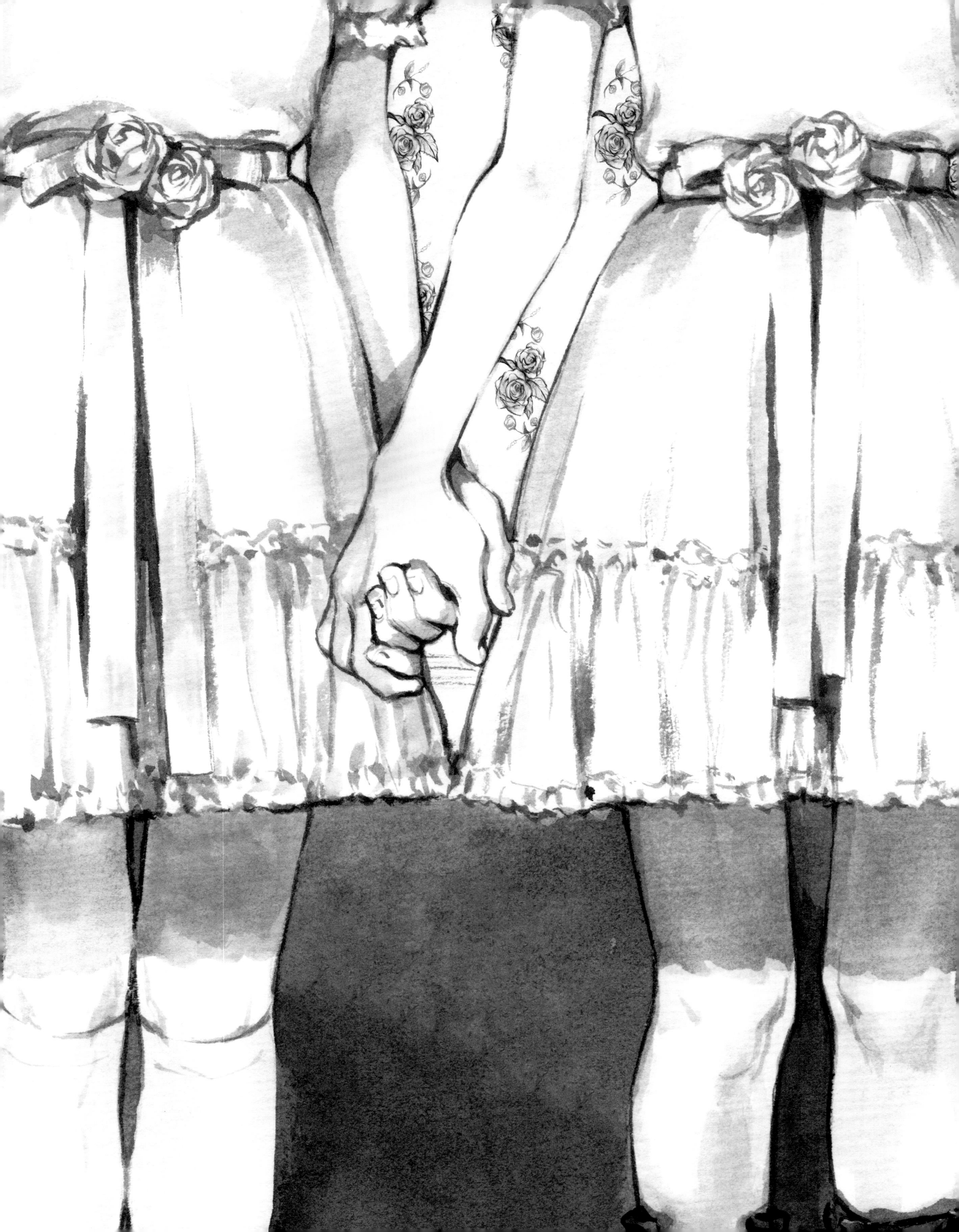

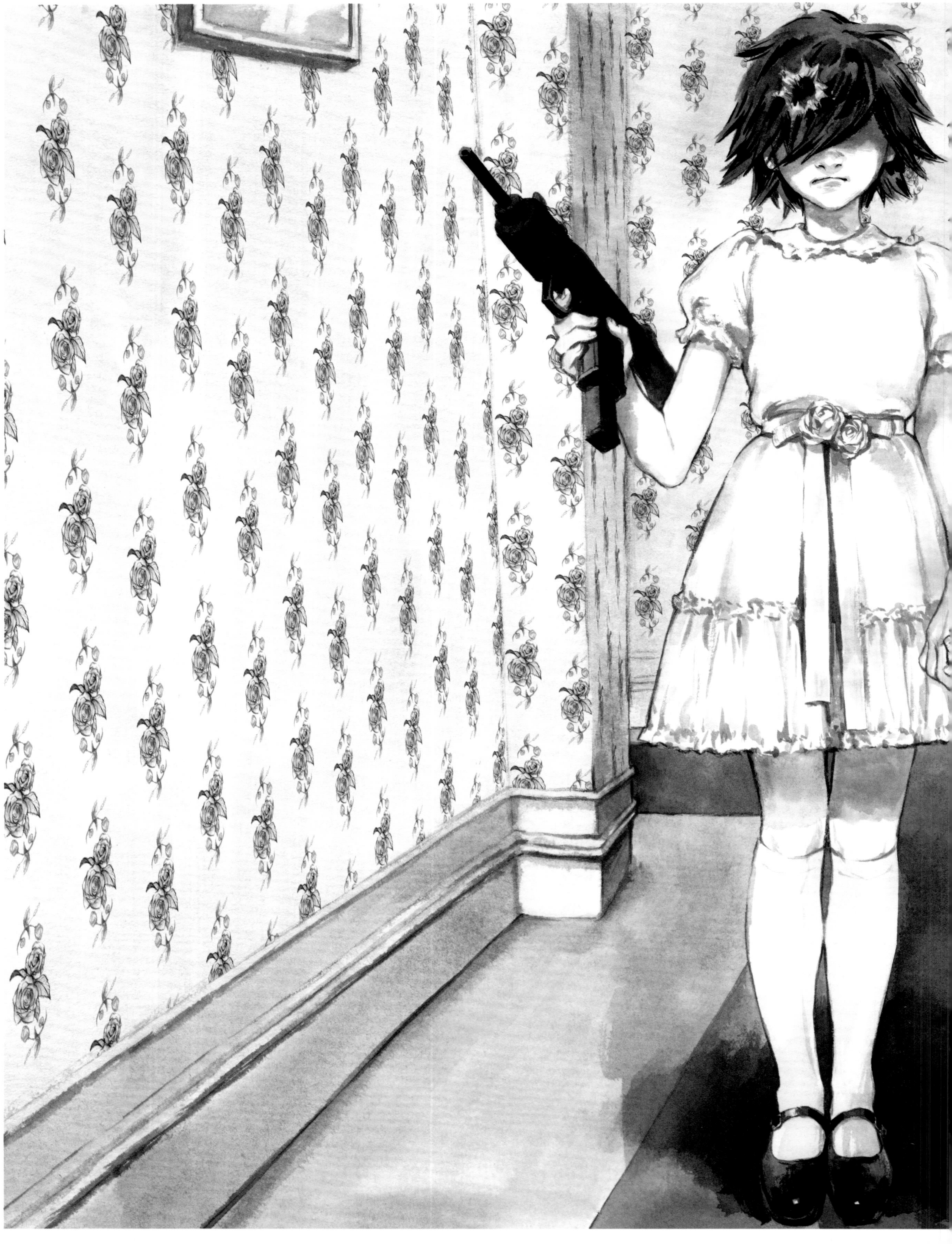

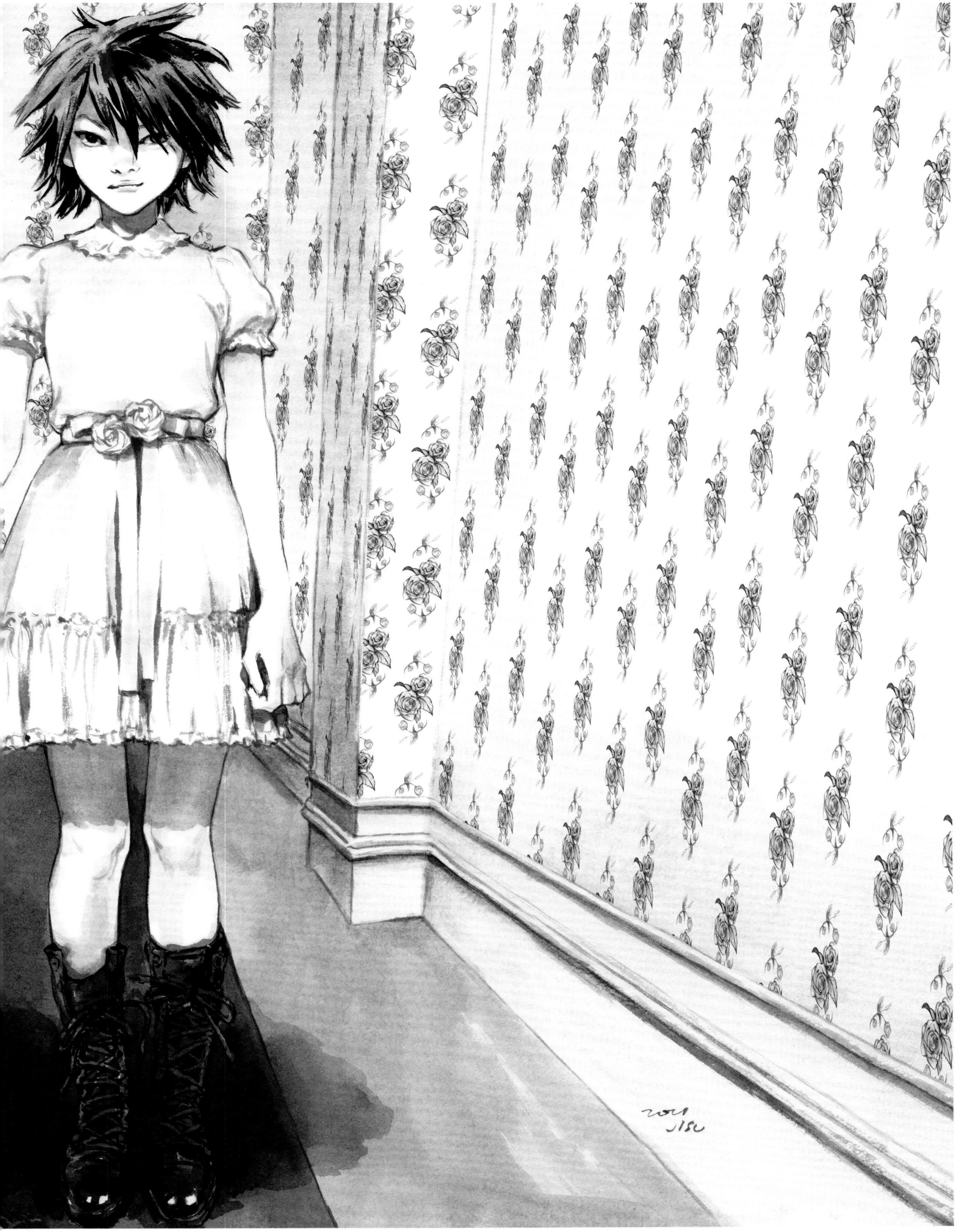

Dana Terrace

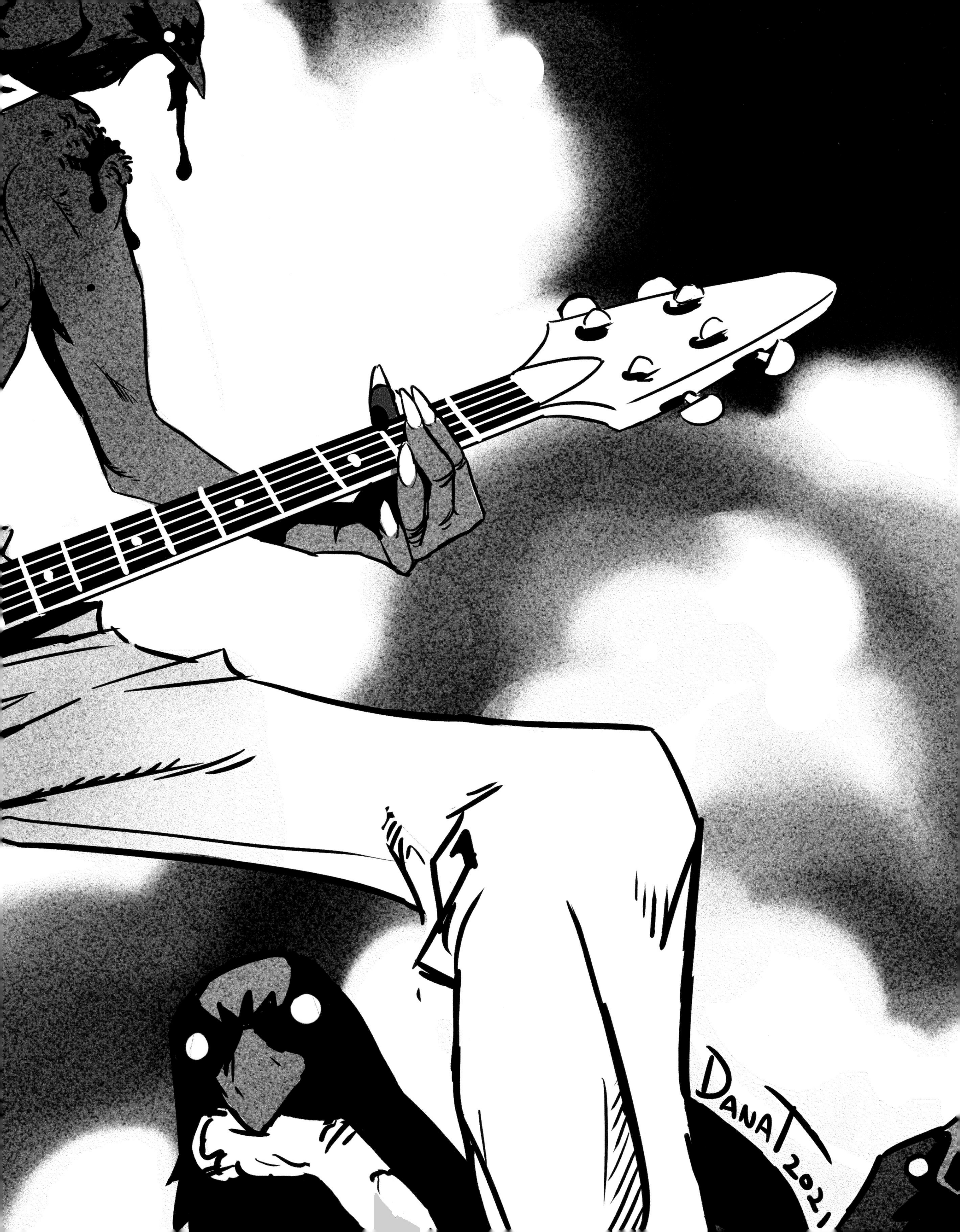
DANAT
2021

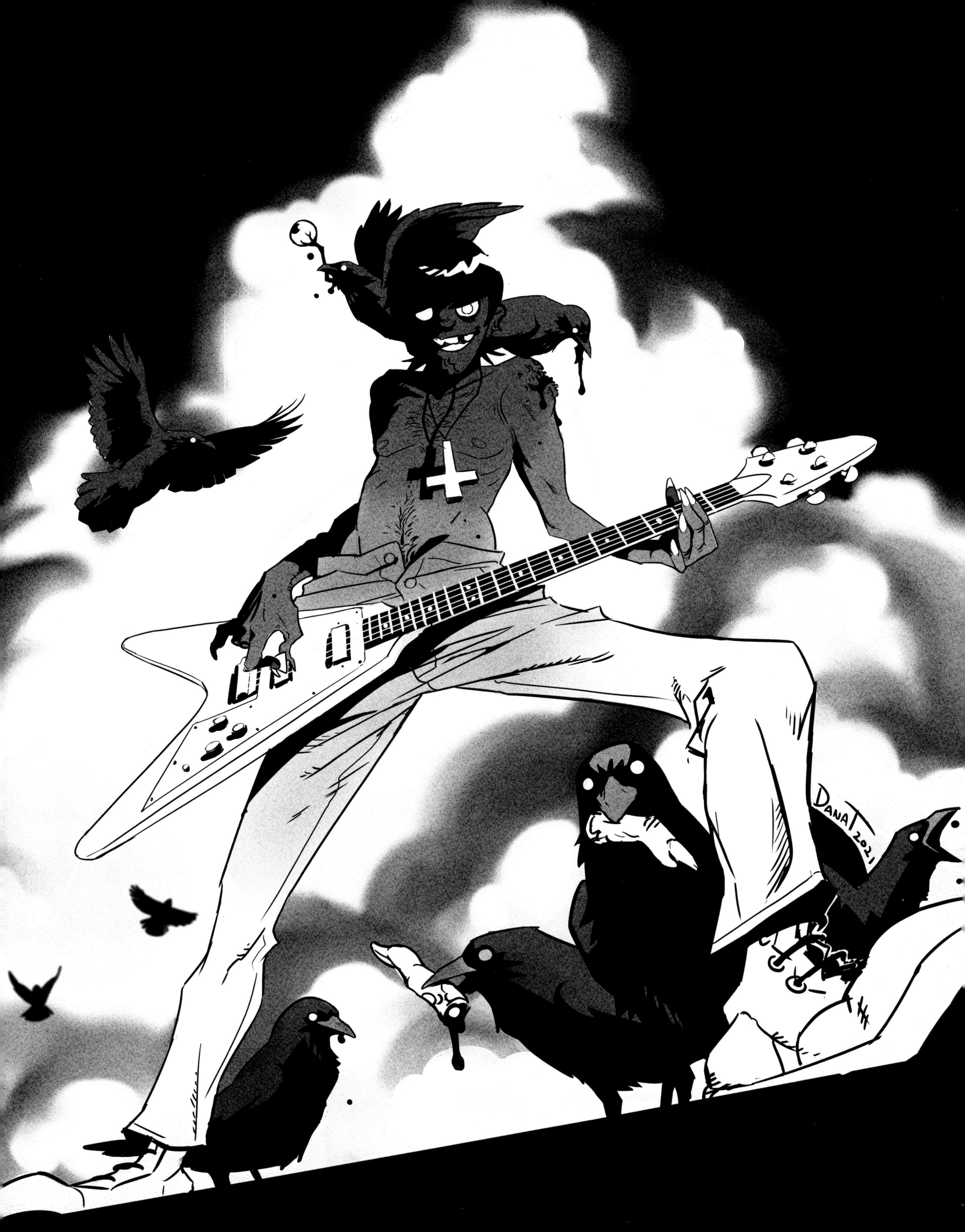
DANAT 2021

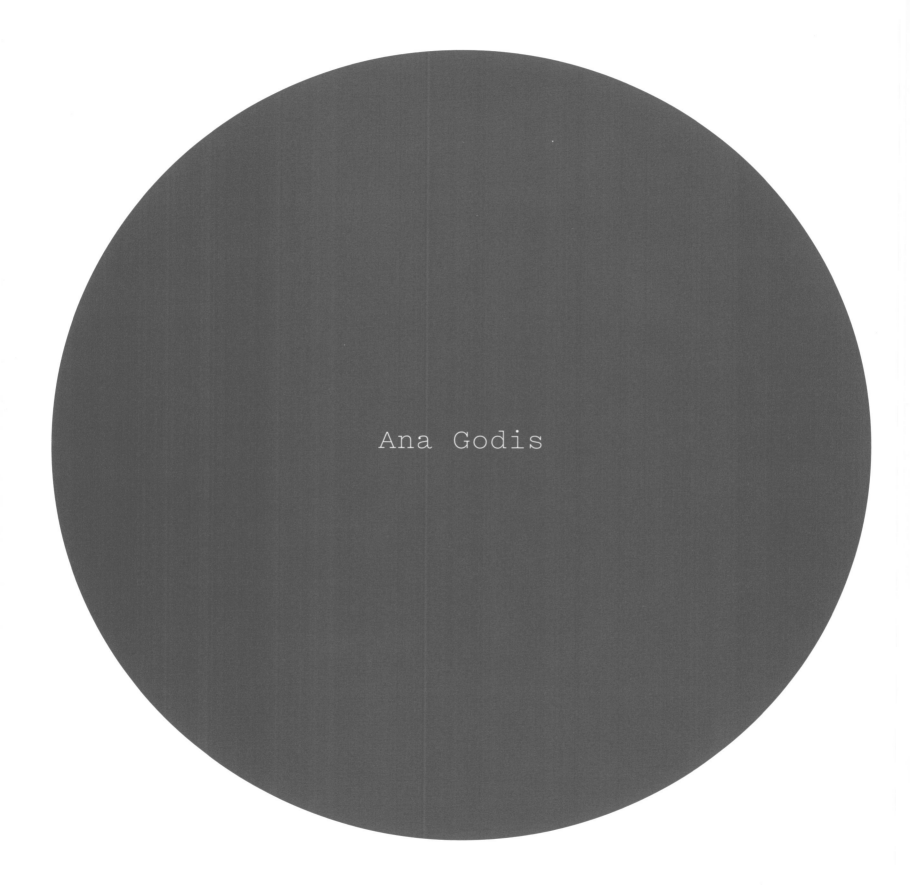

Ana Godis

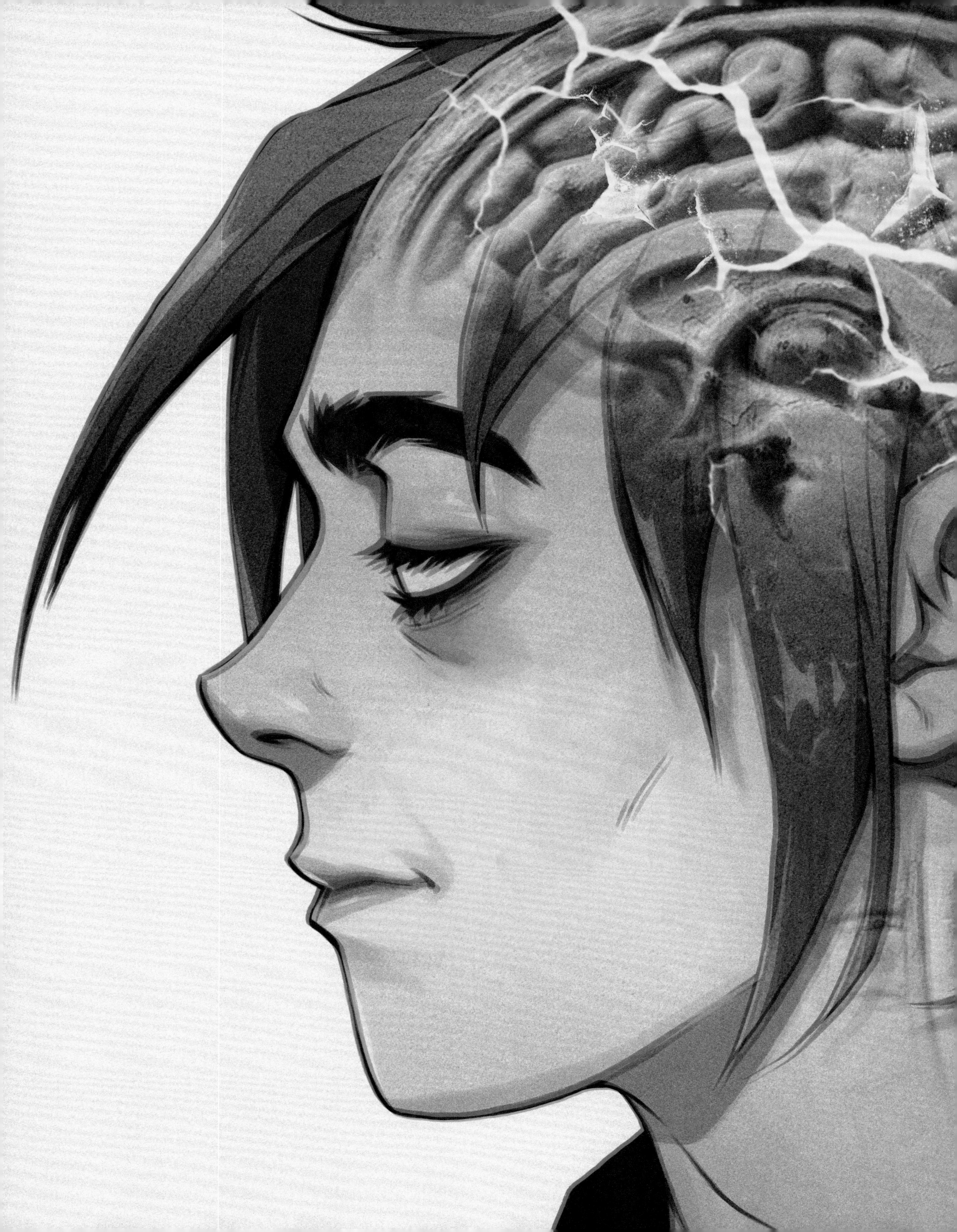

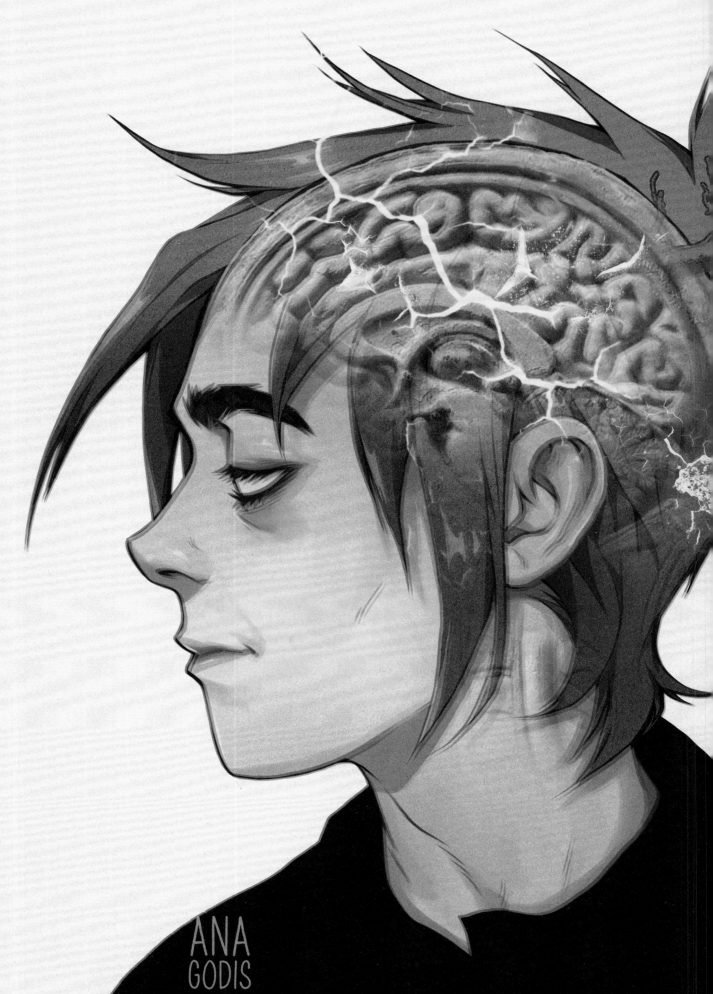

ANA
GODIS

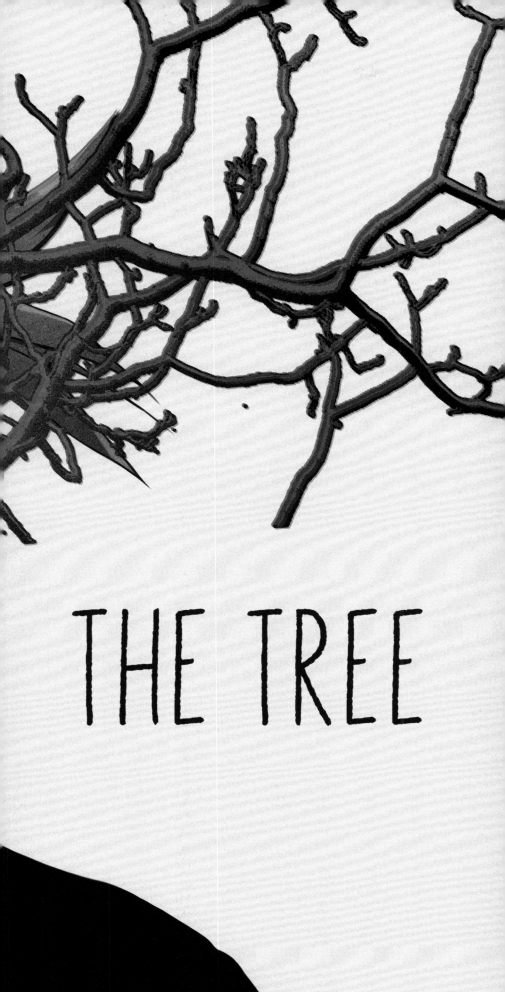

THE TREE

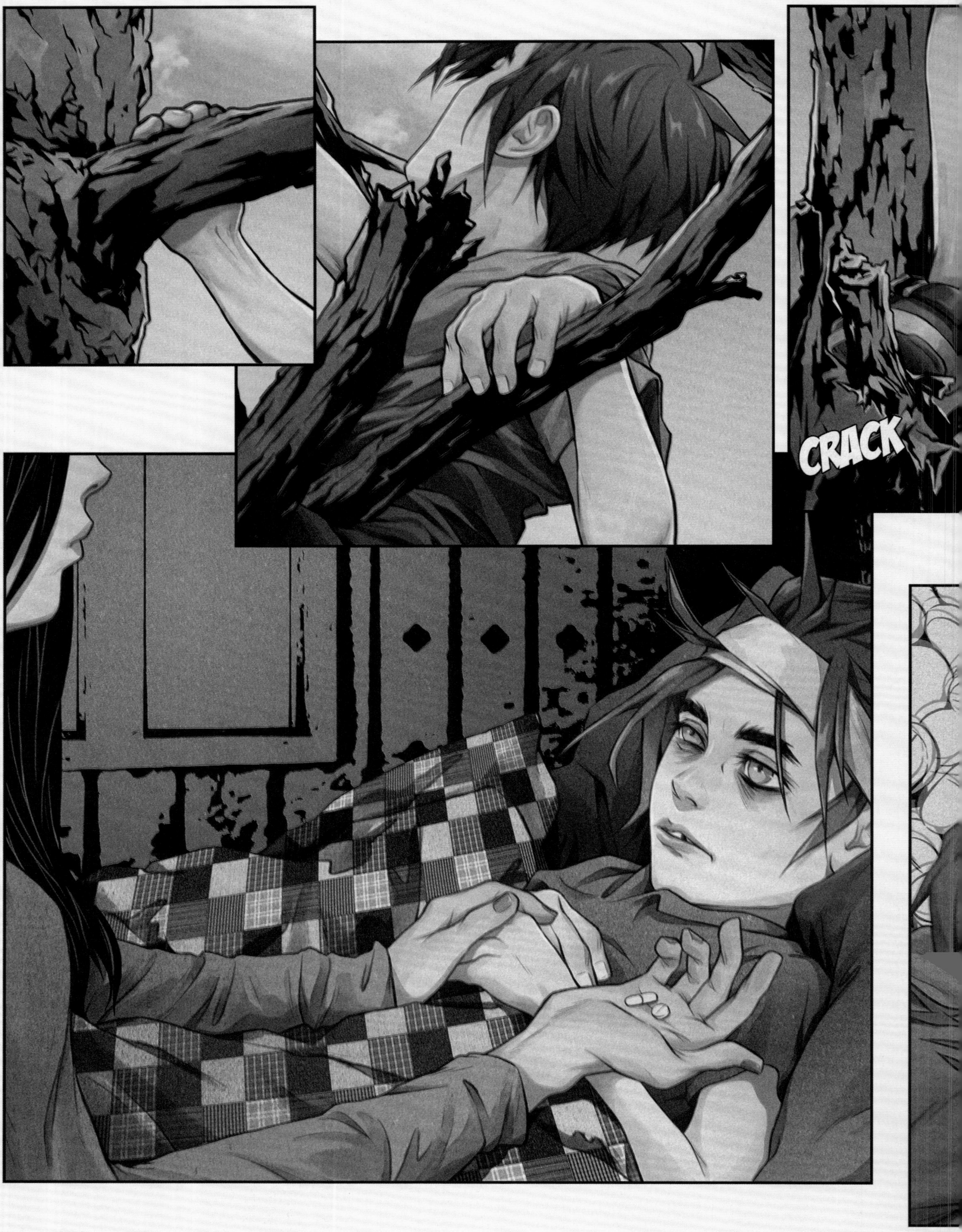
CRACK

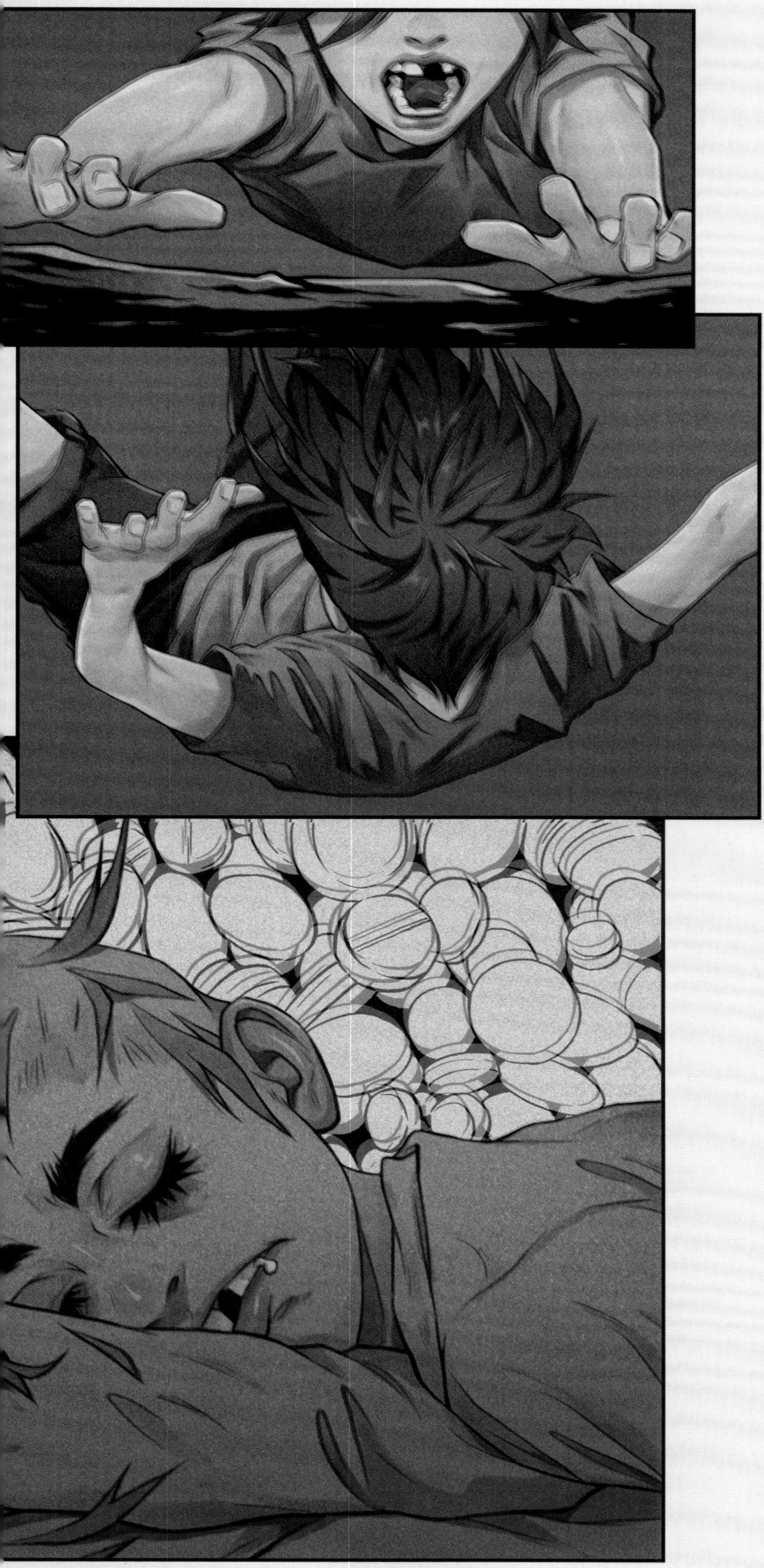

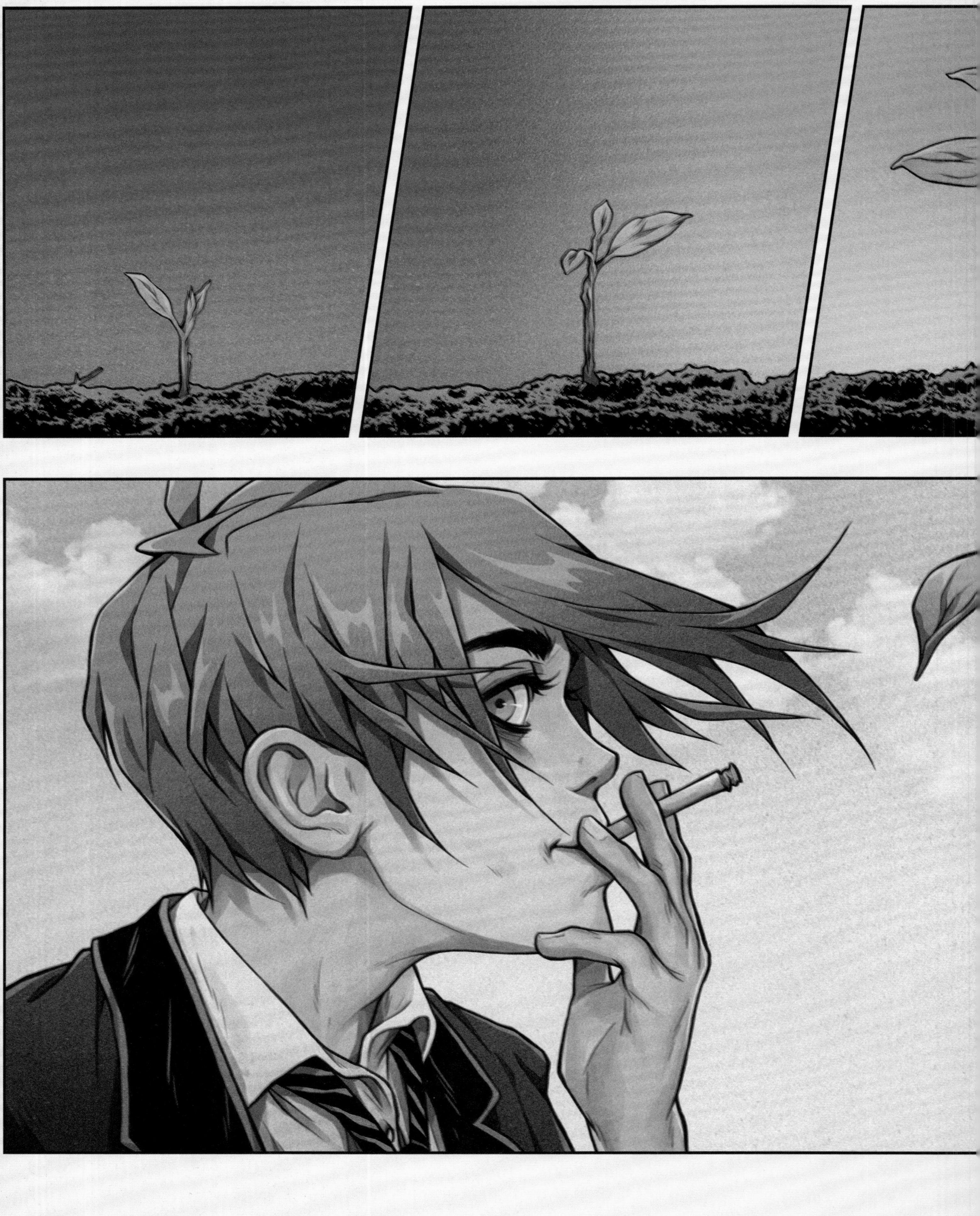

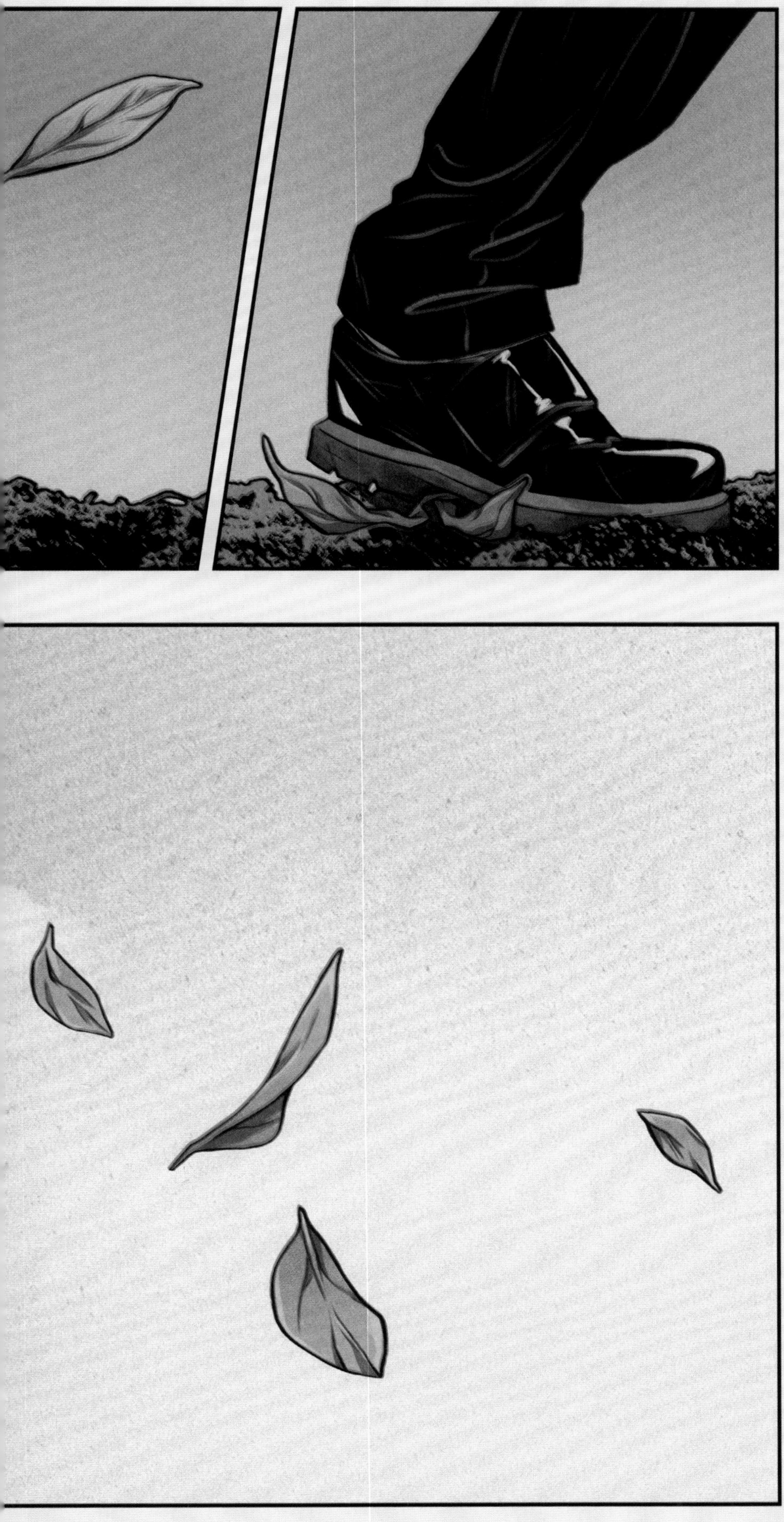

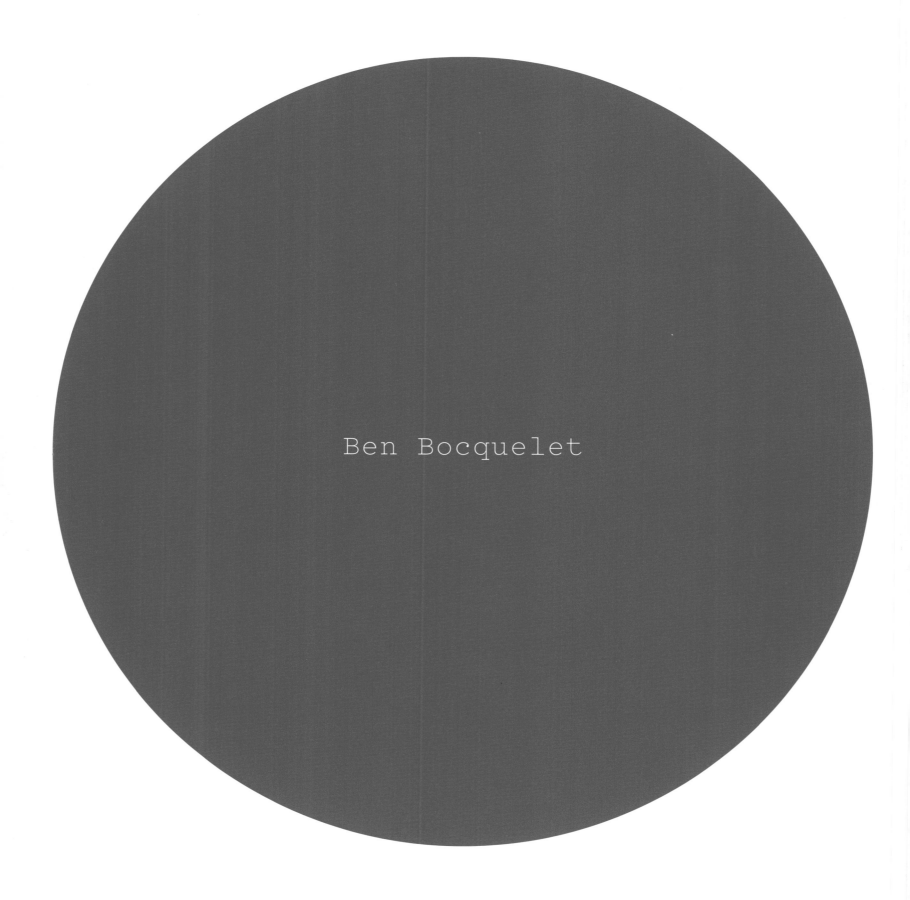

Ben Bocquelet

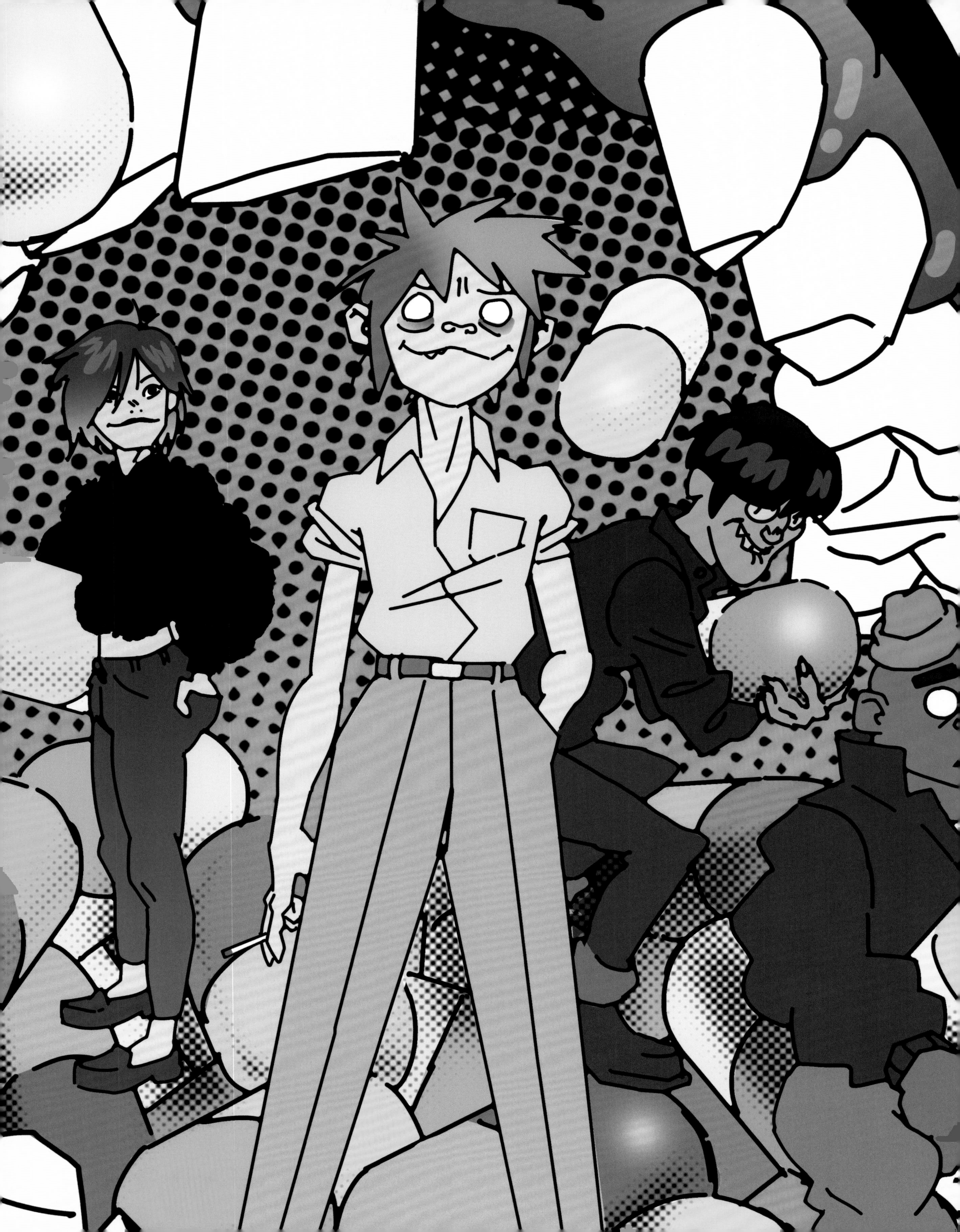

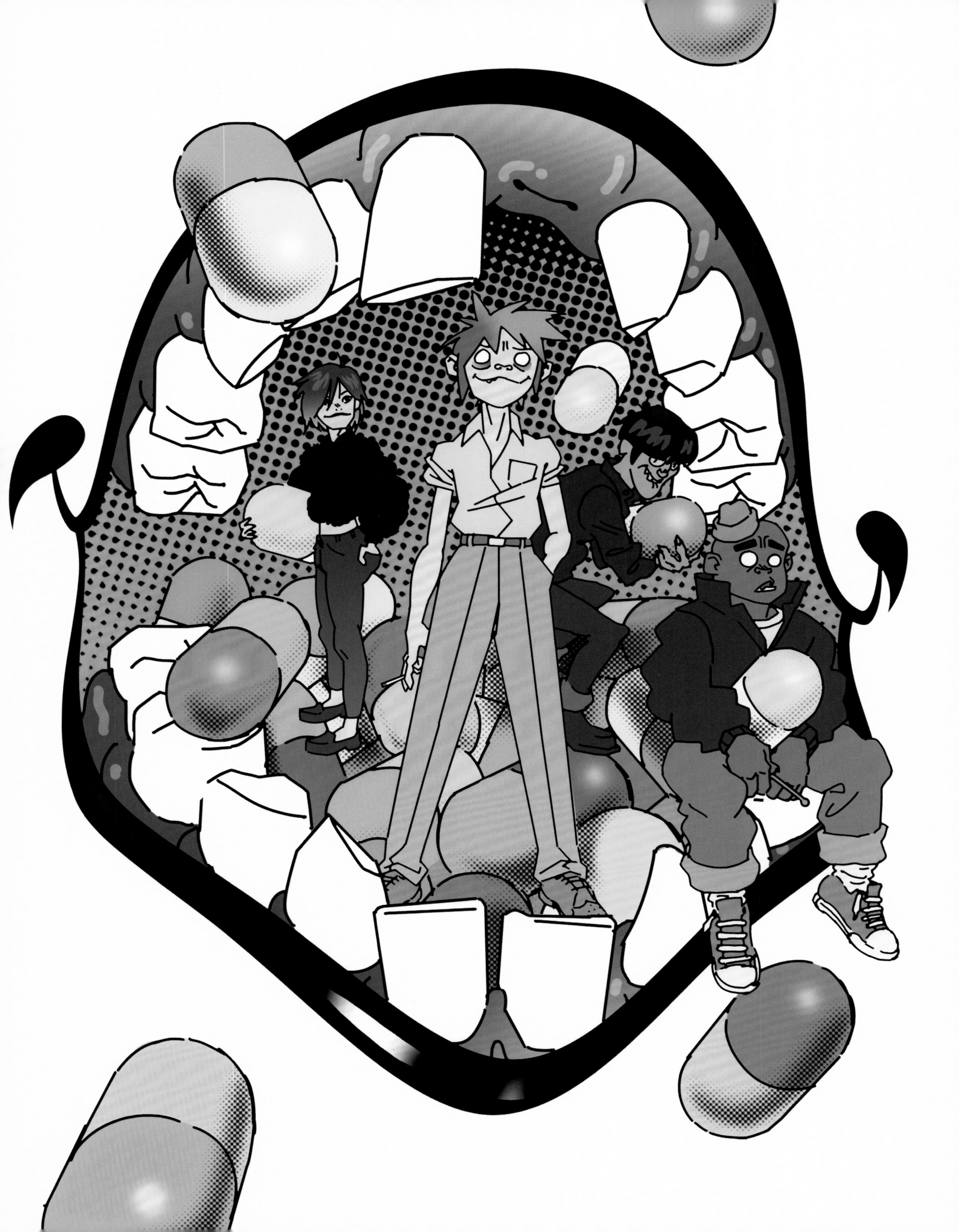

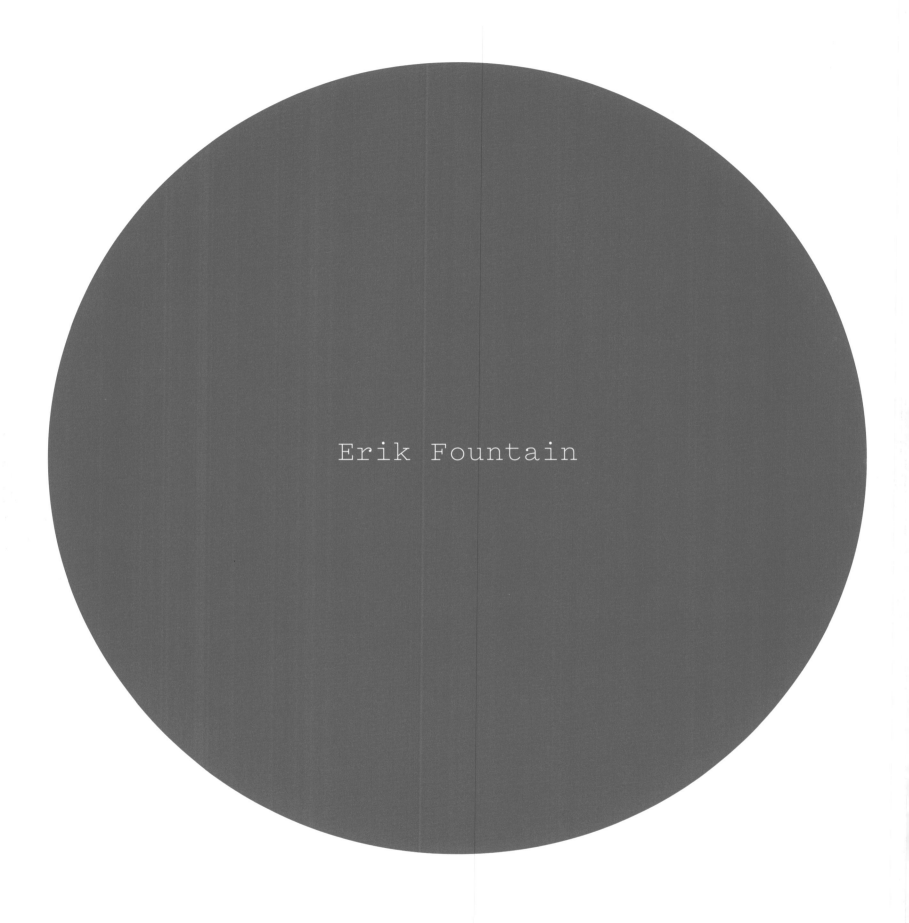

Erik Fountain

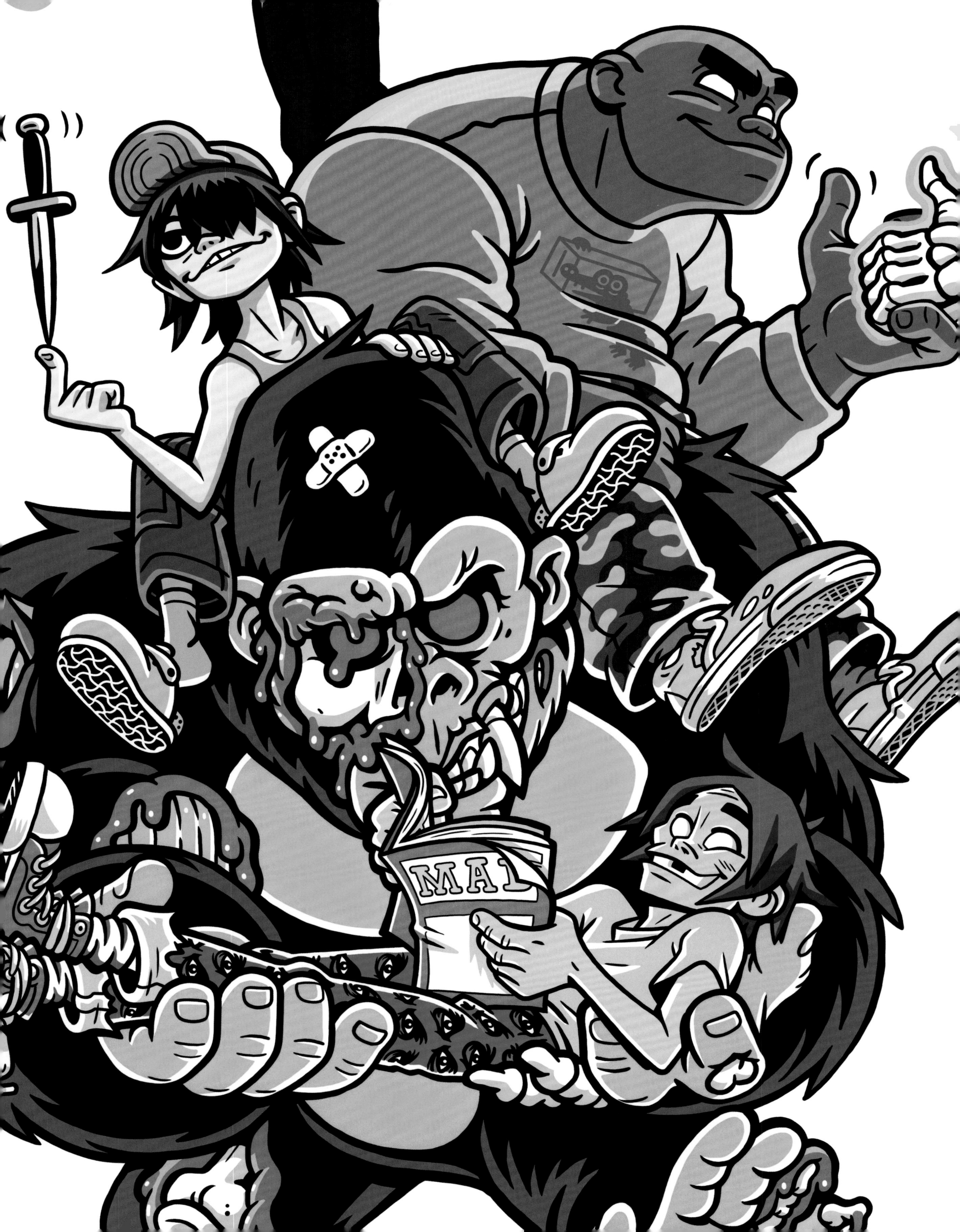
MAD

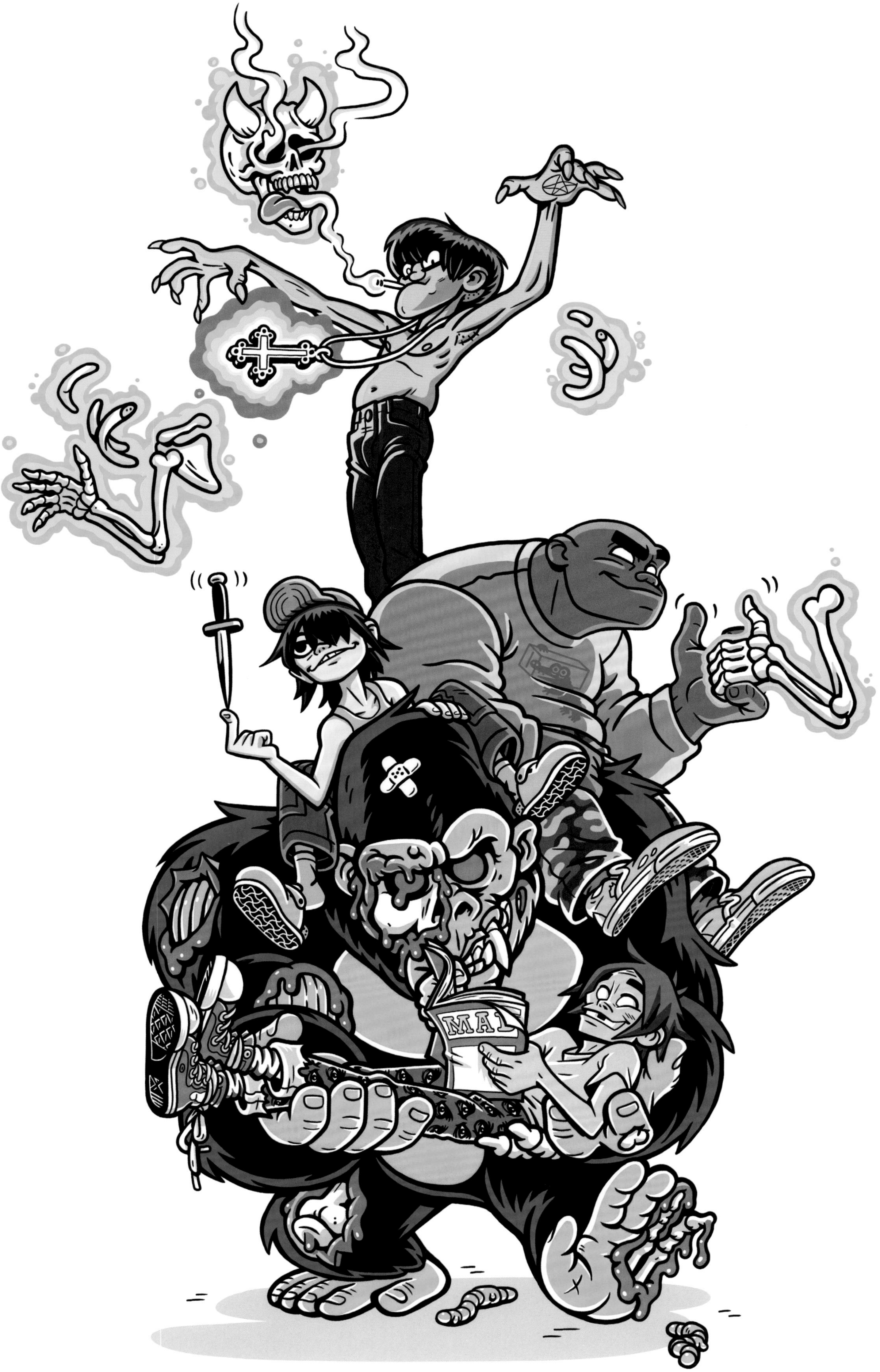
MAL

Holly Warburton

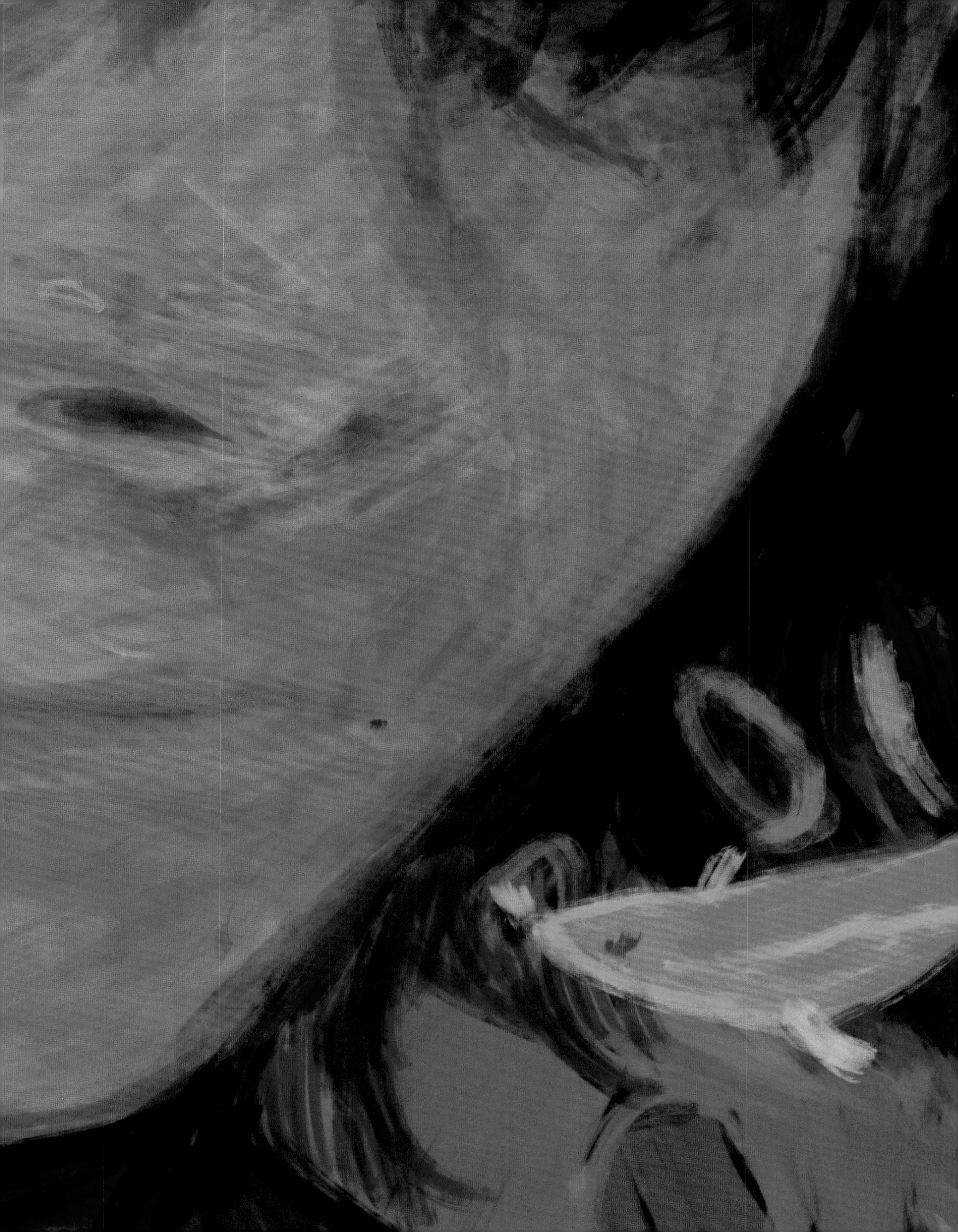

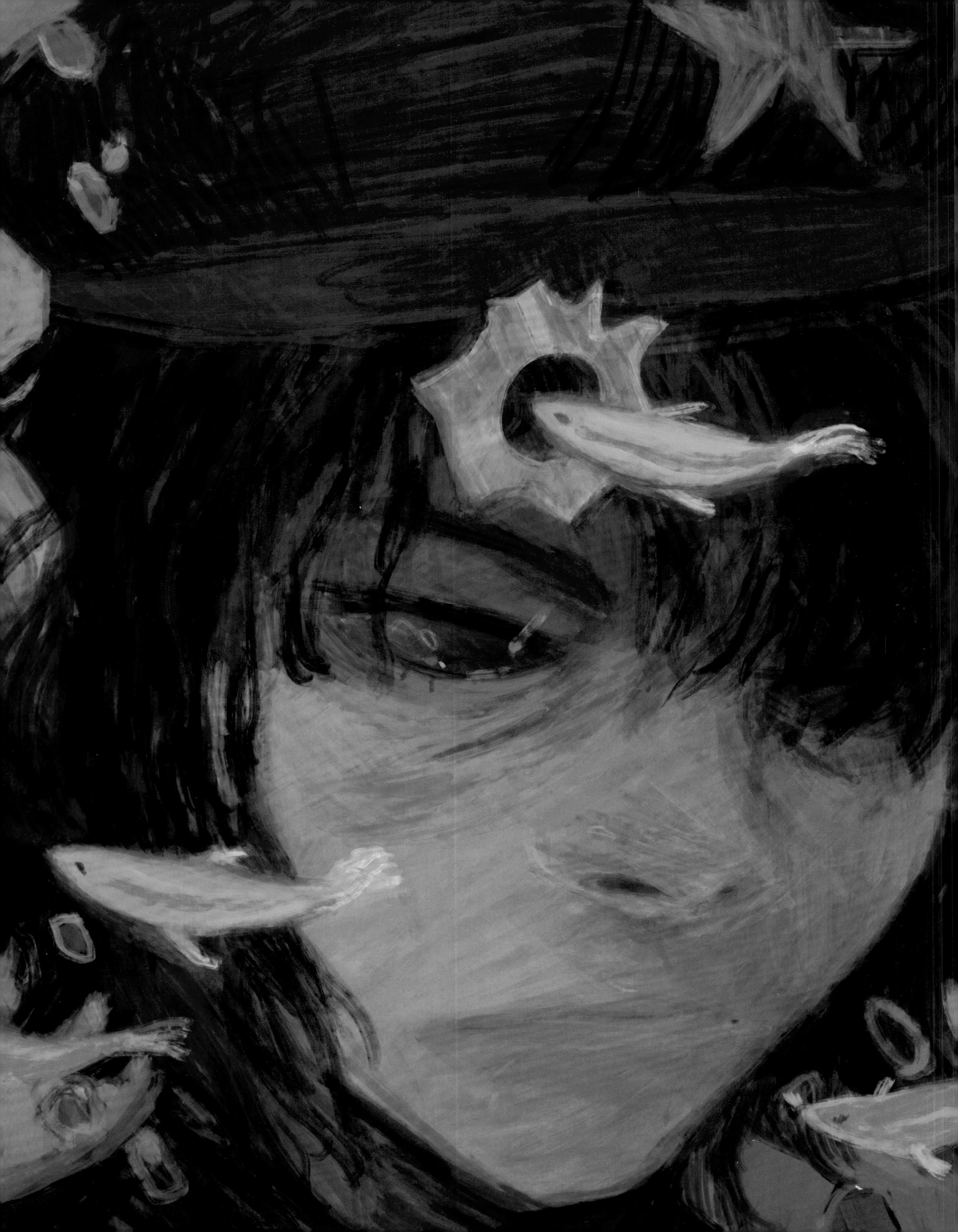

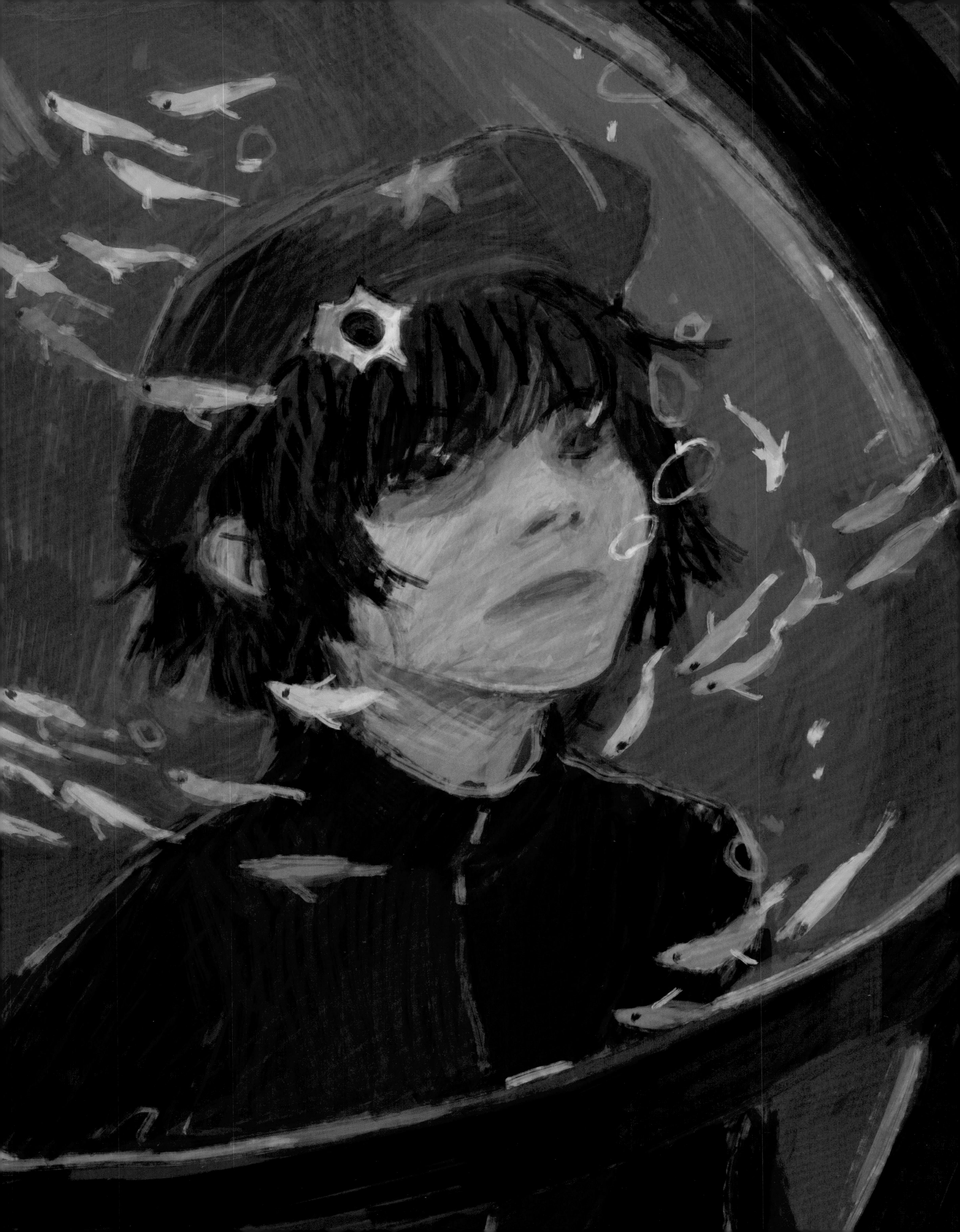

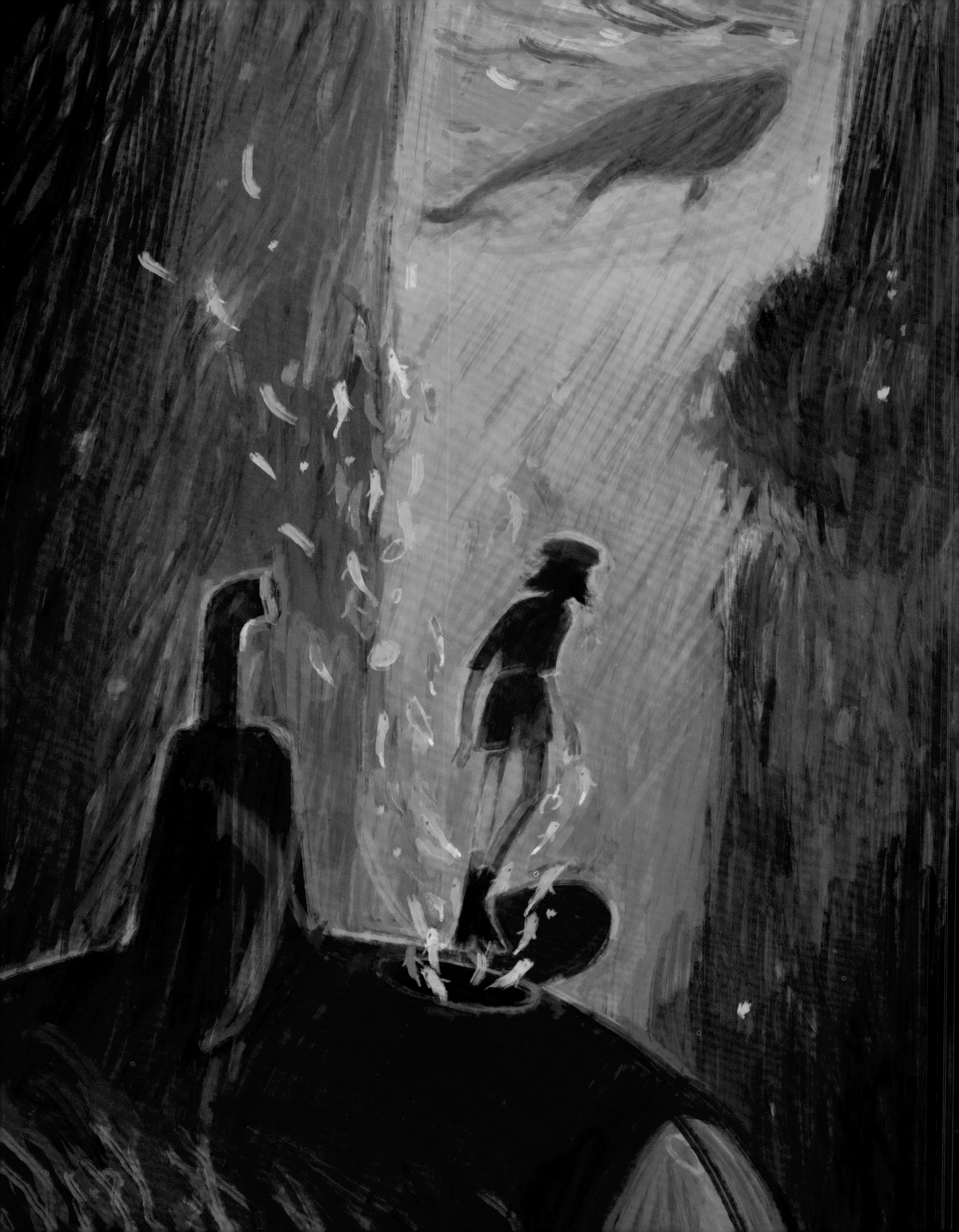

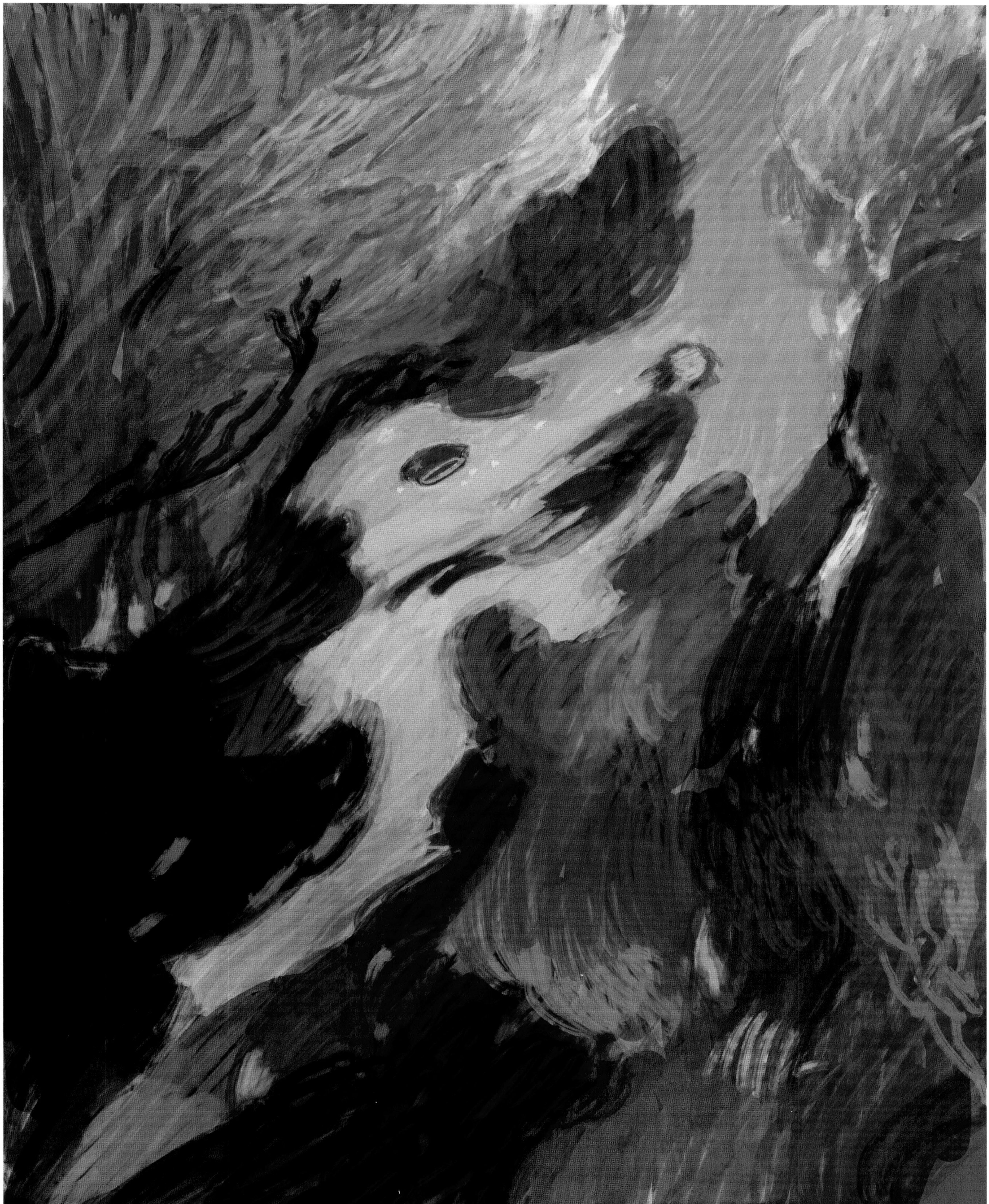

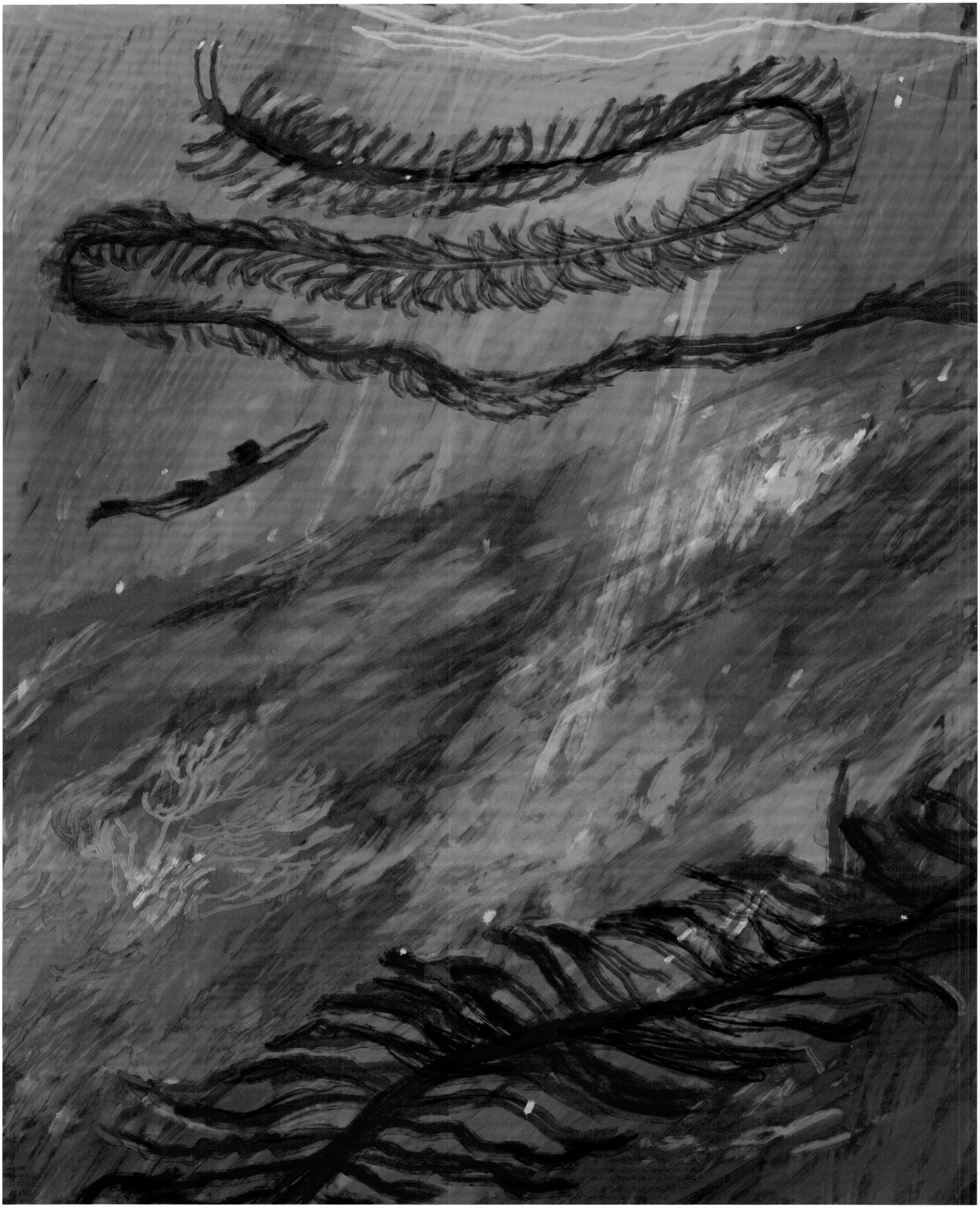

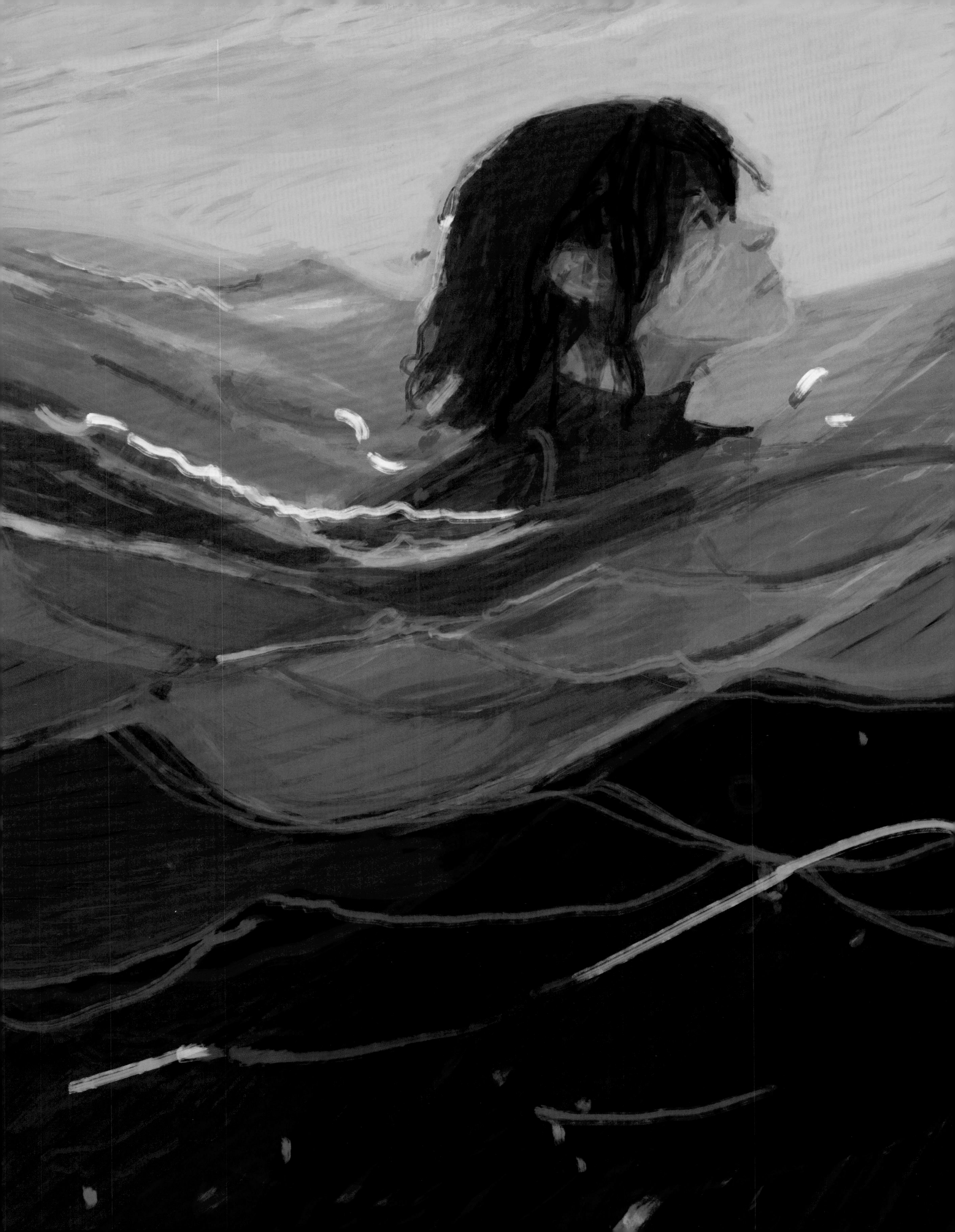

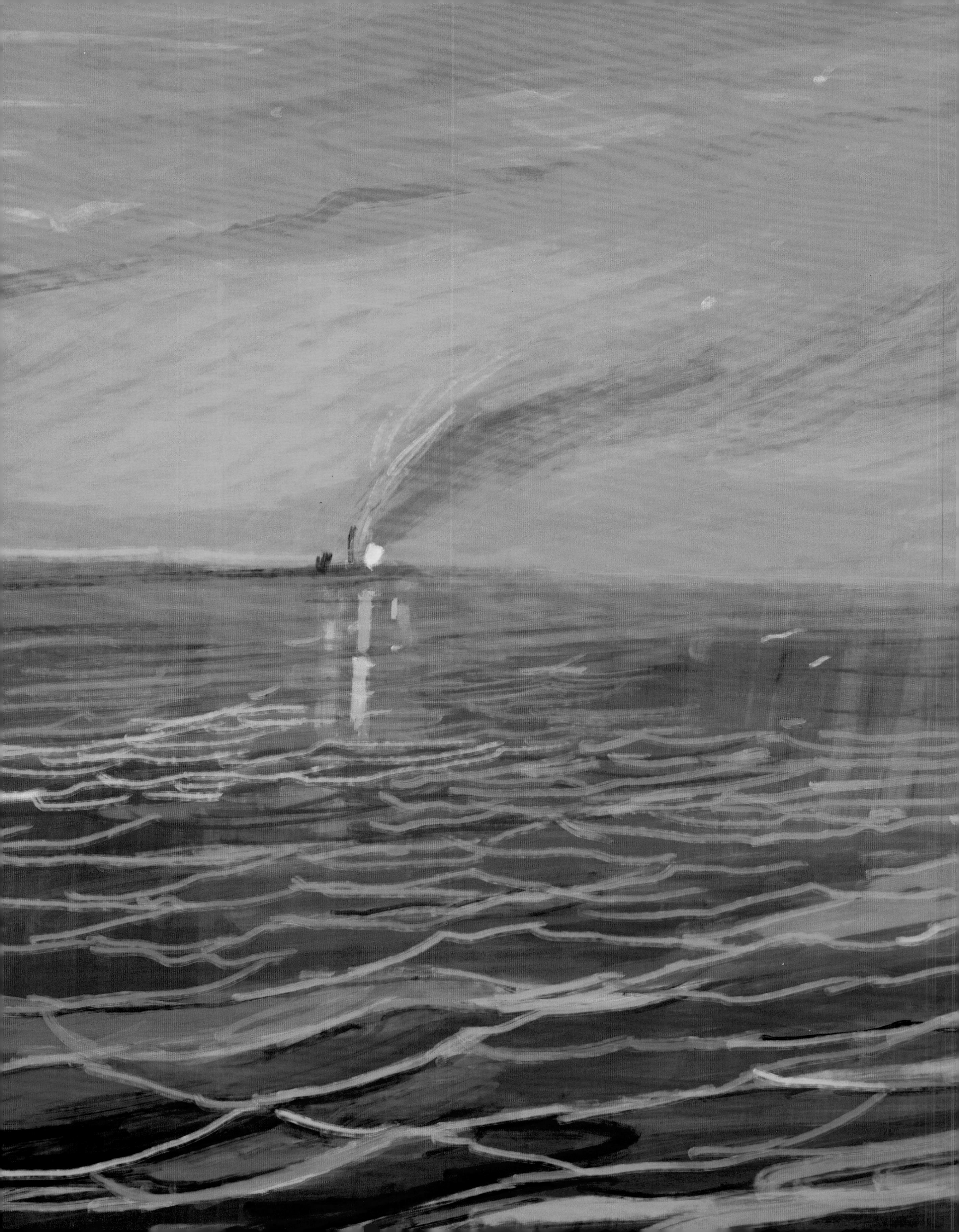

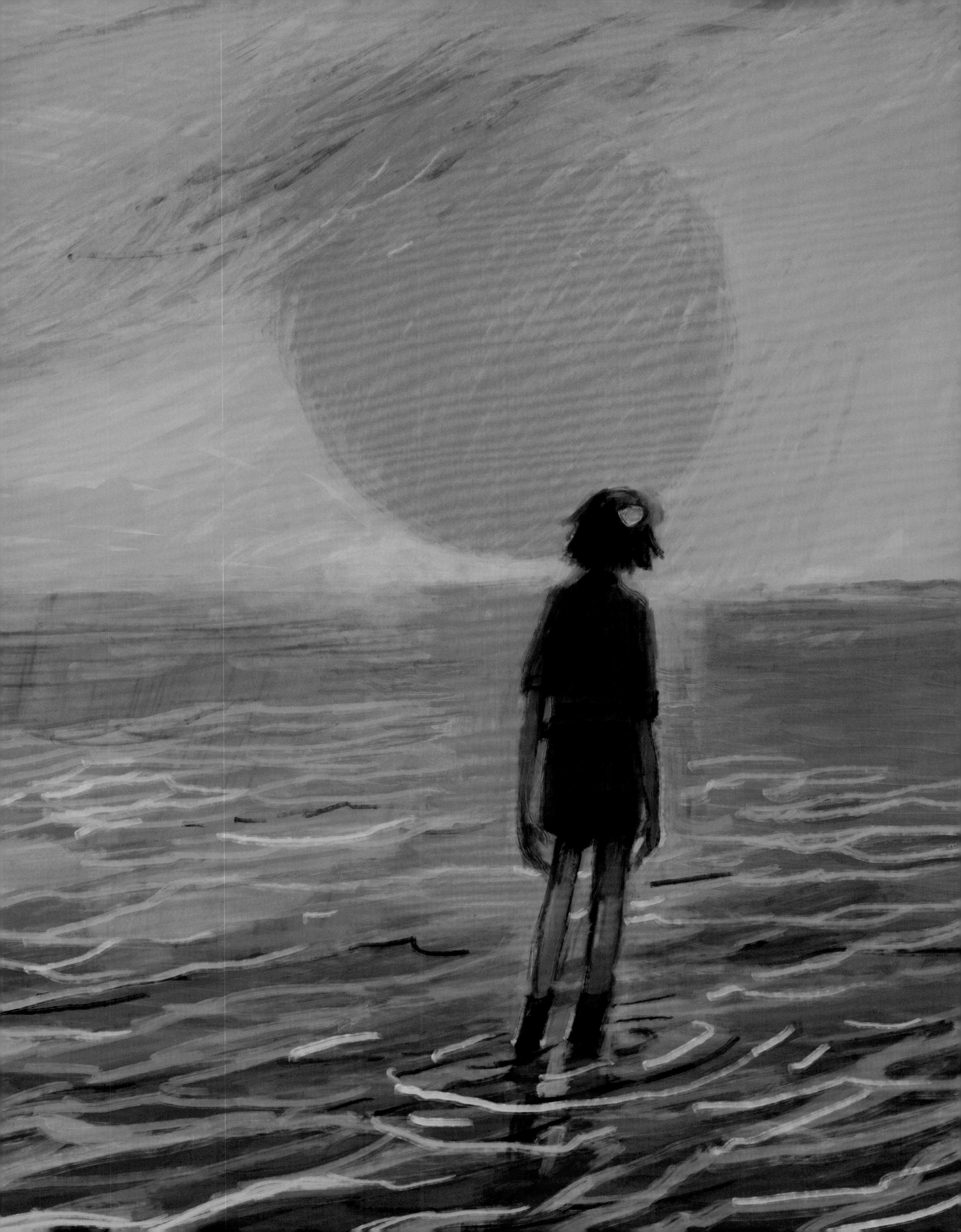

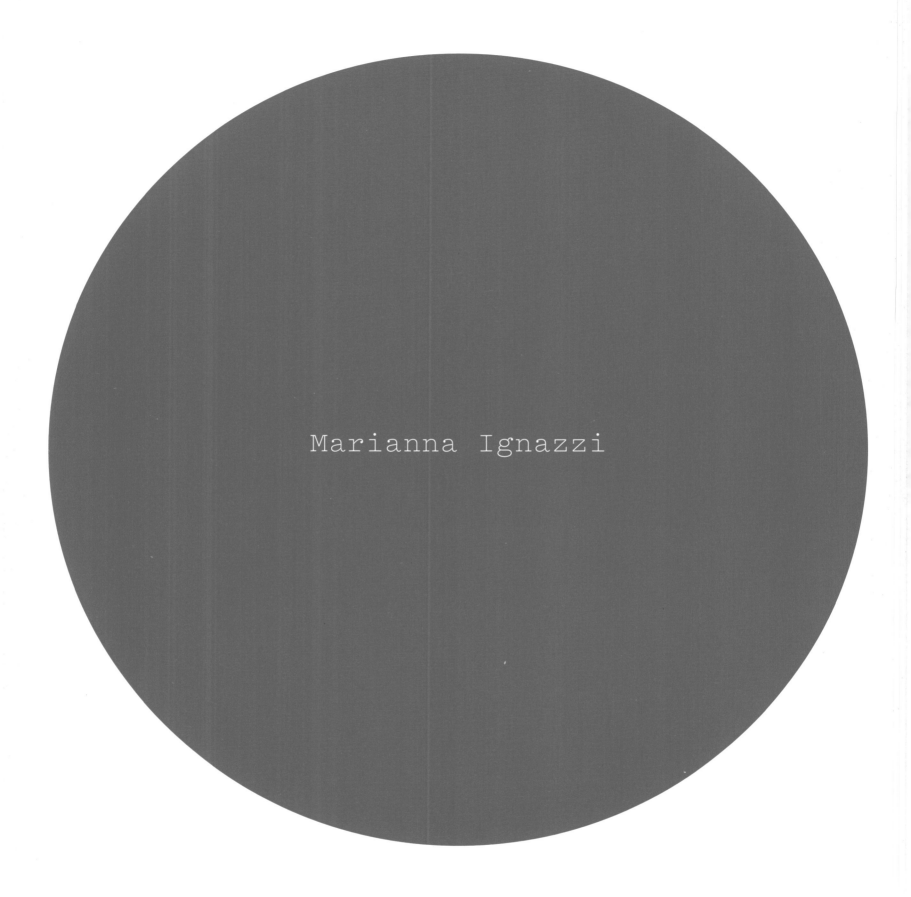

Marianna Ignazzi

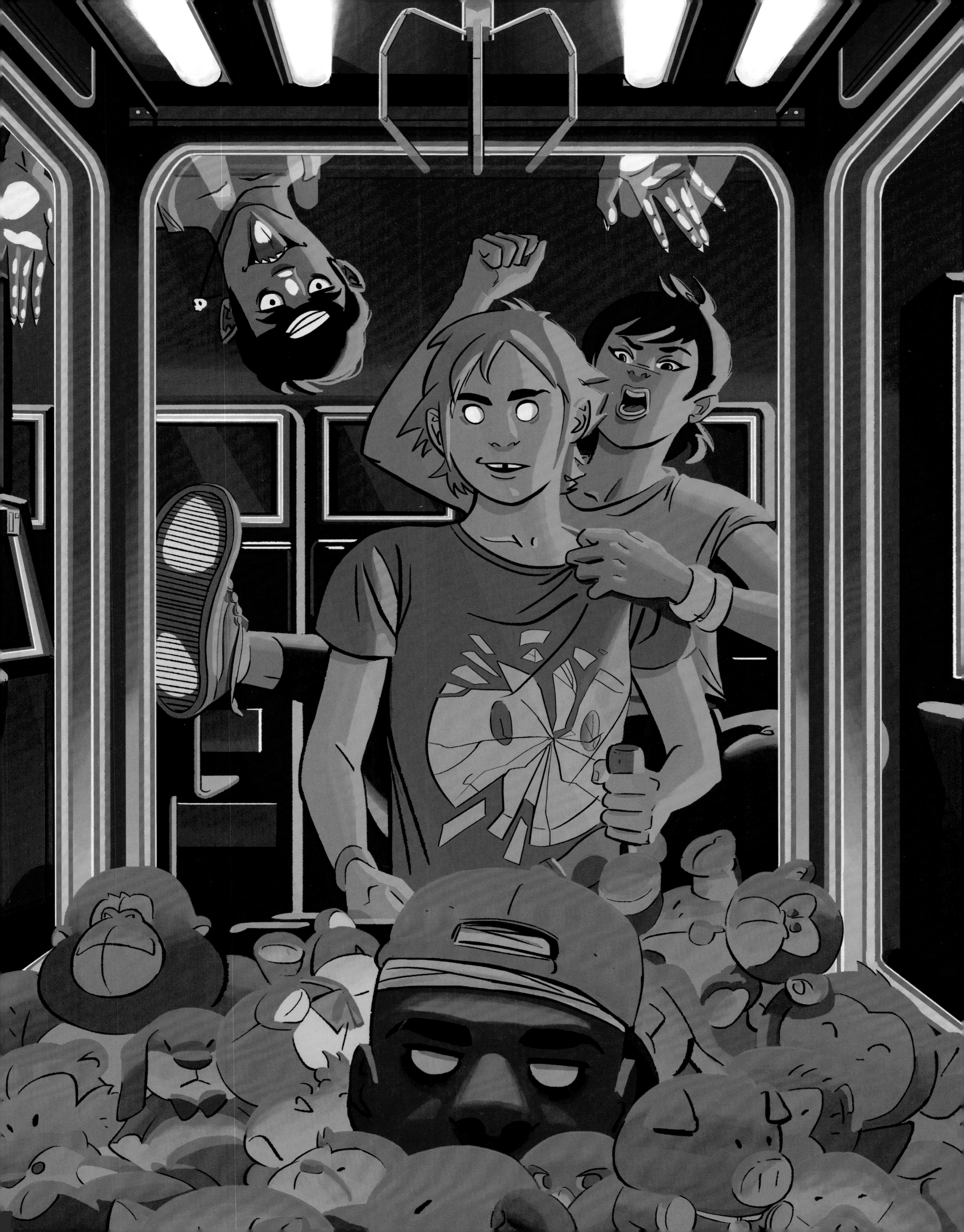

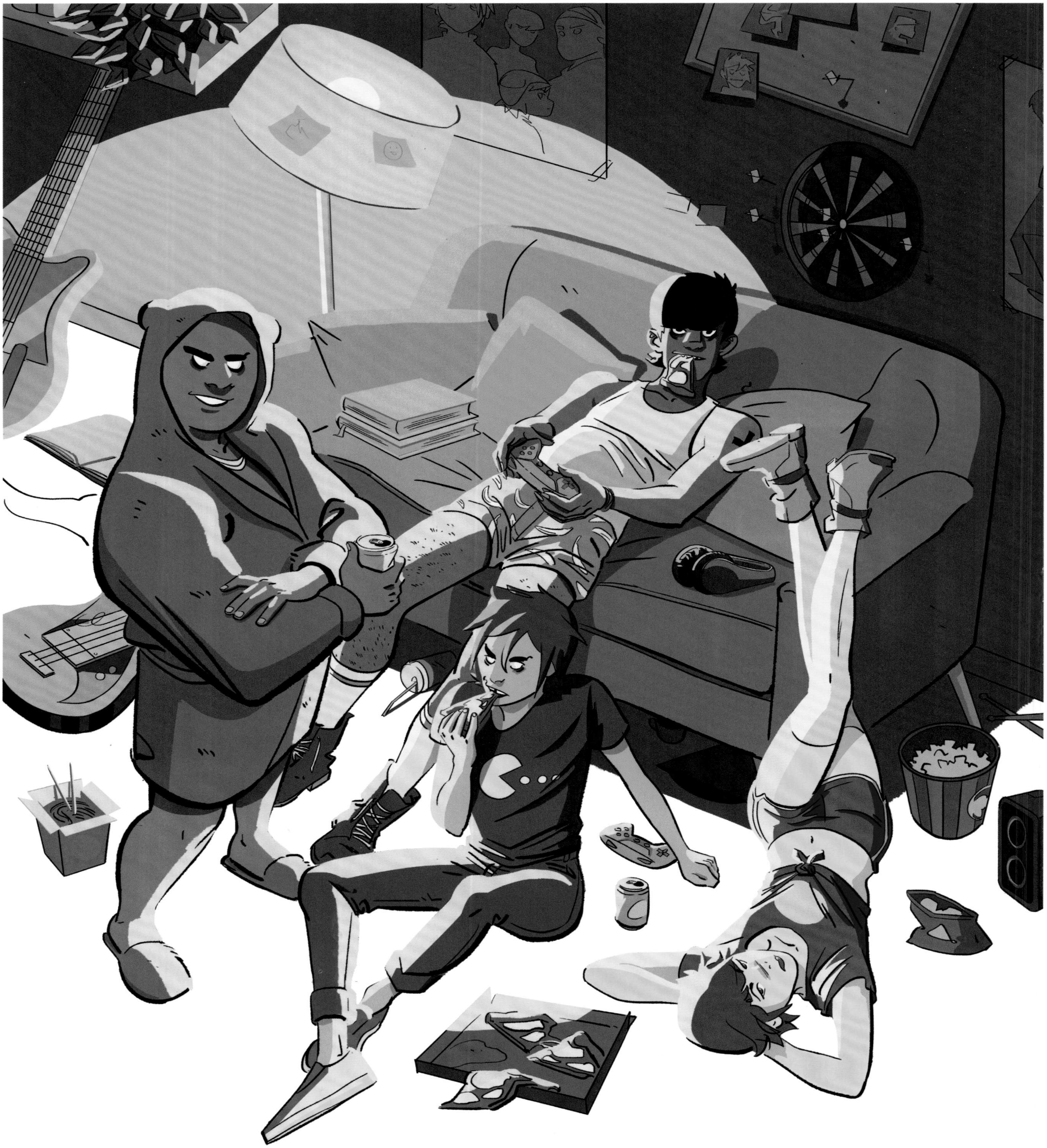

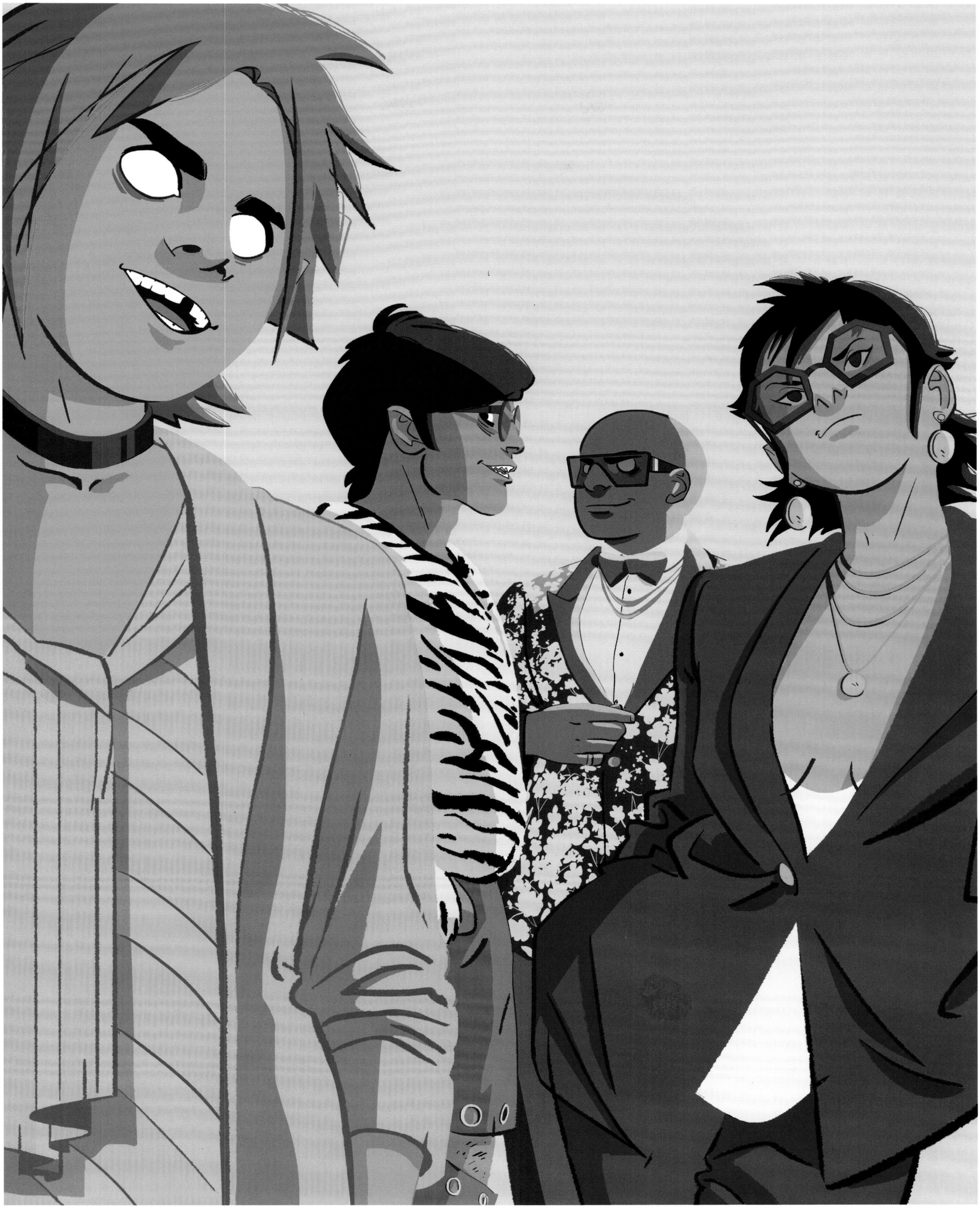

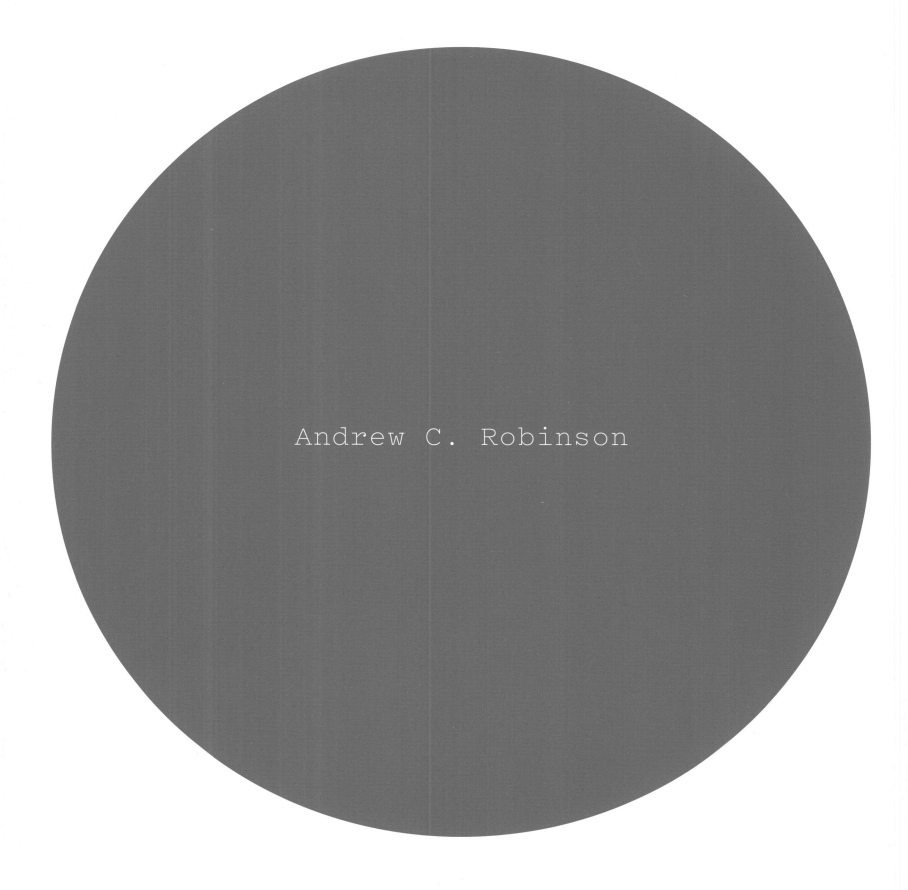

Andrew C. Robinson

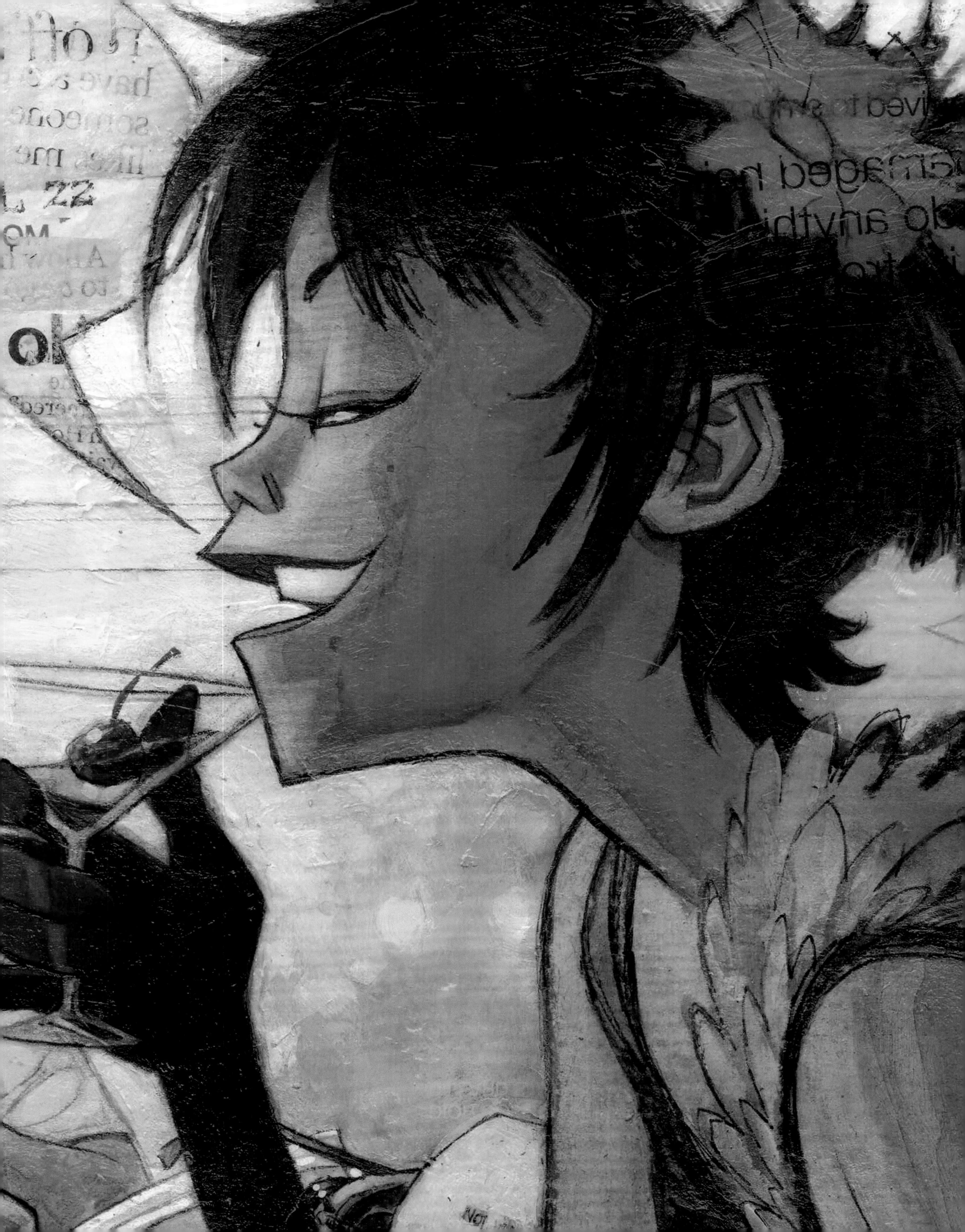

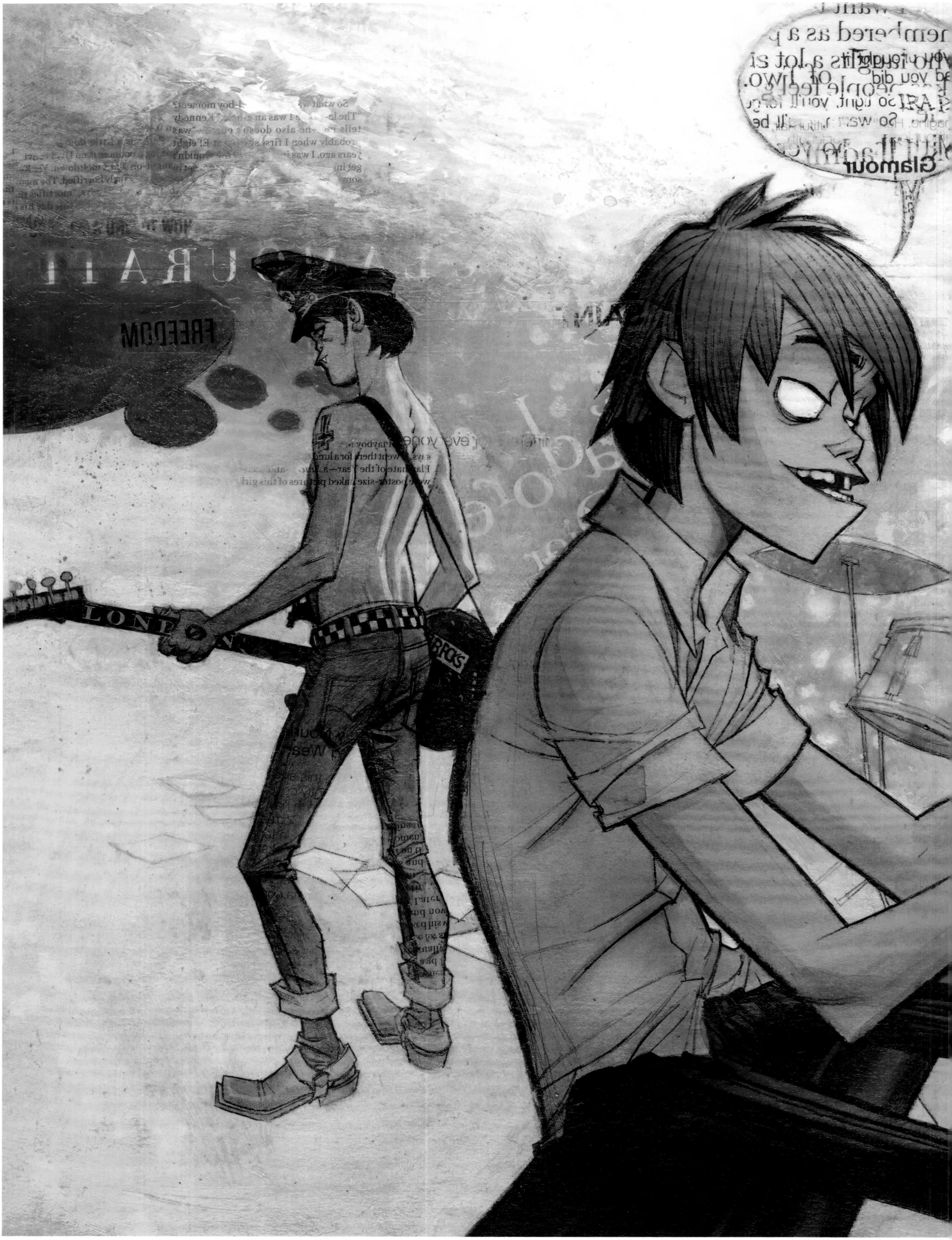

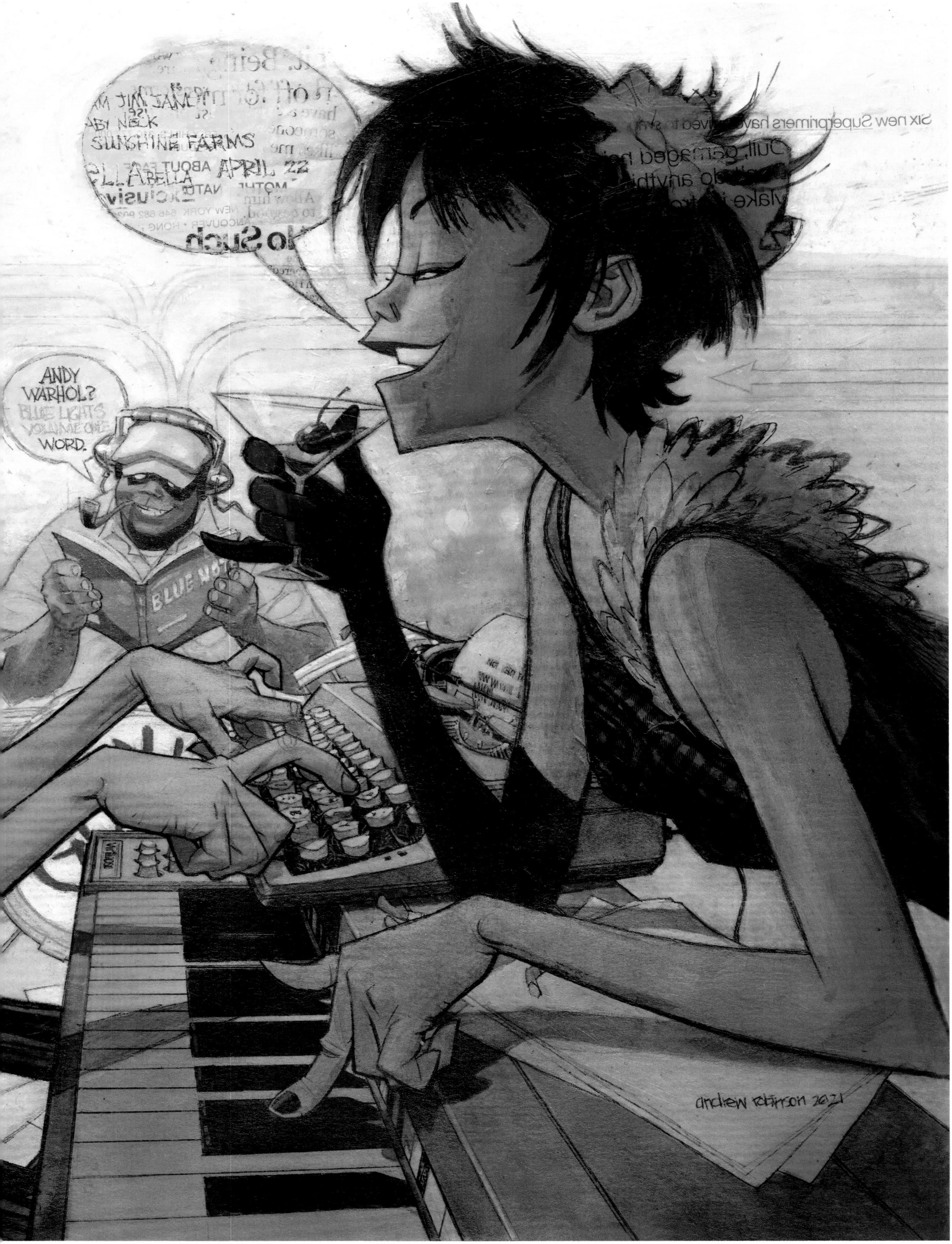
ANDY WARHOL?
BLUE LIGHTS
VOLUME ONE
WORD.
SUNSHINE FARMS
APRIL 22
andrew robinson 2021

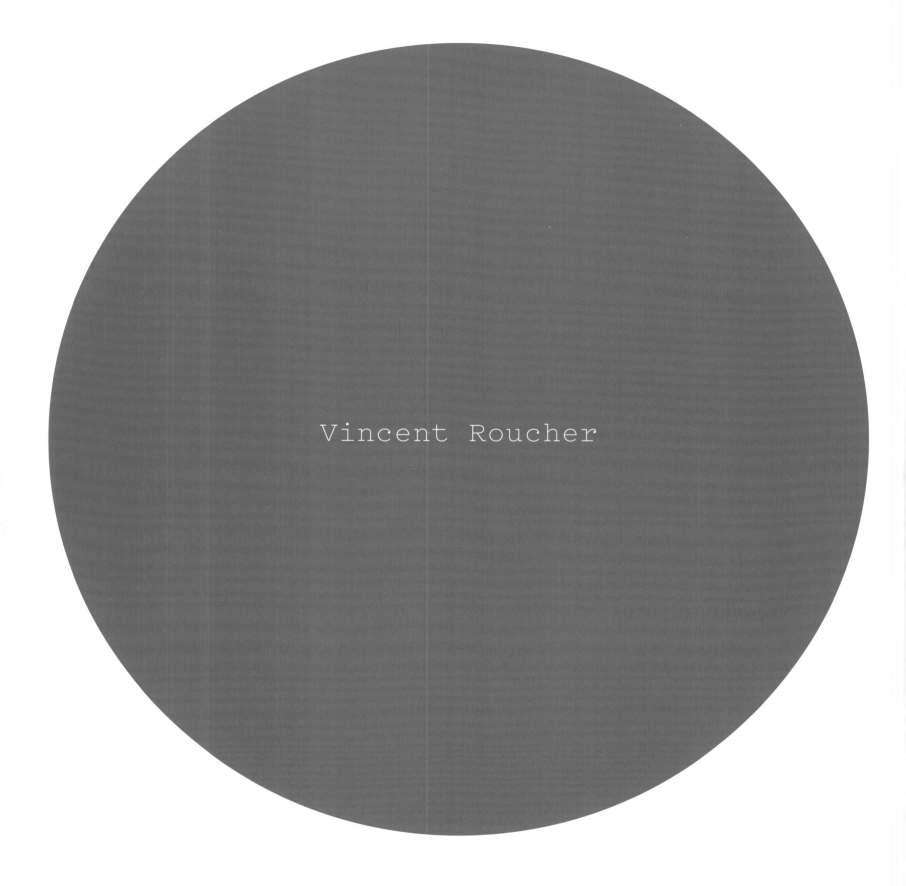

Vincent Roucher

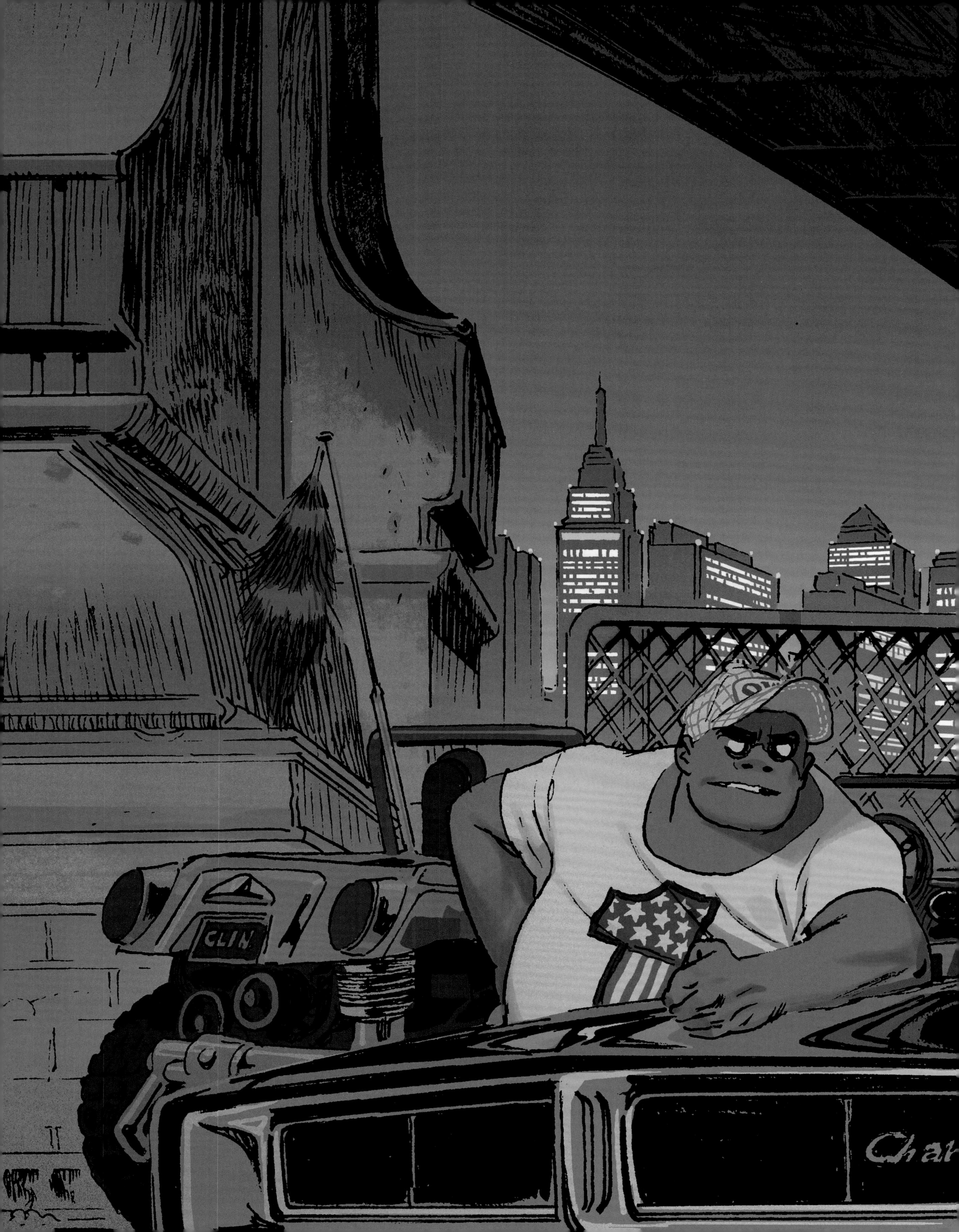

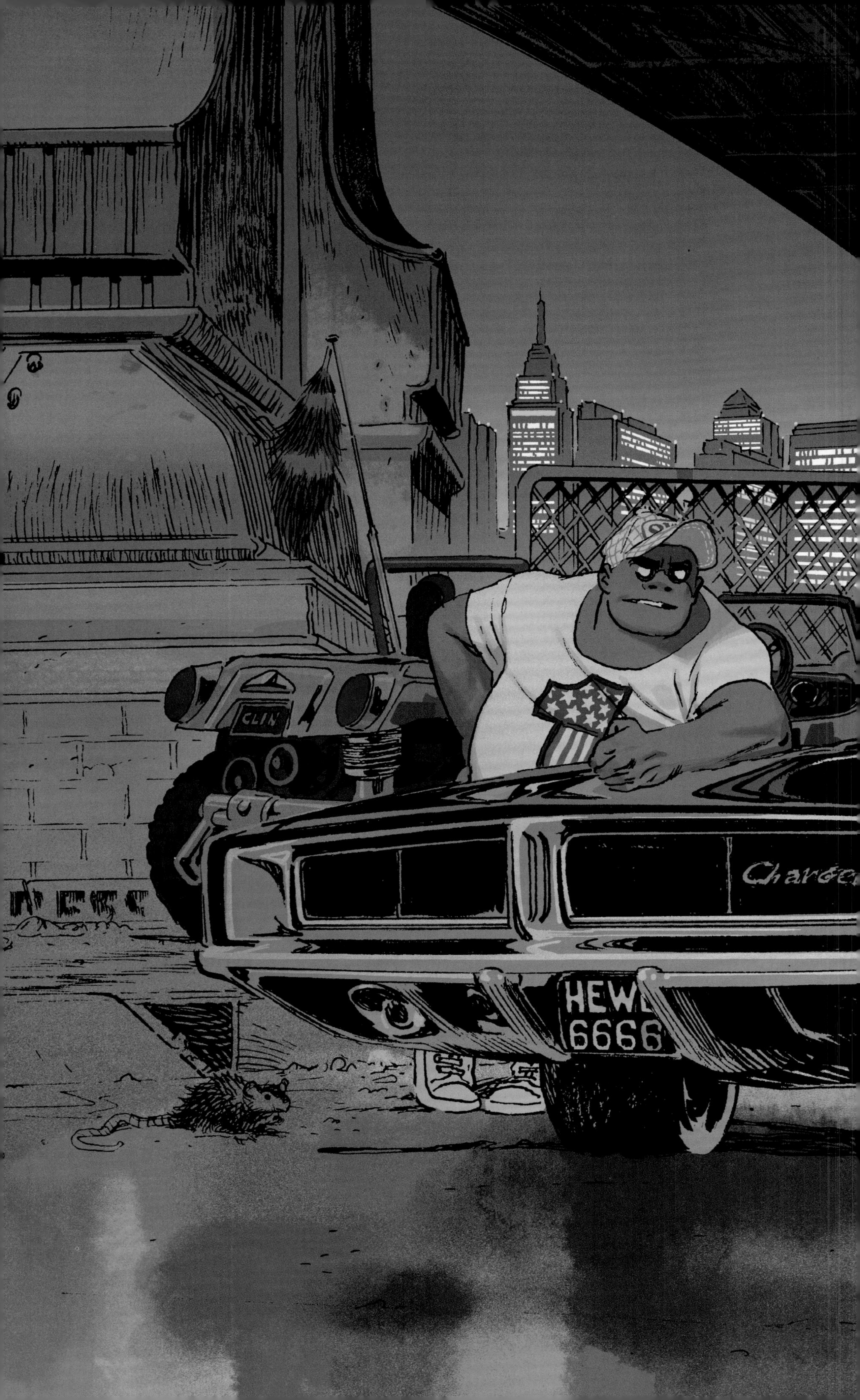
CLIN
6666

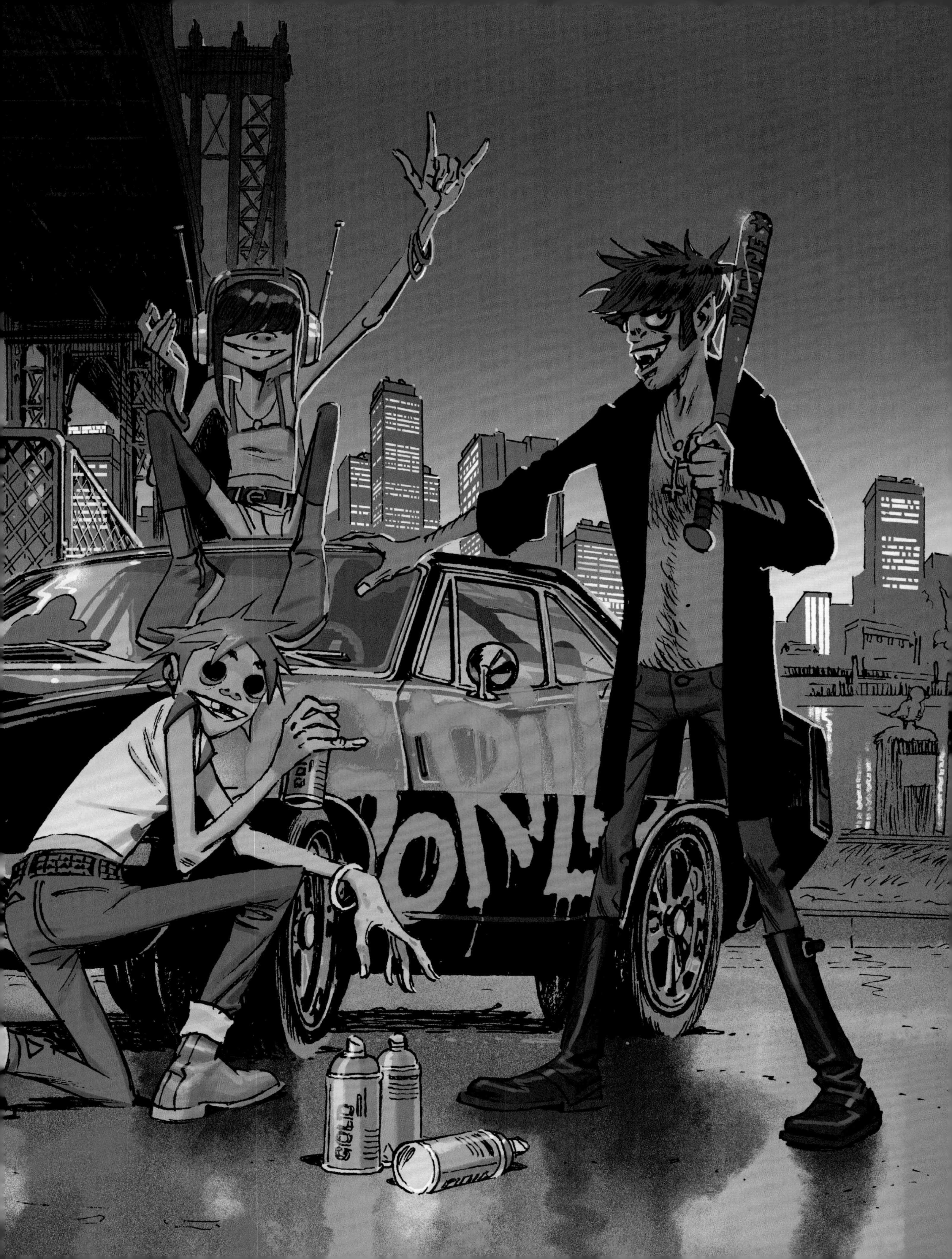

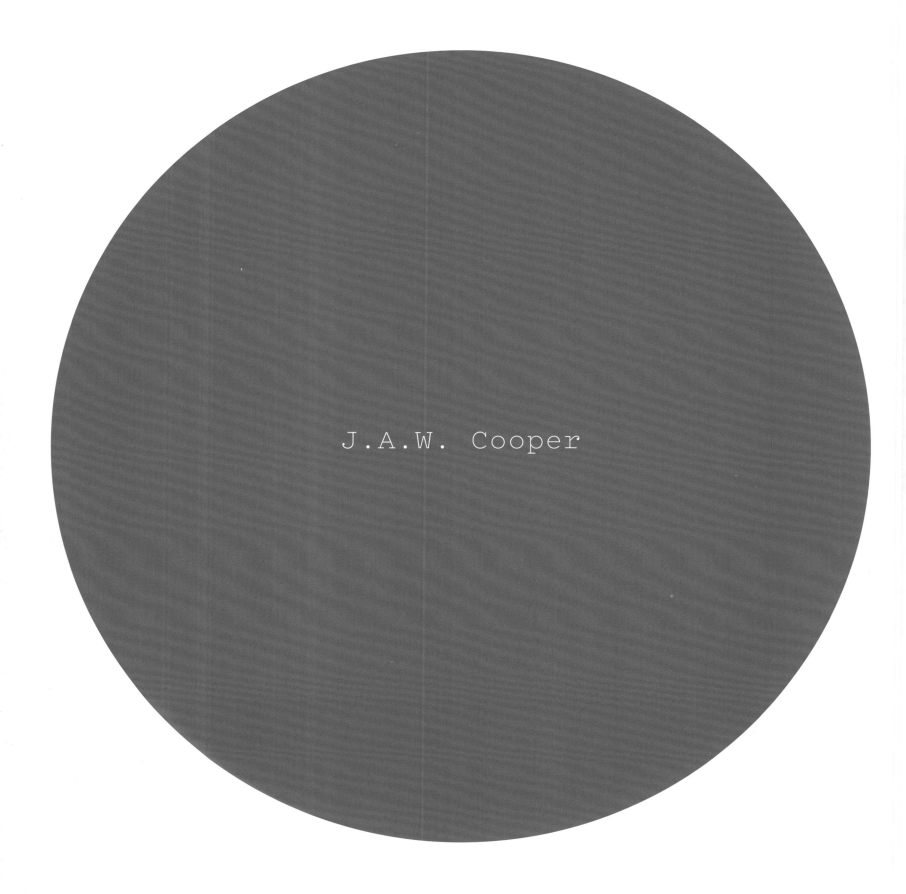

J.A.W. Cooper

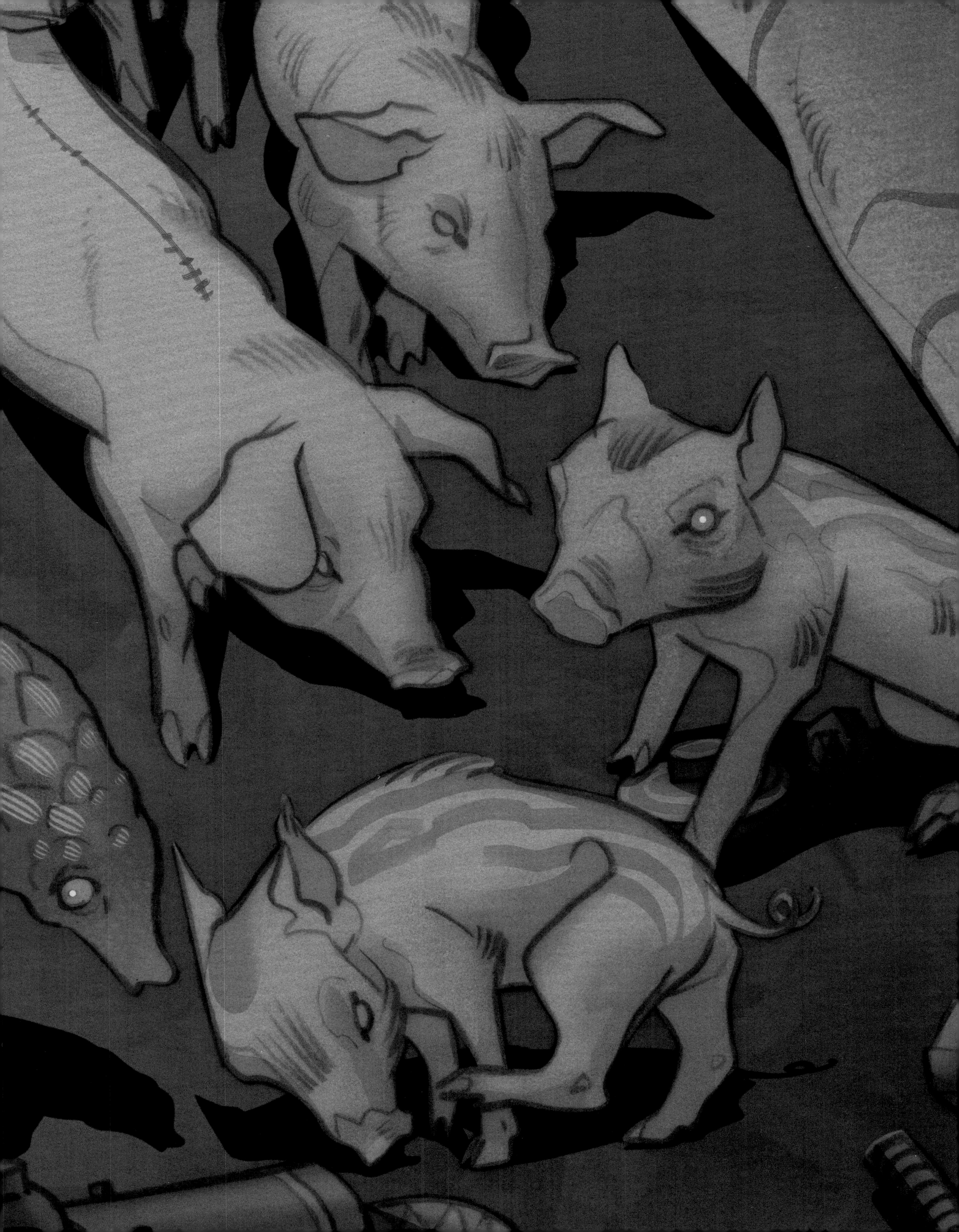

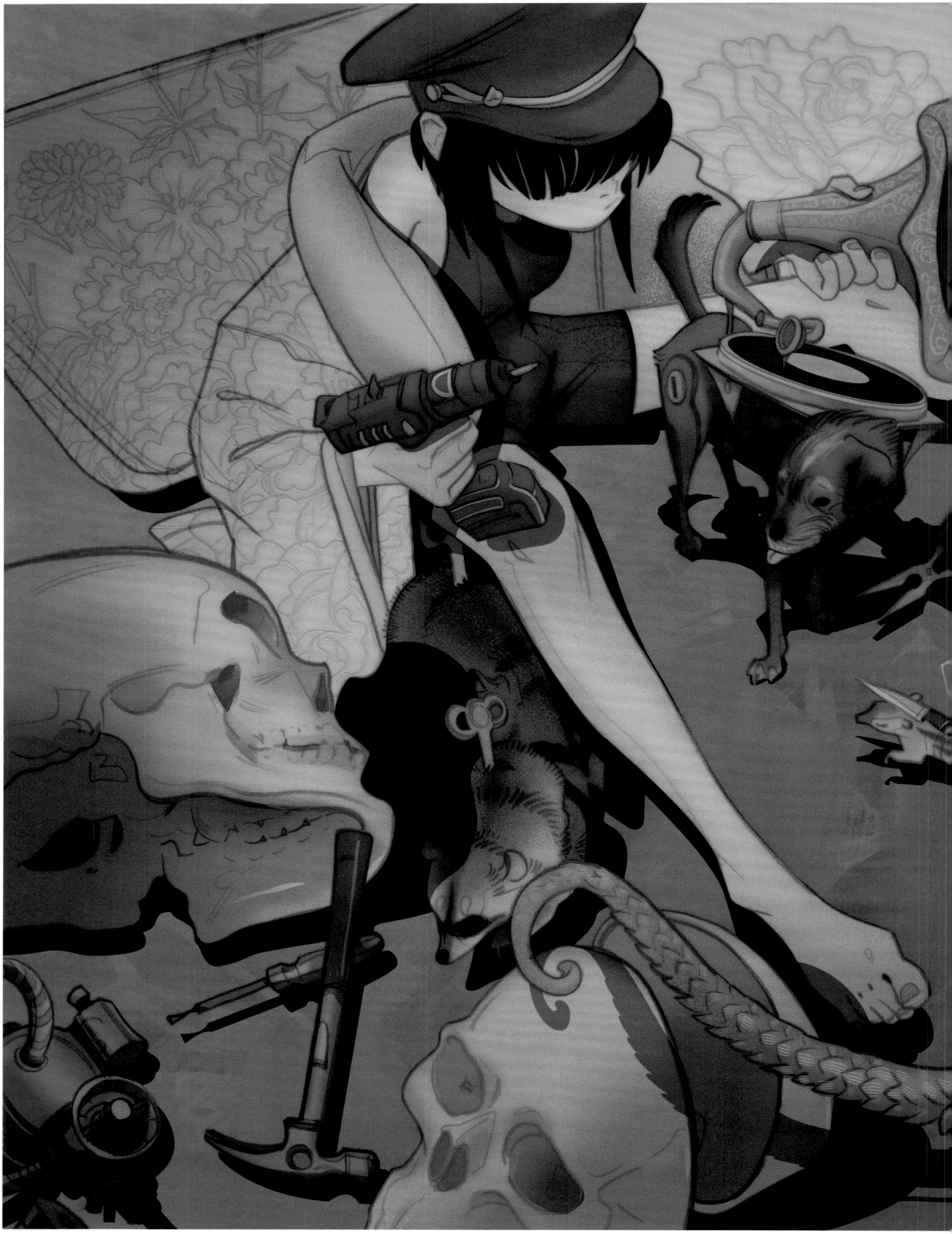

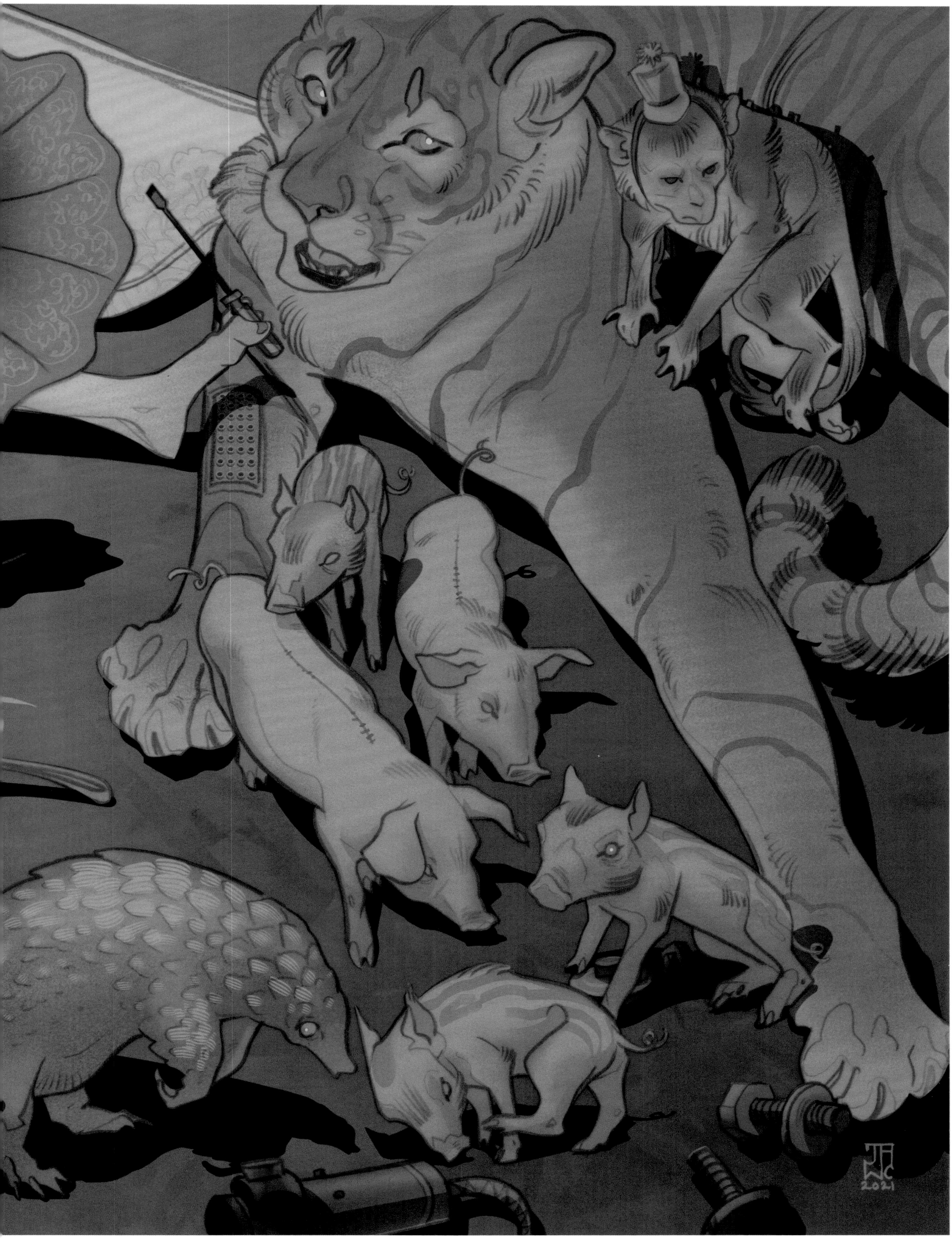

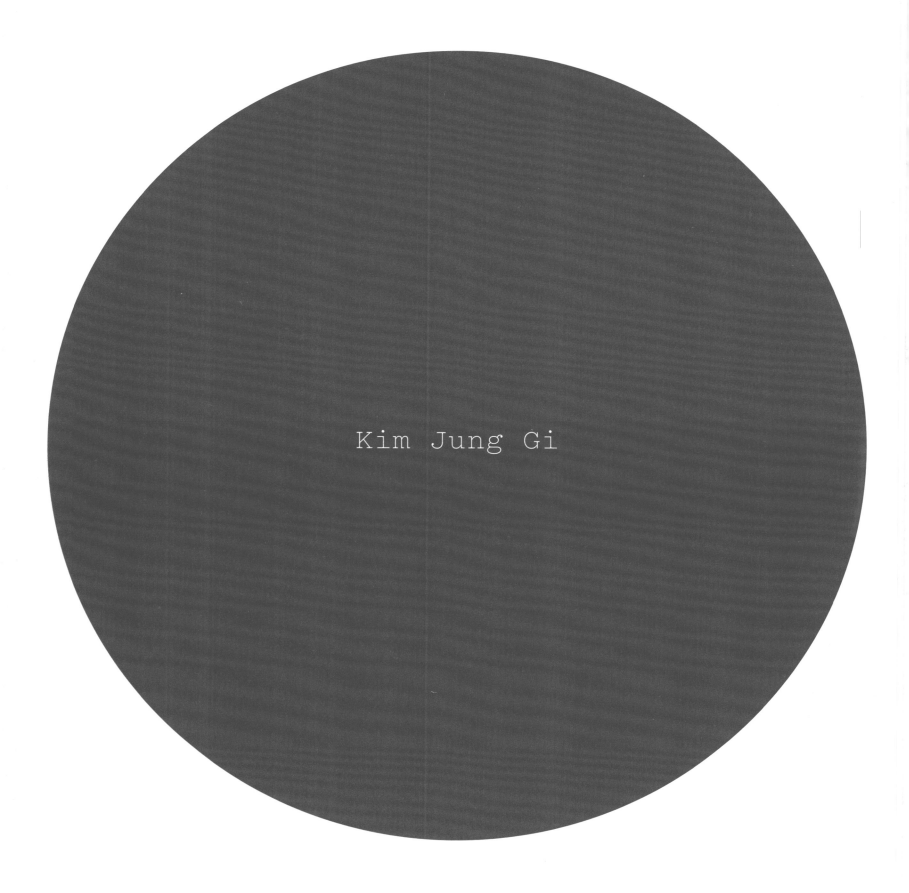

Kim Jung Gi

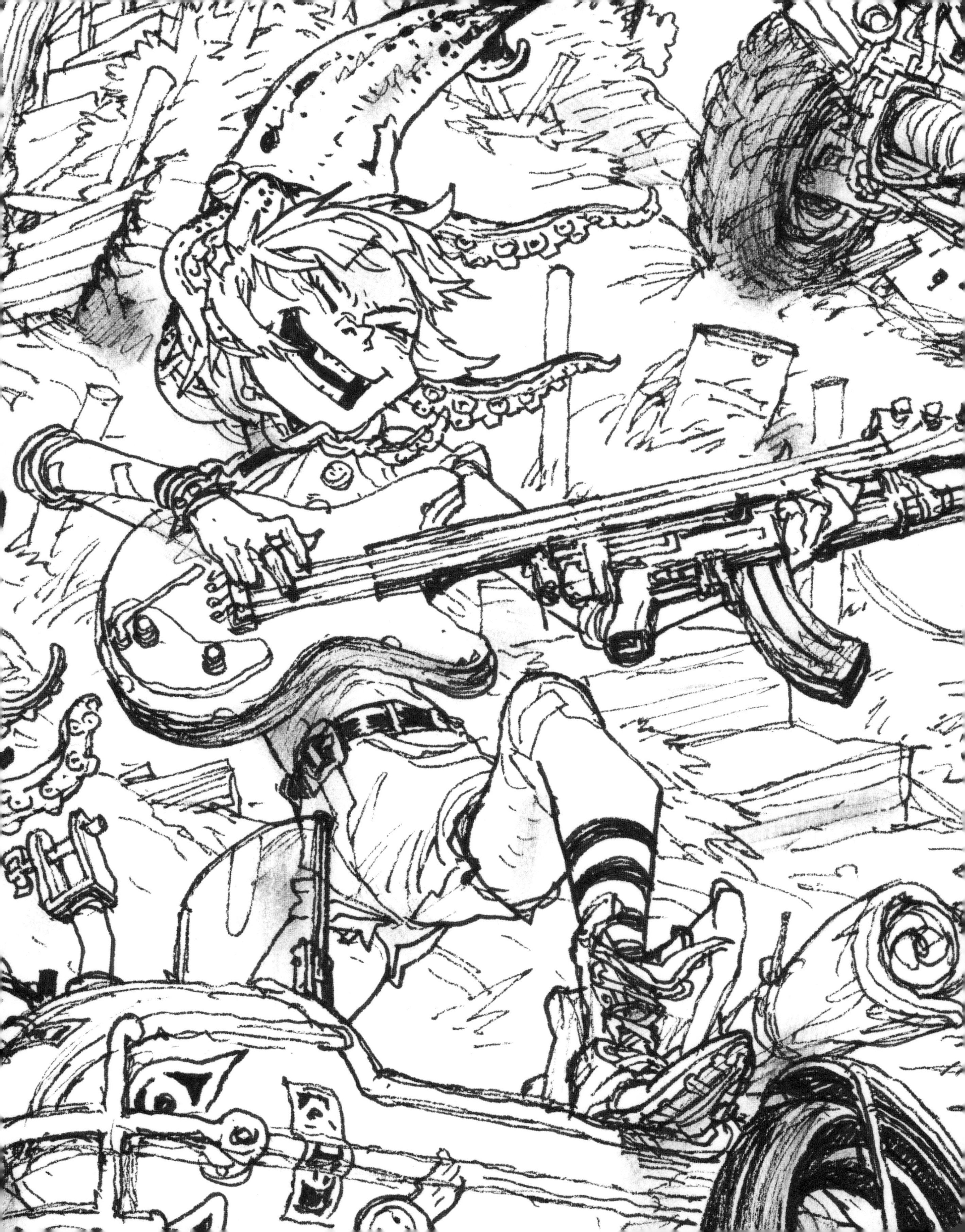

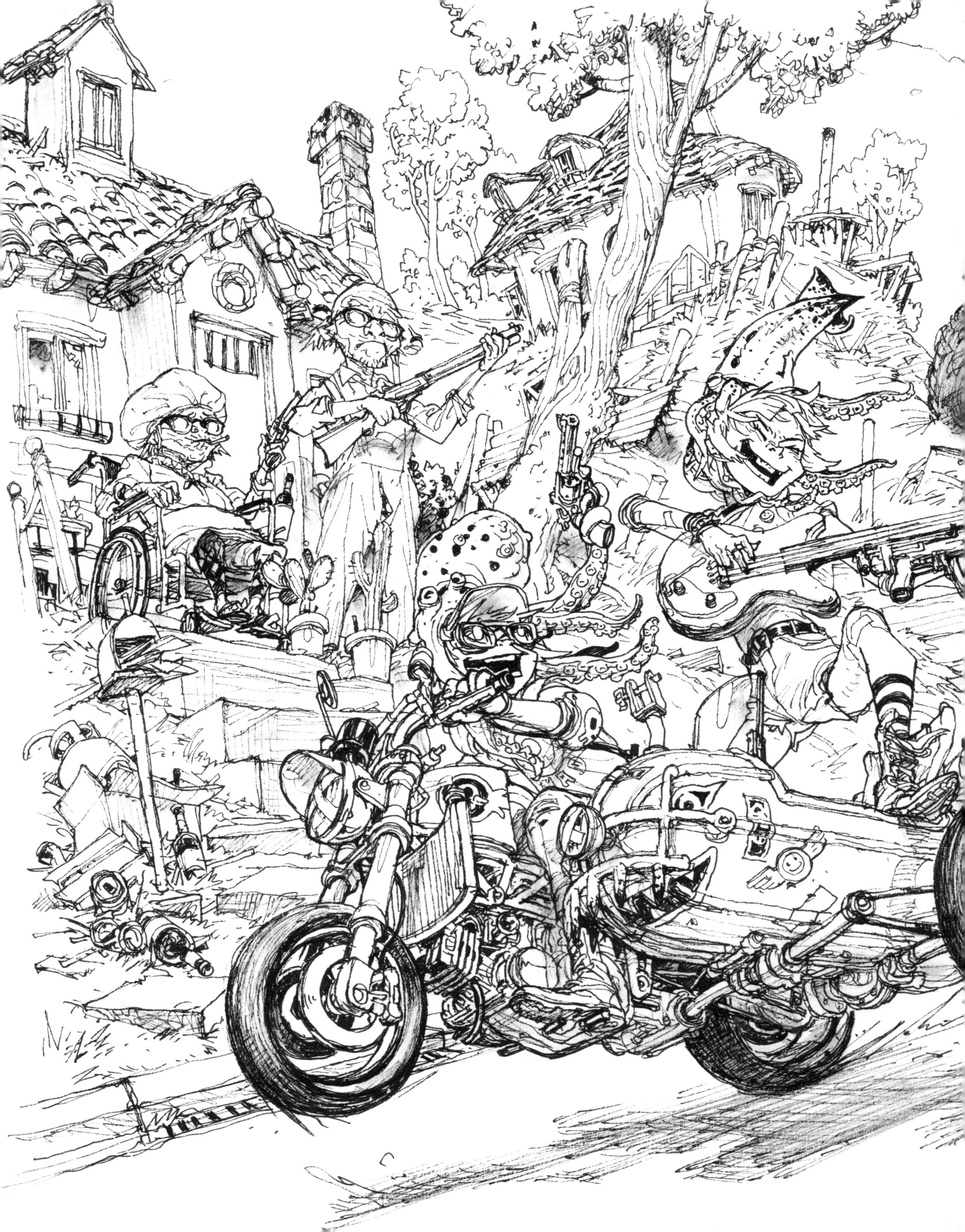

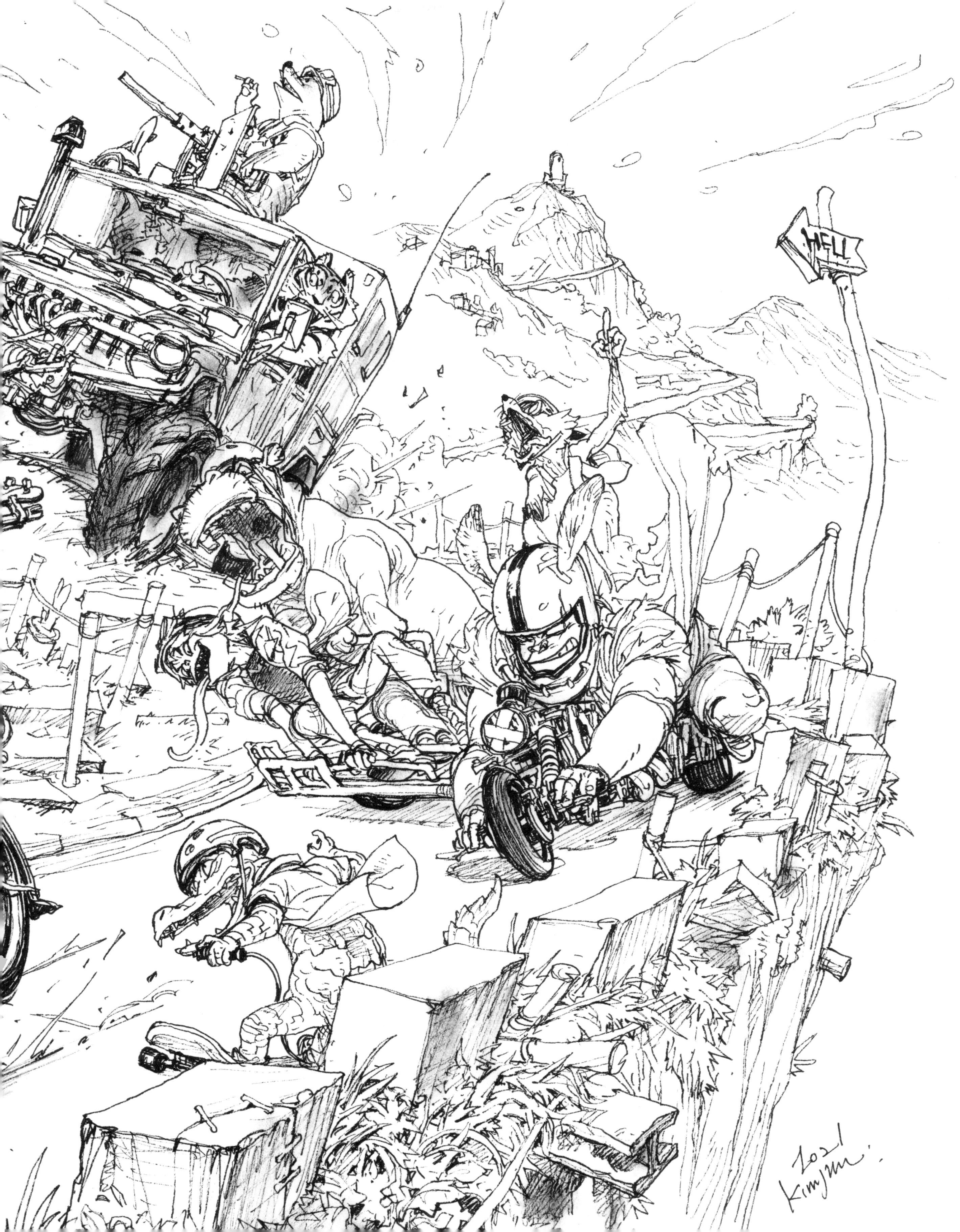
HELL

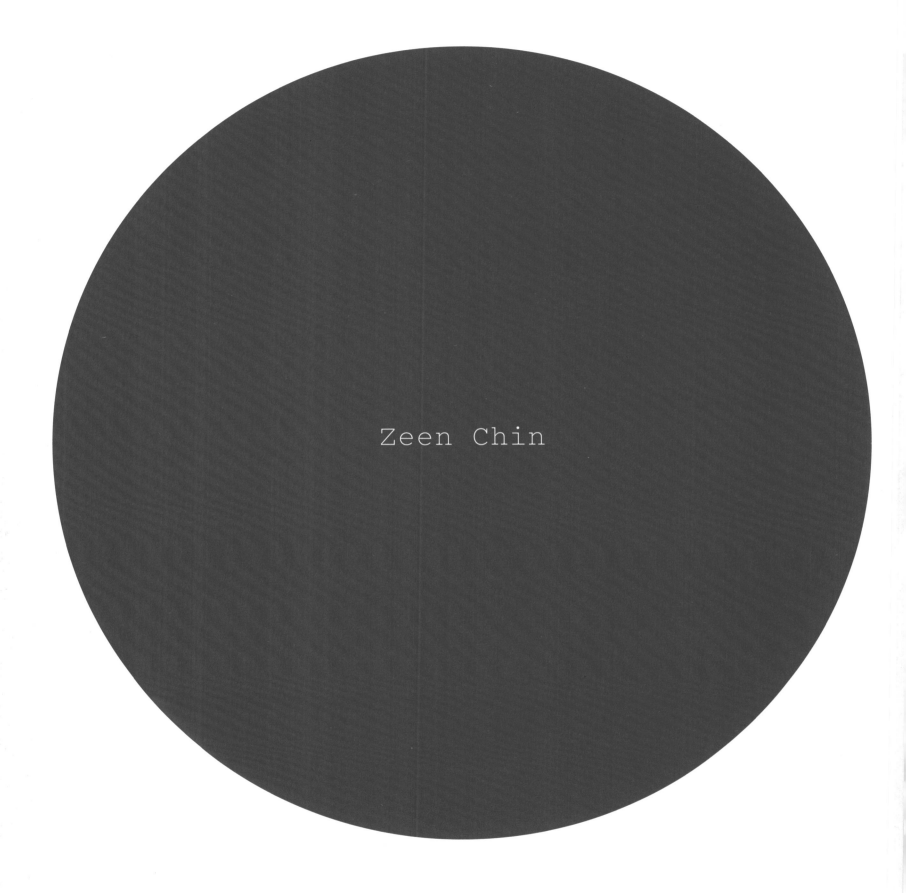

Zeen Chin

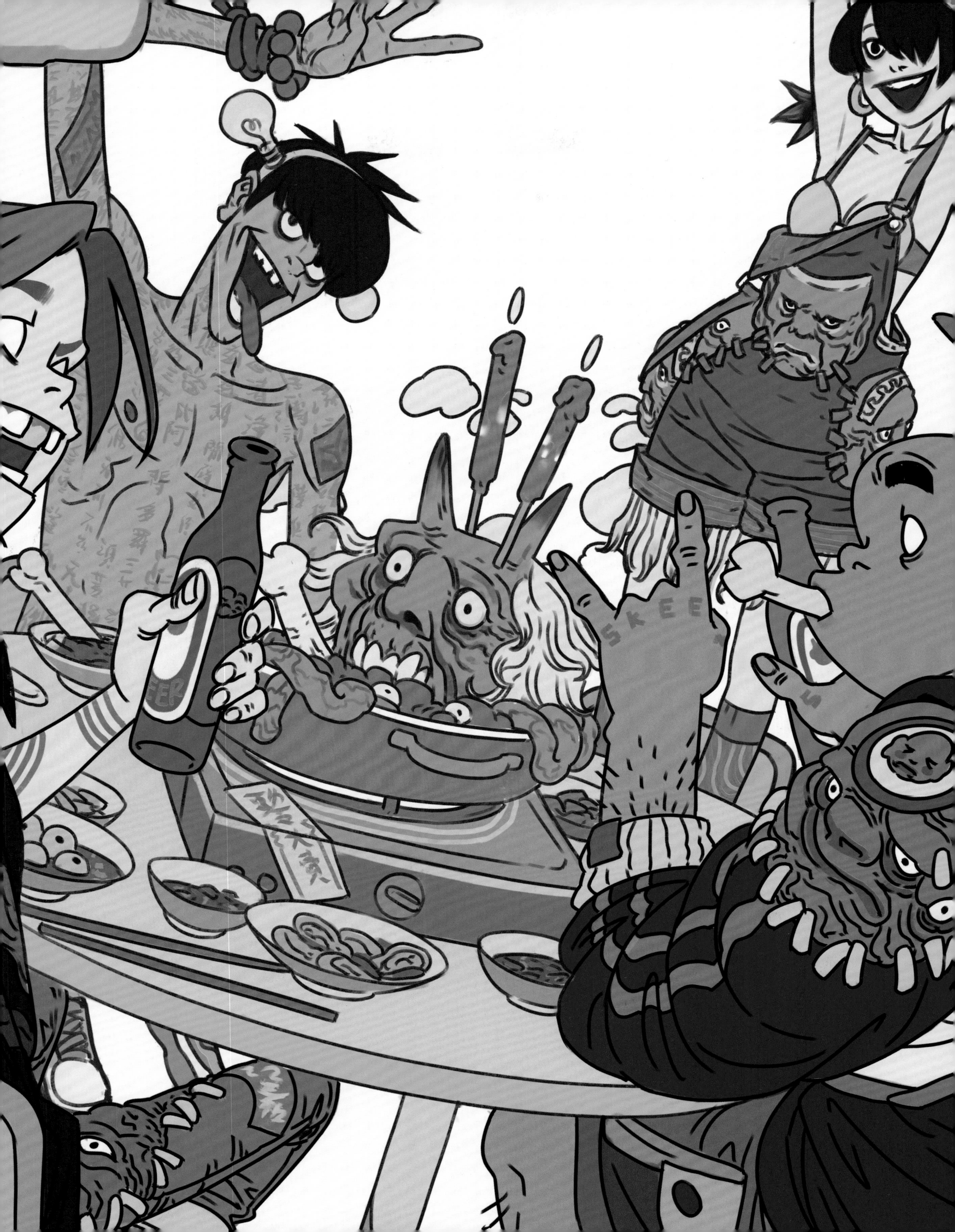
SKEE

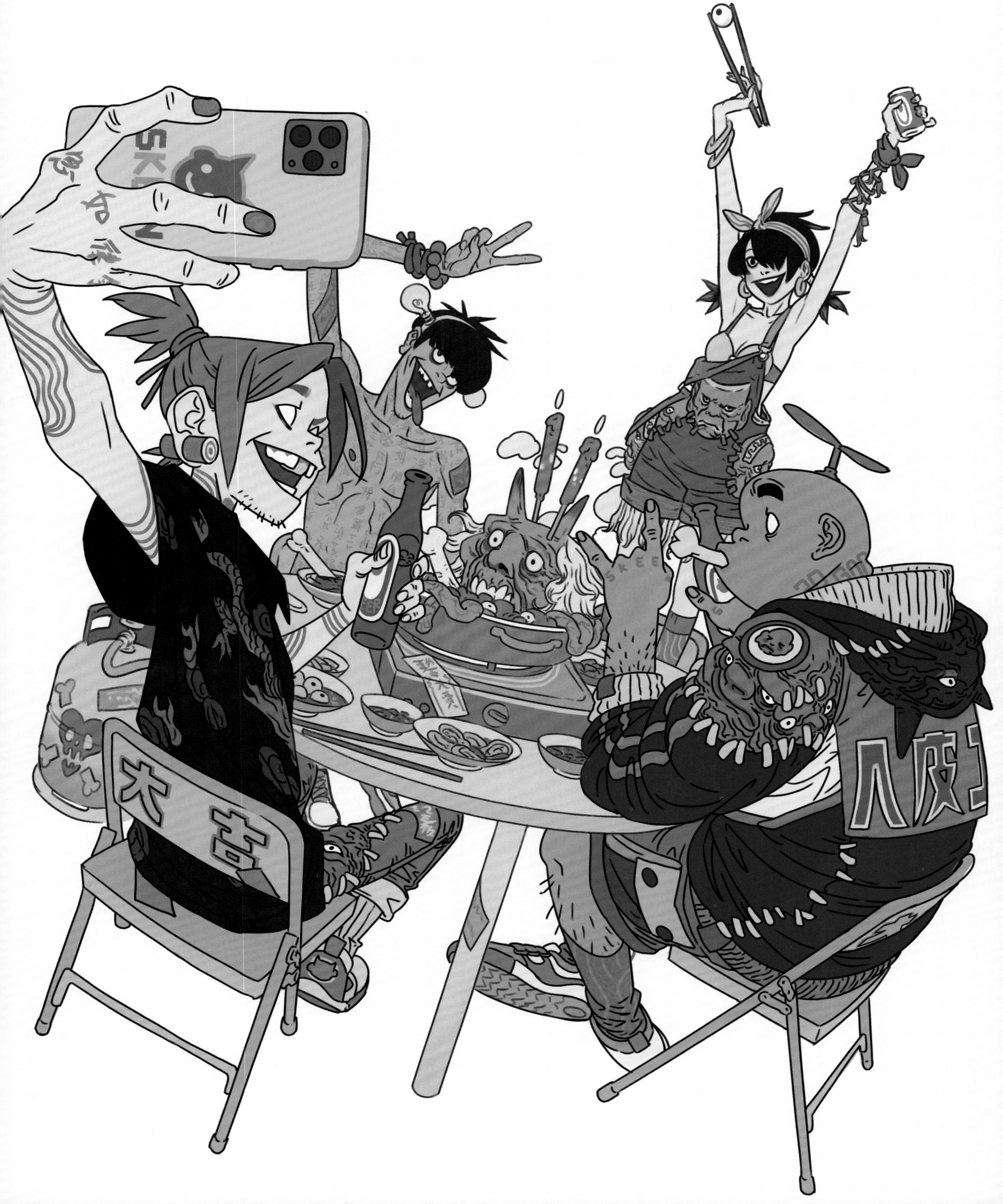
大
吉
SKEE
入夜

Kerbcrawlerghost

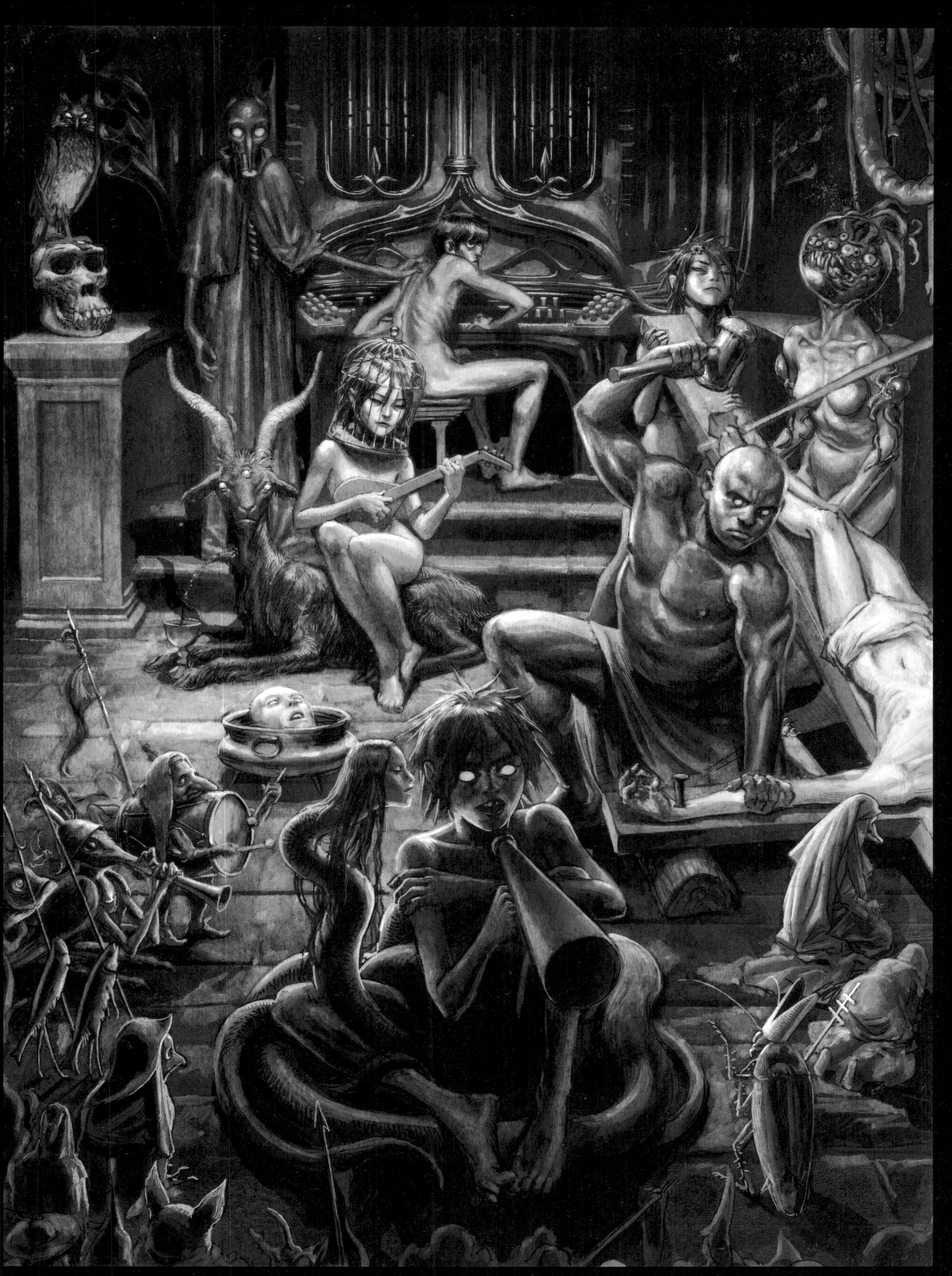

ASCENSION

DRAWINGS BY KERBCRAWLERGHOST

SOUTH PACIFIC OCEAN, APPROXIMATELY TWO THOUSAND FATHOMS BENEATH **POINT NEMO**...

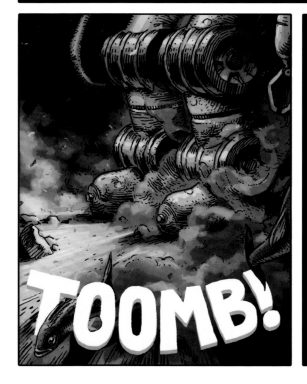

TOOMB!

"PROGRESS REPORT, THREE NINE ZERO. SUSPENSE IS KILLING ME."

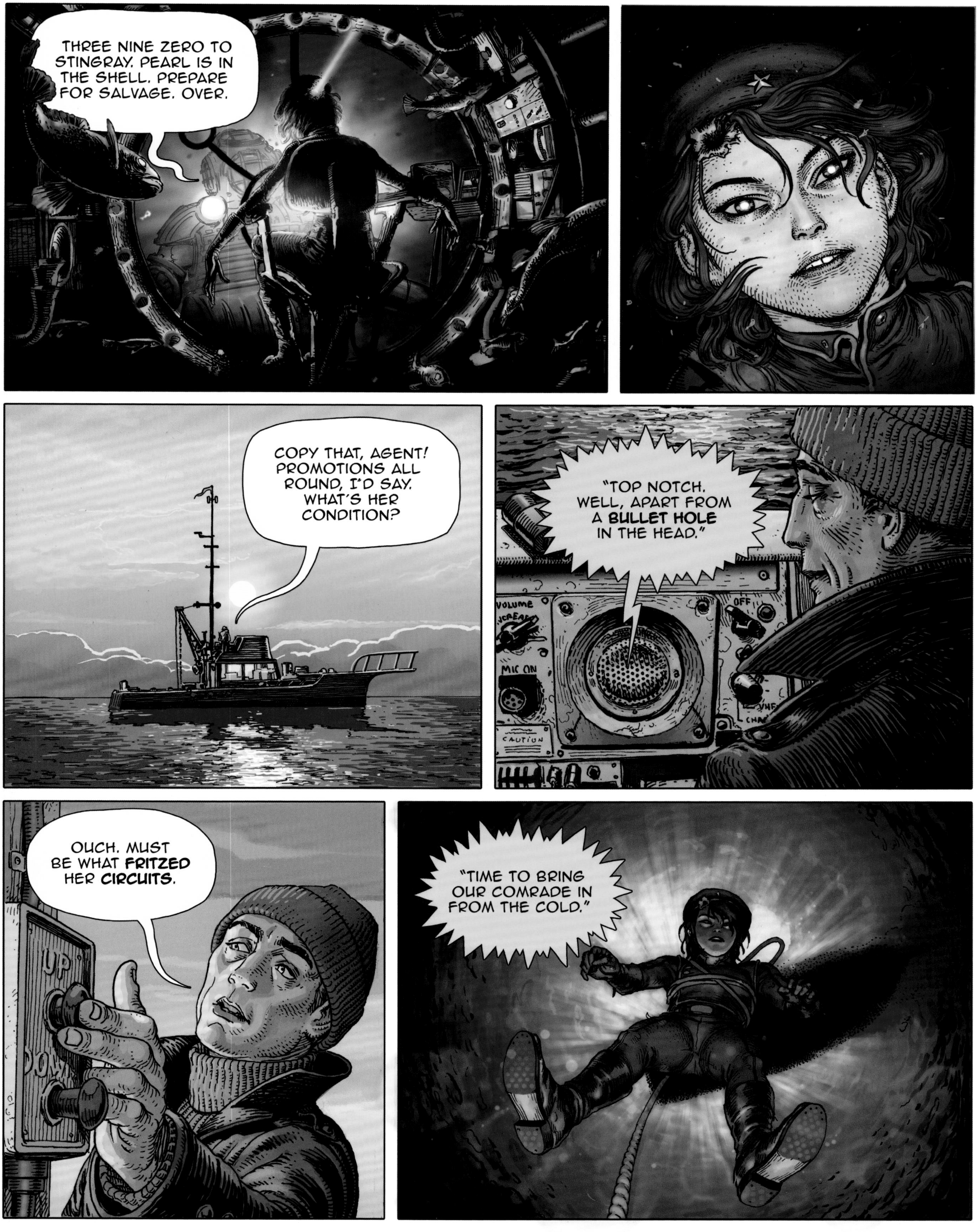
THREE NINE ZERO TO STINGRAY. PEARL IS IN THE SHELL. PREPARE FOR SALVAGE. OVER.
COPY THAT, AGENT! PROMOTIONS ALL ROUND, I'D SAY. WHAT'S HER CONDITION?
"TOP NOTCH. WELL, APART FROM A **BULLET HOLE** IN THE HEAD."
VOLUME
MIC ON
OFF
CAUTION
OUCH. MUST BE WHAT **FRITZED** HER **CIRCUITS**.
UP
"TIME TO BRING OUR COMRADE IN FROM THE COLD."

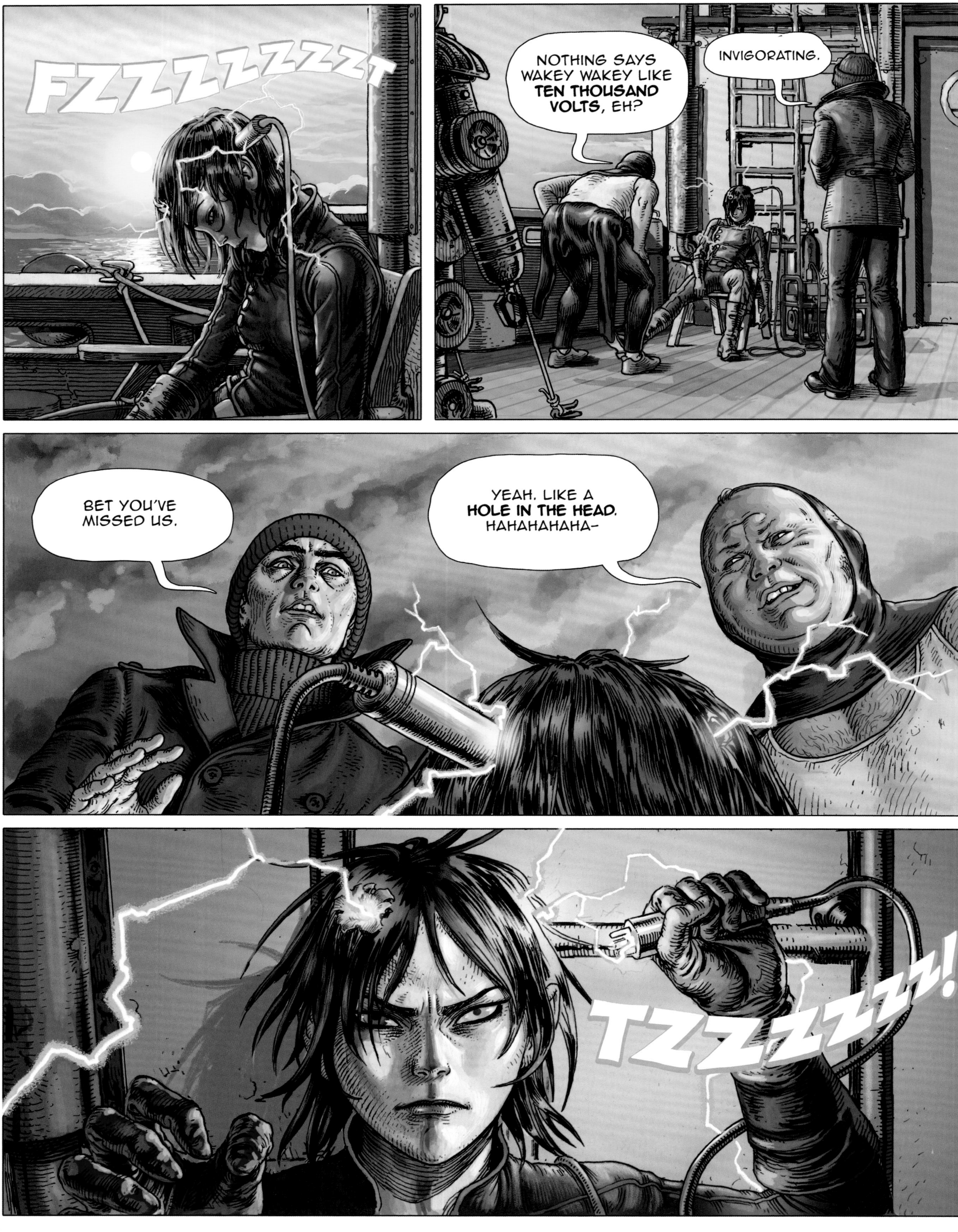
FZZZZZZZT
NOTHING SAYS WAKEY WAKEY LIKE **TEN THOUSAND VOLTS**, EH?
INVIGORATING.
BET YOU'VE MISSED US.
YEAH. LIKE A **HOLE IN THE HEAD.** HAHAHAHAHA-
TZZZZZZ!

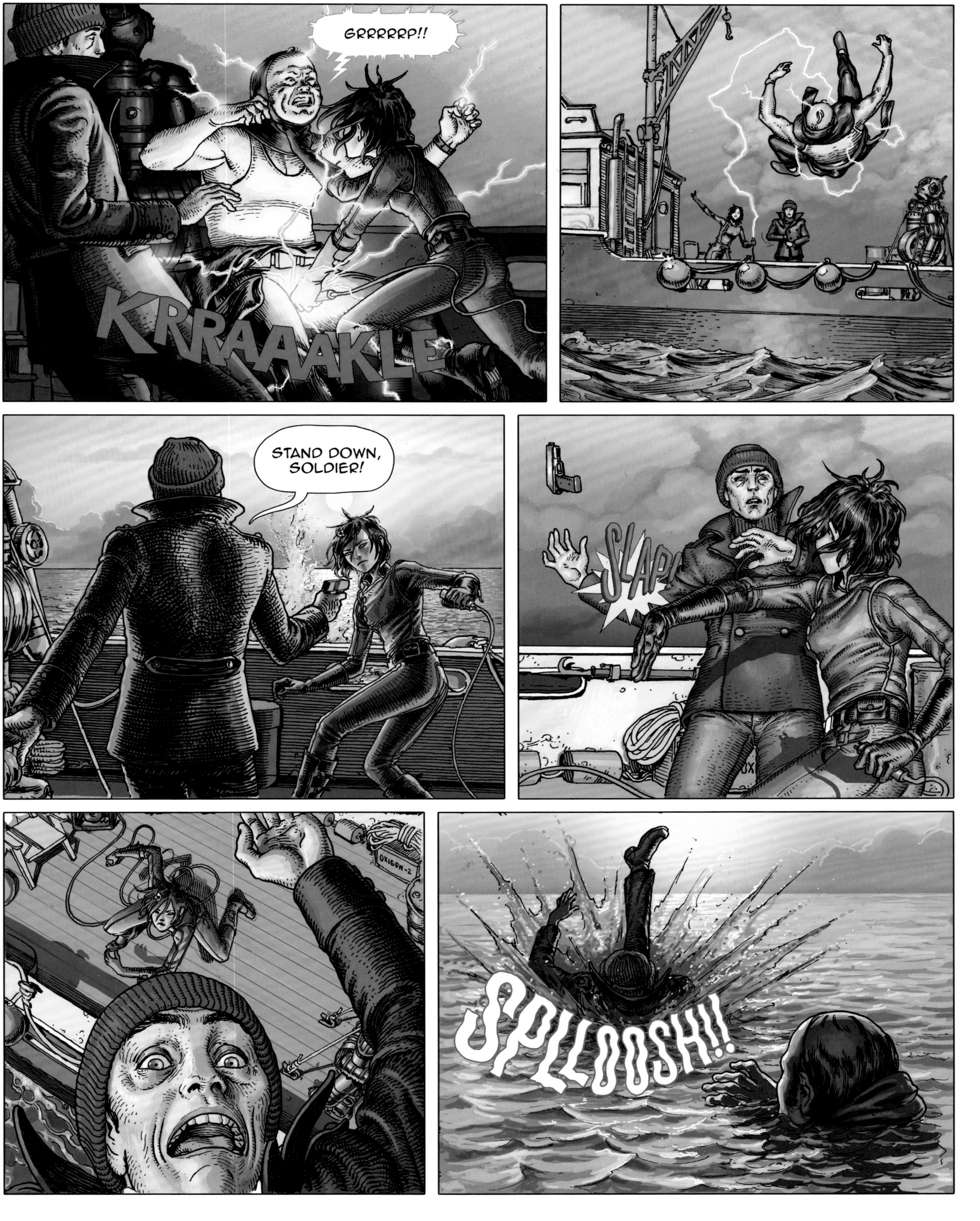
GRRRRRP!!
KRRAAAKLE
STAND DOWN, SOLDIER!
SLAP!
OXIGEN-2
SPLOOSH!!

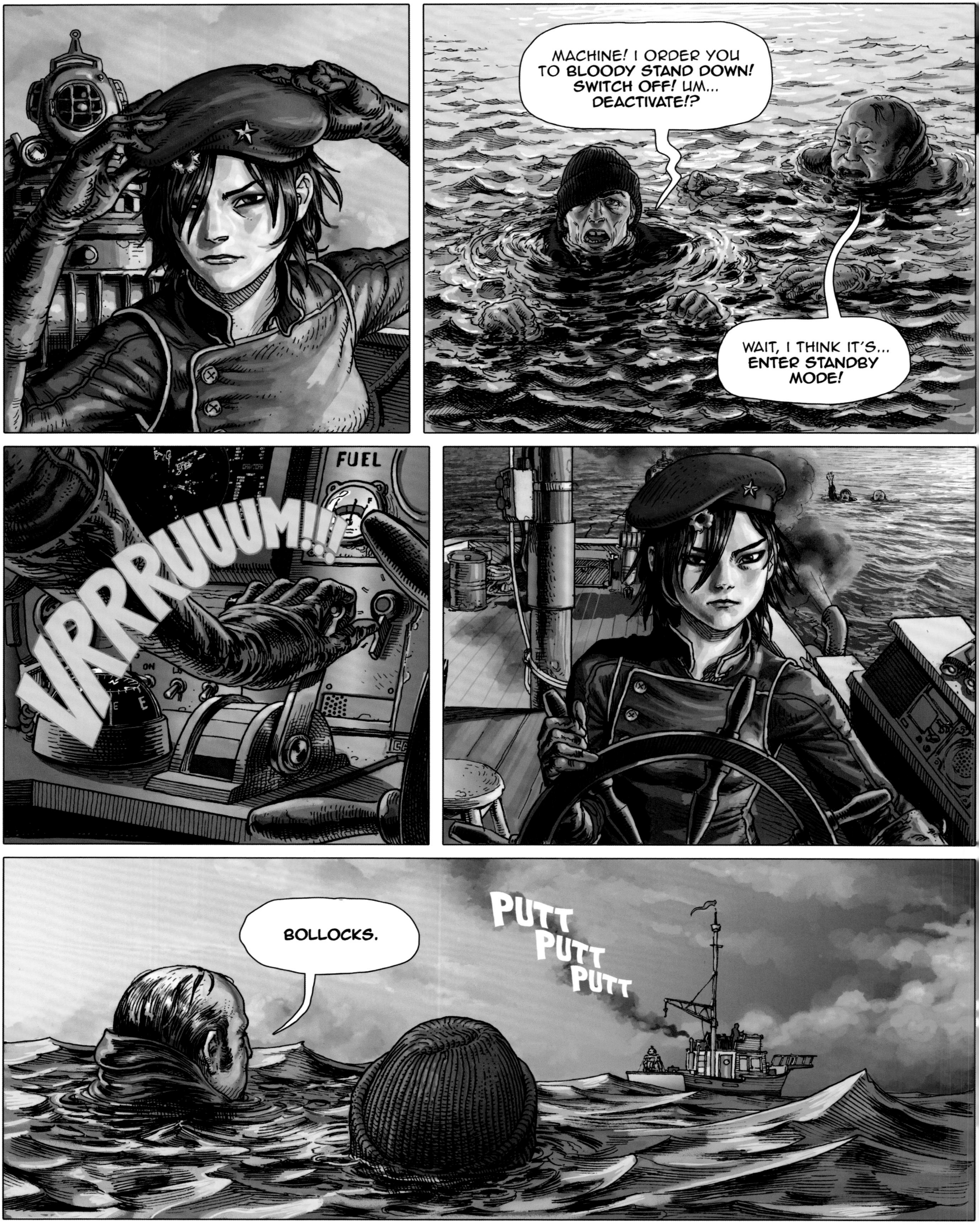
MACHINE! I ORDER YOU TO BLOODY STAND DOWN! SWITCH OFF! UM... DEACTIVATE!?
WAIT, I THINK IT'S... ENTER STANDBY MODE!
FUEL
VRRRUUUUM!!!
BOLLOCKS.
PUTT PUTT PUTT

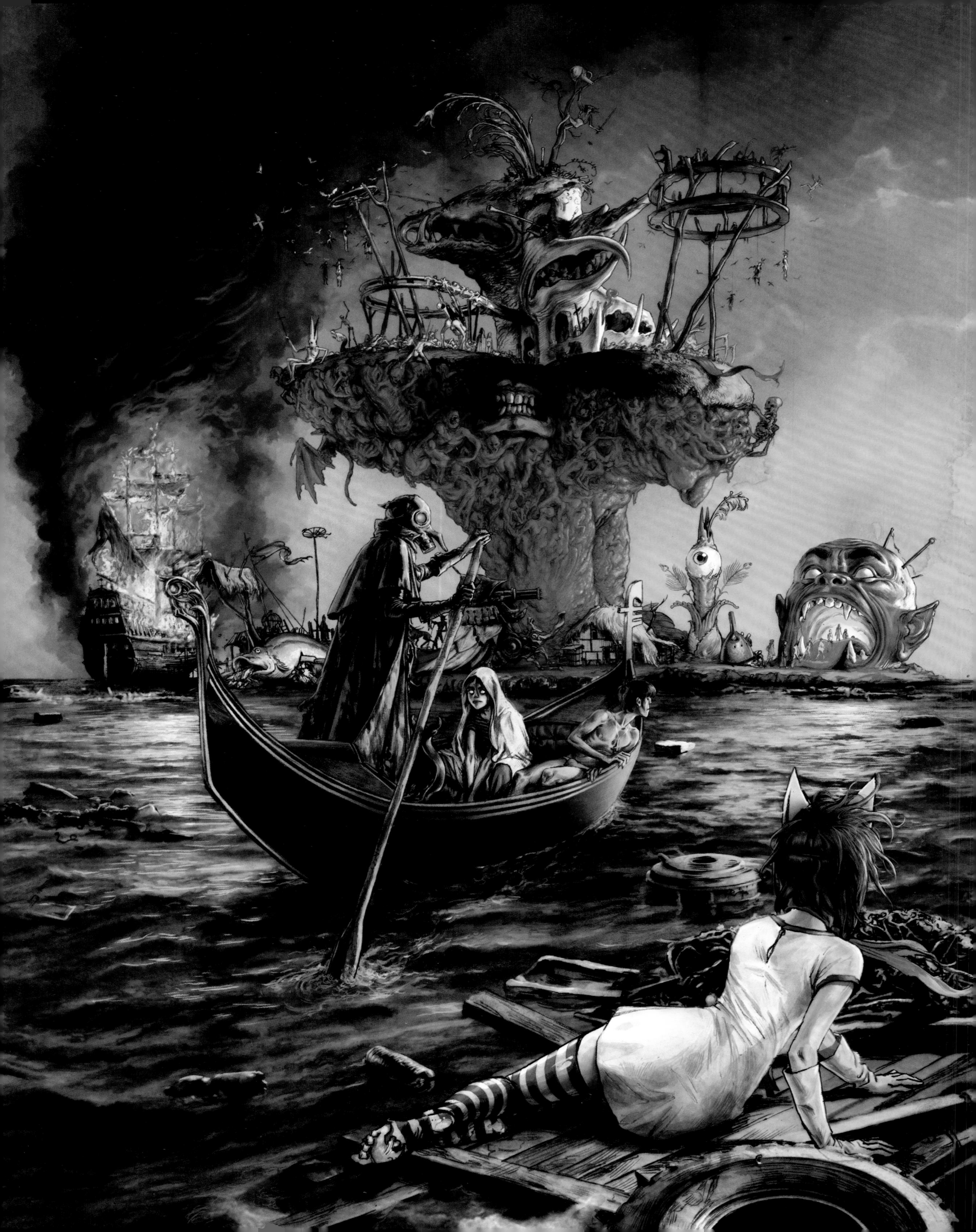

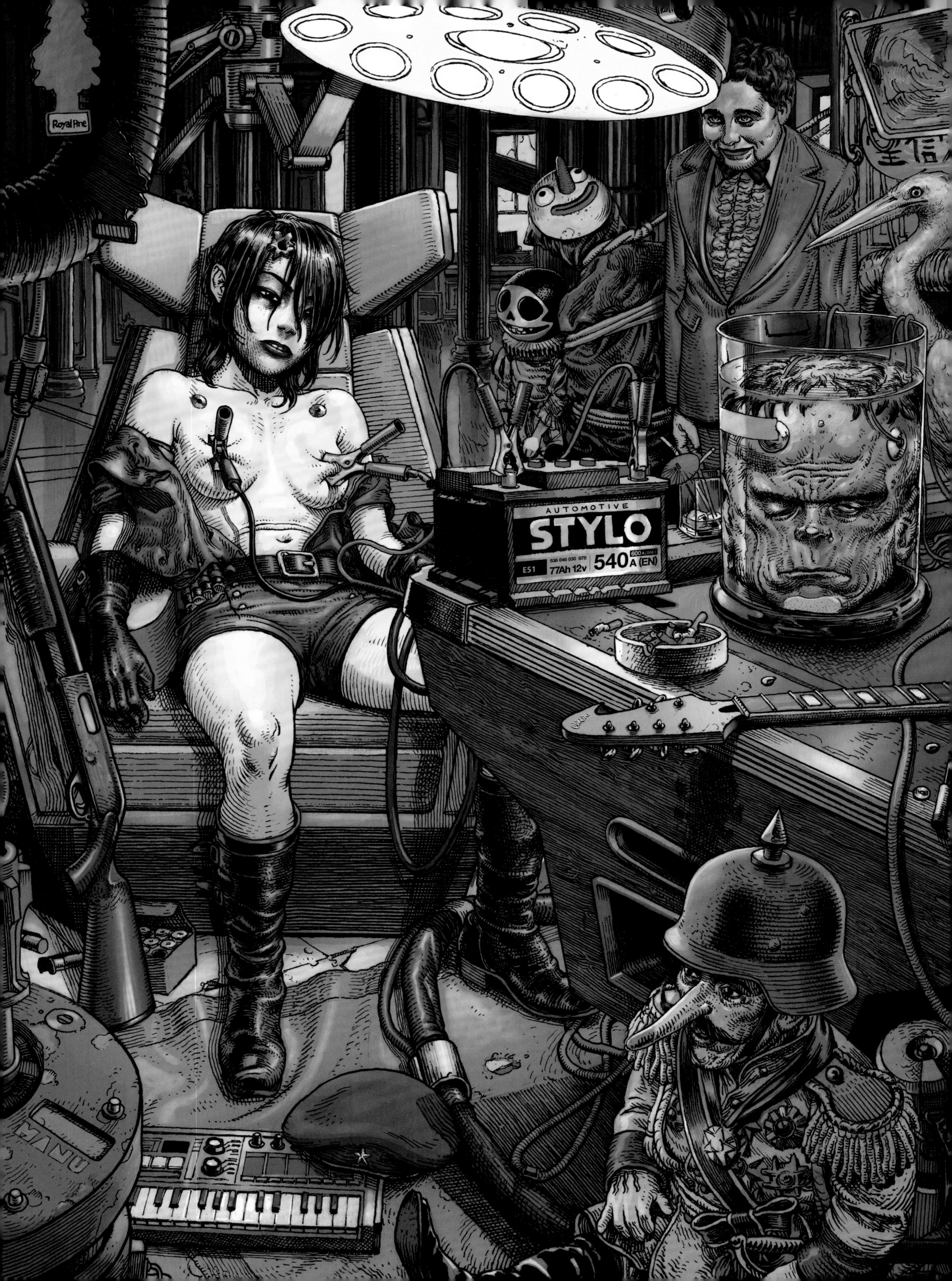
Royal Pine
AUTOMOTIVE
STYLO
536 046 030 078
E51
77Ah 12v
540 A (EN)
600 A (SAE)

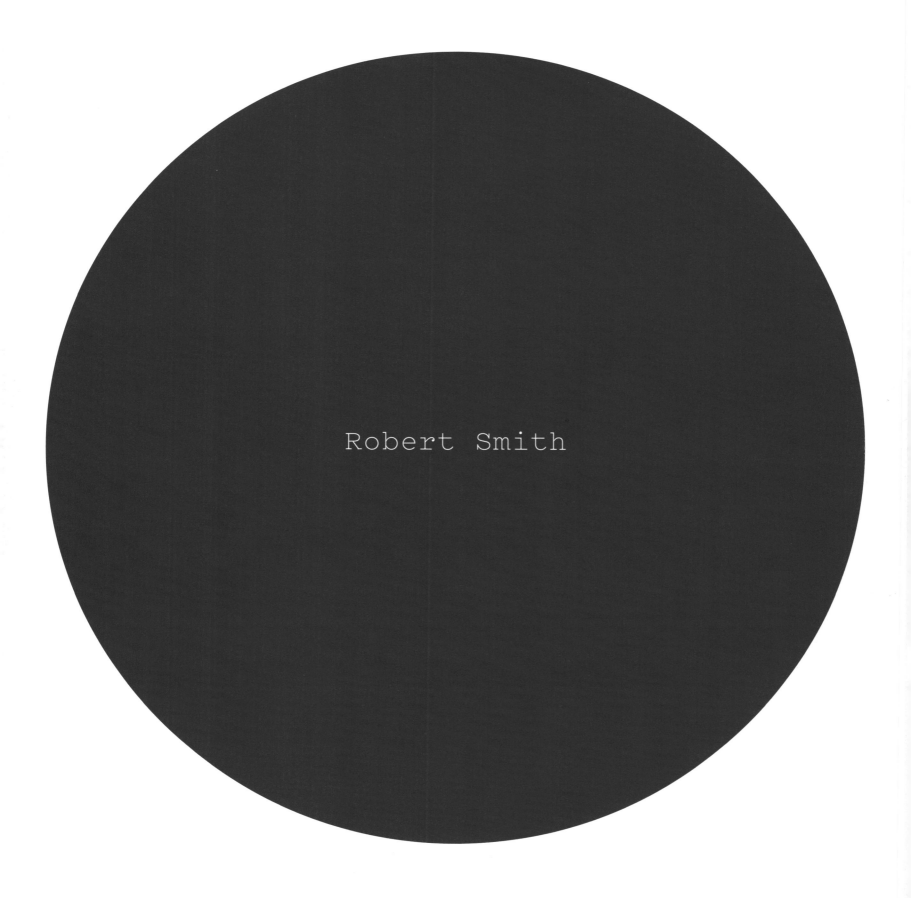

Robert Smith

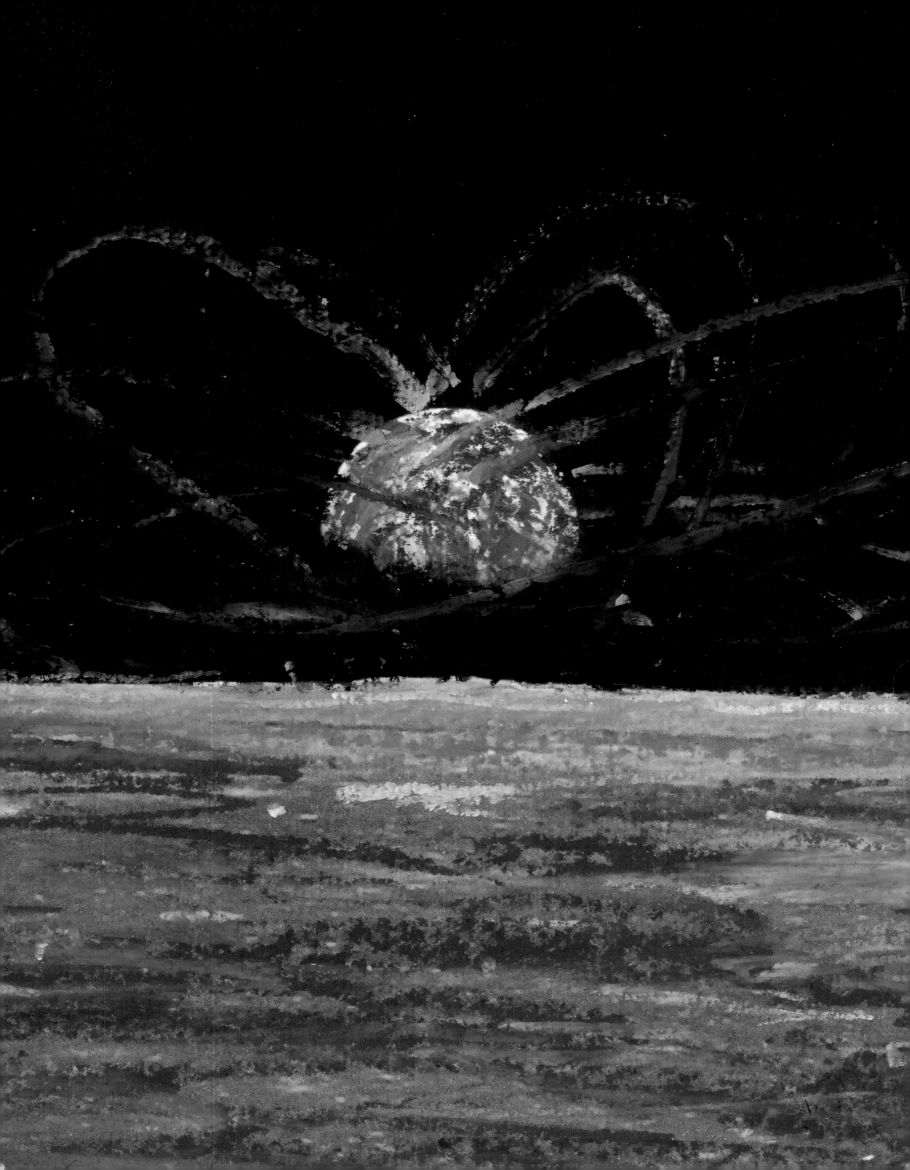

strange **STRANGE TIMES**

strange timez | words by rs

aka

spinning around the world at n

strange time to be alive

strange time to be alive

to be alive th

strange time

to see the light

strange time

to see the light

the sun comes up

until the sun comes up

spinning around until

spinning

around

spinning

spinning

black and white

black and white

spin round in

strange

at night

the world at night

spinning around the world

spinning around

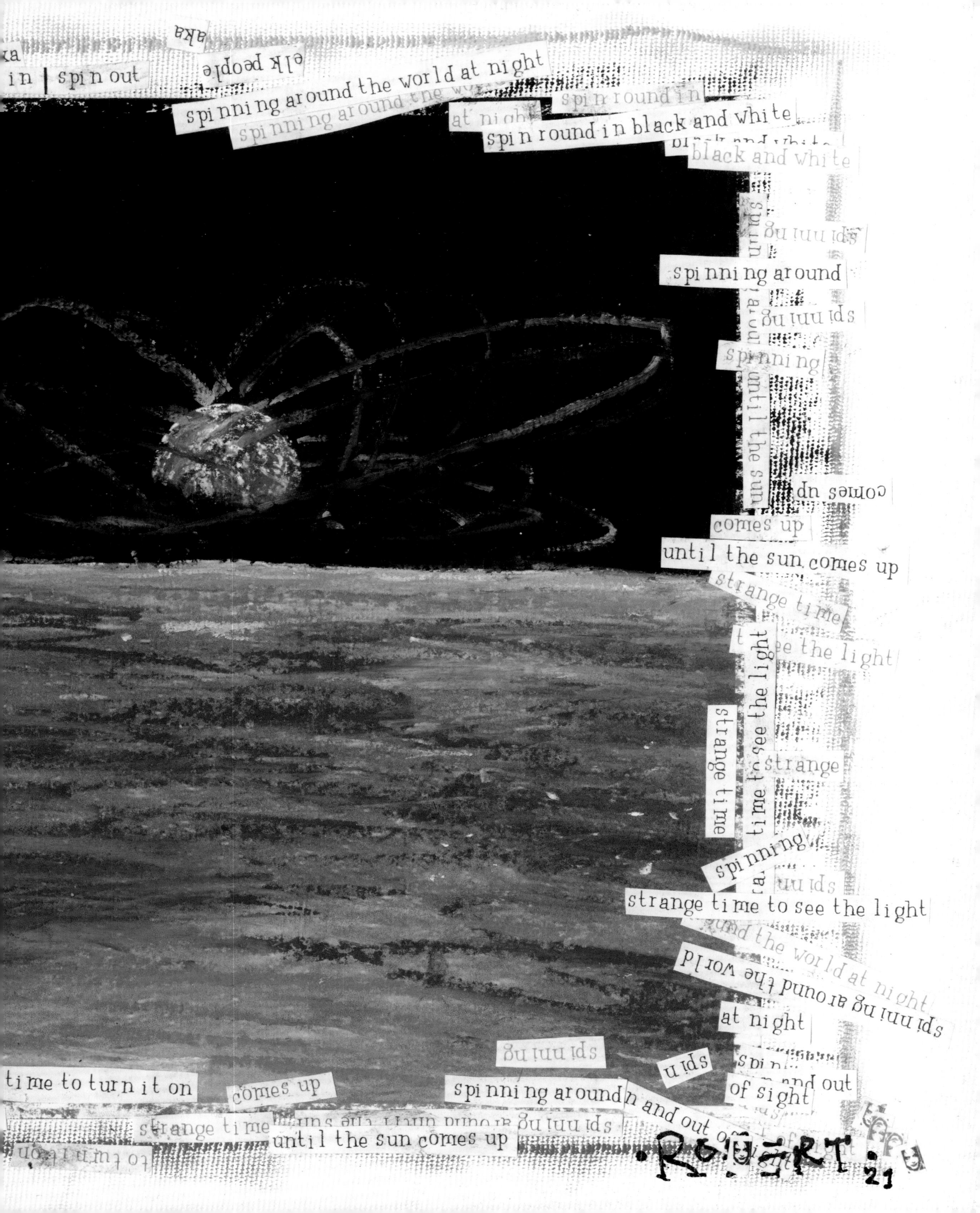
aka
in | spin out
elk people
spinning around the world at night
spinning around the world
spin round in
at night
spin round in black and white
black and white
spinning
spinning around
spinning
spinning
until the sun
comes up
comes up
until the sun comes up
strange time
to see the light
time to see the light
strange time
strange
spinning
spinning
strange time to see the light
around the world at night
spinning around the world
at night
spinning
spin
time to turn it on
comes up
spinning around
in and out of sight
of sight
spin in and out
strange time
until the sun comes up
spinning around
to turn it on
ROBERT
21

Anna Cattish

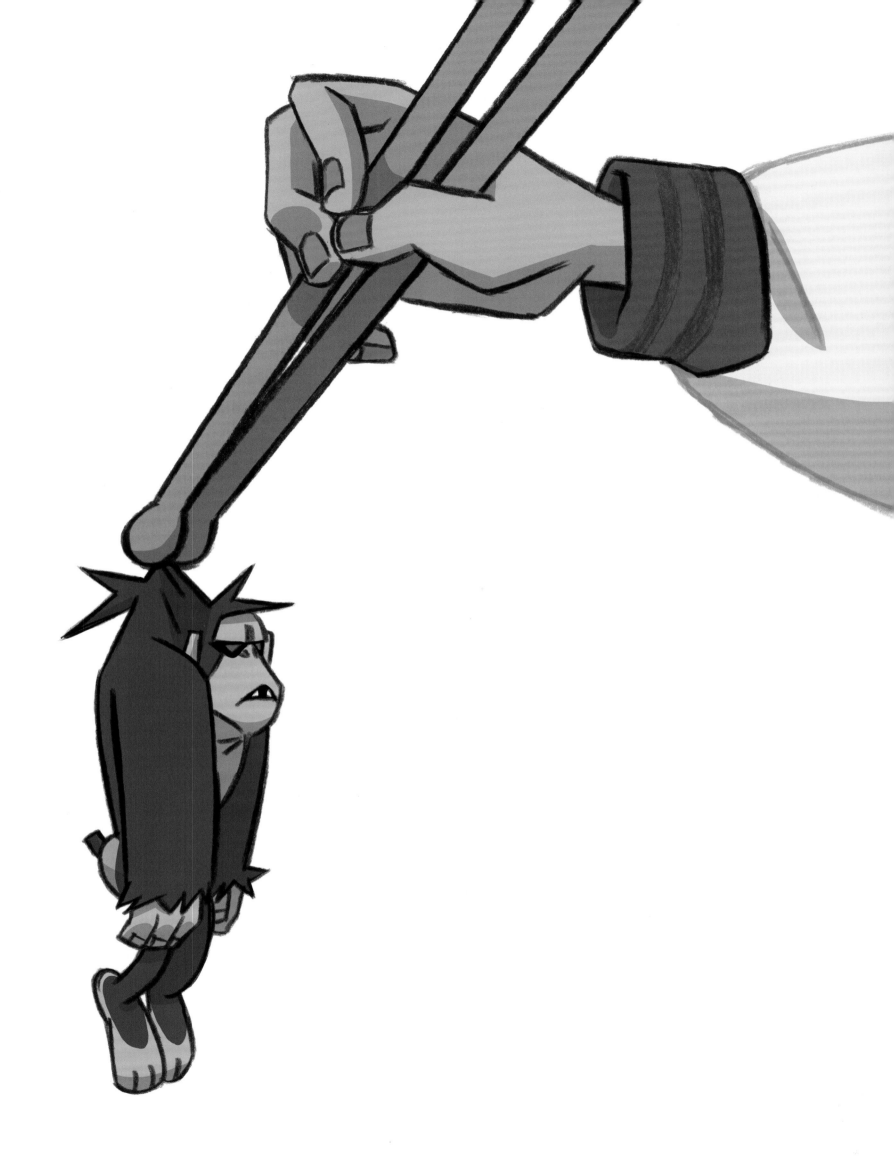

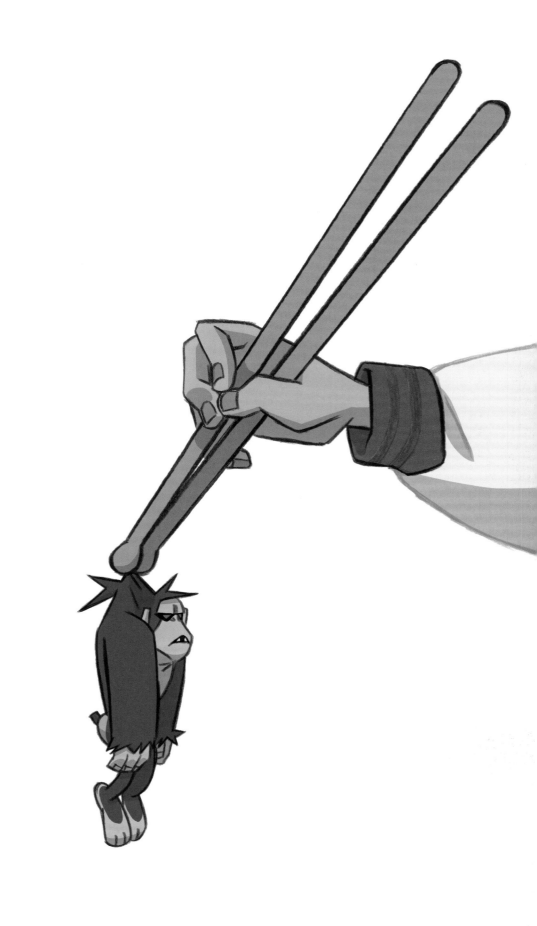
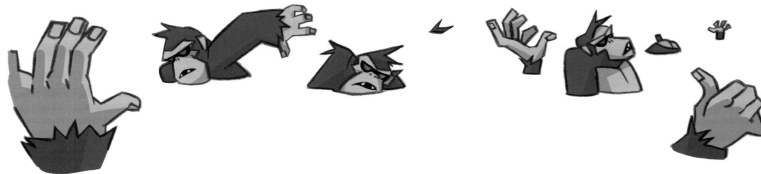

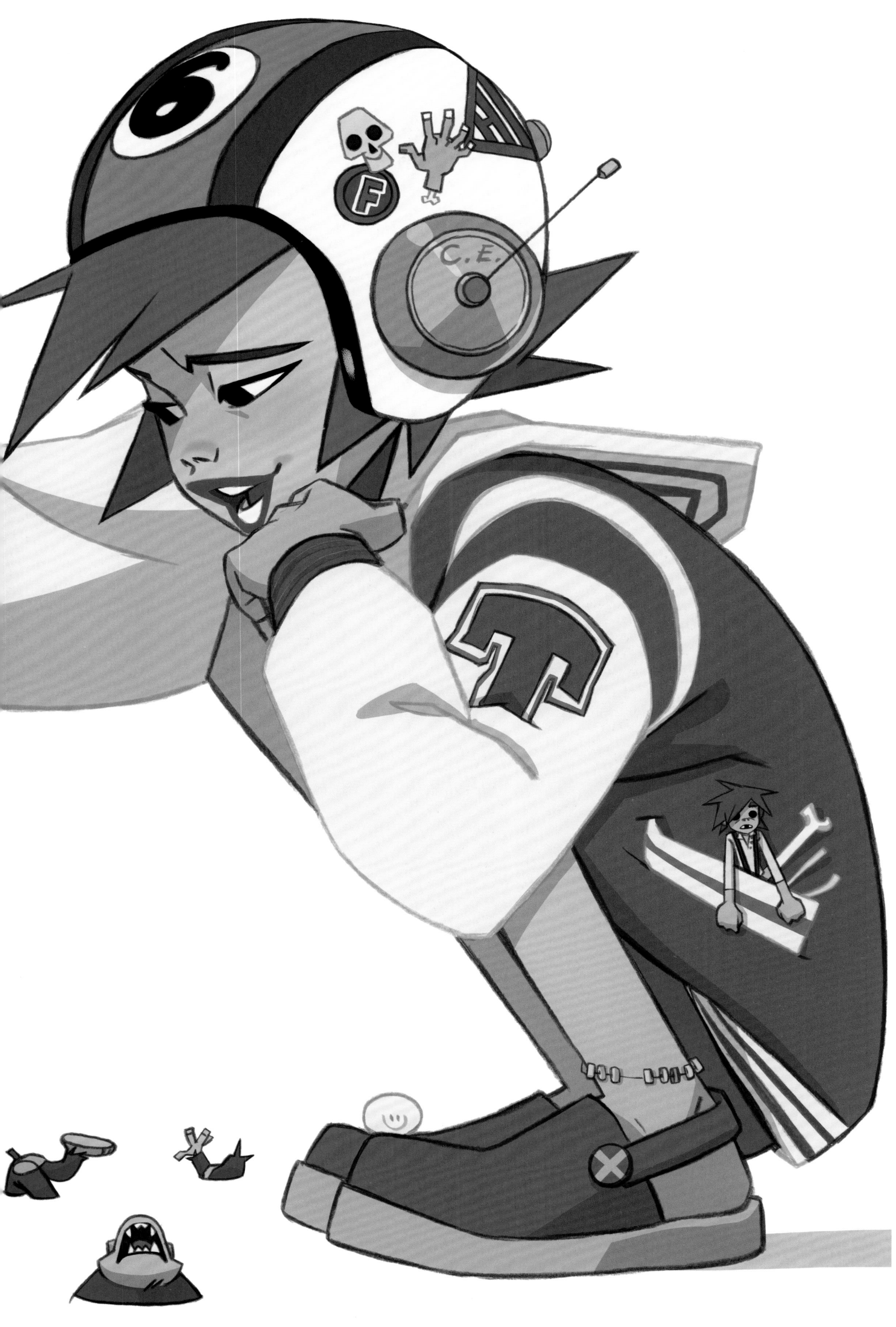
C.E.

Chloe Nicolay

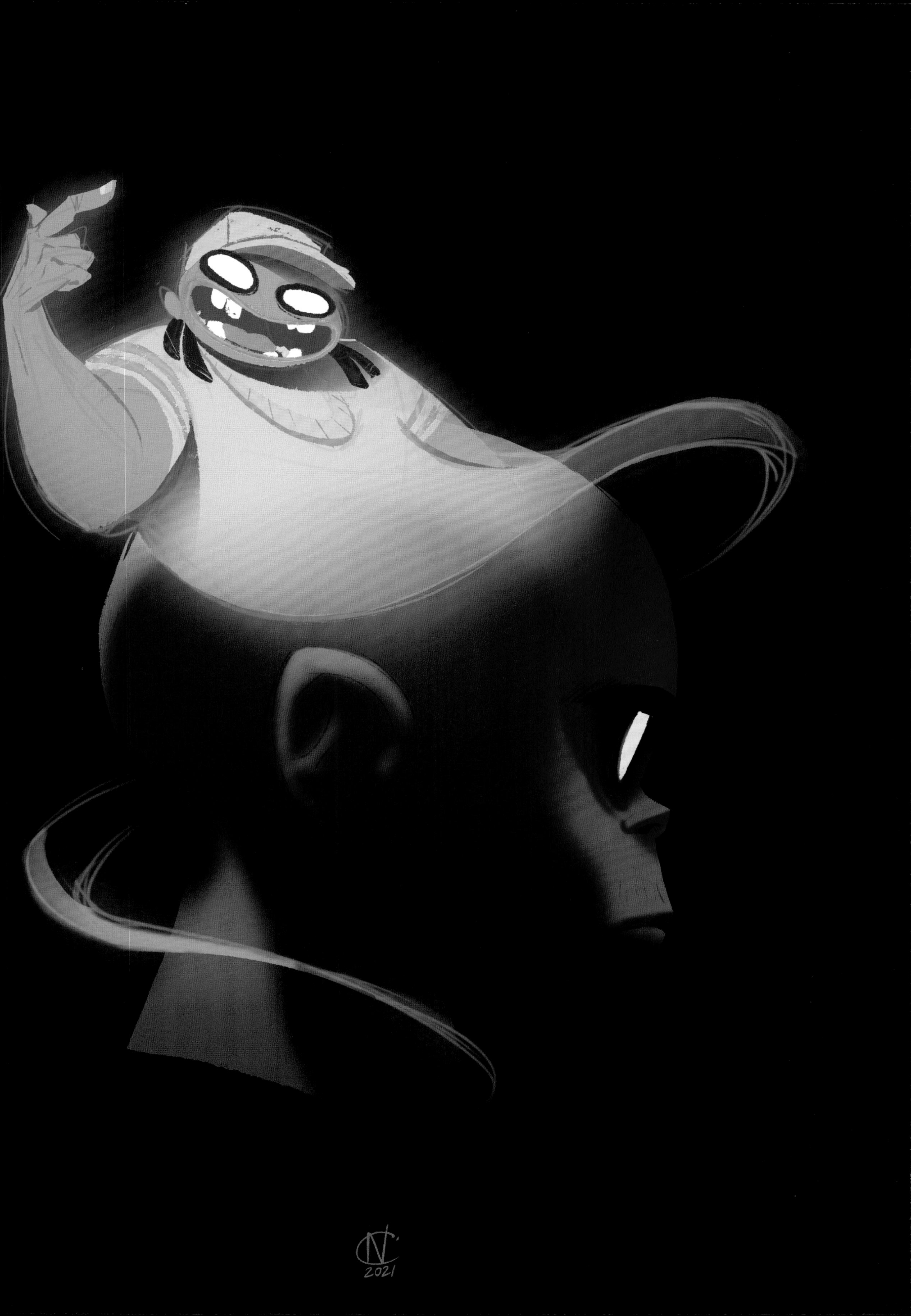
2021

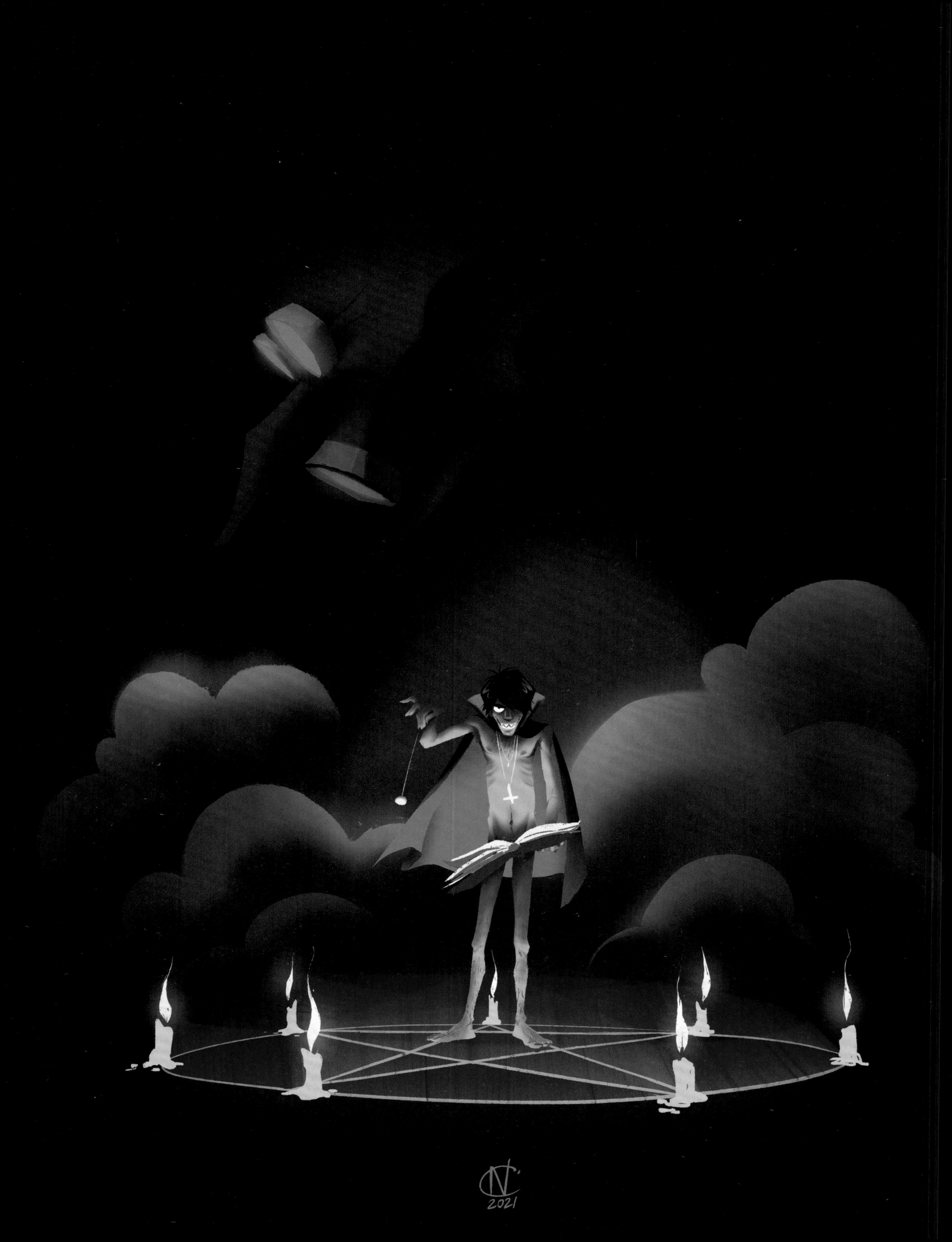
2021

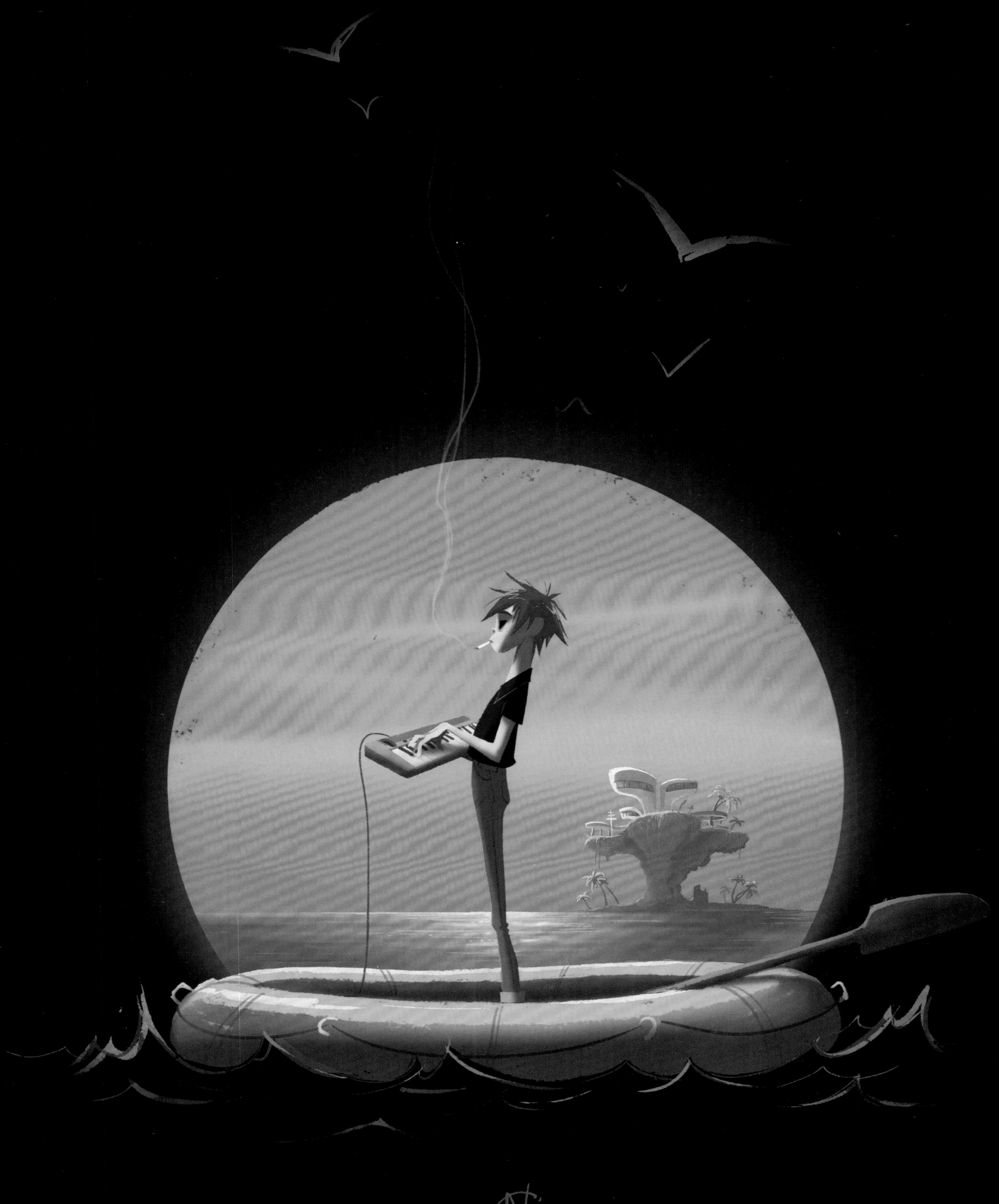
2021

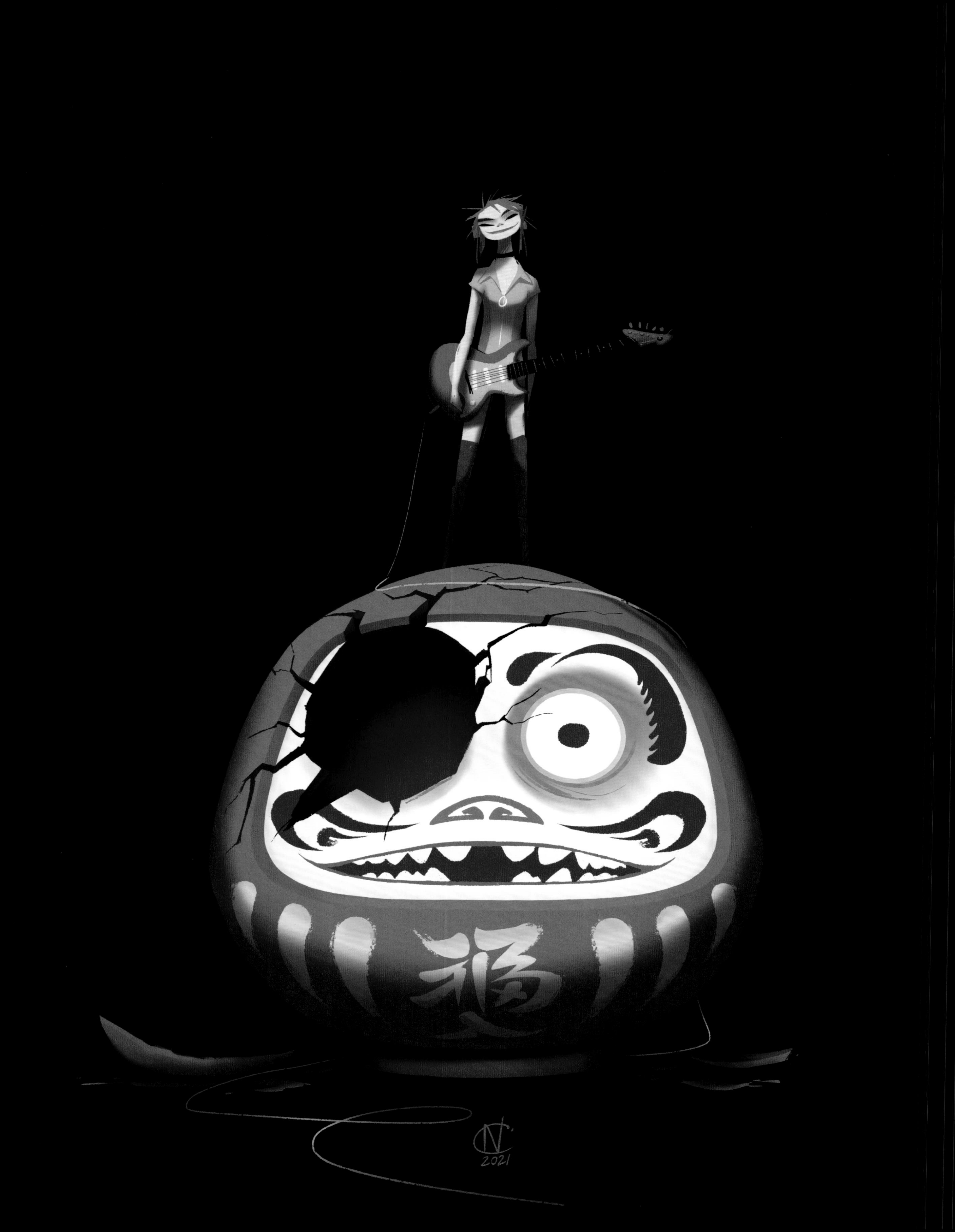
福
2021

RUFFMERCY

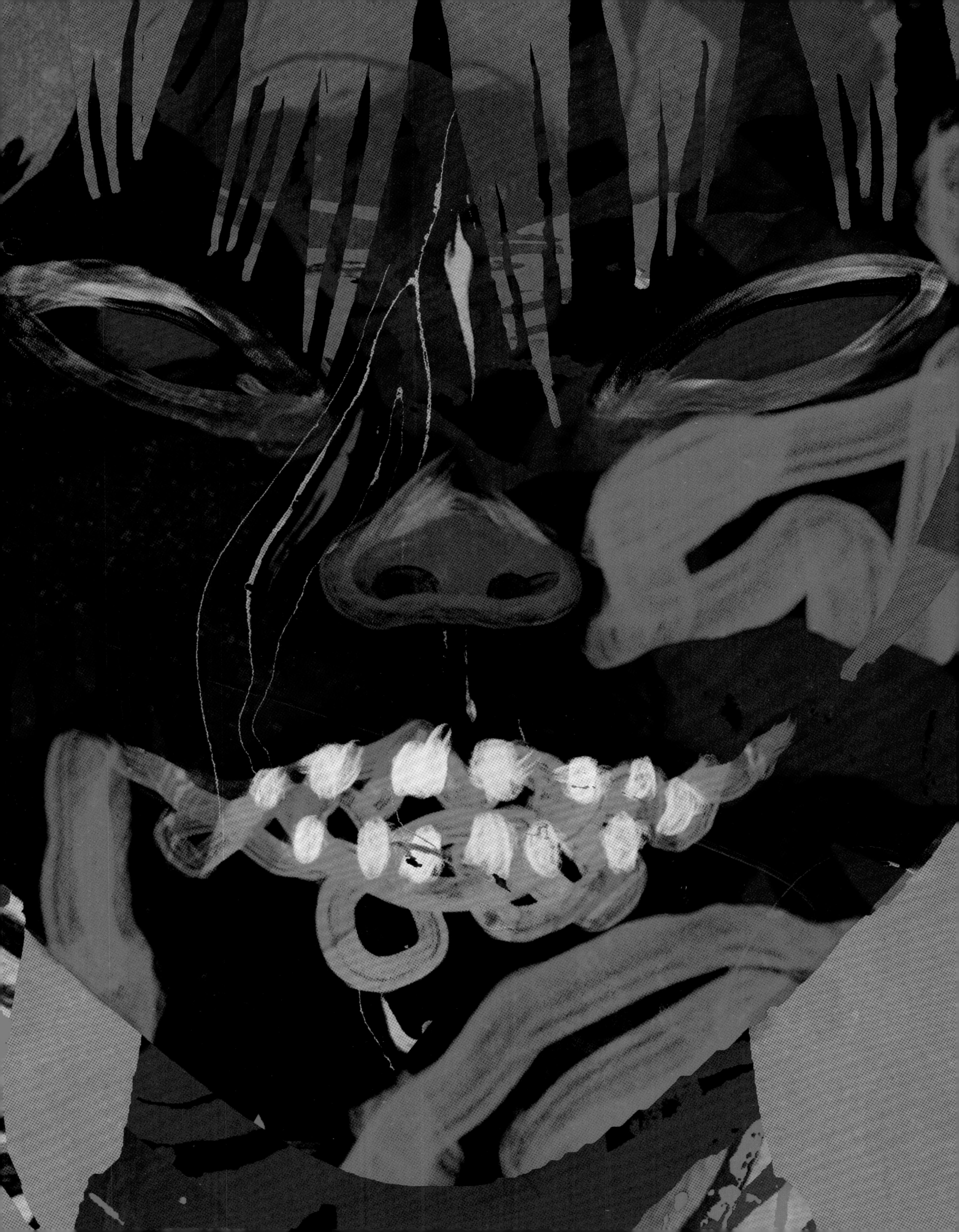

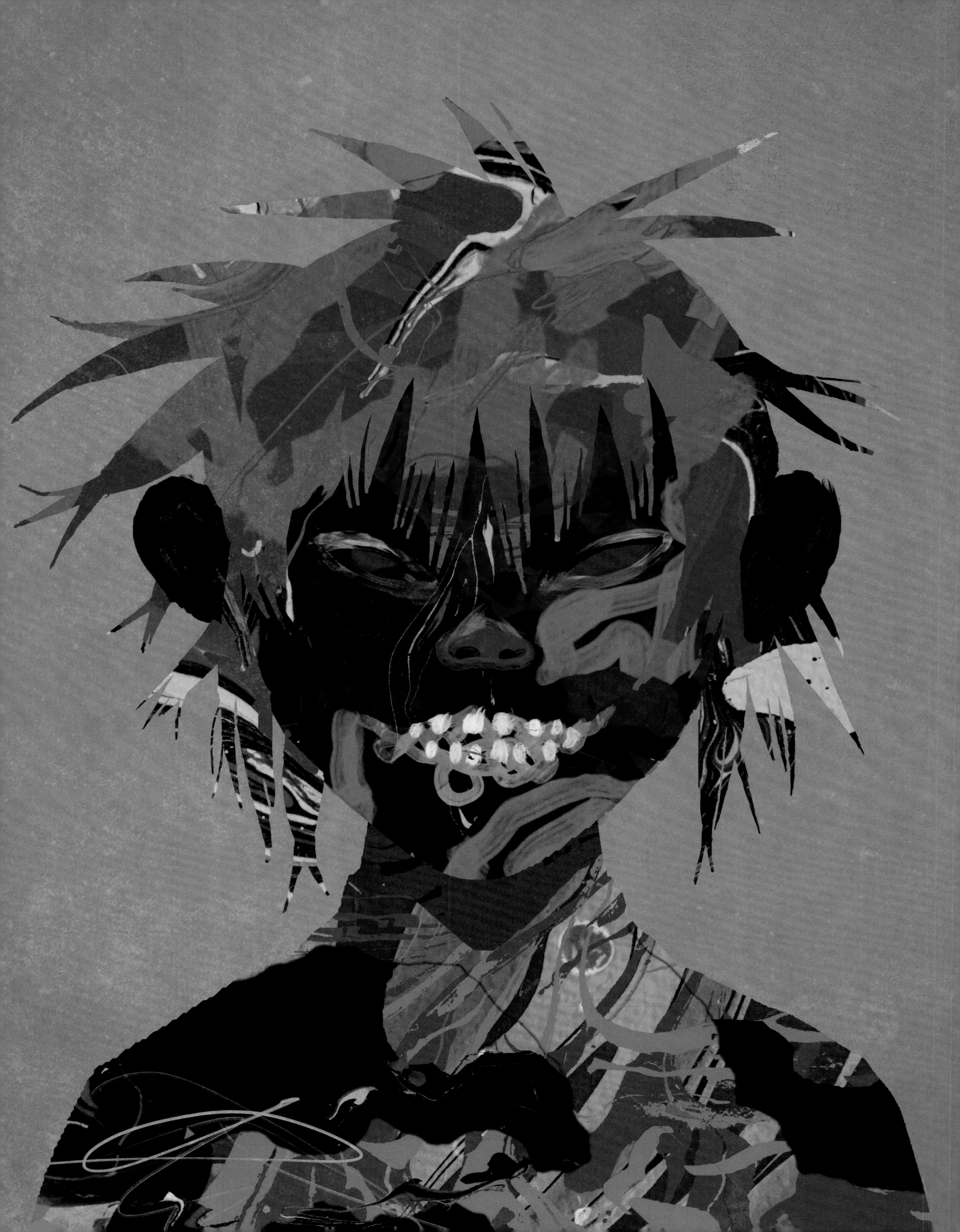

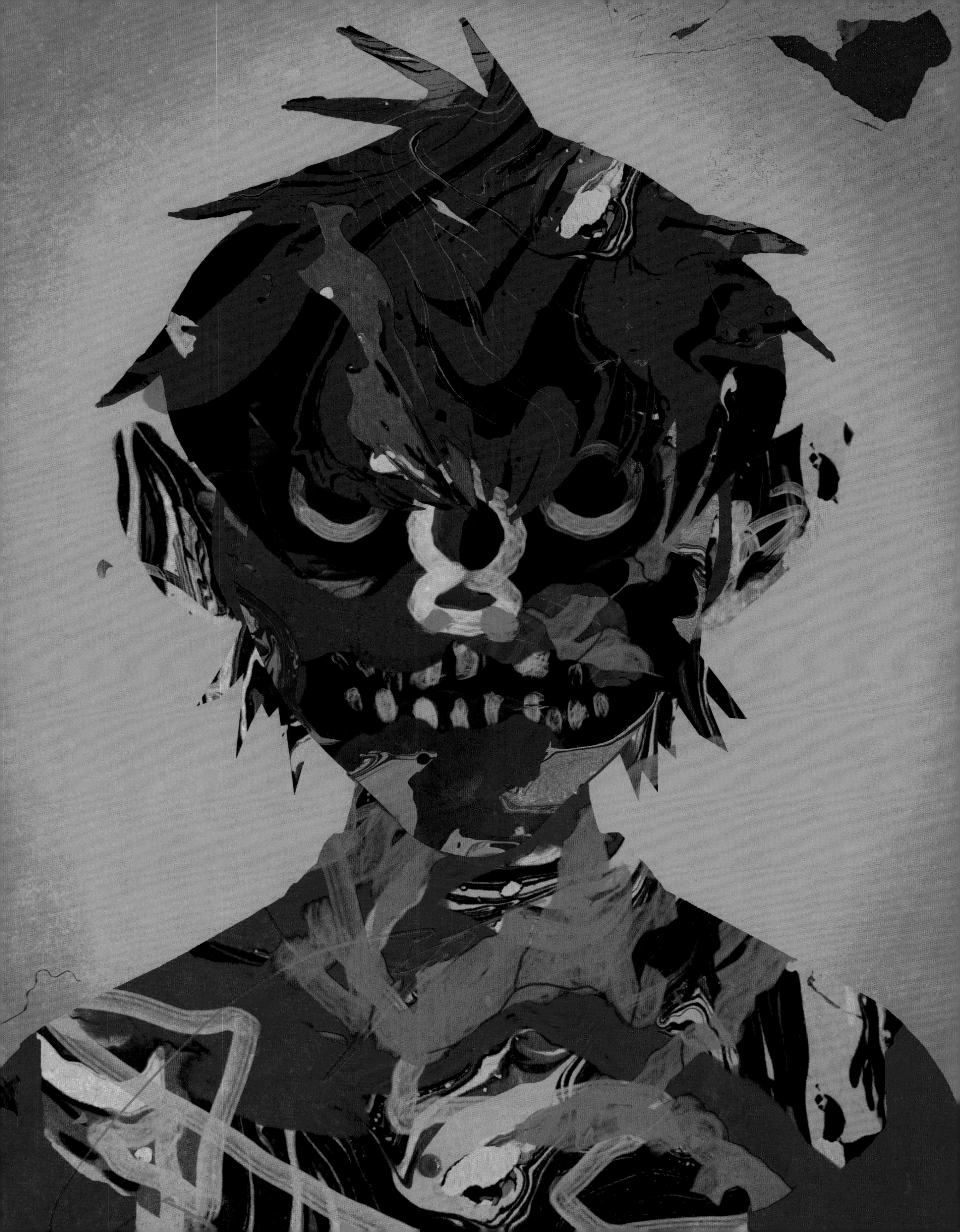

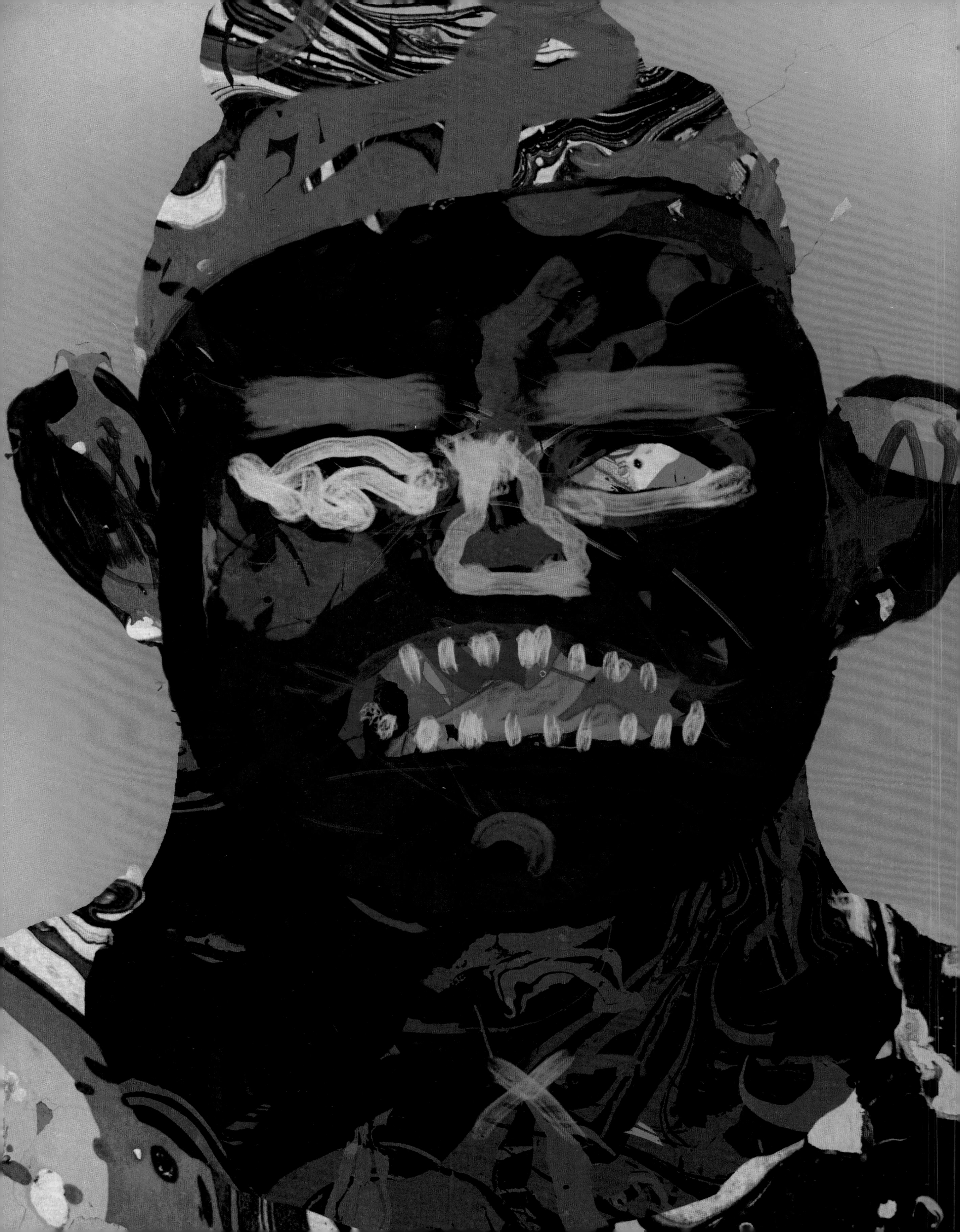

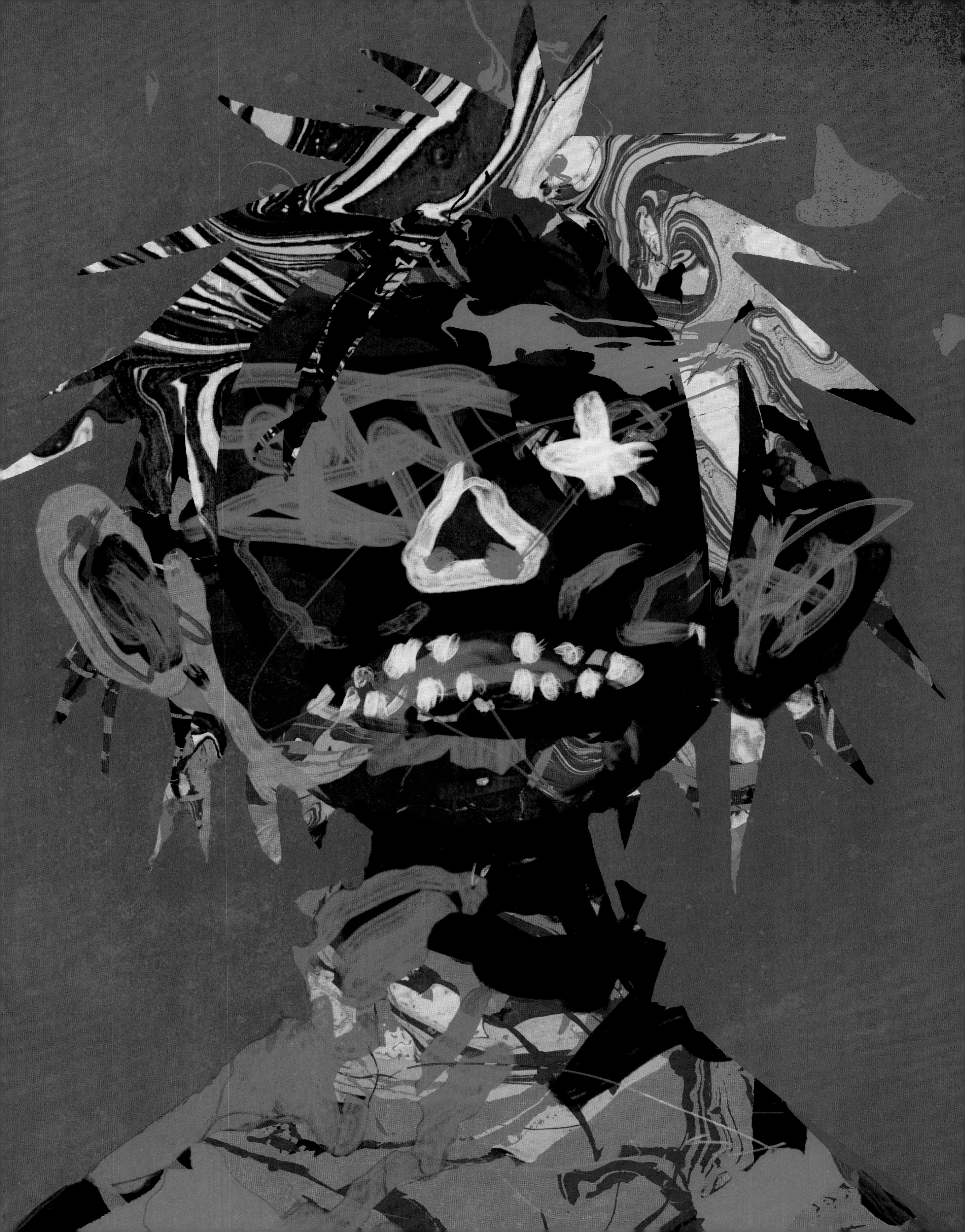

Vanesa R. Del Rey

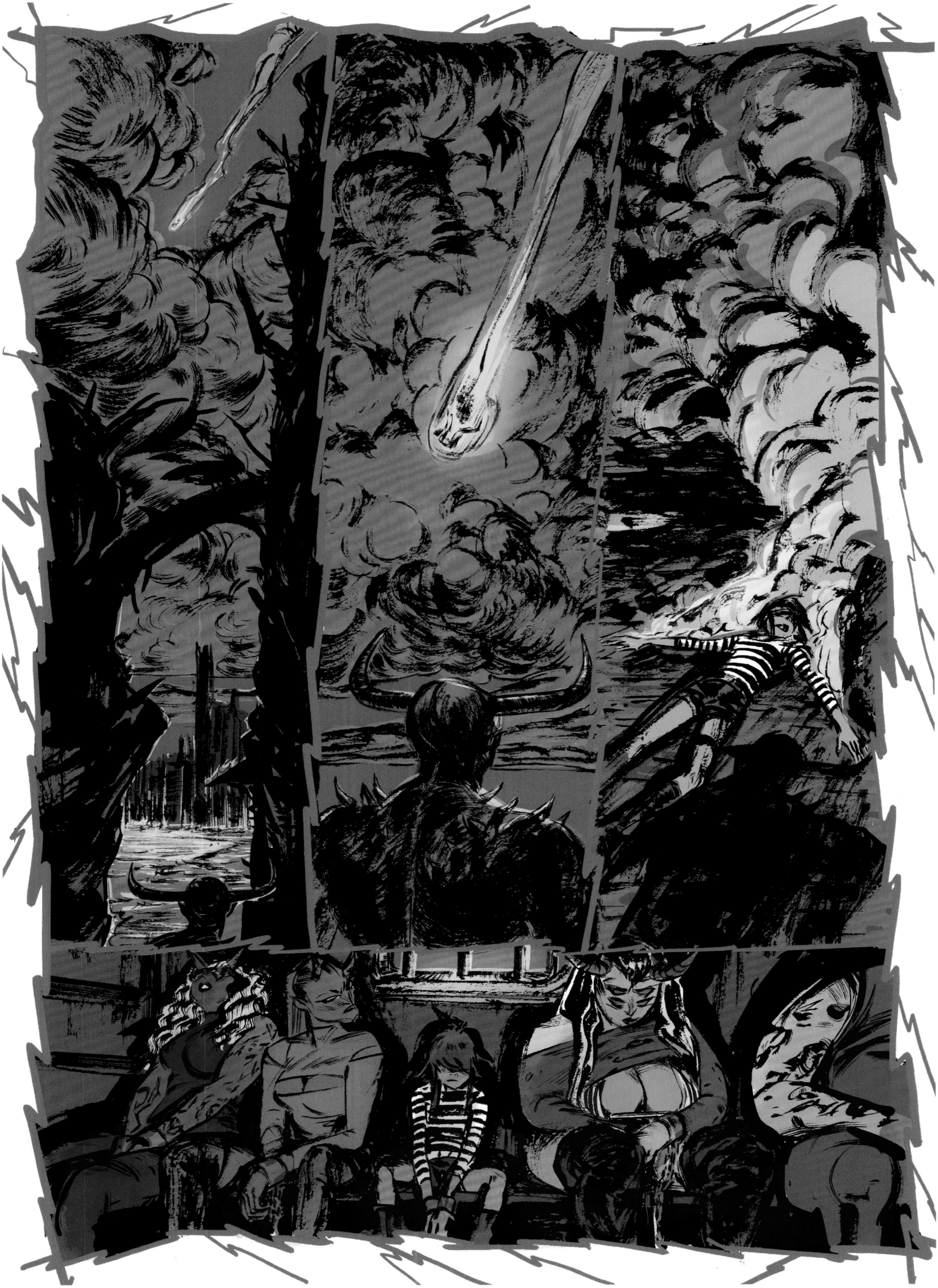

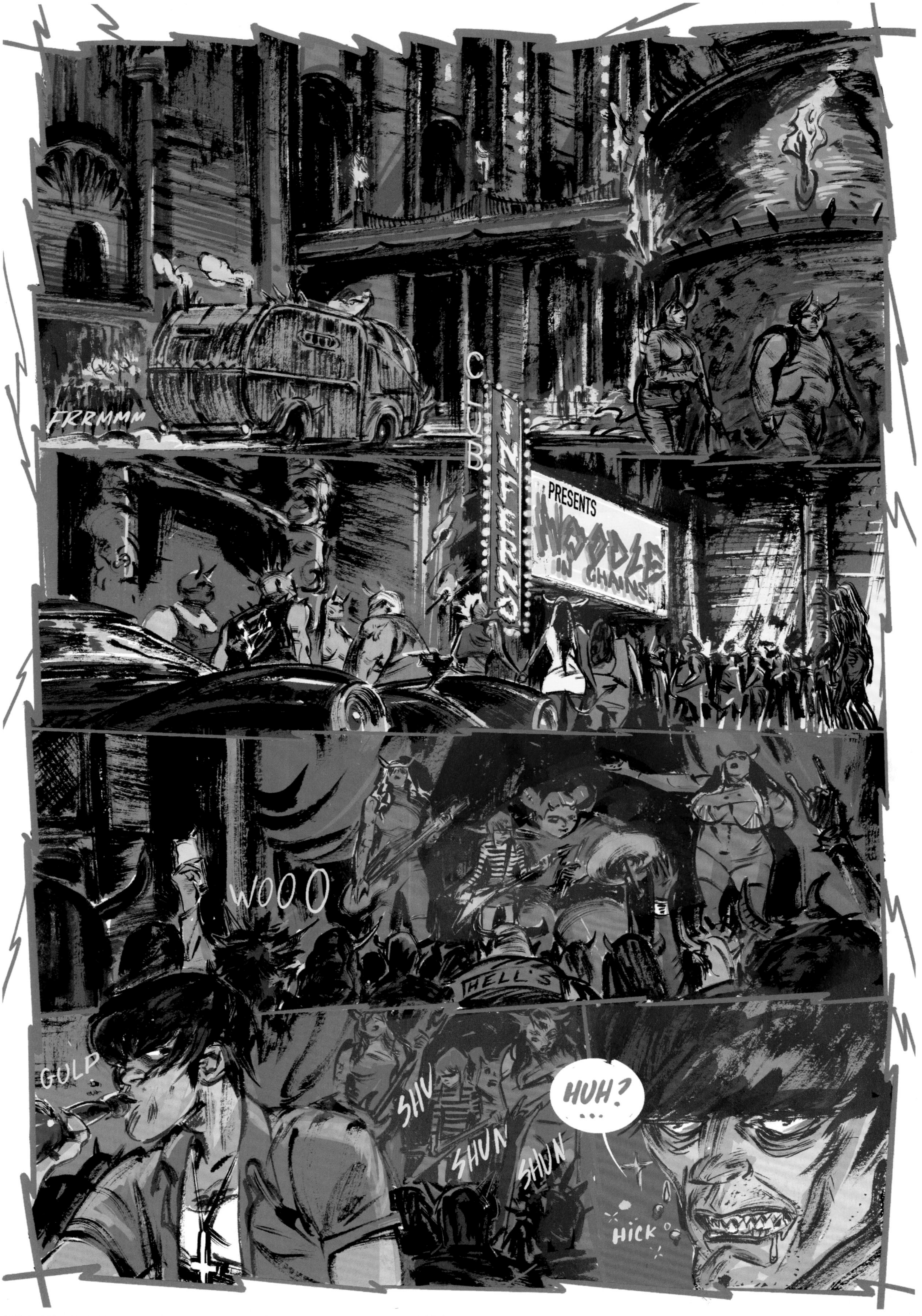
FRRMMM
CLUB
INFERNO
PRESENTS
NOODLE
IN CHAINS
WOOO
HELL'S
GULP
SHU
SHUN
SHUN
HUH?
...
HICK

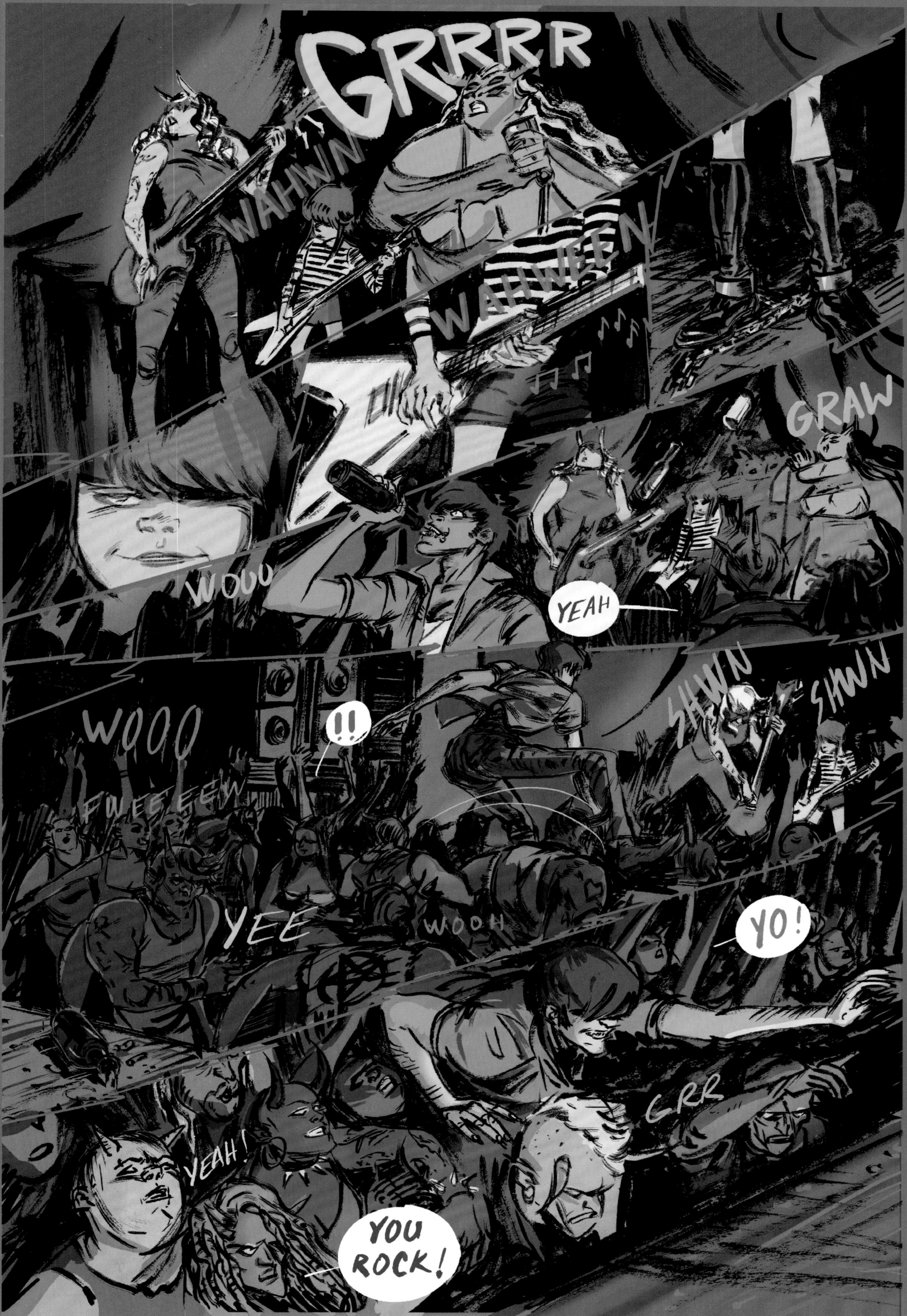
GRRRR
WAHWN
WAHWEEN
GRAW
WOOO
YEAH
WOOO
!!
SHWN
SHWN
FWEEEEW
YEE
WOOH
YO!
GRR
YEAH!
YOU ROCK!

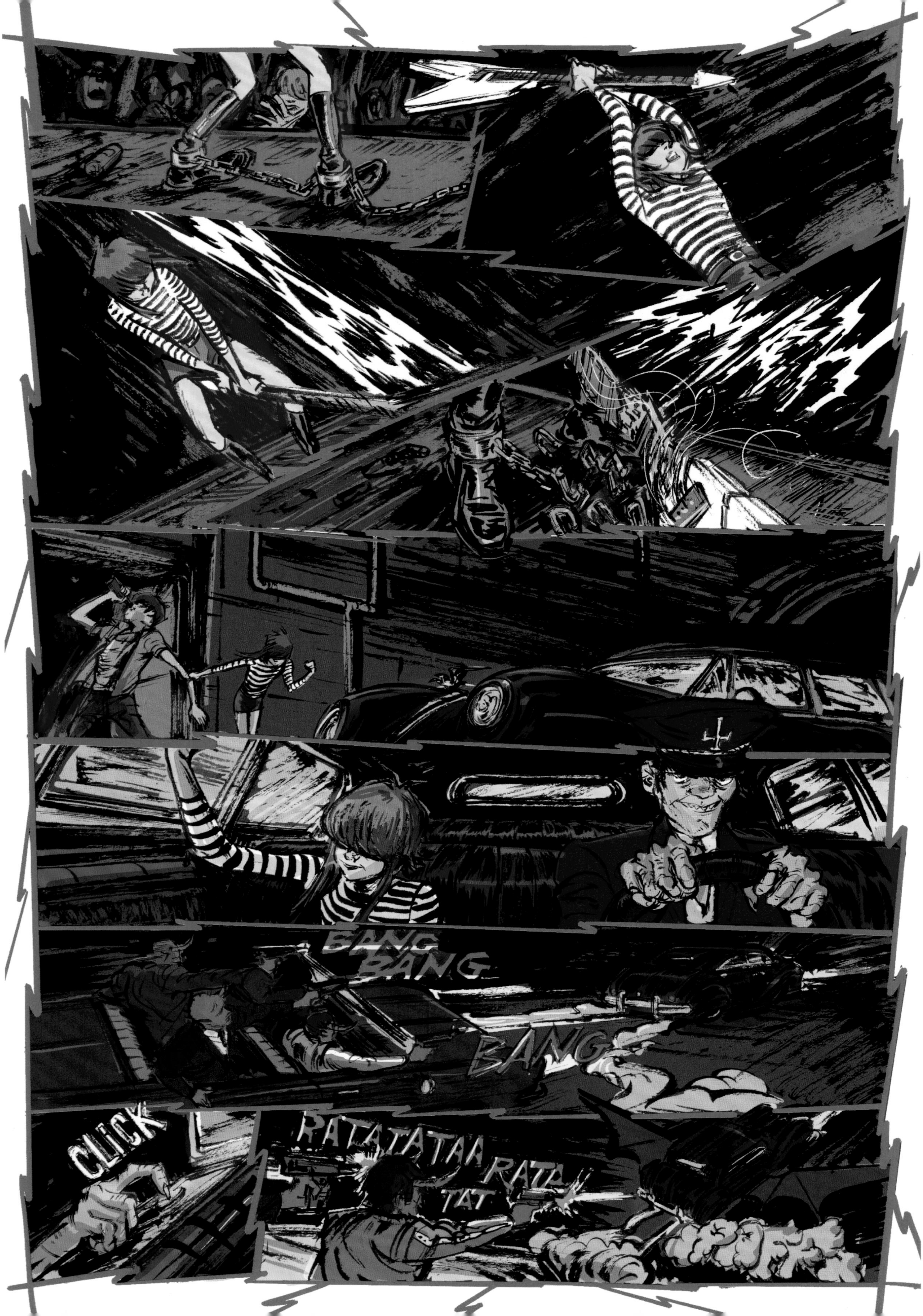
BANG
BANG
BANG
CLICK
RATATATAA RATA
TAT

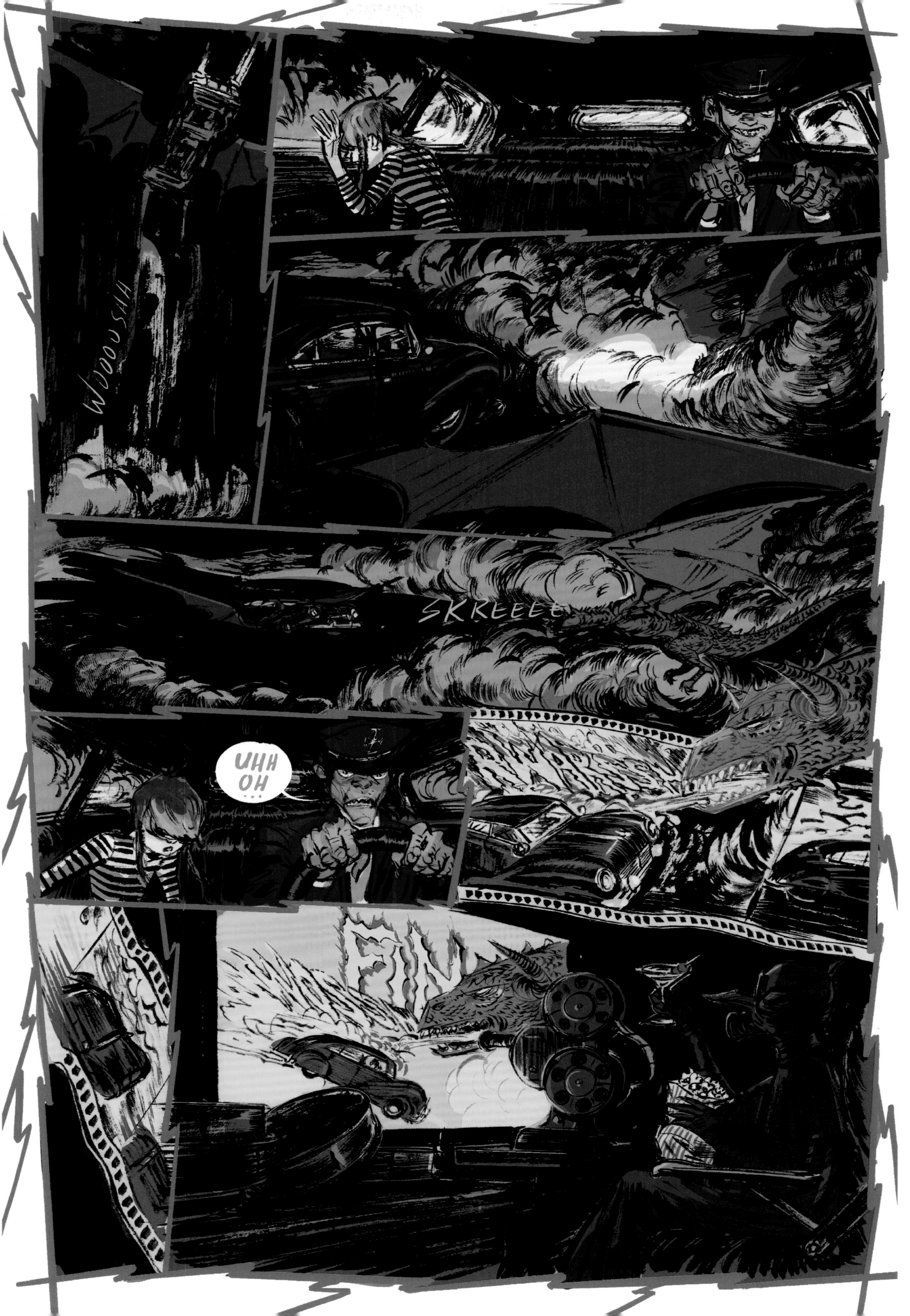
WOOOOUSHH
SKREEEE
UHH OH...
FIN

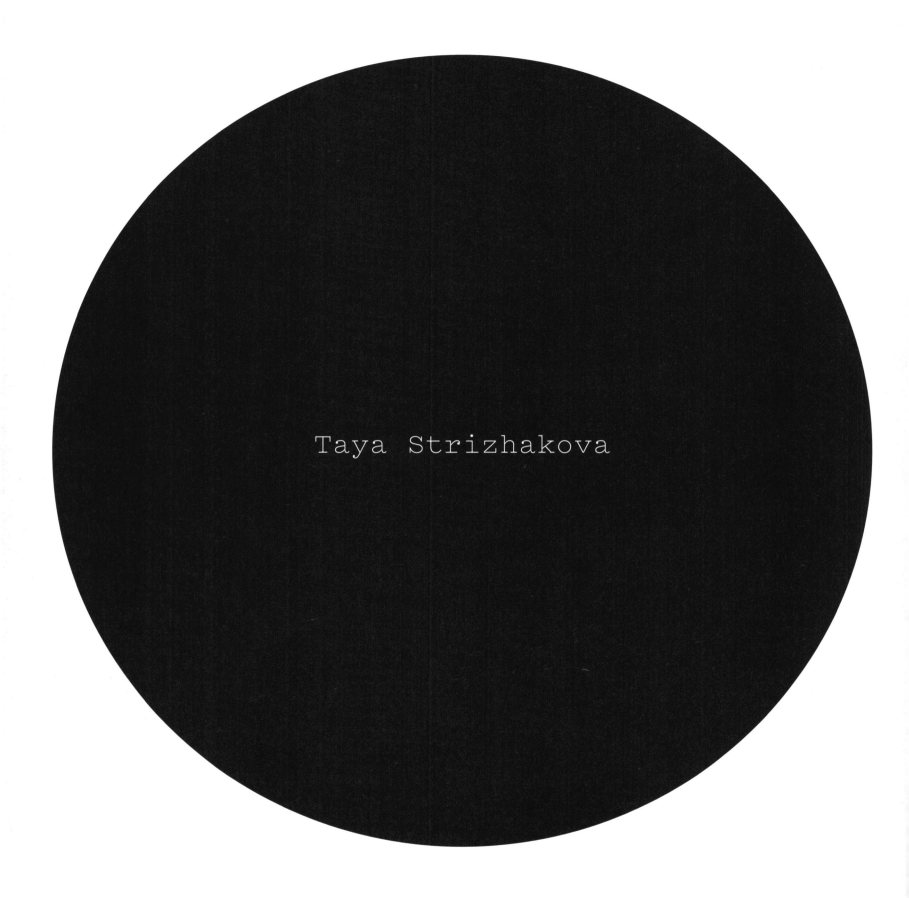

Taya Strizhakova

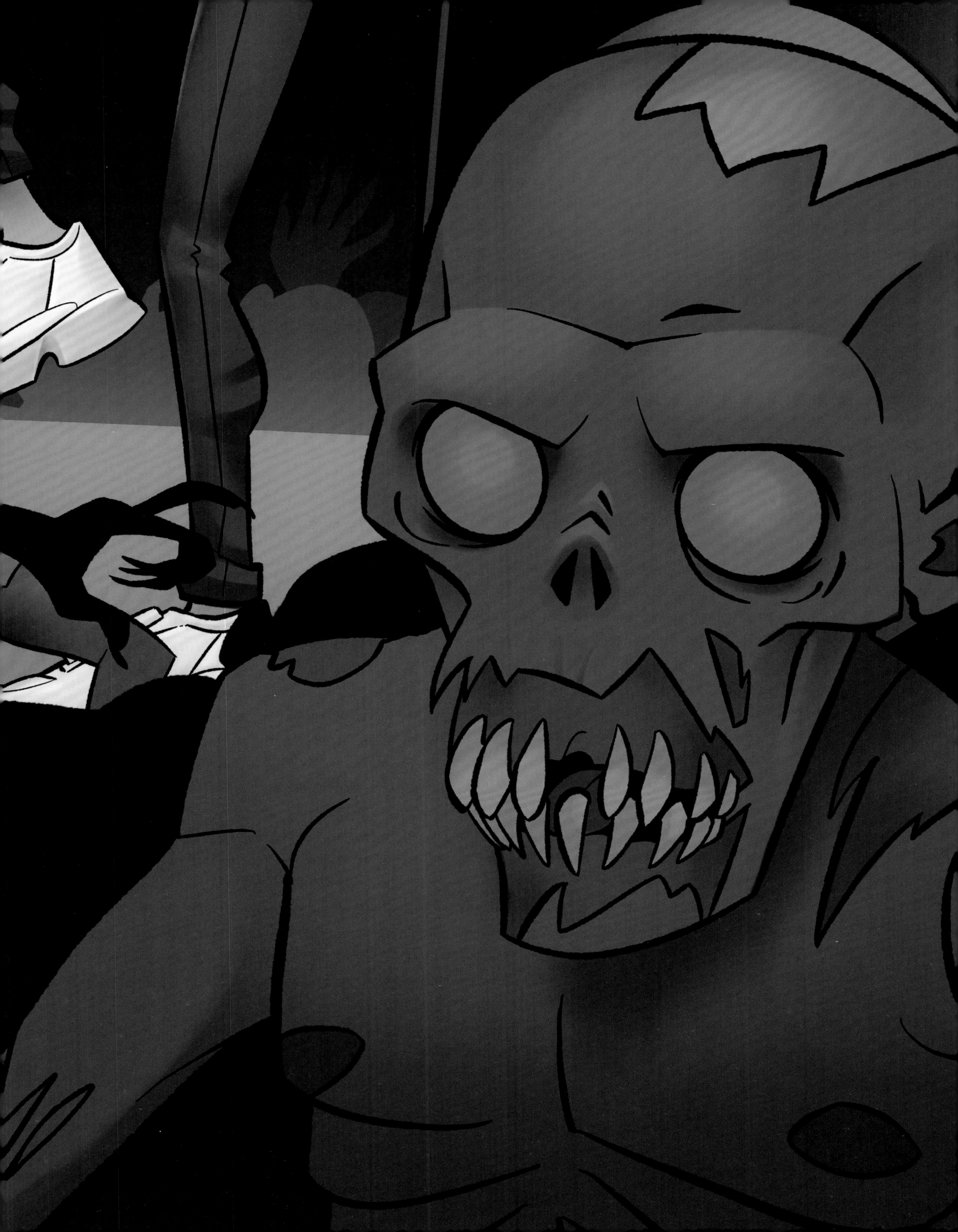

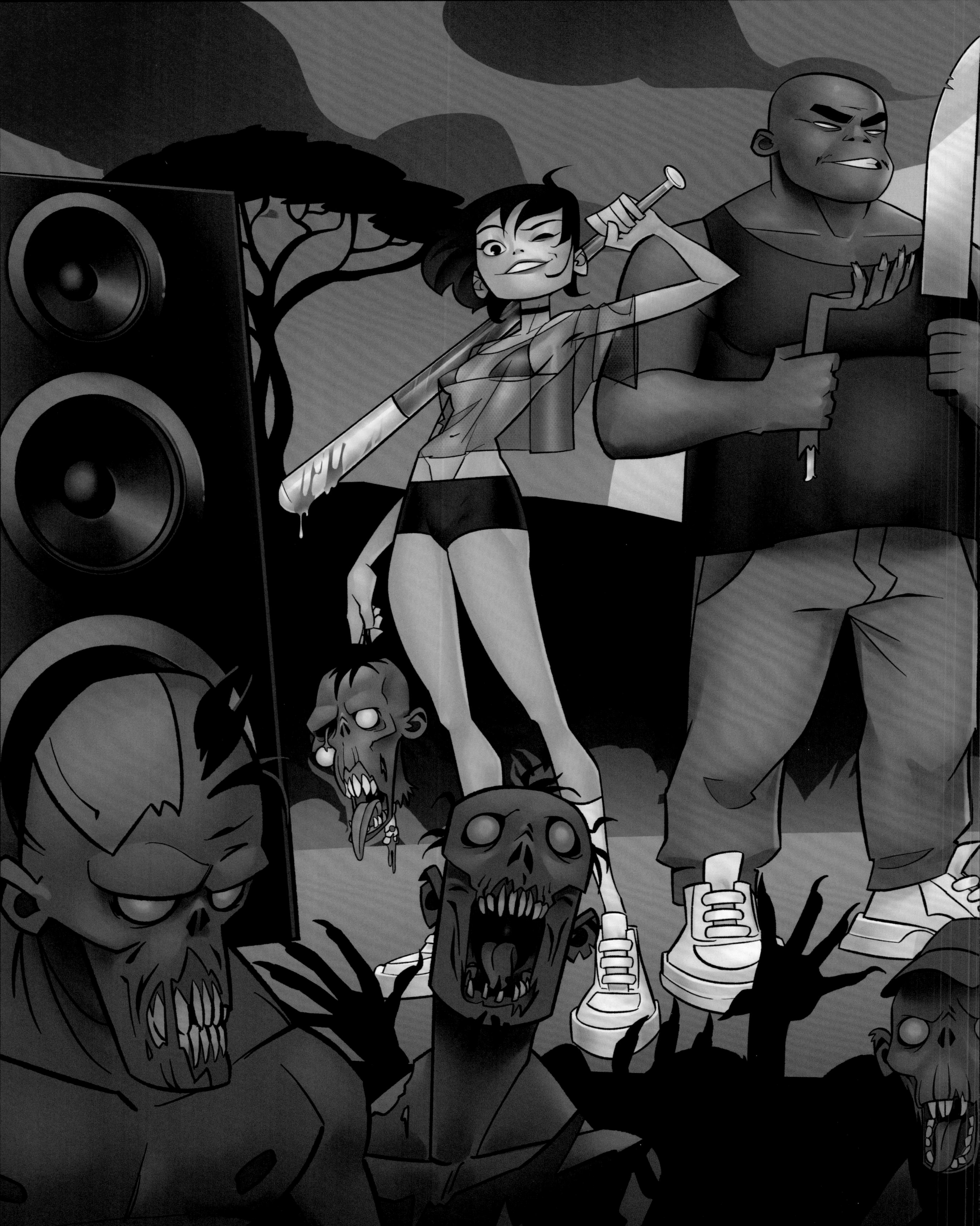

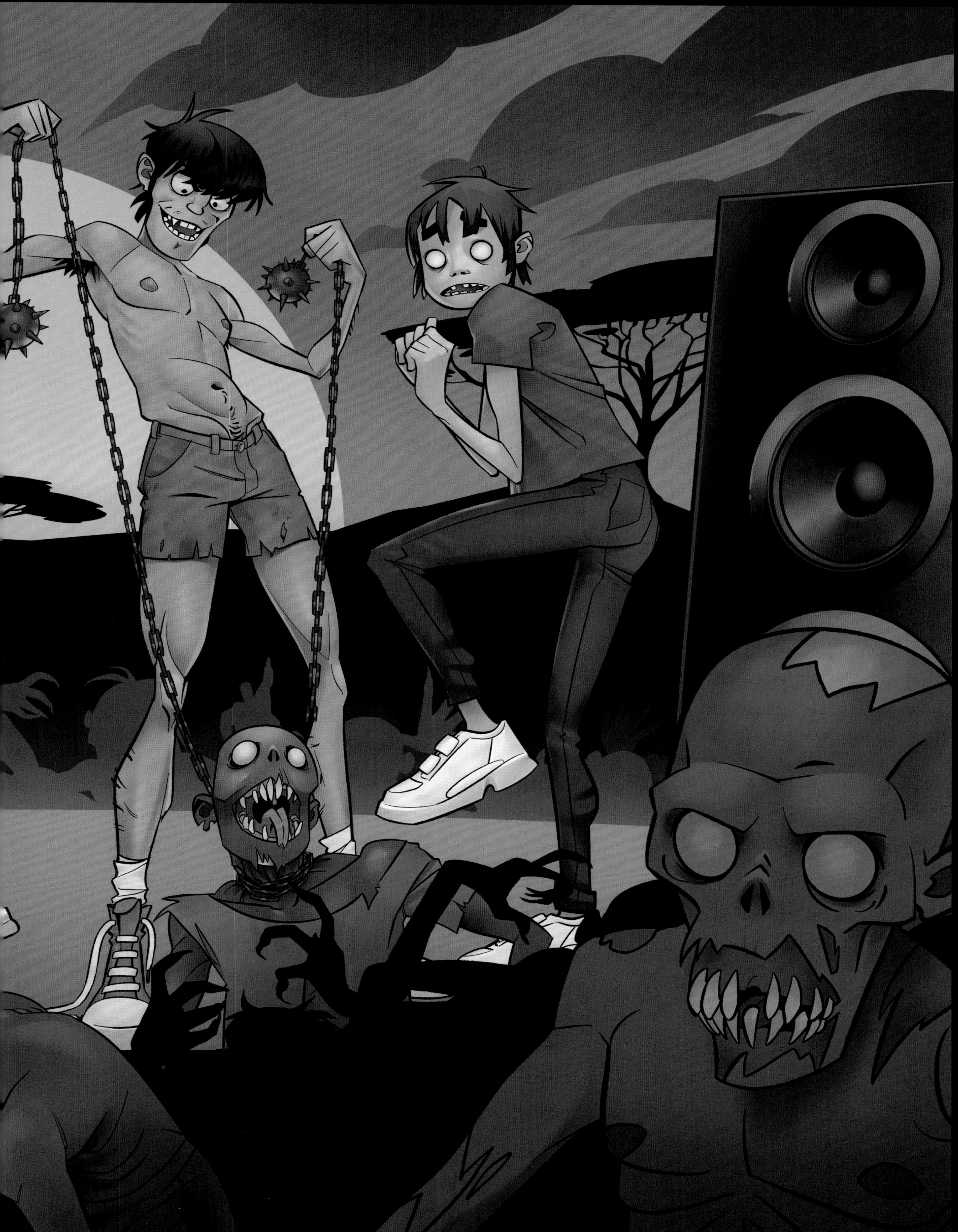

Del The Funky Homosapien

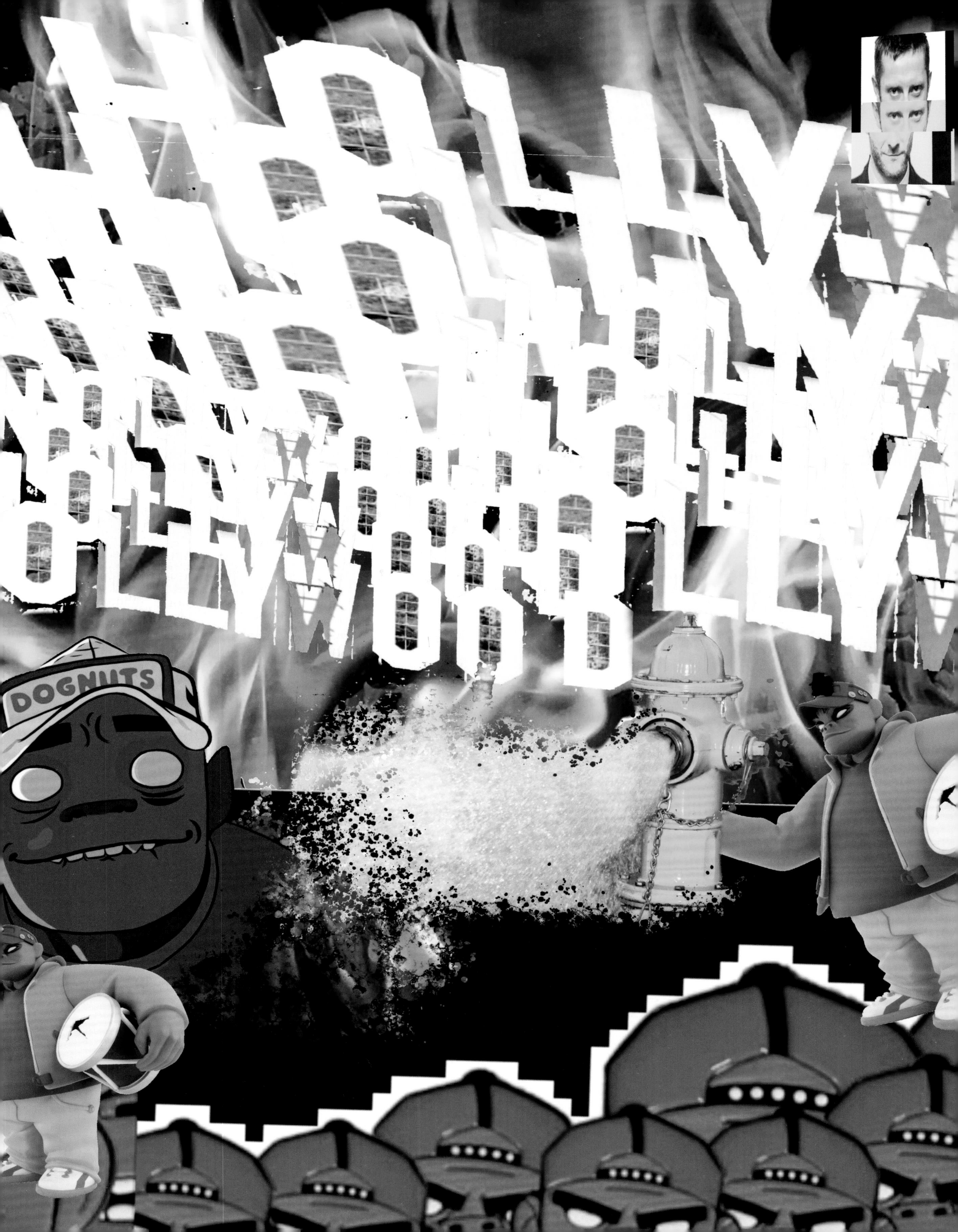
DOGNUTS

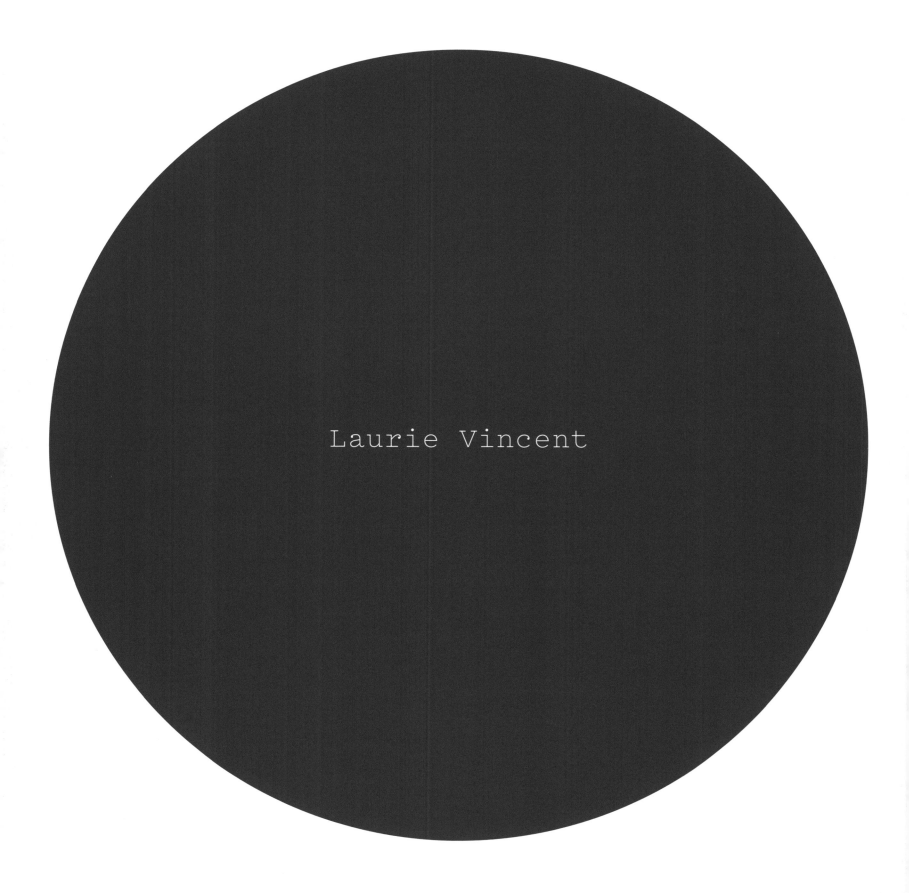

Laurie Vincent

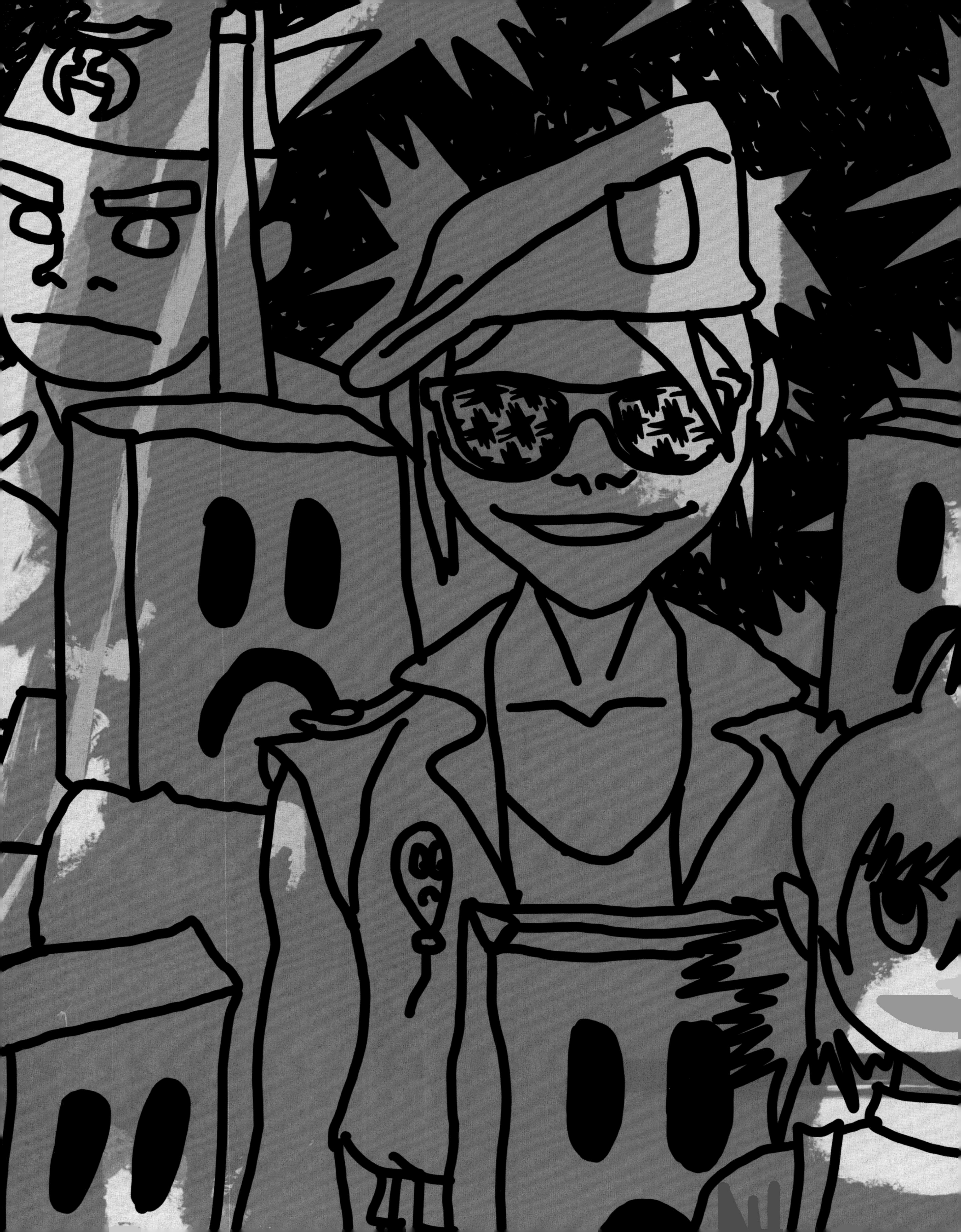

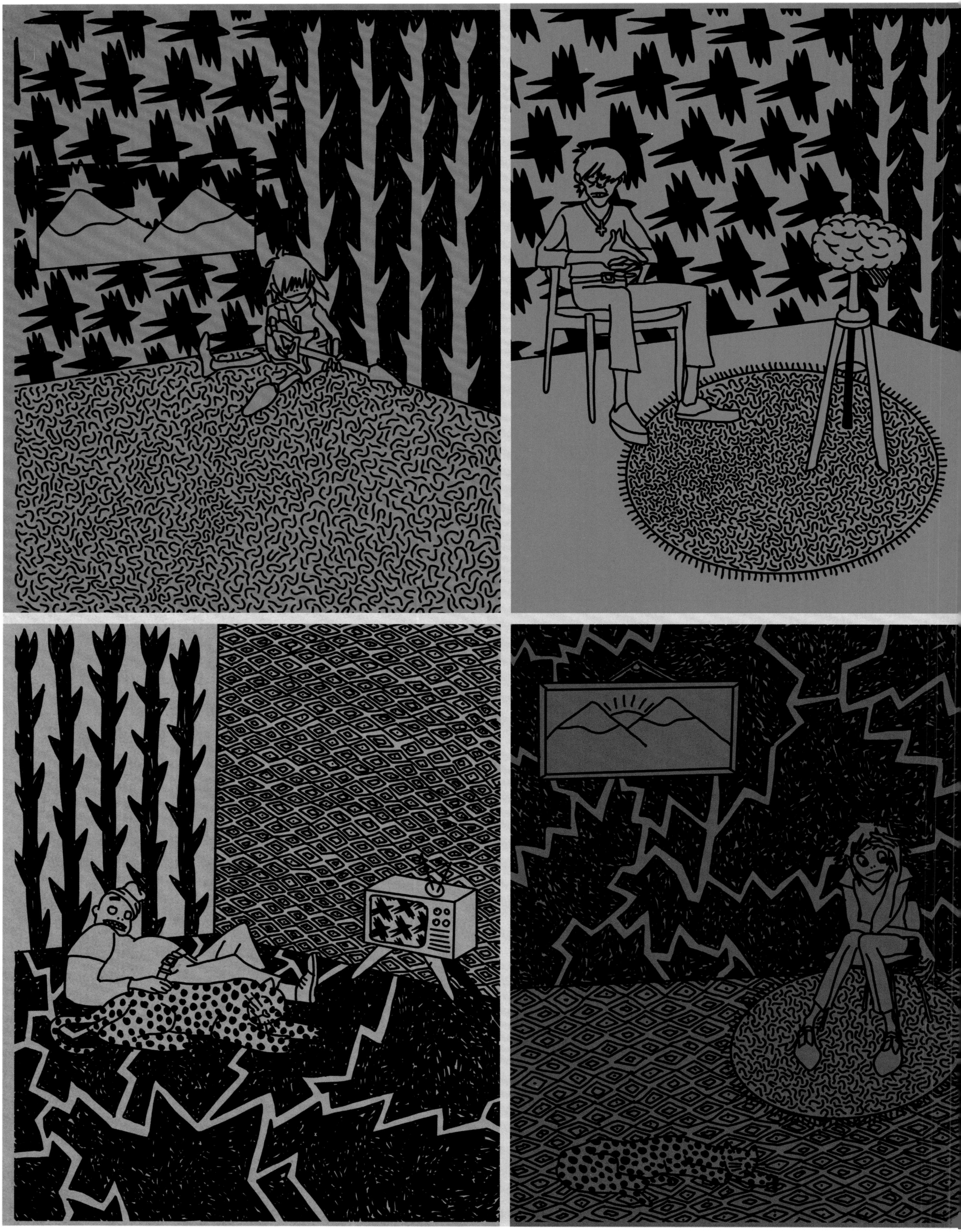

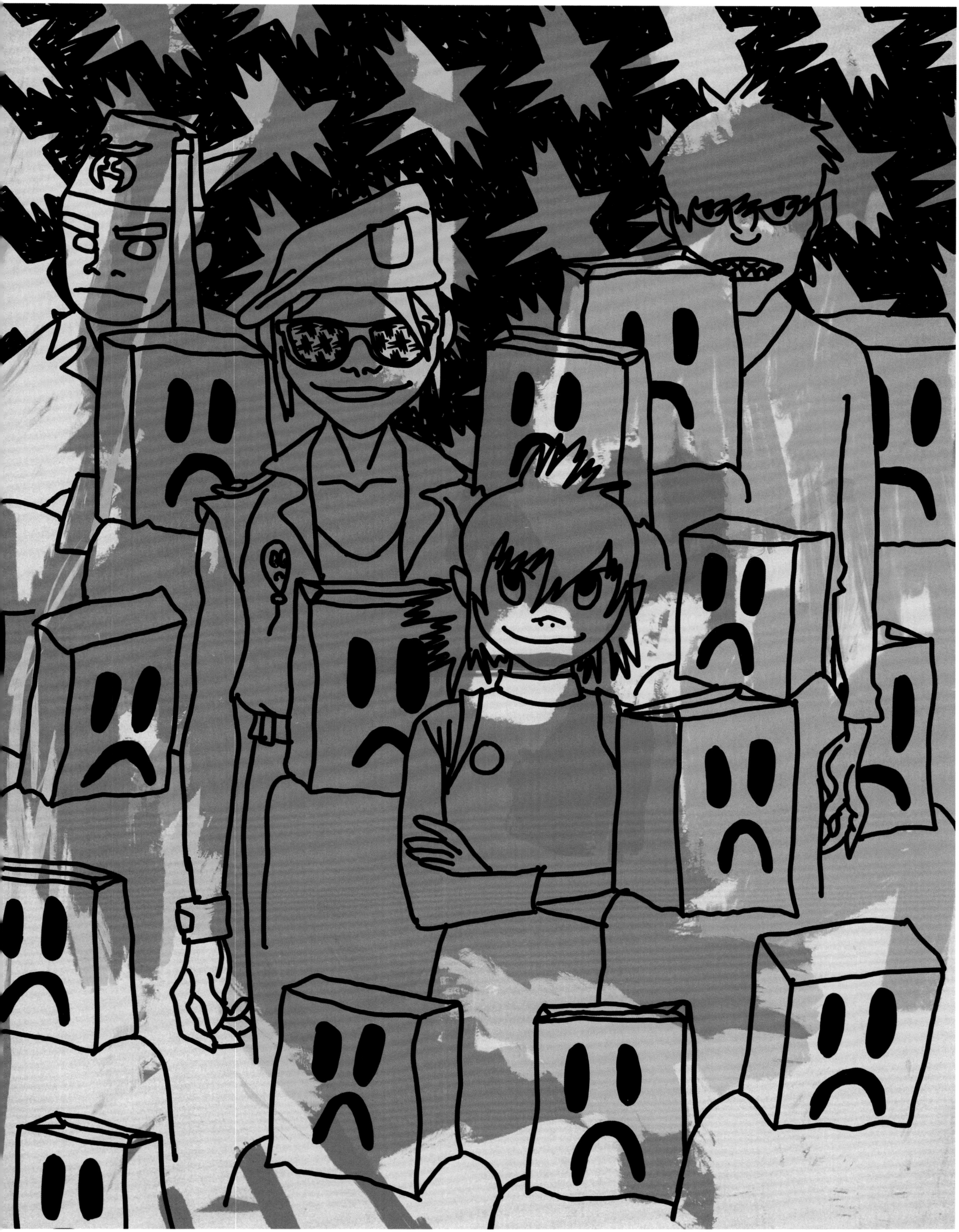

Little Thunder

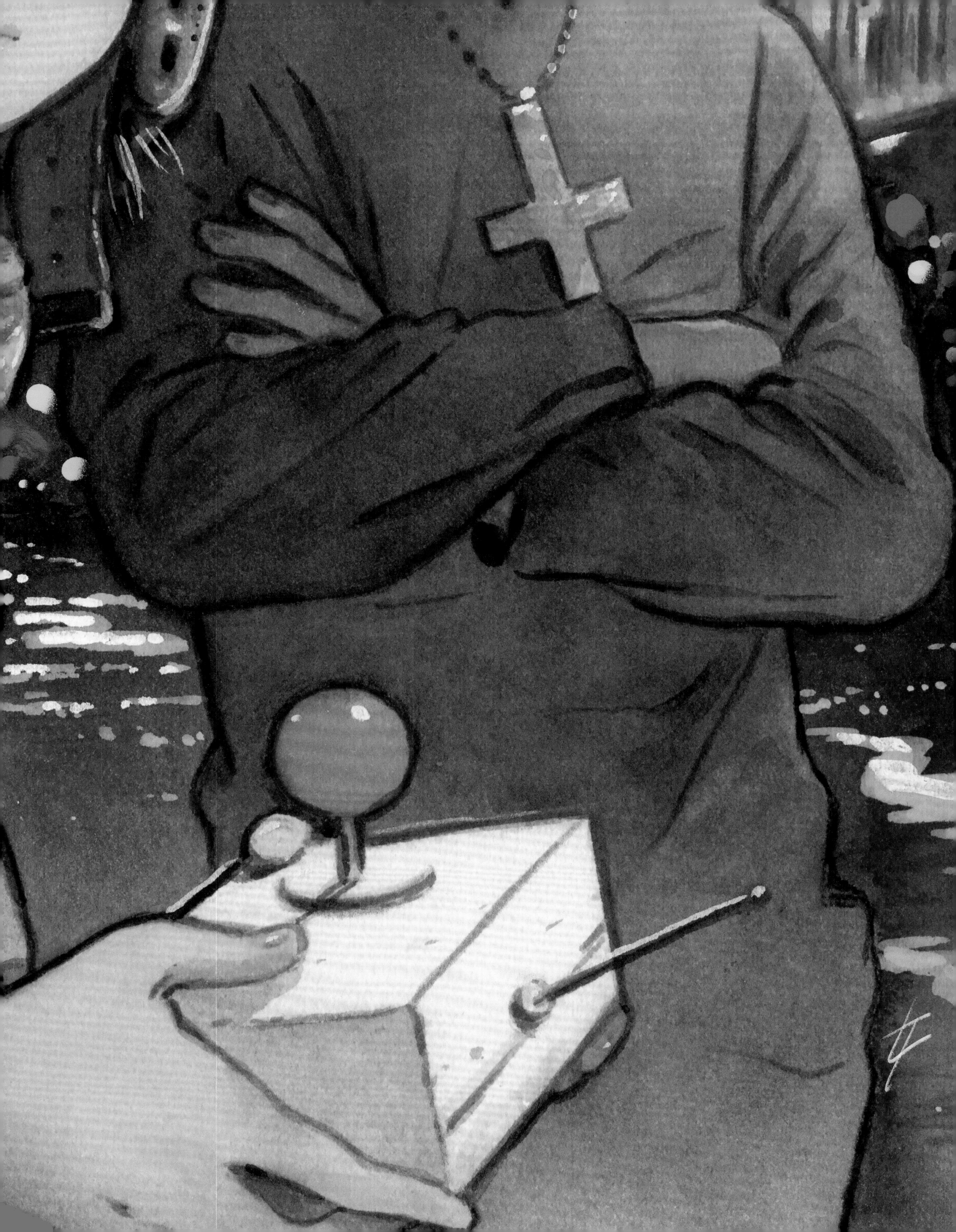

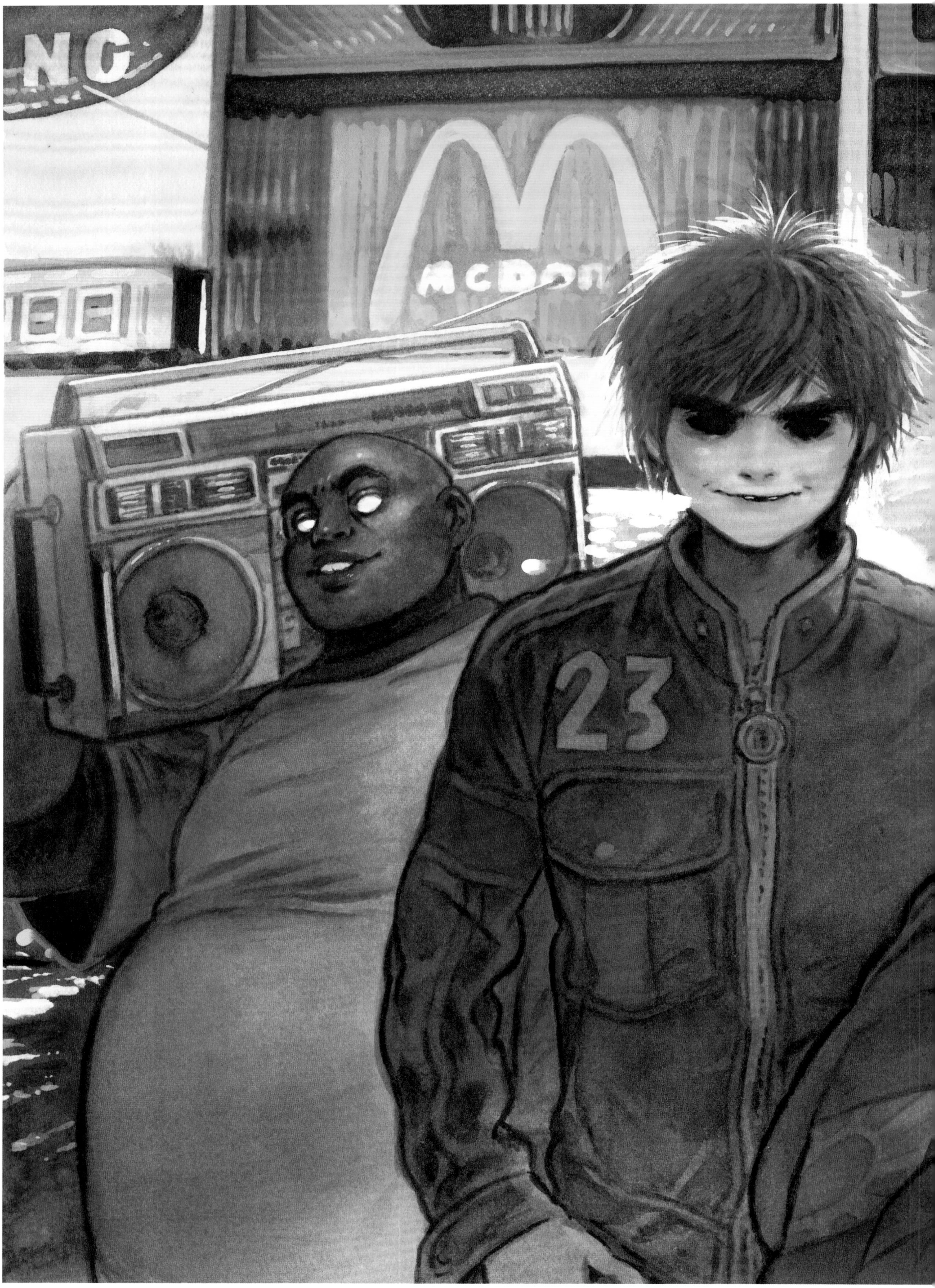
NG
MCDON
23

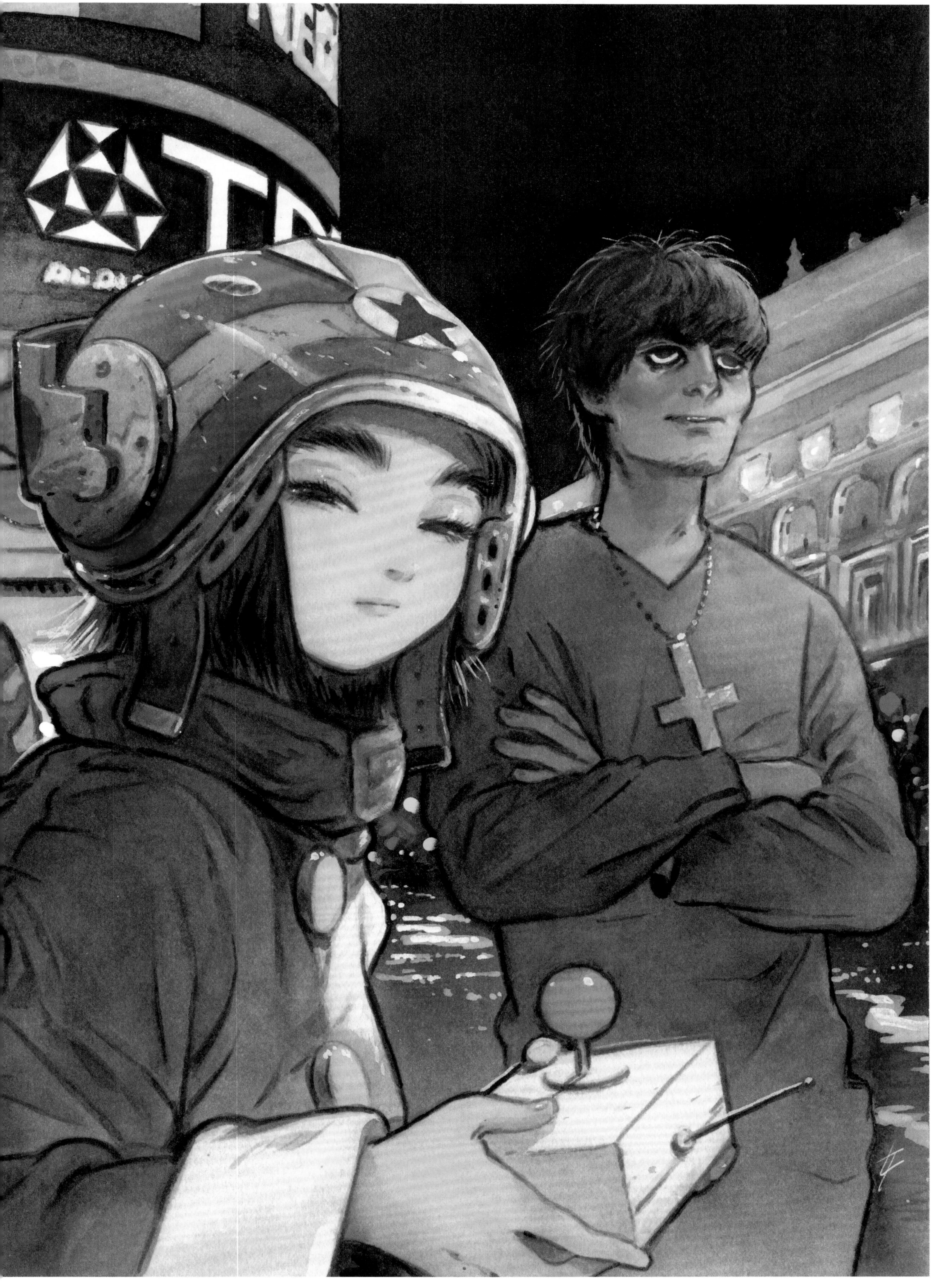

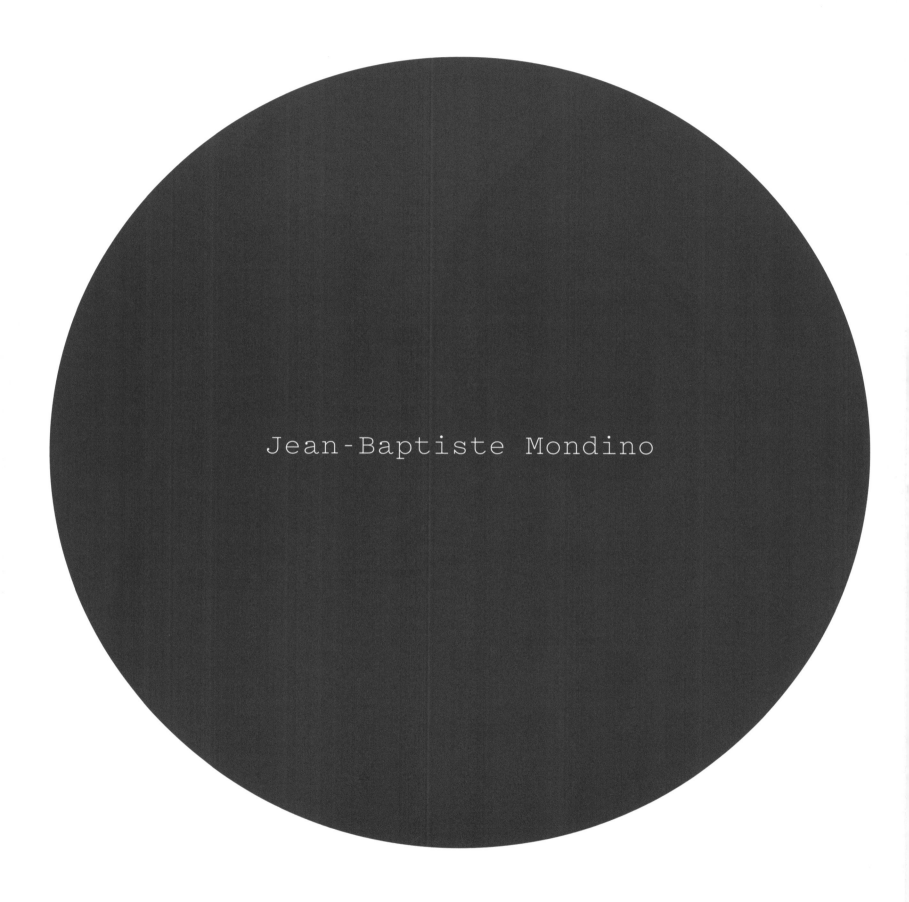

Jean-Baptiste Mondino

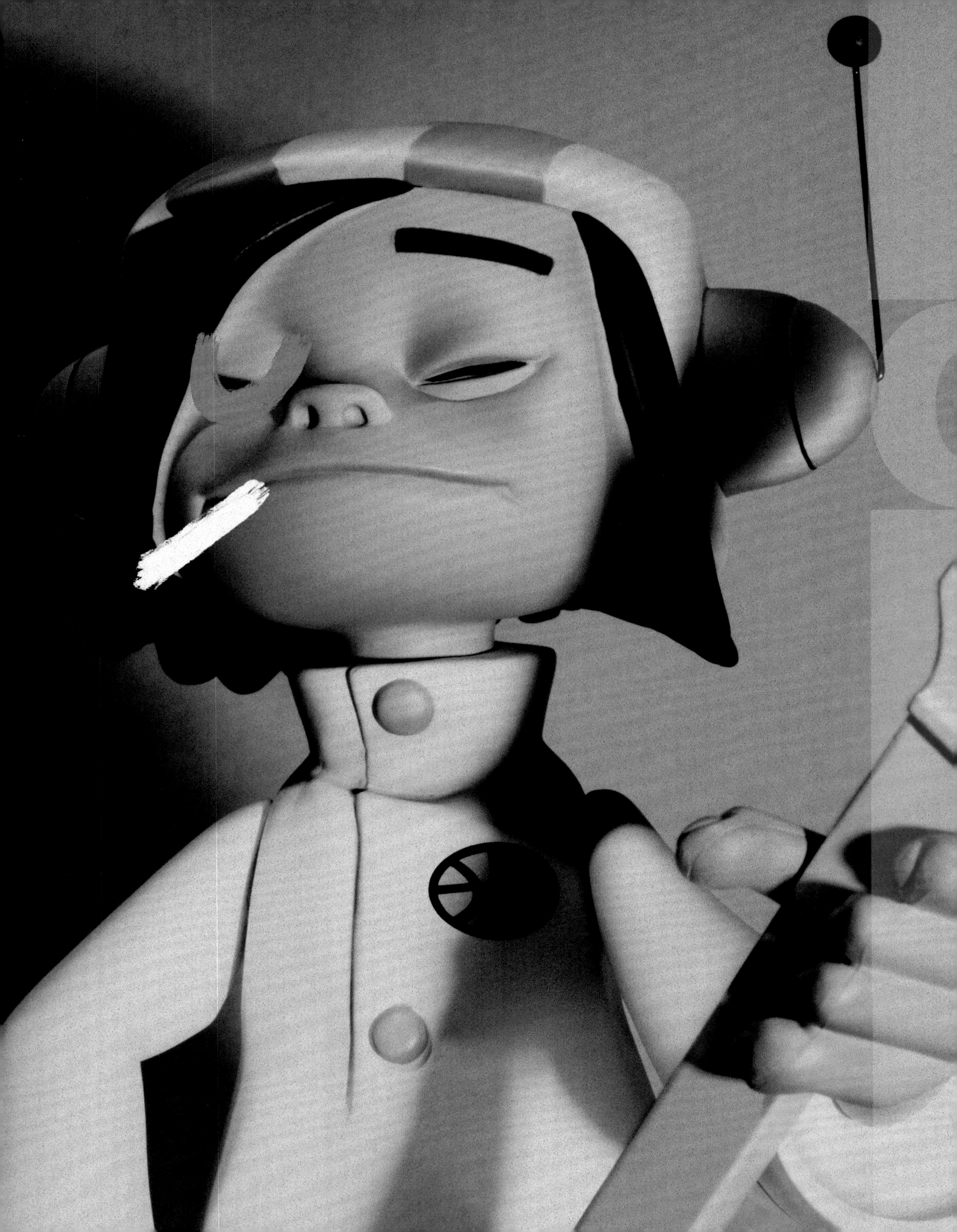

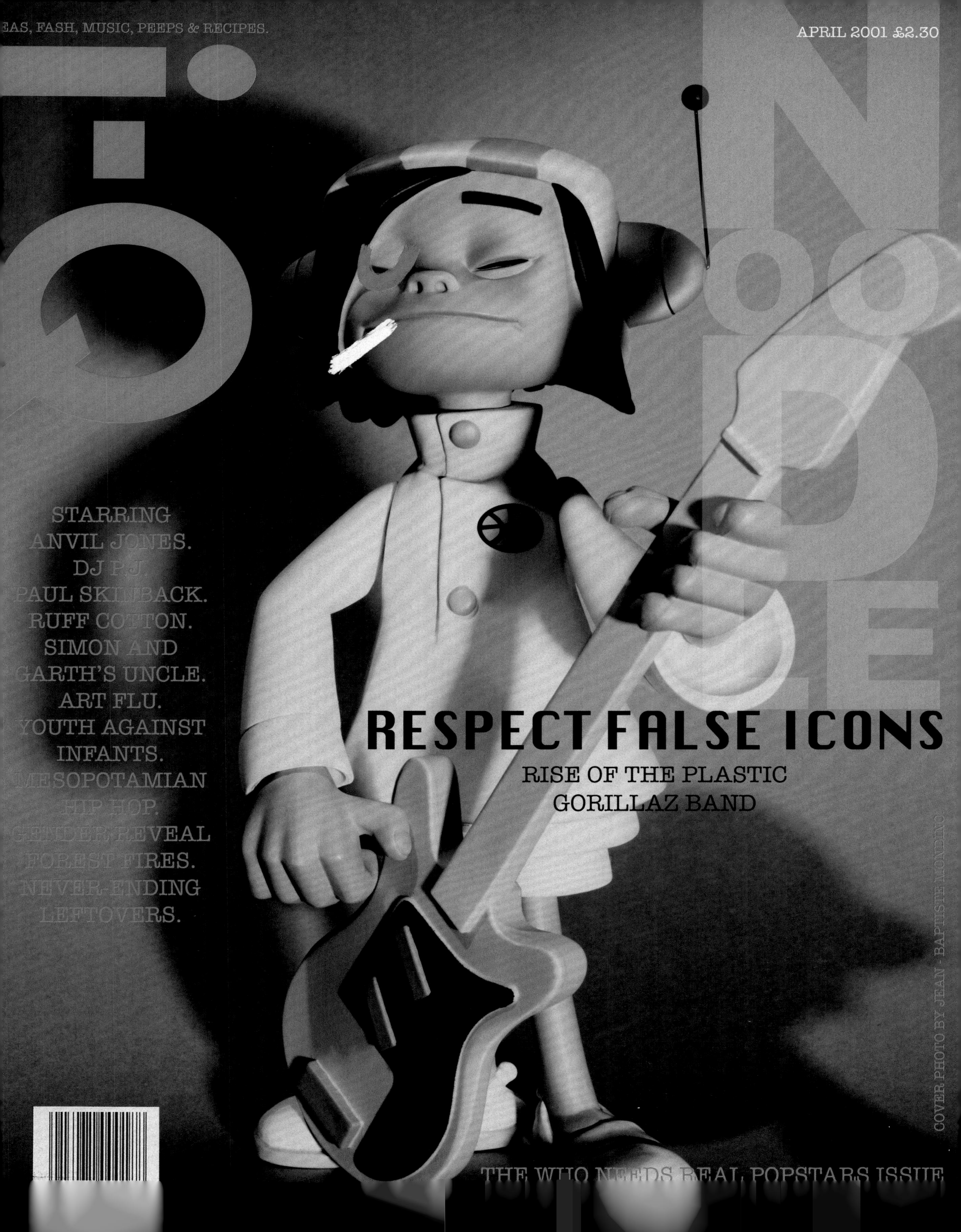

EAS, FASH, MUSIC, PEEPS & RECIPES.
APRIL 2001 £2.30
NOODLE
STARRING
ANVIL JONES.
DJ P.J.
PAUL SKINBACK.
RUFF COTTON.
SIMON AND
GARTH'S UNCLE.
ART FLU.
YOUTH AGAINST
INFANTS.
MESOPOTAMIAN
HIP HOP.
GENDER REVEAL
FOREST FIRES.
NEVER-ENDING
LEFTOVERS.
RESPECT FALSE ICONS
RISE OF THE PLASTIC
GORILLAZ BAND
COVER PHOTO BY JEAN - BAPTISTE MONDINO
THE WHO NEEDS REAL POPSTARS ISSUE

Valéria Ko

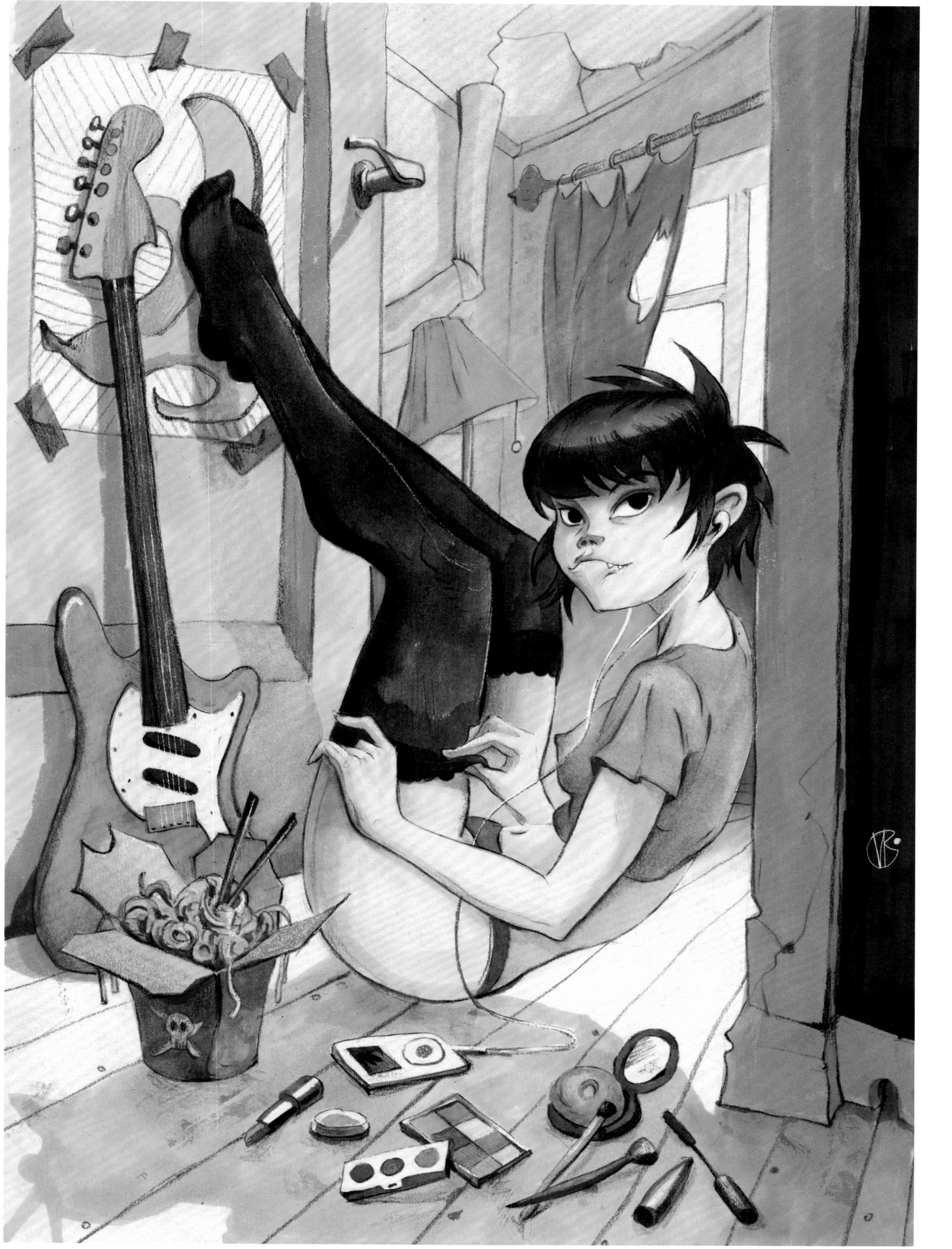

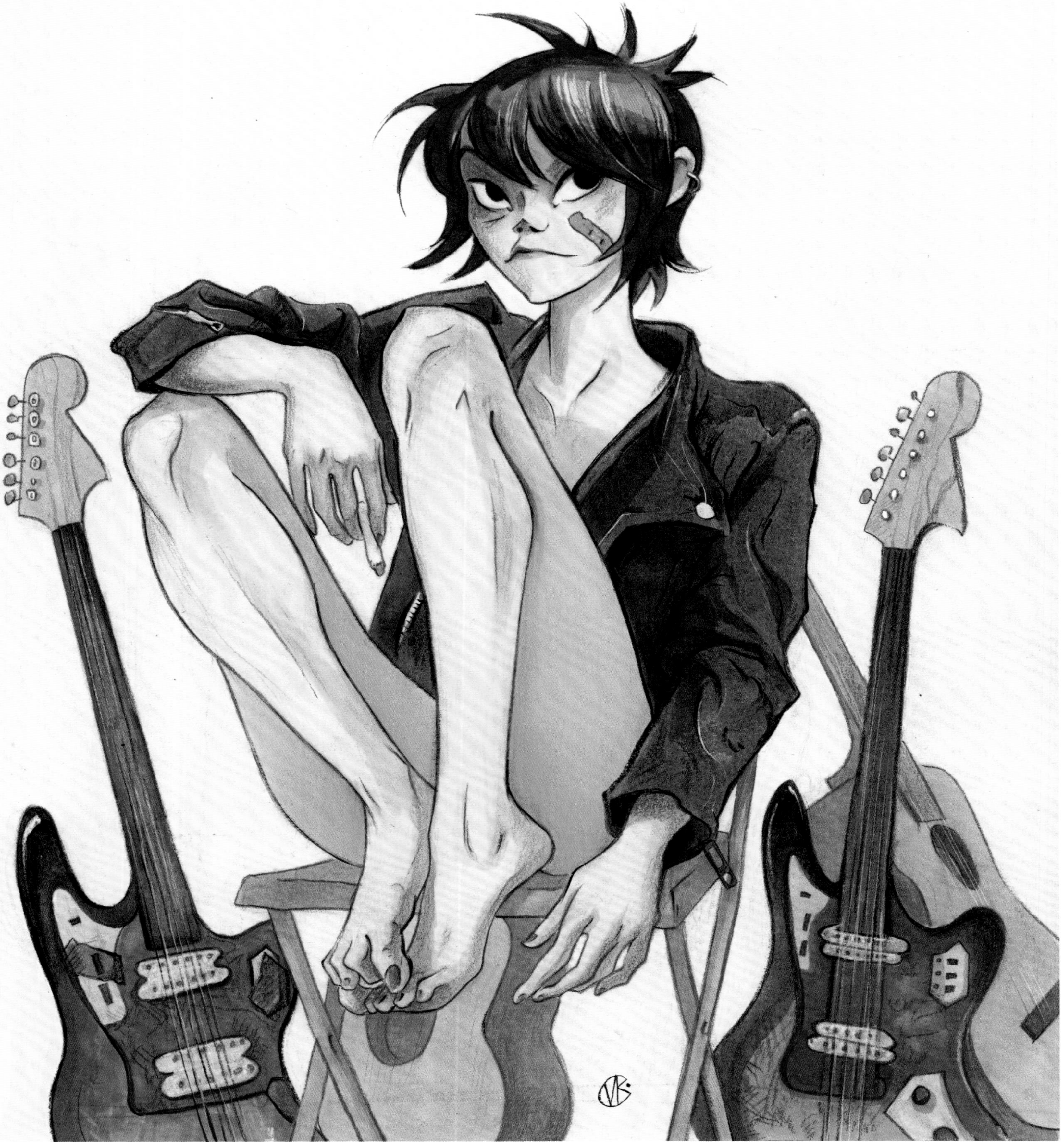

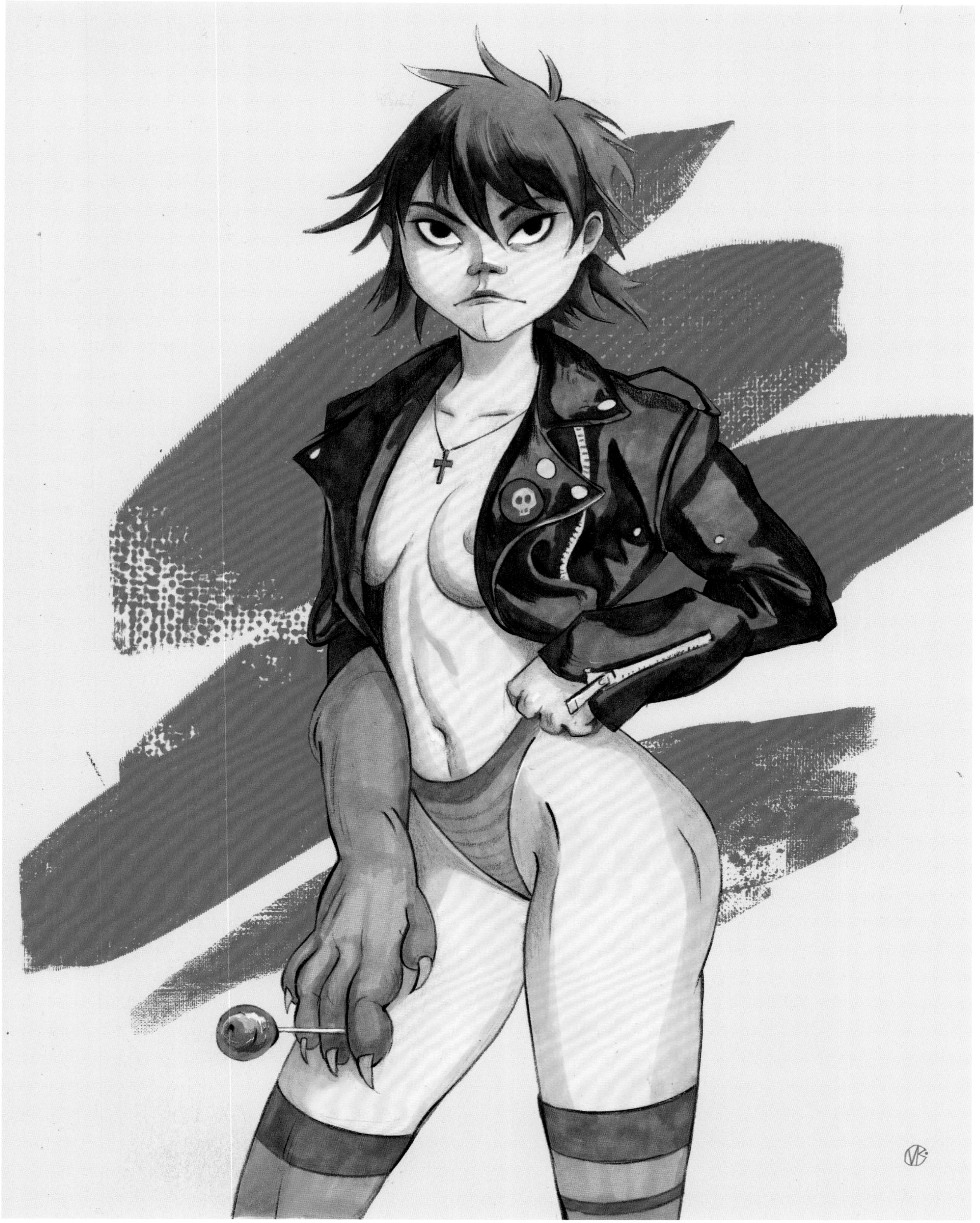

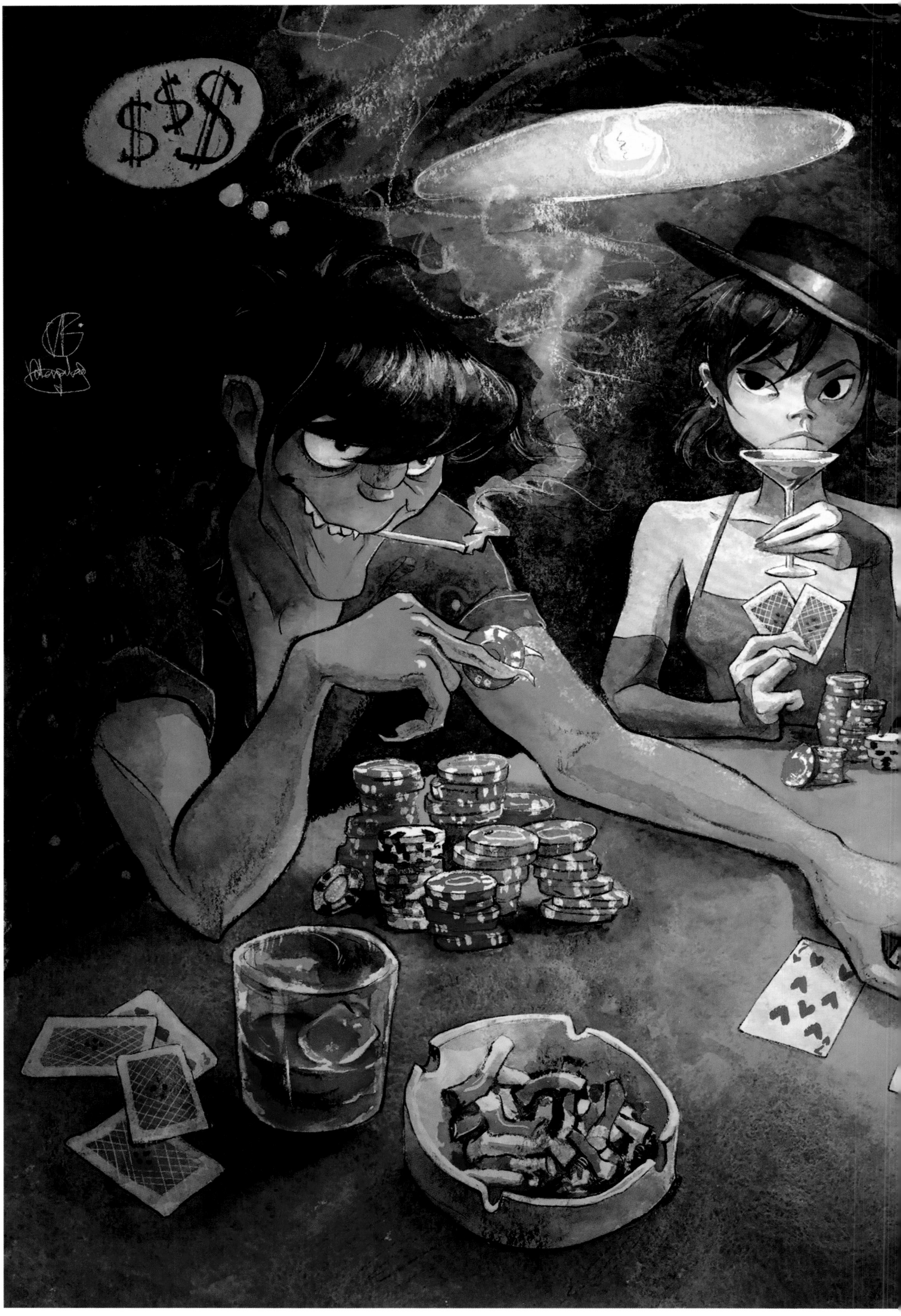
$$$

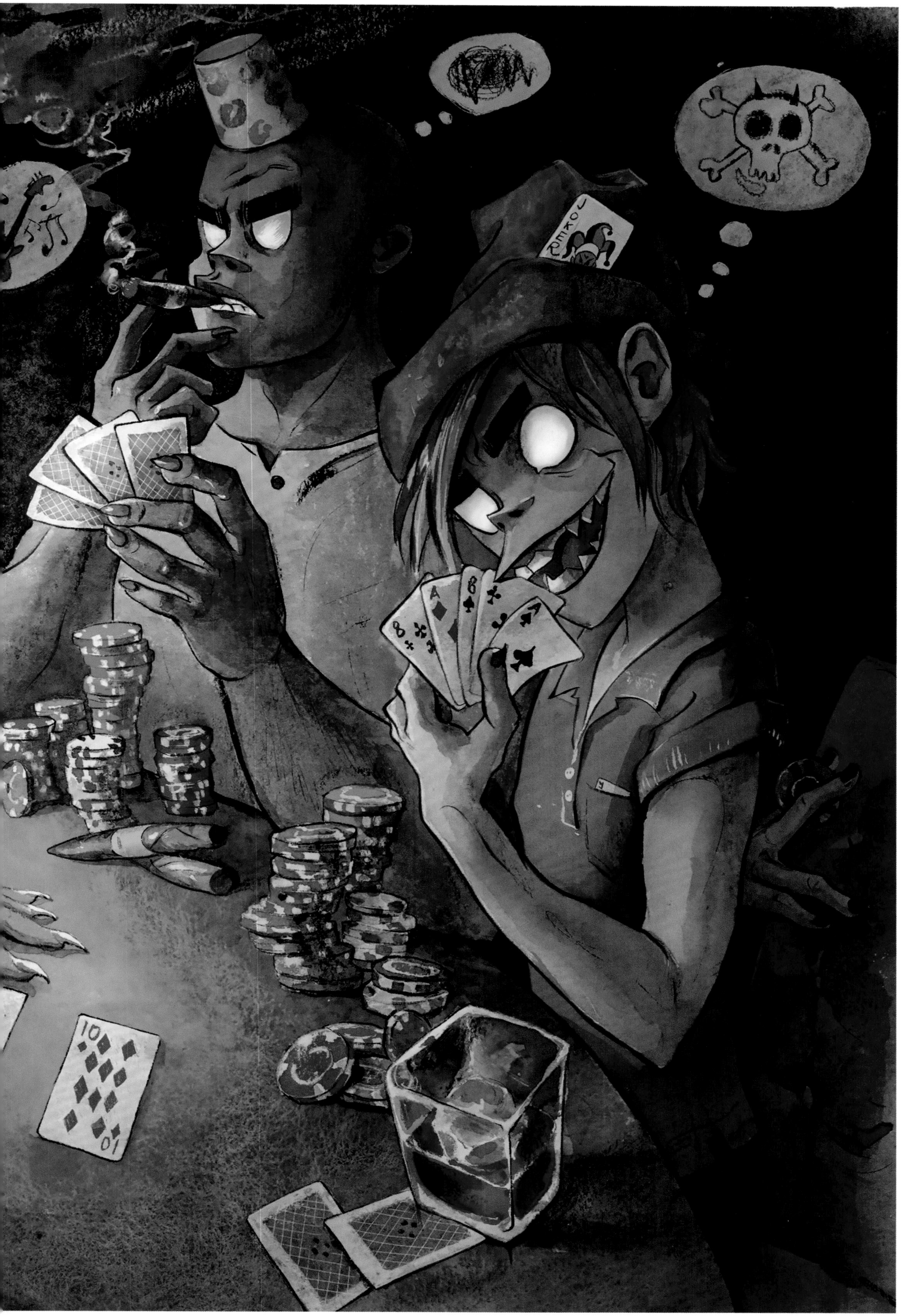
JOKER

Brendan McCarthy

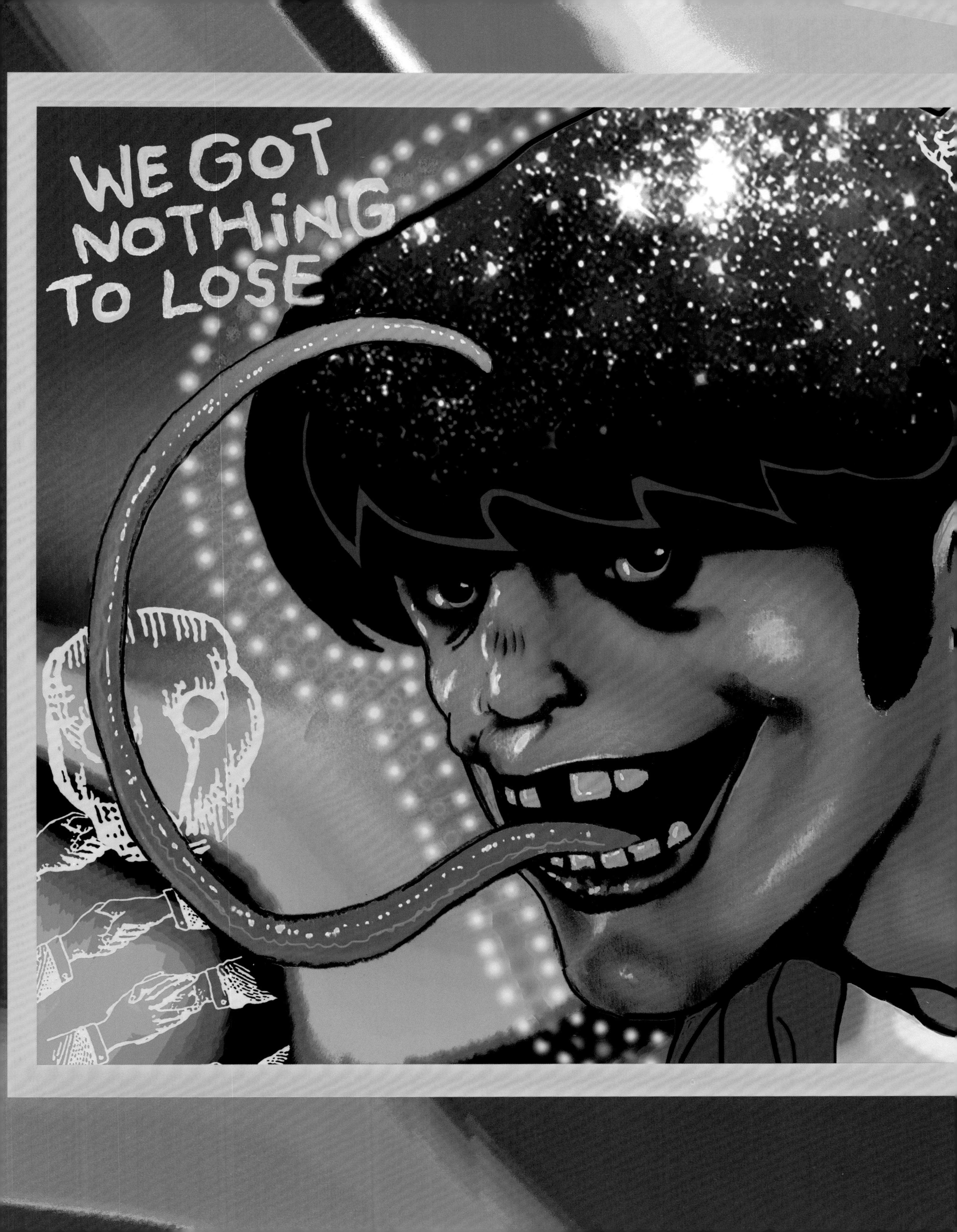
WE GOT NOTHING TO LOSE

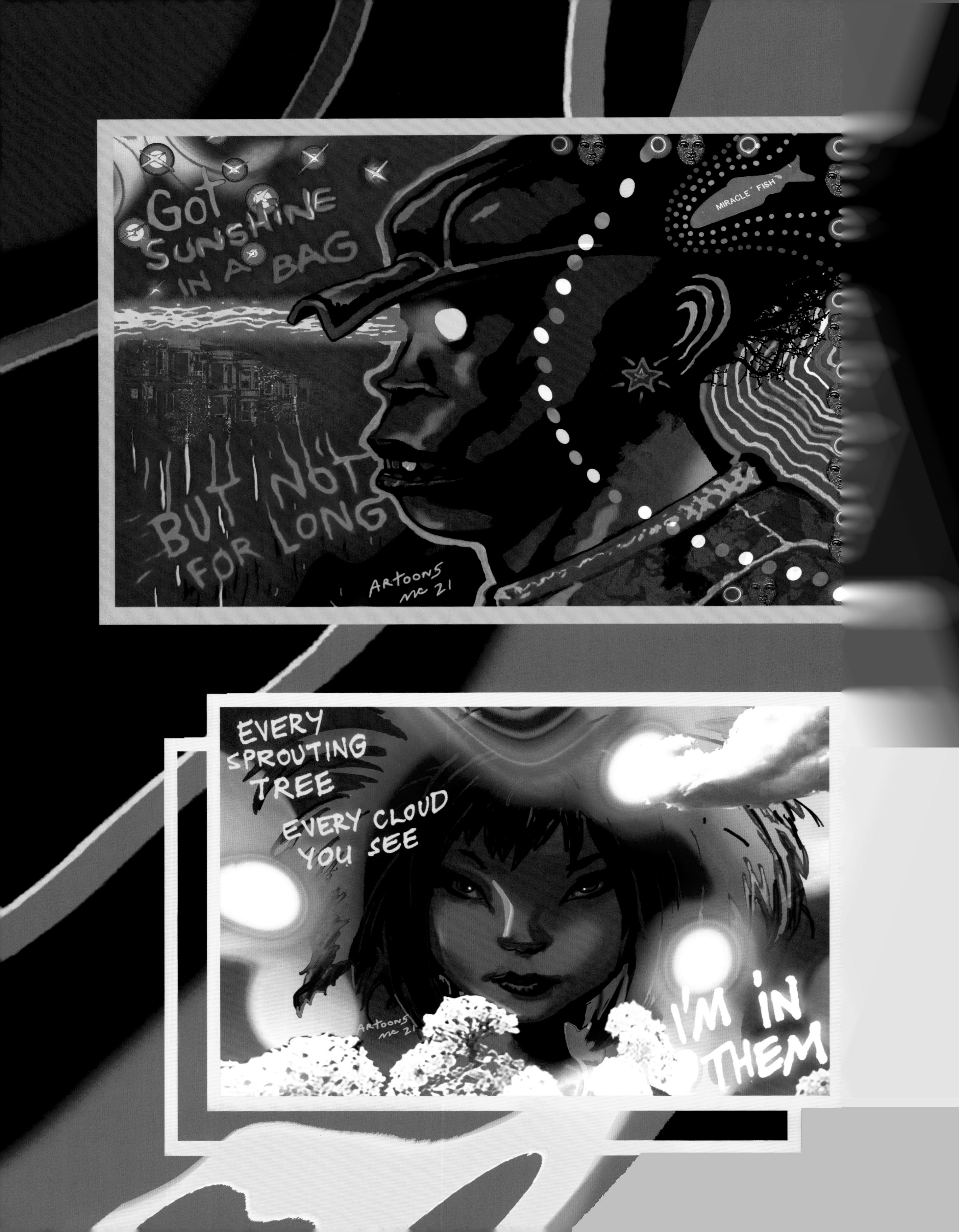
Got Sunshine in a Bag
MIRACLE FISH
But Not for Long
Artoons mc 21
EVERY SPROUTING TREE
EVERY CLOUD YOU SEE
I'M IN THEM
Artoons mc 21

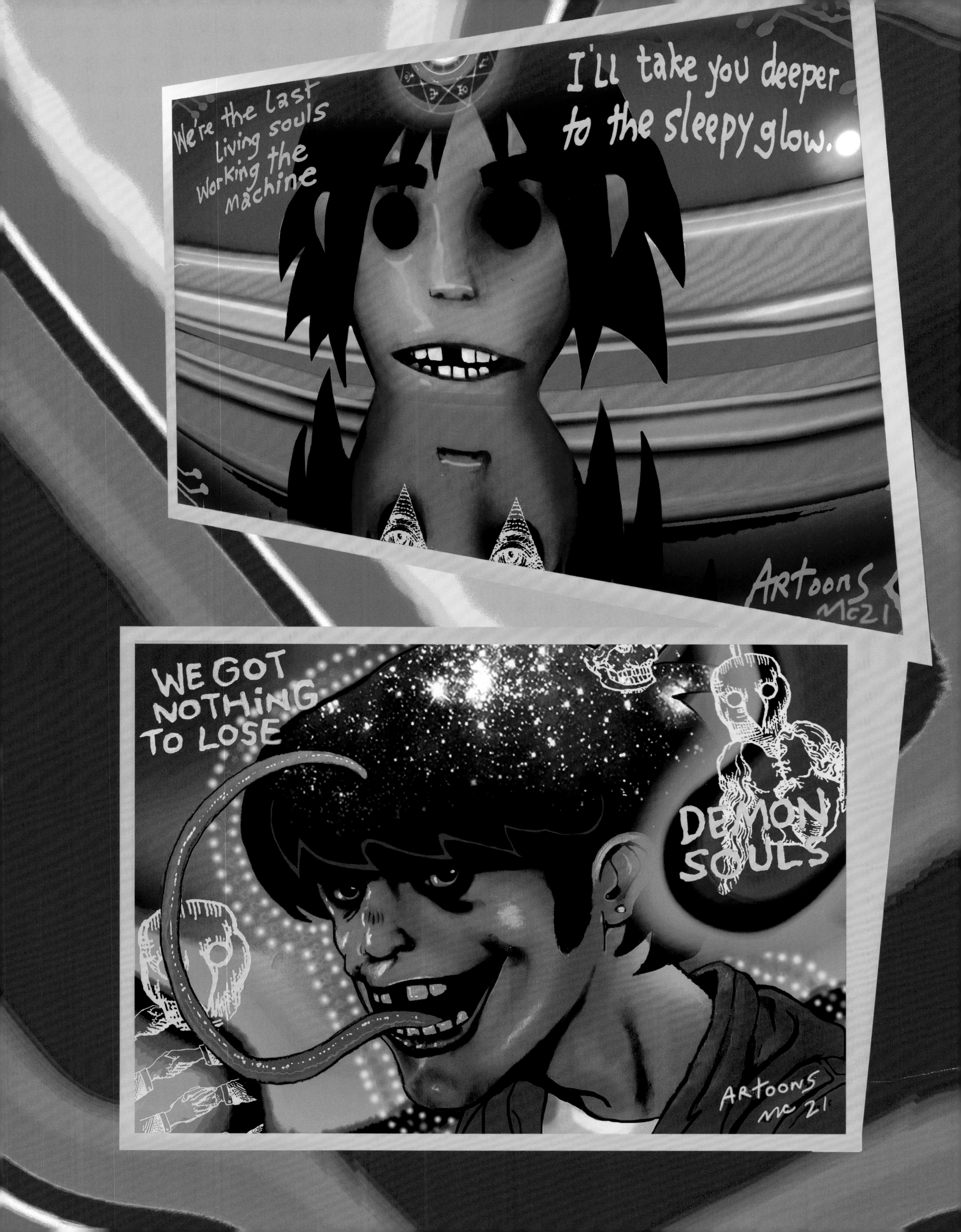
We're the last living souls working the machine
I'll take you deeper to the sleepy glow.
ARtoons MC21
WE GOT NOTHING TO LOSE
DEMON SOULS
ARtoons MC 21

Viktor Kalvachev

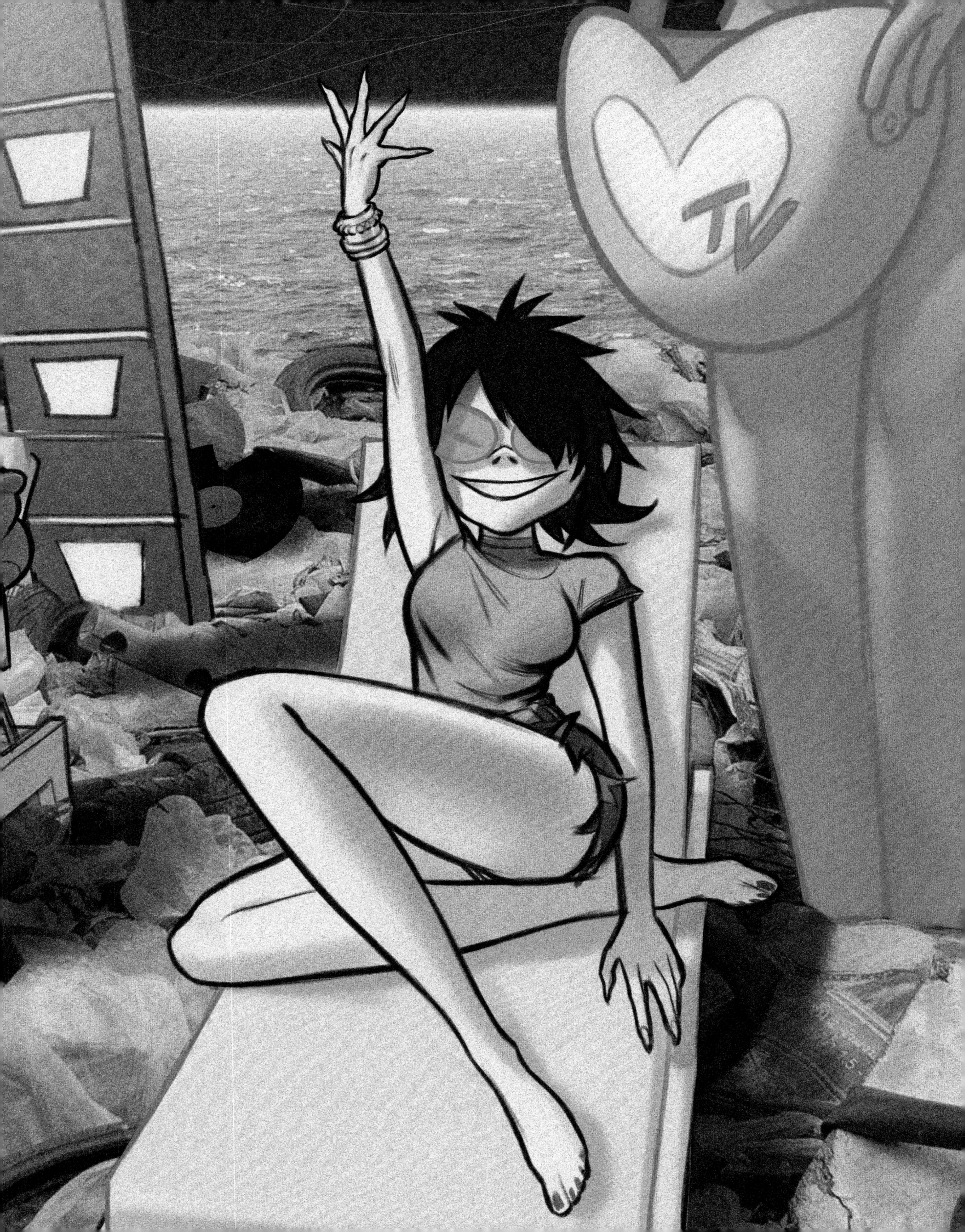
TV

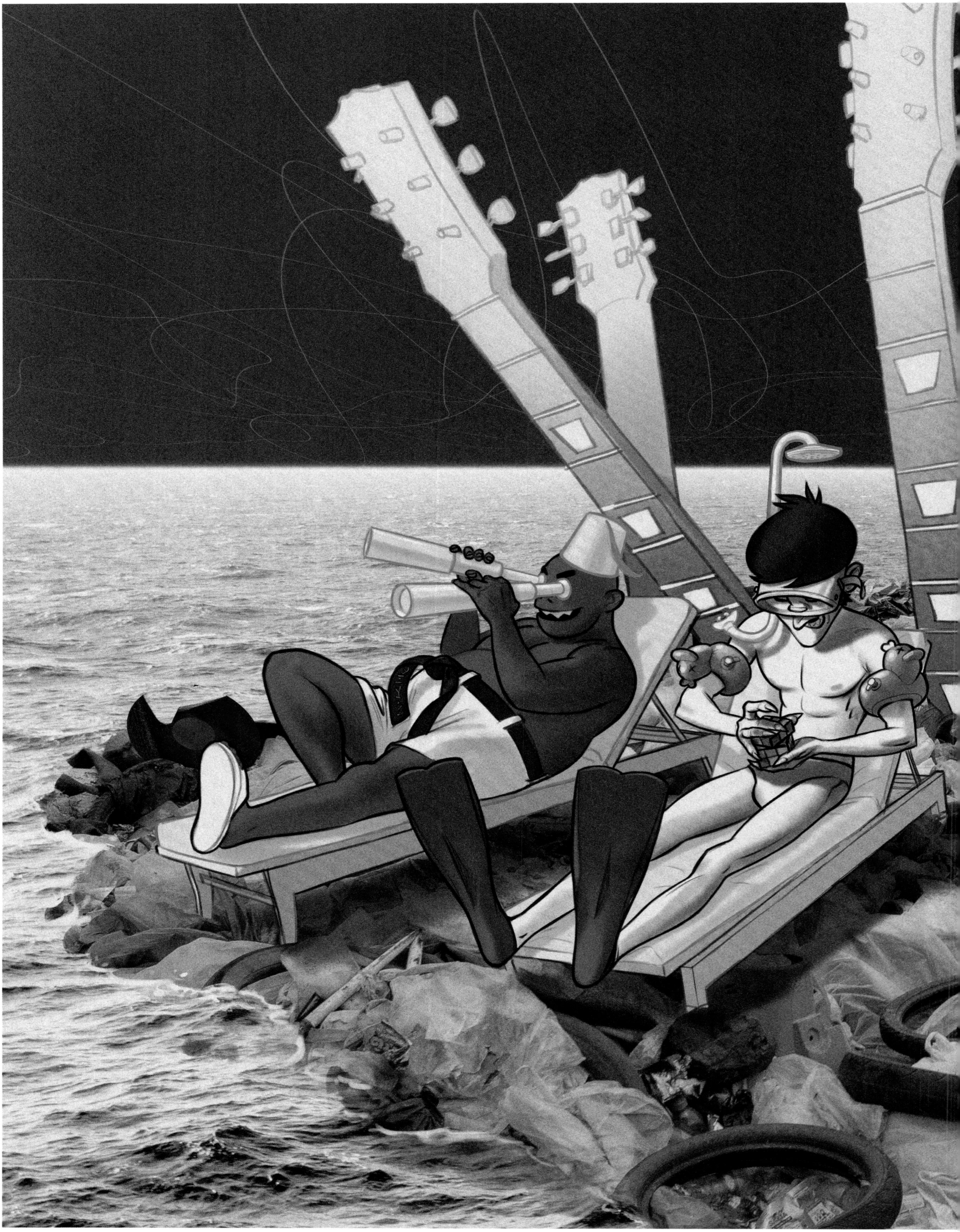

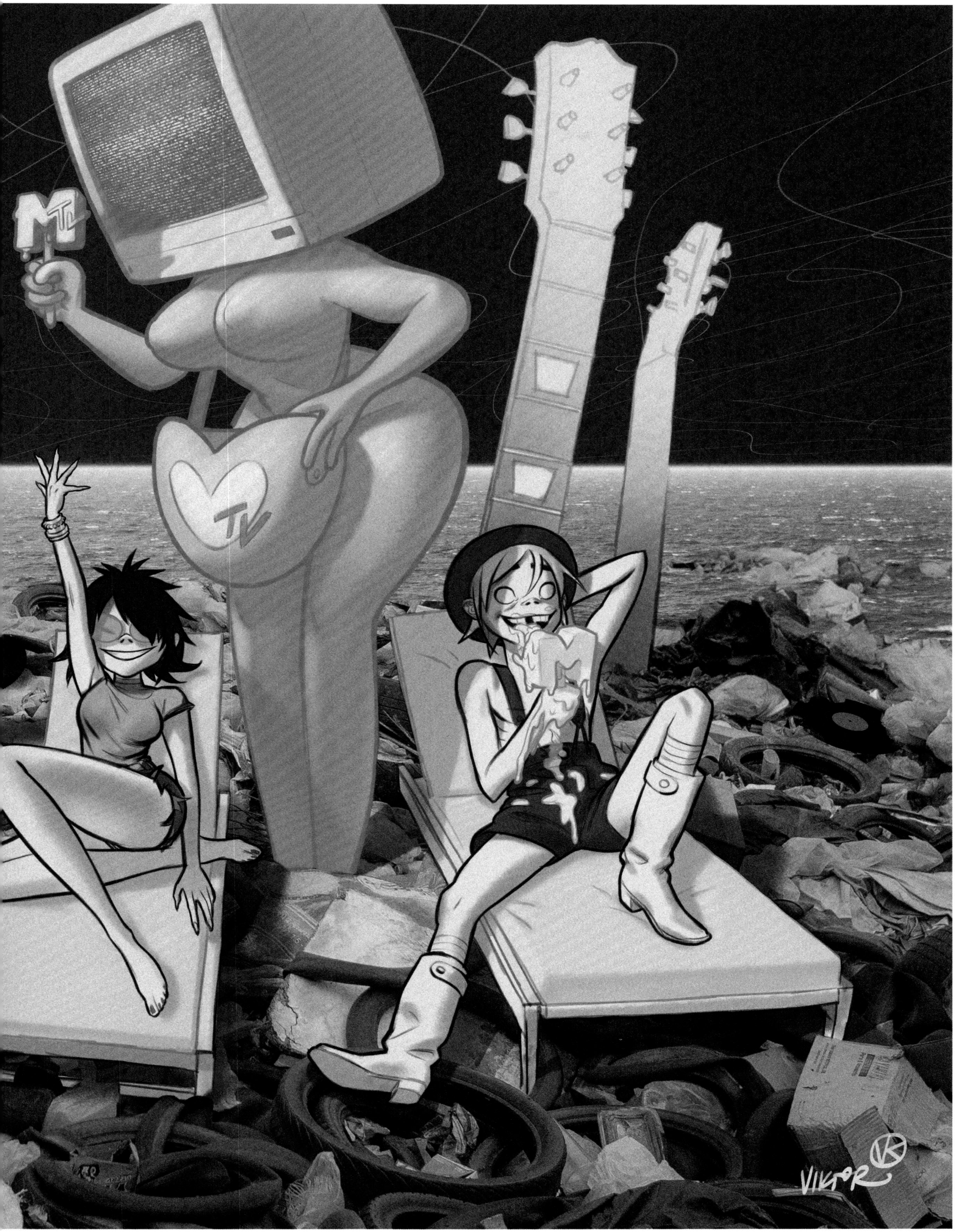
VIKTOR

CREDITS

Jared Cody Wolf
pp.69-75: *Noodle 84*
@jared.cody.wolf
jaredcodywolf.bigcartel.com

William Wray
pp.77-79: *Gorillaz at War*
@william_wray williamwray.com

Craig McCracken
pp.81-84: *Aping Gorillaz (CMcC Cover Versions)*
@cmcccartoons

Glyn Dillon
pp.87-89: *Soon, Like A Wave, Empires Will Fall.*
@glyn__dillon

EPHK
pp.91-93: *Go Go Gorillaz!*
@ephk

Jeremy Enecio
pp.95-97: *A Friend of Horror*
@jenecio jeremyenecio.com

Tara Billinger
pp.99-101: *Batteriez Not Included*
@tarabillinger

André Carrilho
pp.103-112: *Progression*
@andre_carrilho
andrecarrilho.com

Venla Linna
pp.115-117: *Noodle*
@venlarvae

Daniela Uhlig
pp.119, 121: *Noodle I*
p.120: *Noodle II*
@daniela_uhlig du-artwork.de

Sainer
pp.123-126
@sainer_etam sainer.org

Nicolas Dehghani
pp.129-131
@nicolasdehghani

Marella Moon Albanese
pp.133-137: *I Saw That Day*
@marellamoon marellamoon.com

Tim McCourt & Max Taylor
pp.139-141: *Deep Friend Cosplay*
@tim_mccourt @maxtaylordesign
@thelineanimation
thelineanimation.com

Jens Claessens
pp.143-145: *Digital Sketchbook 11*
@jensclaessens
jensclaessens.com

Jack Black
pp.147-149: *Tenacious G*
@jackblack tenaciousd.com

Gregory Herget
p.151: *Gorilla*; p.152: *Gril Girl*; p.153: *Stop Hate*; p.154: *Blue Tarp*; p.155: *Bad* p.156: *Ducati*
@gregoryhergert
gregoryhergert.com

Robert Valley
pp.159-165 @robert_valley

Miss Jisu
pp.167-169: *Come play with us*
@miss.jisu
superanius.com superani.com

Dana Terrace
pp.171-173: *Murdoc*
@danaterrace

Ana Godis
pp.175-181: *Untitled*
@ana_godis

Ben Bocquelet
pp.183-185: *Untitled*
@ben_bocquelet

Erik Fountain
pp.187-189: *RideShare*
@ahhratfarts

Holly Warburton
pp.191-192: *Cyborg Noodle, Awake*; p.193: *Behind Glass in the Depths*; p.194: *Departure from the Submarine*; p.195: *Through Coral and Algae*; p.196: *Sign of Life*; p.197: *Arriving at the Surface*; pp.198-199: *Smoke on the Horizon*
@hollywarbs hollywarbs.com

Marianna Ignazzi
pp.201-203: *Fishin Pink*
@marianna_ignazzi

Andrew C. Robinson
pp.205-207: *THE CREATIVE PROCESS IN THE KEY OF G*
@spacejunkees

Vincent Roucher
pp.209-211: *Rascals on Tour!*
@vinnifantastic
vinnifantastic.company.site

J.A.W. Cooper
pp.213-215: *How To Make Friends*
@jawcooper jawcooper.com

Kim Jung Gi
pp.217-219: *Feel Good*
@kimjunggius kimjunggius.com

Zeen Chin
pp.221-223: *Untitled*
@zeenchin artstation.com/zeen

Kerbcrawlerghost
p.225: *Demon Days*; pp.226-230 *Ascension*; p.232: *Die Toteninsel*; p.233: *Charger*
@kerbcrawlergh0st
kerbcrawlerghost.com

Robert Smith
pp.235-237
@robertsmith

Anna Cattish
pp.239-241: *Klint Eastwut*
@anna_cattish annacattish.com
Animator: **Kristina Poplavskaya**
@revengemeow

Chloe Nicolay
p.243: *Russel Hobbs*; p.244: *Murdoc*; p.245: *2D*; p.246: *Noodle*
@stenopee chloenicolay.com

RUFFMERCY
pp.249-253: *'TOOK IT, SHOOK IT'*
@ruffmercy ruffmercy.com

Vanesa R. Del Rey
pp.255-259: *Club Inferno*
@vrdelrey vrdelrey.com

Taya Strizhakova
pp.261-263
@hey.im.taya
behance.net/heyimtaya

Del The Funky Homosapien
p.265: *Russel Save Us*
@delhiero
del-the-funky-homosapien.squarespace.com

Laurie Vincent
pp.267-269: *Untitled*
@thelaurievincent
laurievincent.com

Little Thunder
pp.271-273
@littlethunder

Jean-Baptitste Mondino
p.275, p.277: *IQ*
jeanbaptistemondino.com

Valéria Ko
p.279: *Noodle's Time*; p.280: *In Bloom*; p.281: *Candy*; pp.282-283: *Dead Ape's Hand*
@valeria_ko_art
valeriakoart.com

Brendan McCarthy
pp.285-287: *4GORILLAZ (Bubblegum Card Mix)*
@Mystic McCarthy
artbrendan.com

Viktor Kalvachev
pp.289-291: *Plastic Beach*
@viktor_kalvachev kalvachev.com

IMPRINT

Gorillaz are
2D, Murdoc Niccals, Noodle & Russel Hobbs

Writing by
Ed Caruana & Thomas O'Malley

Design and Layout by
J.C. Hewlett & Joe Hales studio

Colour separations by
Joe Hales studio

Published by
Z2 Comics

Gorillaz co-created by
Damon Albarn & Jamie Hewlett

Gorillaz are managed by
Eleven Mgmt and the spirit

With thanks to
Niamh Byrne, Astrid Ferguson, Josh Frankel,
Suzi Grossman, Kevin Meek, Courtney Menard,
Regine Moylett, Katherine Nash, Aston New,
Ellie Nolan, Sridhar Reddy, Stars Redmond
and Tanyel Vahdettin.

First printing April 2022
Printed in Italy by Graphicom
ISBN: 978-1-954928-00-8

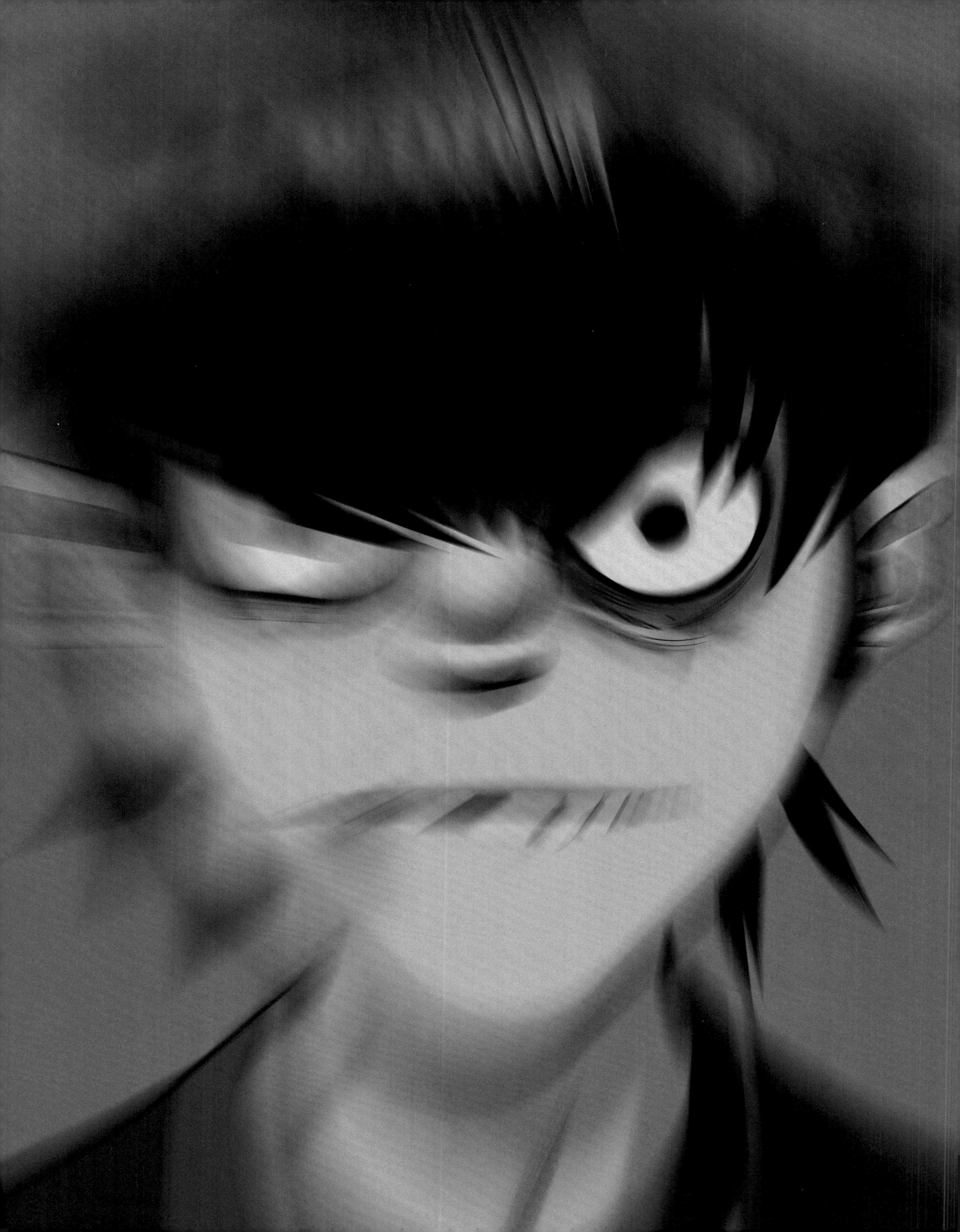

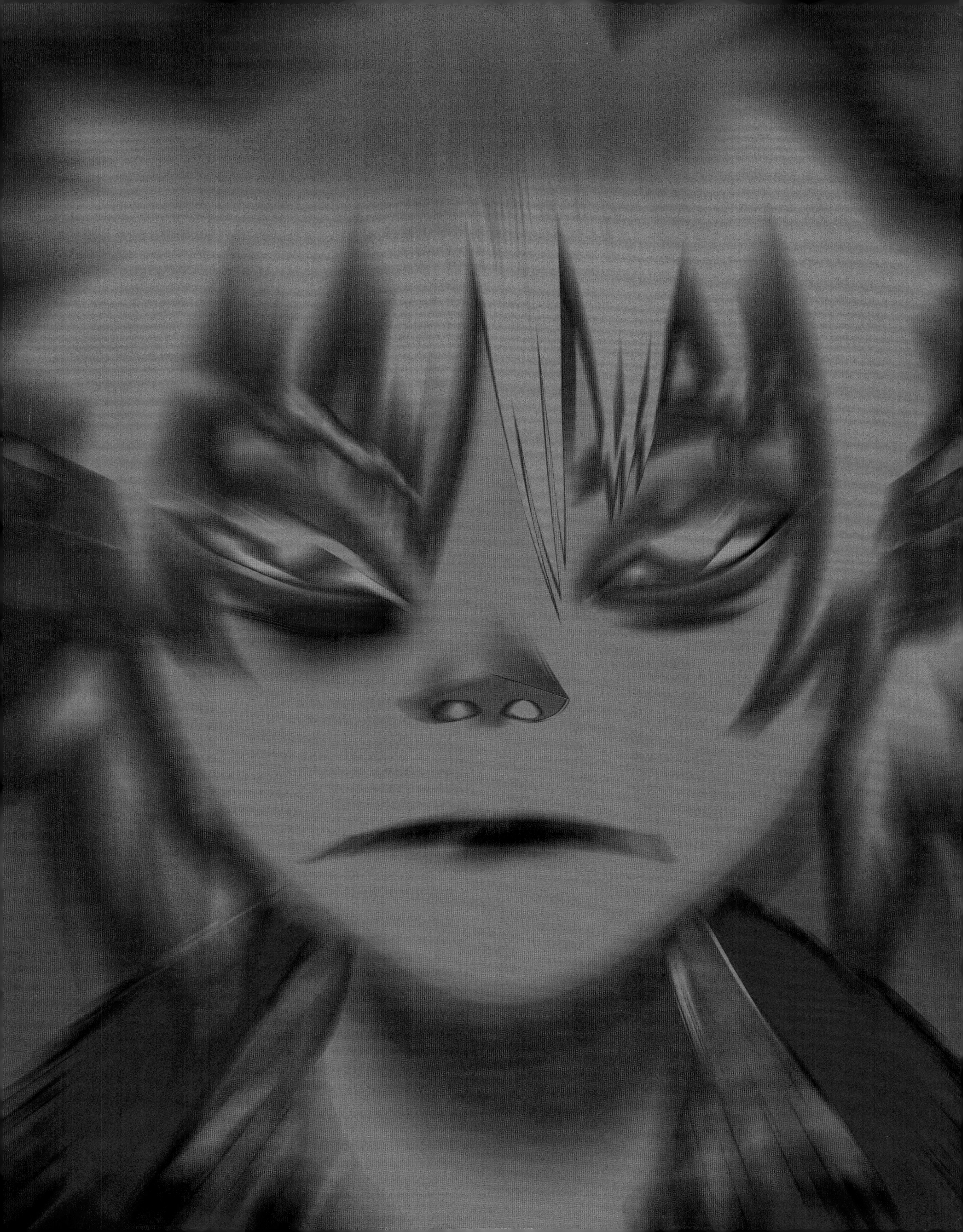